ritish
untry
Planning

# British Town and Country Planning

## Eric Reade

OPEN UNIVERSITY PRESS
Milton Keynes · Philadelphia

Open University Press
Open University Educational Enterprises Limited
12 Cofferidge Close
Stony Stratford
Milton Keynes MK11 1BY, England

and
242 Cherry Street
Philadelphia, PA 19106, USA

First Published 1987

*British Library Cataloguing in Publication Data*
Reade, Eric
   British town and country planning.
   1. City planning—Great Britain
   2. Regional planning—Great Britain
   I. Title
   711'.0941      HT169.G7

ISBN 0-335-15509-X

ISBN 0-335-15508-1 Pbk

*Library of Congress Cataloging in Publication Data*
Main entry under title:
Reade, Eric
   British town and country planning.
   Bibliography: p
   Includes index.
   1. City planning—Great Britain. 2. Urban policy—
Great Britain. I. Title.
HT169.G7R34 1987      307.1'2'0941      87-7640

ISBN 0-335-15509-X

ISBN 0-335-15508-1 (pbk.)

This book was produced on recycled paper at the request of the author.

Typeset by Gilbert Composing Services
Printed and bound in Great Britain by
Biddles Ltd, Guildford and King's Lynn

# Contents

# Preface

If by an academic book we understand one which consists of a careful and detailed enquiry into a relatively narrowly-defined subject, dealing with the various schools of thought on that subject in a way which is as even-handed, disinterested or 'objective' as possible, then I cannot really claim that this is an academic book. There are four reasons for this.

In the first place, there is the fact that those who are involved in town and country planning see it as concerned with an almost impossibly broad range of disparate matters. They do not, however, in general 'break away', establishing themselves around more specialised professional bodies, but tend on the contrary rather strongly, and whatever the nature of the particular problem with which they have become concerned, to regard themselves as 'planners'; this reflects a widespread belief among them that solutions to all these various problems are best sought within the framework of the 'planning' approach. Though quite a number of observers—including myself—have in the past suggested that if they are to achieve greater intellectual credibility planners must considerably curtail their ambitions, and restrict themselves instead to the clarification of the economic implications of governmental intervention in the ownership, use and development of land, the planners have not as yet accepted this excellent advice. Indeed, they continue not only to claim this very wide area of competence, but also to portray their approach as purely technical and professional, while yet at the same time paradoxically explaining that approach in a way which reveals it to be based on very questionable taken-for-granted social and political assumptions.

In writing this book, therefore, I found myself in a quandary. While my object was to show that the substantive field claimed by planners is impossibly ambitious, I was *myself* apparently obliged to review this impossibly broad field of knowledge, precisely in order to substantiate my claim that to do so is impossible. At the same time, and as a result of the profession's above-noted claim to provide technical solutions to matters which are in fact questions of political opinion, I had to enquire into a further range of specialist matters, this time concerned not with the 'substantive' question of *what* it is that planners plan, but rather with the 'procedural' question of *how* such social decisions ought to be arrived at.

To seek to understand the planning profession, in other words, necessitates our trying to get some grasp not only of its multifarious substantive concerns, but also of such 'political science' problems as the emergence in modern Western societies of a fairly significant state-employed salariat, the nature and ideological underpinnings of contemporary professionalism, the social and political attitudes and values of social groups which tend to a 'technocratic' view of the world, and the 'proper' roles, in government, of political motivation and of technical expertise respectively. The need for such understanding is far greater in the case of planning than in the case of other professions, I am suggesting, precisely because its ambitions are greater, and its concerns so very much more diffuse.

To explain 'town and country planning', then, means that we must delve into an impossibly wide range of disciplines and specialisms, a fact no doubt accurately reflected in the faintly ludicrous coverage of the bibliography at the end of this volume. To set the reader's mind at rest, let me say immediately that I make no claim to have understood this mass of material. All I *do* claim, is to have 'mapped out the ground', to have suggested what *are* the major economic, social, political and philosophical questions posed by the existence of planning and planners, and to have suggested where the reader might find his or her own answers to these questions. But though this is all I claim, I must admit that I have not in fact stopped here. In order to *provoke* the reader into finding his or her own answers, I have gone on to suggest fairly unequivocally what *my own* answers to these questions would probably tend to be.

The second reason why this book cannot be a piece of academic work in the normal sense, then, lies not in the impossibly wide range of its subject-matter, but in its being concerned to advance a point of view. Despite having involved myself in more matters than I could properly understand (or perhaps *because* I have done so), I have encountered relatively little difficulty in forming opinions on all these various matters. I have not attempted in this book to examine the evidence for and against each of the various schools of thought on each of the various questions posed by the existence of planning. Had I done so, the book would have been much longer, for as noted above, these questions are legion. Rather, I have tried, after identifying the main issues raised, to show how, jointly, all these various issues can be illuminated from the perspective of a particular philosophical standpoint. As a consequence of this approach, the book contains many statements which may seem somewhat categorical, and to stand in need of some qualification. In many cases, I hope, I might myself have provided the needed qualifications to my remarks, but I do not think that if I had done so, this would have led me to modify in any fundamental way the nature of my case. It would, however, have made this into a very different book. It would have become quite different in style and tone, it would probably have created a much more moderate and 'reasonable' impression, and again, it would have become much longer. It therefore seemed to me much more important just to set out my arguments, in as simple and as unambiguous a way as possible, than to write a careful, 'balanced' and 'academic' book, for these are arguments which in my view are far too seldom even heard at all.

The third sense in which this book is 'non-academic' is closely related to the previous one, and indeed is an extension of it. If we consider the fundamental argument of the book, an argument which might be summed up as a statement of 'the need for politics', it is immediately obvious that there exists an equally valid 'opposite' argument. Where public policy is concerned, there is a perfectly defensible and perfectly respectable case to be made for *less* politics. Too much politicization can easily lead to the oversimplification and even to the trivialization of public issues, it can result in decisions which are short-sighted and ultimately harmful, it can produce outcomes which further disadvantage the already underprivileged, and so on. There is thus a perfectly good case to be made, in principle, and according to one's assessment of the situation, for less politics and more expertise.

It just so happens, however, that I do not consider that this 'opposite' case deserves to be made in relation to this particular area of public policy, in this particular society, at this particular time. On the contrary, I believe that in the case of town and country planning in Britain the ambitions of expertise have been given far too much scope for far too long, and with very harmful effects, and this book is therefore intended as a contribution towards helping to redress the balance. It may be that quite other observers, looking at quite other areas of public policy, may similarly come to the view that the professional ambitions of experts and bureaucrats have outstripped the capacity of the politicians to imbue policy with social purpose, or to subject it to democratic control. In that case, perhaps the present book may suggest the making of useful comparisons.

Fourthly, in saying that this is not an 'academic' book, I mean that I have so far as possible written it in non-technical language. While its approach is broadly speaking informed by a sociological perspective, my hope is that some at least of my readers will find this perspective compatible with what they understand as common sense, or that they will recognize it as consisting of the kind of reasoning from evidence or from stated premises of which any tolerably well-educated person is perfectly capable. There is in my opinion far too little writing designed to bridge the gulf between the social sciences and the public discussion of political issues. Such journalism would not only encourage the public to demand a higher level of objective technical understanding from the politicians, but also help the latter to provide it. In addition, it would reduce the undue power which accrues to bureaucrats as a result of their existing near-monopoly over information. Such popular clarification, however, is unfortunately not rewarded in the academic milieu in which most of the potential popularizers tend to be employed.

Though this book does not claim to be academic, it does in fact summarize arguments which I have put forward in a series of published papers, and which do attempt, between them, to analyse in theoretical terms the major facets of 'planning' as it is practised. These papers deal with questions ranging from the fundamental socio-philosophical presuppositions of planning to the relationship between the structure of society and the creation of the physical environment, as well as such specific things as vandalism, and the dereliction and decay of the urban fabric. My motive, in looking at the various facets of 'town and country planning' in this way, was to try to understand why this governmental activity of 'planning' exists, and with what consequences, and to ask how its existence might be justified. Above all, I was concerned to analyze its intellectual credibility, and to examine the claim that this 'planning' can be a profession and a discipline, and that it can reasonably be taught as a subject in the universities and polytechnics.

To forego the claim to have written an academic book, then, is not to forego the claim to have written an intellectually responsible one. By this last, I meant that the arguments advanced in this book derive fundamentally from one or other of two sources. To some extent, they rest on what is to the best of my knowledge true, in the sense that it can be empirically verified or deduced from theoretical propositions widely regarded as valid. Otherwise, my arguments rest on values, but here I hope to have made clear to the reader that these are indeed values, and not facts. I also hope that they are both mutually consistent and coherent.

A book on 'town and country planning', however, cannot reasonably restrict itself to analysis of the intellectual credibility of what planners *claim* to be able to do. It must also address itself to the matter of what the effects of this 'planning' *actually are*—of what 'functions' planning has in the economy and in society. Though this is clearly discussed at some length in the book itself, it seems necessary, in this Preface, to explain briefly how I approach this question, in order to give the reader some idea of what the book attempts to do.

Probably the dominant view on this matter within the social sciences at the present time, derived from a broadly neo-Marxist perspective, explains the existence of planning as being necessary to the functioning of the capitalist system; it is seen as providing the physical infrastructure necessary to the private sector, thus facilitating capital accumulation, while at the same time legitimating that system by demonstrating that it provides social welfare in the form of a satisfactory environment. I would, however, question this interpretation, largely on the grounds that it appears to rest on a mistaken, and exaggerated, conception of the planners' powers. Planning cannot ensure *that* any development occurs, whether it is infrastructure or anything else. It can only determine *where* it occurs. If, then, we ask what the function of this power to determine the location of development might be, it seems to me clear that it might indeed promote the efficiency of the economic system (for example, by ensuring that infrastructure is located where it is most needed), but that it is on the whole more likely to be used in such a way as to promote class domination and class privilege, even, if need be, at the cost of *reduced* economic and social efficiency.

In any society in which land-use controls exist, my argument suggests, they will tend to be 'misused'; while it may be very difficult to know what spatial arrangements will promote the economic and social efficiency of 'the system as a whole', it is by contrast perfectly easy for all manner of sectional interests to discern those spatial arrangements which will best suit *them*. It is this fact, one might hypothesize, rather than the part it plays in maintaining the 'system', which best explains the existence of planning. If those who tend to monopolize the more favoured milieux can use the *administrative system* to safeguard their surroundings or to get the spatial patterns which suit them, rather than needing to *pay for* these things, they will clearly be tempted to do so, for, in money terms at least, and at least to them, the former method is cheaper than the latter.

One thing which seems to me distinctive about Britain, however, is that in this country both this tendency to differentiate the 'favoured' from the 'unfavoured' environments, and the consequent tendency to spatial class segregation, have developed to such a very marked degree. It is not only particular streets, quarters, or even parts of the cities which are thus socially labelled in Britain, but entire tracts of the national territory, or even regions, which have thus acquired particular predominant class connotations, and I personally find this tendency a little frightening.

A second feature of the British system however, and one which I find peculiarly English, appears to work in precisely the opposite direction. It might be summed up by saying that in its ideology at least, and to some extent even in its attempted practice, the British system has preferred *assimilation* to *exclusion*. One way to preserve social and environmental privilege, quite obviously, is by simple physical exclusion. In American suburbs, for example, class homogeneity tends often to be promoted through legal devices which, by specifying a minimum plot size, make it extremely difficult for those of a lower social class to acquire property in the area. This, however, is a relatively crude method. A second method, therefore, is through what I have called assimilation, and in Britain this second method has been supported by the ideology of 'community'.

In 'community' as thus defined, all classes are welcome, and indeed all are valued for their contribution, but only on the implicit understanding that the working classes do not dominate. Such domination is not, of course, a simple matter of numbers, but centres more on the threat posed by the potential capacity of the working classes to construct an alternative (possibly 'socialist') image of society, and thus to claim for themselves, and to legitimate, some real degree of political power. This ideology of 'community', central to town planning thought, suggests what the desirable socio-spatial pattern ought to be. It is, however, logically linked with two other, complementary, images, one suggesting what the structure of society itself ought to be, and the other suggesting what is the proper scope of politics. In all three cases, there is both the assumption and the assertion of such features as organic complementarity, cohesion, consensus, and systemic order. Class domination in the 'community' is not achieved crudely, through sheer power, but arises 'naturally', out of a widespread acceptance of the 'right' values, and even, therefore, out of a certain degree of deference.

The problem with 'assimilation', however, even when backed up as it has often been by this civilized English middle-class ideology of 'community', lies in the sheer numbers to be assimilated. The sheer scale of the 'industrial districts', even half a century before this arguably rather romantic ideology of 'community' was evolved, was already quite enormous.

It has for many years now been widely accepted that the reason why the town planners' idea of the socially mixed community failed was that people simply preferred to live among those of their own social class. But failed *in what? What* social purpose, in fact, was this idea evolved to achieve? My suggestion is that 'assimilation through community' was evolved as a device for the preservation of class domination and class privilege, but failed; it could not be used, due to its being inappropriate to a large-scale and highly-urbanized society.

As a consequence of this failure, I would suggest, the same objectives were instead sought through the alternative device of physical 'exclusion'. Much of the empirical evidence concerning the *actual* effects of town and country planning in Britain, reviewed in Chapter 3 of this book, clearly demonstrates the considerable extent to which the planning system has been used as a means of securing spatial class segregation. What this research evidence refers to as the 'containment' of the cities is in fact virtually synonymous with what, here, I have called the 'exclusion' of the less privileged.

But even while in practice thus resorting increasingly to the relatively crude and potentially confrontational device of 'exclusion', the British planning system has still tended in its ideology and in its self-image to cling wherever possible to the polite and civilized English notion of the 'community', in which all have their various parts to play. The claim (or the hope) has still in some vague way continued to be that of integrating all the various parts of the whole into a smoothly functioning system, whether these 'parts' be places, artefacts, interests, or social classes. (A socialist approach to land-use planning might *equally* promote a socially mixed spatial pattern, but I would suggest that in this case, it would do so more appropriately under the banner of 'equality' than that of 'community'; if physical milieux perceived as desirable exist, or can be made to exist, then, this socialist approach would suggest, all classes should have equal access to them).

More recently, of course, this vision of planning as systemic co-ordination has faded. From a self-image in which it portrayed itself as based on rational and comprehensive social decision-making, promoting and reconciling the interests of all the various groups in society and securing economic and physical integration, planning has changed its image drastically, now seeing itself as largely pragmatic and opportunistic. From associating itself readily with co-ordination, with a considerable measure of central direction and with government, planning has changed its self-image to that of the maverick ginger-group, encouraging and promoting private or innovatory initiative, however small-scale and sporadic, wherever it raises its head, and even, if need be, *in defiance* of central government policy. From having been originally concerned to control the operations of the property developers, planning has again reversed its preferred role, now portraying itself as promoting the activities of those very same developers.

An activity and a profession capable of such wildly shifting self-images, one may feel, is justifiably viewed with some scepticism. Those capable of portraying their own activity in such markedly varying ways, one suspects, may well be motivated to a large extent by sheer expediency, by their perceived need to define a role for themselves, and thus to keep themselves in employment. At the very least, the purpose of their activity seems long overdue for careful analysis, and the results of this activity seem to call for thorough empirical investigation. For even before these remarkable shifts in self-definition, the purpose of planning was already vague and obscure.

This book, then, asks what the control of land use *does* achieve and what it *might* achieve. Having interested myself in and worked within this field for something approaching 40 years, I have clearly incurred many debts, not only intellectual ones, but also of a more personal kind. As a general rule, I suppose, our perceptions are either reflections of or reactions to the general climate of thought in our field, and I certainly find it very difficult to know to whom I am indebted for very many of the ideas which have stimulated me over the years. This being so, it seems better, rather than setting out any formal expressions of thanks or acknowledgment to particular individuals, to record my appreciation in more general terms. I am grateful for the fact that I was able to work in this field, and thus had the opportunity to think about the problems which it raises. That I have in this book come to conclusions very different from those held by most professional town planners seems to provide an additional reason for declining to link my ex-colleagues in any way with what follows. I would, however, emphasize their fundamental good will, their good intentions, and their sincerity. I would also acknowledge with gratitude the fact that they have often shown me great personal kindness and tolerance, even to a degree which my insistent iconoclasm and disputatiousness may have seemed hardly to merit.

This Preface, then, explains why this book came to be written, and why it takes the form it does. Because it is written within the general framework of 'planning', and is addressed in large part to planners, I have kept to a minimum the conceptual and theoretical apparatus with which social scientists might analyse these matters. But because it is addressed to those whose interest in planning is mainly as an example of the emergence of professional ambition among governmental advisers in general, I have equally kept to a minimum my discussion of the technicalities of planning as planners themselves understand such matters. The result, of course, may be to please neither party. Social scientists may find what follows to be impossibly naive in its conception of the nature of social science, while planners may find it equally deficient in its understanding of planning. Anticipating such criticisms, I can only say that I believe that the approach which I have adopted offers the best hope of improved understanding in this field. The crucial need, as I see it, is to enable both the social scientists and the planners to understand each other's assumptions, concerns, and characteristic ways of thinking, while enabling the politically interested general reader to understand those of both these groups. The need is not to discover how planning might be 'improved', but to direct attention to the much more urgent question as to why this 'planning' should be attempted at all. There clearly is a case for land-use planning, but that case is not served by assuming, as planners tend to do, that that case is so unassailable as to hardly require to be stated. On the contrary, I would suggest that critiques such as the present one, even though they are usually seen by the planners themselves as merely hostile, negative, and unhelpful, in fact offer the only real hope of enabling a justification to be constructed for the planners' own existence.

Eric Reade
January 1987

# 1 Introduction

[T]he system which has existed since 1953 has suffered, from the point of view of the community, from the worst of both worlds. The individual owner, not the public authority, gained the profit. But the public authority did clearly define by zoning the property rights, and it published Development Plans long in advance which substantially reduced the uncertainties facing the developer in deciding whether or not to buy and build on a particular plot of land. The planners attempted to maximise the externalities. The developer attempted to take full advantage of the externalities. The ratepayer and taxpayer have met many of the real costs involved in the creation of externalities. But the value of the externalities created has been translated into market price which has been paid for by the consumer.

Hall *et al. The Containment of Urban England*

## 1. What this book is about

This book is concerned with one of the ways (town and country planning) in which government influences our physical surroundings—but not with *all* the ways in which it does so. There are three main types of governmental influence with which this book is *not* in principle concerned. First, there is *the imposition of physical standards*, as in the case of building regulations under the Public Health Acts, or control of the emission of pollutants.

Second, there are what we might call *'single-purpose'* governmental interventions. In the past, most of these have taken the form of public sector development, as when government agencies build roads, schools, hospitals or housing estates, mainly in pursuance of duties statutorily imposed upon them. This second type of governmental intervention or influence on the spatial pattern, however, also includes a more 'optional' type of initiative, increasingly urged and

1

practised in recent decades, in which central government and local authorities promote development traditionally provided by the market, but which they consider the market not to be providing in the right forms, or in adequate amounts. Town-centre redevelopment schemes are an obvious example, but many other types of such publicly-promoted development are increasingly urged. The extent to which such initiatives reflect a *planning* approach is debatable, however. Often, they seem rather to be opportunistic, or to reflect a concern with a single matter, such as providing employment, and it is for this reason that I have included them in this category rather than seeing them as part of the planning system.

Thirdly, governmental activities affect our physical surroundings in *unintended* ways. The complicated arrangements whereby local government is financed, for example, are not intended to have effects on the physical environment. Yet they do have. By maintaining differences in rate poundages, especially as between cities and their suburbs, they encourage development (and certain kinds of development) in certain places rather than others. Government support of the vehicle-manufacturing and road-construction industries, and subsidization of commuter railways, are other examples. So too is the use by the government of the building societies, both as a means of promoting the social objective of home ownership, and as a kind of general 'economic regulator'. Such social and economic policies can have direct and indirect effects not only on the spatial patterning of development, but even on its physical form.[1]

An important point about these three 'other' types of governmental influence is that they would all exist anyway, whether or not town and country planning existed. The second and third of them probably have greater impacts on our physical surroundings than does planning itself. Nor is town and country planning always even *analytically* distinct from these 'other three'. Aesthetic control in town and country planning, for example, is clearly a matter of the imposition of physical standards, albeit in this case subjective ones. The central idea in land-use planning, however, and the thing which primarily differentiates it from other forms of control or intervention, is that it seeks to determine *where* development of various kinds takes place. By this means, it progressively brings into existence a *pattern* of land use which was presumably intended, or 'planned', and which differs from the pattern which would otherwise have existed. Though I shall therefore concentrate mainly upon this capacity of the planning system to influence location, it is important to note that the planning system can in fact determine the pattern of development in three other ways. It can ensure that physical development is carried out in *forms* it would not otherwise have taken, at levels of *intensity of use* which may be lower (or possibly higher) than the developers had intended, and at *times* other than those at which it would otherwise have occurred. The third of these does not, I hasten to add, refer to the fact that it may on occasion take a long time to get a planning permission, but to the fact that development proposals are sometimes judged premature, since they cannot for the time being be economically provided with public services.

'Freely translating', and summarizing planners' ideas, one could say that they tend to see the planning system as seeking to co-ordinate the constructional and land-use activities of all other agencies, in both public and private sectors, in such a way that all the various elements in our physical surroundings are brought into the best possible spatial relationship with each other.

The existence of town and country planning seems to be predicated on the assumption that there is some pattern of land use which is socially desirable, but which is different from the pattern which either the market, or the three 'other' types of governmental intervention set out above, would produce. This assumption is a constantly recurring theme. We can see it, for example, in the 1942 report of the Uthwatt Committee:

> It is clear that under a system of well-conceived planning the resolution of competing claims and the allocation of land for the various requirements must proceed on the basis of selecting the most suitable land for the particular purpose, irrespective of the existing values which may attach to the individual parcels of land.[2]

We can see it again in the White Paper which preceded the 1967 Land Commission Act, which stated the government's intention 'to secure that the right land is available at the right time for the implementation of national, regional and local plans'[3] and again in the White Paper on land policy issued by the newly-returned Labour government of 1974, which regretfully stated that still, unfortunately, 'the best use of land is not always achieved'.[4] The criteria whereby this assumed socially desirable pattern of land use might be discovered, however, have rarely if ever been very clearly explained. Nevertheless, it is clear that the planning system *does* modify the pattern of land use, or, as I shall say, 'rearrange land uses'.

In fact, of course, it is very difficult indeed to know the extent to which the physical pattern which has emerged since the passage of the Town and Country Planning Acts is the result of planning. Much of it may reflect quite other pressures, influences, or taken-for-granted assumptions. To what extent, for example, is the pattern of residential development the result of planning, and to what extent does it reflect consumers' preferences, developers' economic interests, or the predilections of the building societies? Do branch factories go to 'development areas' because of fears at Westminster of the political implications of unemployment, because of political pressures from the peripheral regions in question, or because 'plans' have been produced, showing the need for them? To ask this kind of question is to ask whether planning 'makes any difference'. It is perhaps because they are unsure of the answer to this question that planners, as I shall argue, are rather prone to blur the boundaries of their activity, and are so anxious to appear to be involved in far wider and far more exciting things than merely operating the Town and Country Planning Acts.

Physical and spatial patterns, then, are not merely the outcome of a multiplicity of economic and political interests and influences. Even within the governmental apparatus itself there is a multiplicity of such interests and influences, and these too may be pushing in quite contradictory directions. And among these various governmental influences the planning system probably plays a relatively minor role. How, then, can one justify a book which concentrates on this 'planning' alone, and which urges that its particular effects should be so far as possible isolated out? One answer to this lies in the vague claims made for planning. I will argue that planners tend to confuse their own activity with that of other people, and that they tend to portray the scope of their competence as being far wider than it actually is. And these things I see as undesirable. They prevent clear thought and public understanding.

It is in part in an attempt to clarify 'planning', then, that I have written this book. Planners themselves, perhaps out of a desire to demonstrate that their activity is creative, and not a matter of merely imposing regulations, often appear to conflate their role with that of the people who design and carry out public sector development. They also quite often portray planning as in some way dealing with currently fashionable problems such as conservation, the control of environmental pollution, or the stimulation of business enterprise. It should be pointed out, however, that they are expert in none of these things. They are not trained in site acquisition and assembly, or the securing of finance, or the designing of buildings, the drawing up of bills of quantities, the comparison of tenders, the hiring of contractors, the supervision of construction, and so on. Nor are they expert in what we might call 'fiscal geography'; others are better qualified than they to assess the ways in which changes in the pattern of government regulations, loans, grants, subsidies, and company taxation might affect the location of economic activity. Nor, of course, are they expert in problems of ecology, conservation or environmental protection, the solution of which demands the contributions of natural scientists, economists, and experts in political science and public administration.

A second justification for concentrating in this book on 'town and country planning narrowly defined' is that despite the vaguenesses and boundary-blurrings just mentioned, planning is in reality a fairly discrete, self-contained and limited branch of government. In their everyday activities, in their occupational socialisation and in their professional ideology, town and country planners are a distinctive group, with characteristic assumptions and values. In portraying their activity in a rather overambitious way, I would suggest, planners not only promote one of the central values of their professional subculture, but also express the wish rather than the reality; their view of planning concentrates on telling us what it *could* achieve, if it were given the scope and the powers of wider coordination which it 'ought' to have. My argument, by contrast, suggests that the best way to discover what planning *could* achieve lies in discovering what it *does* achieve.

A third justification for concentrating on 'town and country planning narrowly defined' is that little is known about it. Even the relatively modest activity which I have summed up as 'rearranging land uses' has very significant economic, political, and social effects. Yet few people have researched these. In urging that planning be widened to embrace the social and economic spheres, or to embrace all environmental questions, planners have neglected to investigate the effects of what they *already* do.

There is a second kind of vagueness to overcome, however, in defining my subject-matter. Even after one has declined to write about every kind of public policy or problem which has 'environmental' implications, and insisted instead on writing only about what town and country planners actually do, there is still this further problem of definition: town and country planners claim to be 'planners' in two distinct senses. In addition to their claim to plan in the 'substantive' sense, of planning the physical environment, they also claim to be planners in a second, 'procedural' sense. They suggest that there is a specific method of arriving at decisions, called 'planning', or 'rational planning method', and that in principle at least, this planning method can be applied not merely to problems of land use or the physical environment, but to *any* problem. This 'planning approach', they suggest, stands in sharp contrast to other possible ways of arriving at decisions, such as basing them on political expediency, or allowing them to be determined by market forces. As compared with these other possible approaches, 'planning' puts greater stress on co-ordination, or comprehensiveness, takes a longer-term view, leads to an outcome which is in some sense objectively optimal, or the 'best possible', and above all, it is more rational.

It is this claim to be planners in a second sense which seems to lie behind the tendency among town and country planners to call themselves simply 'planners', and their activity simply 'planning'. Nor have they hesitated to act upon their belief in their possession of this planning methodology of wider application; the schools of town and country planning have encouraged their graduates to regard themselves by virtue of being 'planners' in this second sense as qualified for jobs as managers in the public service more generally, and even in industry and business at large.

In this book, I am clearly not concerned with the applicability of this 'rational planning method' to anything other than governmental intervention in land and property development. Nevertheless, it seems necessary to outline my view on it, which is as follows. Rather than being a body of knowledge arising out of research and practice, it is largely a set of prescriptive ideas. In so far as it *does* derive from scientific work, it has its roots in systems theory and cybernetics. These last, however, were not intended to explain human actions, but only the behaviour of such things as mechanical or electronic systems, or unreflecting organisms. It is therefore very difficult to reconcile this notion of a rational planning method with the kinds of knowledge produced by the social sciences.

Three further points can be made, concerning this notion of 'rational planning'. First, since it is based on a conception of human nature which omits all that distinguishes us from animals or mechanical systems, its use poses a threat to political freedom. Second, since town and country planners do claim to use it, their claim should be taken seriously. Third, as I will also argue later, the attempt to use this method has the paradoxical effect of making government and administration *less* rational than they would otherwise be. Public policies in general have more or less understandable aims, and because they can be publicly challenged, and discussed in plain language, the extent to which they are achieving these aims can be assessed by independent research. 'Planning', by contrast, since it attempts or purports to render the implementation of policies into a supposedly

continuous process of 'feedback' and policy readjustment, carried out from *within*
the governmental apparatus, renders this rational public challenge and independent
critical research virtually impossible.[5]

Town and country planners, in summary, are not trained as specialists, but as
generalists, and see themselves as coordinating all the various pressures on land.
But in their attempts to justify this role, they tend to avoid any concrete
description or explanation of the land and property development process, or of
exactly how 'planning' intervenes in that process. Instead, they often attempt to
legitimate their activity in terms of this notion of 'planning' as an approach to
social decision-making in general. Thus, I have argued, their professional ideology
is vague and confused. But it is in part this very vagueness and confusion, in their
patterns of socialization, in their taken-for-granted assumptions about government
and society, and in their practice, which distinguishes town and country planners
as a distinctive group in society, and justifies our studying them.

## 2.  The theoretical justification of town and country planning

So far, I have identified the subject of enquiry. On the one hand, I have
distinguished it from other, wider, 'environmental' policies, problems and
concerns, with which it is often conflated, not least by planners themselves. On
the other hand, I have said that I am mainly interested in planning in the
'substantive' sense of the governmental control of land use, and in the notion of a
general planning method only in so far as it is an ideology used by land-use planners
to enhance their own professional power.

To be able to discuss land-use planning sensibly, one first needs some *theory*
about it. By this is meant some reasonably credible account as to why it might be
attempted, and what it might achieve. Planners themselves have failed to develop
such theory. It might help, therefore, if before we go any further, we at least try to
think about how such a theory of land-use planning might be constructed.

Why might government 'rearrange' land uses? A very simple type of argument,
but one which has played an important part in planning thought, is aesthetic:
towns and villages simply *look* better, it has for example been argued, if they are
compact. Planning powers have therefore been used to ensure that development
has become concentrated rather than scattered. A second type of argument is
'functional', in the sense in which engineers speak of the functioning of a
mechanism. Roads can carry future traffic volumes more easily, for example, and
with a minimum of disturbance to other nearby land uses, if generous swathes of
land are set aside for them, and kept free of all development. A third type of
argument, however, is expressed in economic terms. Land and buildings differ in a
fundamental way from other 'factors of production', or other 'goods'. Much of
the benefit we get from using or owning any particular building or facility derives
not so much from its inherent qualities, but rather from its location in relation to
*other* buildings or facilities, and from *their* inherent qualities. Also, buildings are of
little use without infrastructure; this too means that spatial arrangements are

crucial, for land must be set aside for (not directly profit-making) things such as roads and services. Moreover, land and buildings differ fundamentally from other commodities in that it seems virtually impossible to use them without affecting the pattern of other people's benefits and costs. The market, however, at least if unaided, seems bad at dealing with such things as these. It is difficult for public authorities to claim payment from those whose accessibility they improve, it is difficult for them to claim payment from those they provide with improved infrastructure, and it is equally difficult for you to claim compensation from your neighbours when they reduce the market value of your house by allowing their own houses to become neglected and unattractive.

Suppose that for convenience we classify all such land-use problems for the time being as *externalities*.[6] Could we then explain town and country planning purely in economic terms? Could we perhaps hypothesize that planning is the process of maximizing the aggregate margin of positive externalities over negative ones, by 're-arranging land uses'?[7] Is this third type of explanation, in economic terms rather than in terms of aesthetics or function, capable of subsuming the other two? Scattered development, for example, (at least to those who do indeed find it ugly) is certainly a negative externality; when enjoying the use of *one* bit of land, their enjoyment is reduced by the appearance of *other* bits. And similarly, it is obvious that traffic noise, fumes, and the reduced speed and increased fuel costs which congested vehicles impose upon each other are negative externalities.

In practice, the language of economic externalities is not much used in planning. Instead, the problem is often discussed in physical terms, as a matter of reducing the 'nuisance' which land uses impose upon each other. Even more commonly, and even more vaguely, it is discussed as a matter of safeguarding 'amenity', and of ensuring that land uses do not destroy this 'amenity'. What all this reflects, of course, is a reluctance on the part of authority to say *who* gains, and *who loses*, and by *how much*, when land uses are rearranged as a result of planning. To be both more open and more accurate about the matter, expressing costs and benefits in money terms or at least attempting to quantify them, would, however, obviously help us to understand town and country planning far better than we do.

If planning is best *conceptualized* in terms of what it can do about externality effects, I am suggesting, it might also be most logically *justified* in these same terms. Planners would then justify the giving of permission for one piece of proposed development, and the refusal of permission for another, by showing that in each case the effect would be to add something to the aggregate margin of positive over negative externalities in the neighbourhood.

In reality, as I have however noted, this is *not* the way in which planning decisions are usually justified. Is this because the estimation of such externality effects is too difficult, in purely technical terms? The answer to this seems to be that this is *not* the reason. Such impact assessment is undoubtedly difficult, but not impossible. In the case of major public sector proposals, it has often been not merely used, but taken to almost absurd lengths, in the sense that prices have been put on artefacts and even vaguely defined environmental qualities of the most intangible and subjective nature.[8] In the case of the planning control exerted over ordinary private sector development, by contrast, it has paradoxically hardly been used at all.

The real reason why development control decisions are not normally justified in terms of such costs and benefits is rather that the planning system rests fundamentally on what might be termed a kind of 'institutionalized coyness', so far as private and sectional material interests are concerned. This involves not merely a reluctance to consider or to discuss *financial* losses and gains, but even extends to a reluctance to make any serious attempt to assess the losses and gains of the affected parties in material terms at all. Instead, the system has always tended to rest on a concern for the physical environment itself, summed up in the concept of 'amenity' or the 'right use of land'; the assumption (or the legalized fiction) has always apparently been that all sections of the community will benefit equally if 'the environment' is protected and enhanced.

Increasingly in recent years, however, attempts have been made, first to discover the extent to which planning decisions do in practice, despite this 'coyness', reflect concern for economic and material considerations, and second, to discuss the possibility of constructing a rationale for town and country planning, based explicitly on welfare economics. These attempts, however, have not been made by planners, but rather, by lawyers and economists.[9] While the political convenience of what I termed 'institutionalized coyness' is obvious, the fact is that it also carries with it grave dangers. In particular, it has led other observers, and notably political scientists and sociologists, to hypothesize that hidden behind this facade of concern for the physical environment in its own right, the planning system may in fact operate in such a way as to help powerful economic interests and the more privileged members of society, both financially and by safeguarding their privileged environments.[10] Sheer self-interest, therefore, may ultimately compel change. Those who operate the planning system may themselves begin to feel it necessary both to find out more about the redistributive effects of their decisions, and, having found out, to make this knowledge public.

We could also, of course, ask whether this statutory 'rearrangement of land uses' *is* necessarily so very embarrassing in its effects as to necessitate such 'coyness'. Is the redistribution of environmental externality effects *of necessity* a 'zero-sum game', in which benefits can only be conferred upon some at the cost of taking them away from others? What, for example, of the case where we do not merely reroute a road with the consequence that it annoys one lot of people rather than another, but manage to find a *third* alignment for it, where it annoys nobody? And if a new landscaped open space is created where none previously existed, does not this create positive externalities for those living nearby without reducing those enjoyed by any other groups?

The fact would seem to be that there is inevitably a *relative* redistribution, if not always an absolute one. Some groups, after all, have *not* had traffic removed from their *door steps*, some have *not* had a new park provided near their homes. Since there will always be relative redistribution and sometimes absolute redistribution, then, it seems possible to conclude that it can hardly make sense to adopt land-use planning at all, unless we have first decided what social redistribution we wish to achieve.

One should, however, add that while it may seem reasonable for the planning system to seek to redistribute *physical-environmental* costs and benefits, it might seem less legitimate to use it as a means of deliberately redistributing property values, or the incomes derived from property values. If redistribution of wealth or income is the object, it may be argued, town and country planning would seem neither the most legitimate nor the most effective way of pursuing this aim. Indeed, it might be argued that the physical planning system should seek only *relative* redistribution, even of environmental 'goods', in the sense of ensuring that the environmental conditions of those affected by development are always improved, and never reduced. But even this apparently modest aim would have quite radical implications. A reduction of environmental standards in absolute terms, and as a direct result of planning decisions, is at present a common experience, and especially of less privileged groups in society.

Land-use planning, however, also has quite another type of redistributive effect, not yet mentioned. Quite apart from its tendency to enhance or reduce both physical and financial costs and benefits in an indirect way, as a consequence of what it permits to happen on other, nearby, land, it also has a more direct effect on property values. The very act of drawing up a plan, and thus showing which land can and cannot be developed, quite obviously takes virtually all value away from certain sites and presents it as a 'free gift' to the owners of others. This might seem to be an unfortunate 'side-effect' of planning, however, rather than a justification for adopting it.

But let us return to this idea that land use decisions can be made in accordance with social criteria or 'needs', for it is at the very heart of the problem of the theory of planning. Let us suppose that the wishes expressed in the official statements cited above were in fact fulfilled. Let us assume that (for example as a result of the taking of all land in the country into public ownership), the planners were able to have their way, and instead of allowing land use to be determined as at present on the basis of an almost unbelievably complex web of market forces, 'single-purpose' interventions, 'unintended' interventions and 'planning', it were to be determined by 'planning' alone. How would we then proceed? How would we then decide how to allocate land as between competing users? Those who urge planning, as the above-cited official pronouncements do, must presumably believe that there are principles from which we could derive our decisions. Indeed, they cannot logically urge this 'planning', unless they believe that there is a characteristic pattern of land use, which planning would produce, and which differs from the pattern which the market together with all the 'single purpose' and 'unintended' interventions characteristically produces. If there were, of course, there would be a theory of land-use planning. And from this, principles could be derived, on the basis of which the specific decisions could be made.

I would argue, however, that there cannot be any such theory of land-use planning. One way of demonstrating this is by looking at the communist countries, where the market clearly does not decide. Yet despite this, their characteristic patterns of land use are not unlike ours. Like ours, they reflect on the one hand certain economic imperatives, which mean, for example, that they do not usually use land of the highest accessibility in the centres of big cities for grazing sheep, any more than we do. On the other hand, their land-use patterns reflect the outcomes of competition and bureaucratic infighting between ministries and governmental enterprises, acting either on self-interest or on their various differing conceptions of the public interest—just as our land-use patterns, similarly, reflect the effects of what I have called 'single-purpose interventions', 'unintended' governmental influences, and 'planning'.

And, furthermore, it is apparent that in the communist countries the market is 'missed', in the sense that those concerned often find it difficult to make land-use decisions in the absence of that information on opportunity costs and consumer preferences which a functioning market can provide. Indeed, this is so much so that they often advocate or attempt 'shadow' pricing, or the estimation of 'shadow' rents.[11]

On the basis of such evidence, I conclude that there cannot be an alternative way of ordering things, which reflects 'human needs' or 'social considerations' rather than the laws of economics. Planners, however, behave as if there were such an alternative set of principles. They do not point to *specific* types of problem or 'market failure' in the 'modified market' pattern of land use which prevails in Britain, and they do not on the basis of their analysis of these specific problems come up with specific remedies. On the contrary, they justify 'planning' in *global* terms. Planning, it is asserted, can point to the best use for *every* piece of land. *All* changes in the use or in the intensity of use of land are therefore subject to planning control, and not just those changes which are in defined categories, which pose specific problems for society. If planners did *not* purport in this way to offer a supposed set of criteria for overall guidance, they would in terms of their own ideology run a grave risk—the risk of appearing not to be planning at all, but merely engaging in *ad hoc* interventions. They very notion of 'planning' would thus collapse. It would be seen to resolve itself into a long series of disparate, specialized and highly technical questions—of how best to combat *this* particular problem, and *this* one, and *this* one.

Yet in asserting (or giving the impression) that they *do* have criteria on the basis of which overall guidance can be operated, the planners run an equally grave risk; they may be asked what these criteria are, and from what coherent body of theory they derive.

From the above brief discussion of the possible theoretical justification of land-use planning, I draw two conclusions. First, it would seem that there could be no justification for an overall system of control, but only for intervention in specific types of situation. Secondly, any such specific intervention could only be justified in terms of political objectives, since it must of necessity have redistributive effects. The British planning system, however, rests on diametrically opposed assumptions, in both respects. It purports to control *all* land use, and any redistributive intention is broadly speaking denied. But before we can go any further, we need some basic facts concerning this planning system.

### 3. The British town and country planning system: an outline of institutions and practices[12]

The planning system as it still exists at the time of writing consists essentially of the vestiges of legislation of 1947, 1953 and 1959. In this system, the relevant central government ministry (at present the Department of the Environment) has general supervisory and policy-making powers, and also acts as an administrative 'court of appeal', but the main powers rest at the local level, being divided in England and Wales between the counties and the county districts. In the metropolitan areas, where no county-level authority exists, these powers rest with the local authority. In Scotland, they are divided between the regions and districts. The basis of the whole system lies in the fact that the local authority, statutorily defined for the purpose as the 'local planning authority', must grant permission before any 'development' is carried out. And 'development' is defined broadly, as 'the carrying out of building, engineering, mining or other operations in, on, over or under land, or the making of any material change in the use of any buildings or other land'.[13] The system has three fundamental features:

*Firstly,* it rests on a high level of administrative discretion.[14] To make this clear, we can imagine a spectrum, from *pure rule of law* at one end to *pure administrative discretion* at the other. 'Pure rule of law' describes a system in which the rules on which control is based are clear, and public. In such a system, there is a plan, and accompanying regulations, from which anyone can see what is permitted and what is not. Such a system obviously does not require a high level of expertise among those who administer the controls 'in the field'. All that is required is that they can read the plan and regulations, and explain them, and that they have the power of enforcement. A high level of expertise *is,* however, desirable at the level of the system as a whole, both to advise on objectives, and to discover by research the extent to which these objectives are being achieved. *Pure administrative discretion,* by contrast, describes the situation in which there is no such obligation on the part of the planning authority to provide a clear statement of what is, and what is not, permitted, and in which, instead, 'each case is determined on its merits'. This leaves those who actually administer the system at the local level free to decide what 'merit' is when they see it. It also leaves them free to bargain with developers, extracting whatever concessions seem to them in the particular circumstances to promote the aims of good planning as they interpret those aims at the time.

A system which emphasizes 'pure rule of law' has the virtues of simplicity and comprehensibility, and is also manifestly fair, in the sense that all can see what the rules are (this is not, of course, the same as saying that the rules themselves are necessarily fair or equitable). It may, however, become rigid, if its purposes and its effects are not constantly challenged by researchers. A system which emphasizes 'administrative discretion', by contrast, should have greater flexibility, and should thus permit the planners to take advantage of opportunities as they arise, but it will probably appear unclear in its rationale and in its operations, it will probably be relatively slow, it lacks political accountability, and it is much more open to corruption. Above all, those who administer it may come to get such a high level of psychological gratification out of exercising their powers of administrative (or 'professional') discretion, of operating as 'fixers', that they may lose sight of the objectives which the system is politically intended to pursue.

Clearly, no actual land-use planning system corresponds to either of these 'ideal types'. But most comparable Western countries have planning systems which lie much closer to the 'pure rule of law' type than does Britain's. Both the main cause and the main consequence of this lie in the relatively strong position in the British system of the planners themselves, and especially, in the fact that they are organized as a 'profession'. The members of a profession clearly cannot be seen to be merely enforcing clearly stated regulations, in the way that minor officials do. On the contrary, they must appear to be resolving complex matters, in ways which demand highly developed capacities of expertise and judgment. Another crucial consequence of this high level of administrative or professional discretion is that, as noted above, specific permission must be obtained in Britain for each piece of development. In most other comparable countries, the *plan itself* confers permission upon any development which accords with the plan.

The *second* major feature of the British planning system relates to its categorization of land uses. As we saw above, permission is required for any 'material change of use'. But the use categories defined for this purpose are from a certain point of view rather vague, since they relate to 'nominal' uses rather than to socio-economic realities. Here, then, we see again the 'coyness', or embarrassment concerning the redistributive effects of planning, noted in Section 2 above: residential use, for example, is simply 'residential', whether it is slum dwellings or extravagant luxury apartments, and a shop is a shop whether it sells everyday food needs in small amounts, or expensive antiques for export to North America. Since permission is not required for changes of use within the defined categories, profound socio-economic changes can occur in the urban fabric, but they are no concern of the planning system. An area can be 'gentrified', for example, and its original working-class population displaced.[15] In defence of this definition of use categories in 'nominal' rather than socio-economic terms, however, one should perhaps point out that it derives from perfectly reasonable and impeccably egalitarian conceptions of social justice. The basic premise was that residential uses should be protected against the encroachment of 'nuisance' uses, such as industry, and it was in the belief that *all* residential areas should have this protection, irrespective of their social status, that 'residential' was defined as a single category.

The *third* major feature of the British planning system is that the country's major land use, agriculture, is excluded altogether from planning control. As long as land which is allocated in the plan for agricultural use *remains* in agricultural use, no permission is required for its development, even if such development involves the erection of buildings or other plant, or the intensification of this agricultural use. The significance of this exemption, of course, lies in the fact that new and more intensive forms of agricultural production can often have profound effects, both ecologically and on the landscape, and for this reason, a number of commentators have urged that agriculture should be brought under planning control like everything else.[16] To date, however, the exemption continues. Indeed, it has been reinforced; under recent legislation, provision has been made for payment of compensation to farmers in certain areas for *not* farming their land more intensively, a measure which conflicts with the otherwise well-established principle that no compensation is payable in Britain for the imposition of planning restrictions.[17]

As regards its legal and administrative arrangements, we can distinguish three main components in the British planning system, *development plans*, *development control* and its *financial provisions*. I will discuss each of these in turn.

At the time of writing, and outside the former 'metropolitan' areas, development plans must be prepared at two levels. Each county must prepare a 'structure plan', covering its entire area. District councils within each county must prepare 'local plans'. Structure plans are supposed to be the means whereby national policies are translated into proposals at county level. They are based on stated assumptions, looking some 10–15 years ahead, concerning population and employment trends. But they make only broad diagrammatic proposals for land use. One is not supposed to be able to see from the structure plan what is the intended use of any specific plot of land. Indeed, the major part of the 'structure plan' consists of the statement of policy in words, the diagrams of intended land use being purely ancillary.[18] It is the local plans which translate these broad statements of policy into actual land-use allocations.[19] The main weaknesses of structure plans, and of their relationship to local plans and development control derive from the 'two-tier' system of local government in 'non-metropolitan' England.

This system of structure plans and local plans was introduced in the late 1960s, when it was confidently expected that following the recommendations of the Redcliffe–Maud Commission, a single-tier system of local government would be established everywhere except in the largest conurbations. Thus, it was anticipated that both the structure plan and the local plans would be prepared by one and the same planning department. In the event, however, the Conservative government which took office in 1970 rejected the Redcliffe–Maud proposals, and instead retained a two-tier system of local government. (Later, paradoxically, the Conservatives abolished in 1986 the two-tier system which *had* been recommended by Redcliffe–Maud, and established, in the 'metropolitan areas'). Thus, structure plans became the responsibility of the counties, and local plans of the new, enlarged, districts. The districts were also given the major powers of development control. Given this division of powers, it was inevitable that conflicts would arise. The districts inevitably tend to resent the way in which the county can decide which of them will get the desirable development. The county, for its part, almost inevitably mistrusts the districts' intentions faithfully to pursue the objectives set out in its structure plan.[20]

Some observers also consider that structure plans have been weakened by being deprived of any real economic or social content. At the time they were introduced it was widely assumed in planning circles that government was about to embark on a programme of 'economic and social planning', with which physical planning would be increasingly integrated. But this assumption too, like that concerning the future pattern of local government, proved misplaced. Many planners in the early 1970s still tried to include statements concerning their authorities' social and economic policies in their structure plans. The Department of the Environment, however, has increasingly firmly insisted that these plans should be concerned only with questions of land use.[21]

'Local plans' are prepared by the district councils. They can be 'subject plans', concerned with such specific matters as mineral extraction, tourism, or sites for industry, or they can be 'action area plans', related to specific localities. These should be prepared wherever it is anticipated that there will arise significant demands for private sector development, or where proposed public sector development will require to be integrated with surrounding land uses.

It may also be mentioned here that there usually exist *regional* plans of various orders of authority and credibility. Under all post-war British administrations there has been a greater or lesser degree of commitment to 'regional policy', the attempt to ensure that economic development is shared more evenly between the prosperous South-East and the peripheral regions. Structure plans are supposed to reflect these wider policies. Regional planning is, however, beyond the scope of the present book. It is a sphere of public policy in which town and country planners regard themselves by training to be competent, but in which in practice they are not normally employed.[22]

*Development control is* the power to decide whether or not specific development takes place on specific sites, to control the intensity of the development thus permitted, and to control its layout and design. A very important part of the development control system, it should be made clear, lies not in the power to grant or to refuse permission, but rather in the power of the professional planners to persuade the applicants to modify their proposals, even before they submit these for approval. Thus, the planners will usually advise informally on what is likely to be welcomed by 'the committee', and what, by contrast, the committee are likely to 'frown upon', and will even themselves spend time producing alternative sketches, which the applicant, if he accepts them, can then work up into a formal submission. Formally, then, decisions on such applications are made by the planning committee of the local authority in question, advised by the salaried professional planners.[23] Central government, however, has certain overriding powers. The Secretary of State for the Environment can 'call in' specific applications, deciding them himself rather than allowing the local planning authority to decide them. This power, however, is used only in the most unusual circumstances, in relation to politically sensitive cases. Much more important in normal circumstances is the Secretary of State's duty to decide so-called 'appeals', those cases in which the applicant does not accept the local planning authority's refusal of permission, or does not accept the conditions on which permission is granted. Such conditional permissions, it may be noted, are issued in order to achieve such things as tree planting, or minor modifications in design and layout. Where the planning authority wishes to secure objectives which are not of this physical nature, but which might be thought 'social' or 'economic' in character, it usually seeks to achieve this not by such conditions, but by 'voluntary' agreement, for which provision is also made under the planning legislation. Such legal agreements are used, for example, where it is desired to restrict the occupancy of houses in rural areas to local workers, to prevent their sale as 'second homes'.[24]

Most 'appeals' are decided by an inspector, appointed by the Department of the Environment on the basis of 'written representations' put to him by the appellant, the local planning authority, and other interested parties, if any. In less straightforward cases, the inspector appointed to deal with the case may decide to hold a local inquiry, an administrative hearing which is open to the public, and at which all interested parties may present their cases both orally and in the form of written evidence. In major planning appeals, the various parties employ lawyers, and the proceedings take on some of the outward trappings of a court of law. It is important to note, therefore, that these procedures are not legal, but purely administrative ones. The inspector is not required to decide the case in terms of equity, or in response to the force of the arguments put forward. Rather, his job is to ensure that the final decision is a correct interpretation of *policy*, as laid down by central government and as set out in the local authority's statutory plans.[25] The major element in this system of plans, the *structure plan*, is itself subject to approval and possible modification by the Department of the Environment.[26]

Thus we see how in principle all the various parts of the planning system fit logically together. In exercising its development control function, the local planning authority is of course guided by the development plan, and especially by the local plan, if one exists. But it need not necessarily be, and can indeed refuse or grant permission in ways which conflict with that plan, if it has good reasons. What 'good reasons' means here, of course, is reasons which the DoE inspector would seem likely to uphold, if the case were to come to appeal. Here again, in the local planning authority's right to go against its own statutory plan, we see reflected the high degree of administrative discretion which characterizes the British system.[27]

It should also be added that in principle *public* development is also subject to development control.[28] Thus local councils as 'housing authorities' are required to consult with themselves as 'planning authorities' before resolving to put council houses on particular sites, and similarly all public sector agencies and statutory undertakers are required to consult with the local planning authority before commencing any development. Planners often complain that these consultative arrangements give them insufficient powers of control, however, especially over such powerful central government agencies as the Central Electricity Generating Board and the Department of Defence.

The third component in the planning system, as identified above, consisted of its *financial arrangements*. These, however, have occasioned far more problems than have the arrangements for the making of plans or for the carrying out of development control. Rather than simply describing these financial arrangements, therefore, it seems more appropriate to explain them within the context of a wider consideration of the relationship between land-use planning and land values. This forms the next section of this chapter.

## 4.   Land-use planning and land values[29]

Imagine a steadily expanding city. To the north, south, east and west of this city is agricultural land. The owners of this land will each hope that at some time in the not too distant future, their own particular bit will be in demand for development. Now let us imagine that a system of land-use planning is introduced, and that with the exception of that relatively small proportion of it judged adequate for the development which is actually needed, all this agricultural land is allocated in the plan as remaining in agricultural use. All the owners, on every side of the city, will feel that their own particular land might well have been developed, had the plan not come into force. They will therefore claim that the plan has destroyed the *development value* in their land, the difference between its value in its existing agricultural use and the price which a developer would have paid for it as building land.

In the case of a relatively small proportion of all these landowners, the claim is in fact true. But we have no means of knowing which. We have no means of knowing where this development *would* have settled in the absence of planning, for planning has indeed been introduced. If we add up the claims of all these owners, we will find that, in total, they are many times the amount which developers could have been expected to spend on land purchase for many years ahead. To meet all these claims, therefore, would be not only financially impossible but in any case socially unjust. This is the problem of 'floating value'; we cannot know where the floating value would have settled, had we not introduced planning. We therefore cannot know whose interests have been damaged by the plan, and we thus do not know who should be compensated.

Next let us consider the land on which the plan *does* permit development. Development values which in the absence of planning might have been realised in many different places, on all sides of our city, will all be 'shifted', concentrated by the plan within this relatively small area. In the case of any particular owner, however, it will be quite impossible to *prove* that it is the imposition of planning restrictions elsewhere which has produced his enhanced development value. It might just have happened to be his land which would have been most in demand for development anyway, he may suggest, even had planning *not* been introduced. And we have no means of showing that his suggestion is unfounded. This is the problem of 'shifting value'; it is mainly the existence of the plan, we strongly suspect, which has placed these windfall gains in development value in the hands of particular owners, and in terms of sheer equity, therefore, they should pay back this money. But we cannot *prove* that these owners have gained at others' expense.[30]

How has the British planning system dealt with these closely related problems of 'floating' and 'shifting' value? Before we can answer this, we must first deal with a confusion in the use of the term 'compensation'. In the literature generally, this word is used to mean two quite different things. First, it is used to describe payments made to owners in recognition of the fact that planning restrictions are applied to their land, as in the above example. Second, it is used to describe payments made to owners when their land is purchased from them, compulsorily, by the state, for the purpose of building such things as roads, schools, hospitals or whatever. This dual use of this single term, 'compensation', seems confusing. I shall therefore use it only to describe payments made in recognition of planning restrictions, and where there is no change in ownership. Payments for compulsory purchase, I shall call the compulsory purchase price.

Until the Second World War, the assumption was that the only fair way to deal with the problem of 'floating value' was indeed to compensate (in *my* sense) the owners of all land allocated in plans for agricultural purposes, and which therefore could not be developed. But this made planning almost totally ineffective. Even in a country as densely populated as Britain, the land *not* allocated for development was obviously many times greater than the land which *was* allocated, and the potential cost of compensation was therefore astronomical. To avoid paying this compensation, local planning authorities used various subterfuges. One, for example, was to allocate vast stretches of countryside not for agricultural use, but for extremely low-density residential development. Thus if one house already existed in an area of many acres, no more could be permitted. By 1937, about half the country was covered by plans. But within even this area, sufficient land was allocated for residential development to house about 350 million people. Clearly, this approach to 'planning' made very little sense.[31]

An apparent solution, however, was to be found in a long-standing economic doctrine, clearly enunciated by social theorists as long ago as the eighteenth century. This suggested quite simply that increases in land values in general are not produced by the efforts of the owners, but by society. To tax them away, this doctrine therefore suggests, would be not only ethically just, but also efficient in economic terms. With the emergence of town planning, then, in the twentieth century, there presented itself an obvious possibility. Where *planning* increased land values, as in the case of the 'shifted' values discussed above, this could be equated with the increases in value attributed by this long-established doctrine to 'society'. A tax could be imposed on these planning-created increases in development value, and out of the revenues thus produced, compensation could be paid to those owners who had had the development value of their land reduced or destroyed by planning.

Before we can examine this apparently very neat solution, however, we need to look a little more closely at this idea that increases in land values are in general socially produced. We can in principle distinguish three ways in which this occurs.

The first of these is due to an increase in the level of economic activity in the country as a whole. Land in every kind of use, everywhere, will in principle be in greater demand, and there will be considerable economic incentive to convert much of it from less profitable to more profitable uses. The second case concerns land in a specific area, such as that in the vicinity of our expanding city discussed above. As development creeps out into the countryside, the prices which can be obtained from developers will soon be many times the agricultural value. The third type of case concerns the expenditure of public money. In many cases, the potential for development can be attributed specifically to such things as the provision nearby of an access point onto the motorway system, or main drainage, electricity or telephone cables, or the construction nearby of planted and landscaped parks or open spaces.

In practice, however, increases in development value will usually be due to a combination of all three types of cause, and it will usually be impossible to show what proportion of any given rise in development value is attributable to the expenditure of public money on infrastructure or amenities. But the principle is clear, nevertheless. Because *other*, nearby, land is developed, owners reap development value on their own land, but without having themselves done anything or incurred any expense. Unlike the increases brought about by 'shifting values', above (which seem best described as a kind of 'direct' transfer), the increases in value brought about by all three of the types of factor mentioned here are *externality effects*.

What we *call* these socially or publicly produced increases in value brought about by factors of the above three types, is itself a source of further confusion. John Stuart Mill termed all three of them 'the unearned increment', and argued that since they were economically unproductive, corresponding to no expenditure of resources on the part of those to whom they accrued, they could be taxed away in their entirety without any harmful effects on the economy. In more modern times, they have been termed 'betterment', but here there is further confusion. Some writers use this term to describe *only* those increases in value which are specifically due to public works, while others use the same term to describe all such increases in value, whether attributable to public or to private investment. For simplicity, and because it is in any case difficult to attribute specific parts of the increase in value to specific causes, I shall follow this last usage. In fact I shall go further. I shall use the term 'betterment' to describe *all* increases in land values, whether due to factors of the three types mentioned above, *or* to what we have called 'direct shifts' produced by planning, *or* to the effects of planning in ensuring that neighbouring land uses are mutually compatible, and thus provide positive externality effects for each other. Following this usage, of course, betterment can for all practical purposes be simply equated with *development value*, the difference between the value of land in its existing use and its value if it can be converted to a more profitable use.[32]

What in fact happens if we follow the advice of Mill, and tax away betterment? This is a complex question, but much, apparently, depends upon the particular form which the tax takes, and especially, upon its timing. If it is imposed in the form of a periodic levy on increases in site value, for example, (that is, on the value of the site but ignoring the value of whatever building is upon it), this should in principle encourage the development of all land for its most profitable use. An owner of agricultural land which, due to urban growth, has acquired a development value, for example, simply *cannot afford* to keep it in agricultural use, if such a tax is imposed.[33] If, on the other hand, the tax takes the form of a single payment imposed either upon the seller or the buyer at the time the land is bought for development, this may well have the opposite effect, and remove the incentive to develop. The reason for this is that both landowners who sell for development, and developers themselves, *expect* to share between them some of the development value; developers, in Britain, do not usually distinguish between the profits which they make from 'unearned' increases in site value, and the profits which they make out of organizing the construction process.

Let us now return to our area of land on which development *is* permitted, and onto which 'shifting' value has therefore been concentrated. Since we now *have* a planning system, we can say that it is planning which has produced all the externality effects, too, which *also* play a part in increasing the value of this land. For it is planning, after all, which has permitted, (or promoted) all the neighbouring development, and all the infrastructure, which previously, we simply attributed to 'economic growth', or 'society', or 'urban expansion'; in a society which *has* planning, it is planning which, supposedly, decrees where growth and expansion shall occur. Above all (as argued above), planning should have produced a 'better' pattern of surrounding uses than would otherwise have existed. It should have maximized the margin of positive externalities over negative ones, for the development which is to go upon it, or in other words ensured that it will have 'useful neighbours', nearby uses which do not constitute 'nuisances', or destroy 'amenity', but which, on the contrary *increase* 'amenity'.

We are now ready to return to the argument that a tax on all this betterment could provide the funds out of which compensation could be paid, where planning prevents land being converted to a more profitable use. It may seem fairly obvious that the former should not only pay for the latter, but that the two should, at least in principle, balance, in a strictly financial sense. The purpose of land-use planning, after all, is certainly not to reduce the volume of construction activity which is going on, but merely to 'rearrange' it spatially, presumably in order to increase in some way the benefits it gives.[31] By the same token, then, it would seem to follow that it is not the object of planning either to increase or to decrease that proportion of the nation's wealth which is invested in or produced by land and property development. If this wealth, too, has inadvertently *also* been 'redistributed spatially', as a result of ensuring that all land has been put to its 'best' use, then it too can, as it were, be returned to its rightful owners; the 'unearned increment' presented as a free gift to the owners of the land allocated for development can be recouped by taxation (logically at 100 per cent), and used to compensate those owners who have *lost* development value.

Unfortunately, however, the logic is illusory. This becomes clear, as soon as we remember that in logic as well as in terms of ethics, and law, society is obliged to give a clear answer to what we can call the 'fundamental' question: to whom should development value belong, to property owners, or to the state? Above, I have set out arguments which lead to the conclusion that it should belong to the state. There is, however, an alternative point of view, and this alternative view also can be convincingly justified. It can be pointed out, for example, that the processes whereby land values are created, whether 'market' processes or forms of government intervention, should be well known to those who own or trade in land, or develop it, and that it is therefore *their* business to avoid being left with unprofitable land on their hands. Their legitimate function in society, this alternative view suggests, is to take advantage of these processes, in order to make profits; since they can make such profits only if they provide that pattern of development for which the public is prepared to pay, this is itself the proof and the guarantee that their actions in buying, selling, holding and developing land are in fact socially beneficial.

And this 'alternative' view, of course, leads to the conclusion that development value (or at least some part of it) should be the property of developers. It is in practice virtually impossible, this view suggests, to distinguish between that part of developers' profits which comes from increases in land values, and that part which comes from the construction process, and it is therefore better to leave the *whole* of their profits in the hands of the developers, since this is likely to increase economic efficiency.

Which of these two answers we give to this 'fundamental' question is immaterial, from the viewpoint of the present argument. All that is being established, for the moment, is that according to whether we accept the one view or the other, we are obliged to accept those conclusions which follow from it. If we decide that development value should belong to the state, then it follows that it should be brought into the possession of the state. It does *not* follow, however, that those who are prevented from developing their land, and thus realizing its development value, should be compensated. After all, one does not compensate people for the loss of something which is not theirs.[35] If, on the other hand, we think that development value should be the property of owners or developers, then it *does* follow that any who are not permitted to realize it should indeed be compensated, but equally, it follows that there can be no 'tax', or recoupment of this development value by the state.

We can conclude, therefore that it is logical to have *either* compensation, *or* a tax on betterment. But it is not logical to have both. Nor is it logical to have neither. And which of these two logics we adopt, must depend on the answer we give to the 'fundamental' question set out above. It is very common to discuss the financial problems raised by the existence of town planning under the heading 'compensation and betterment'? A less confusing heading might be 'compensation *or* taxation of betterment'.

We are now ready to look at the 1947 Town and Country Planning Act, the first major attempt, in Britain, to find a solution to these problems. There is of course no doubt as to which of the two possible answers this Act gave to what we have called our 'fundamental question'. In taking away from owners the legal right to develop their property without express permission, the Act quite logically also gave this legal restriction economic expression: it in effect simply expropriated the development value in all land, both that existing at the time, *and* all that development value which would be created in the future. If owners *were* given permission to develop their property, they were therefore obliged to pay a 'development charge', which was to be calculated as 100 per cent of the difference between the value of the land *with* this planning permission and its value *without it*. What all owners kept, was the existing use rights in their land; no land was to be allocated in plans for a *less* profitable use than the existing one.[36] But in the case of all those owners who could show that their land had development potential at the time of the passing of the Act, provision was made for payments to be made in recognition of their financial loss, out of a £300 million fund set aside for the purpose.

It is important to stress that the Act *did* simply expropriate the development value in all land, and did not purchase it against compensation, for there is some confusion over this. Even the Uthwatt Report itself, widely if mistakenly regarded as having provided the logic for the Act, discussed compensation and betterment as if they could logically be 'balanced'. Indeed, it even went so far as to produce accounts, showing that if money were borrowed at the then prevailing rate of 3 per cent to pay the compensation claims, the taxation of betterment could cover the combined costs of these payments plus the cost of borrowing.[37] It was apparently mainly the representatives of the Labour Party who at the time of the passage of the Act pointed to the fallacy in this argument, and who insisted, therefore, that the payments made out of the £300 million fund *could* not logically be compensation, and should therefore be regarded as *ex gratia*, or 'hardship' payments.[38] That there could not logically be compensation, if it were the state which in fact now owned the development value in all land, was of course obvious in the provisions made under the Act for the refusal of planning permission; here, quite logically, there was to be no compensation.

It is also necessary, however, to say something about the way in which the 100 per cent tax on betterment, or 'development charge', was actually collected, for this is widely seen as the reason for the failure of the 1947 Act. The essential point here is that, unlike developers themselves, the Act made a very sharp distinction between the profits to be made out of rising land values and the profits to be made out of organizing the construction process. It assumed the former to be 'unethical', but the latter it saw as perfectly legitimate. What the government intended, therefore, was that from the time when the Act came into force, land would change hands at existing use value. Since the developer who purchased land for development *knew* that he would be required to hand over the whole of its development value to the state in the form of the 'development charge', it was assumed he would not be so foolish as *also* to pay any part of this development value to the vendor. Within a short time, it was also assumed, the market would adjust accordingly; all sales of land would be taking place at existing use value.

What happened in practice, of course, was that vendors demanded more than existing use value, and that developers, competing for land, paid more. As they thus paid development value twice over, development costs increased. Another problem arose from the timing of the development charge. Since it was payable at the time that development was carried out, it could be, and was, portrayed as a 'tax on development', a pejorative description which the Conservatives were obviously able to exploit to their own political advantage. What seems to have helped the Conservatives even more, however, was their simple assertion that 'nobody understood' the rationale behind the development charge. By an Act of 1953, therefore, two years after returning to office, the Conservatives simply abolished the development charge.

What the new Conservative government did *not* do, however, was to alter the principle that no compensation was payable for planning restrictions placed on land by the zoning provisions made in plans, or for refusal of planning permission. They thus ushered in a long period of 'town and country planning', extending right down to the present day, in which the entire system of control has been both illogical and unjust.[39] That no compensation is payable implies that, in law, development value belongs to the state. That no taxation of betterment exists, on the other hand, implies that in law development value belongs to the property owner. In practice, what this muddled approach means is that development value belongs to the property owner *if* he can get planning permission, but that where he *cannot* get planning permission the development value is in effect expropriated.

Faced with a planning system so muddle-headed in its basic principles, so unfair in the way it discriminates between 'fortunate' and 'unfortunate' property owners, and which so clearly functions in such a way as to use the power of the state to create near-monopoly price levels, one's first reaction is to wonder how it could be justified at all. In the first place, it was justified by further confusion. Under legislation of 1954, accepted claims on the £300 million fund would be paid *not* as intended to all owners who had been able to show that the introduction of planning had decreased the development value in their land, but only where planning permission was expressly refused. This presumably helped, by giving the false impression that in some way or other compensation *was* after all a feature of the new Conservative dispensation.[40]

Mainly, however, justification was achieved by reliance on two contradictory doctrines. To justify the publicly-created near-monopoly profits enjoyed by the 'fortunate' owners, these were portrayed as rewards to enterprise. To justify the fact that the 'unfortunate' owners were not allowed to realize the development value in their land, the 'good neighbour' principle was resuscitated. This, a principle traditional to British property law, suggests that it is indeed reasonable to deny owners the right to use their land in certain ways, if these proposed uses would cause nuisance to others. Taken together, however, these two principles constitute a remarkably odd social-philosophical basis on which to erect a land-use planning system.

The thesis advanced here, then, is that from 1953 to the present day, the British planning system has been vitiated by being operated in conjunction with a free market in land—or rather, often with a near-monopoly market, for this is the inevitable result of attempting to combine the two opposed logics of 'market' and 'plan'. Given such a contradiction of principles, it is not surprising that considerable problems have ensued. The profits to be made in such a system are largely *created by* planning, a situation which is obviously socially unjust. But the public sector, in such a system, also creates problems for *itself*. The land which must be acquired for non-profit-making public purposes has itself had its price pushed up by planning restrictions, and that taxpayers must pay these inflated prices is an added injustice.[41] Twice in this long period, first in the early 1960s and again in the early 1970s, tremendous 'property booms' have gathered force in Britain, and land and property prices have risen to levels which many observers have considered damaging to the economy as a whole. Two subsequent attempts by Labour governments to reintroduce the taxation of betterment (1967 and 1976), as well as various rather less wholehearted attempts by Conservative administrations at the height of the property booms to impose taxes with similar intentions, can all be seen as political responses to these problems, created by the '1953 system'.

To suggest that little has really changed in this area from 1953 to the present day may seem a little too simple, for as noted above subsequent Labour administrations have twice attempted to establish extremely ambitious schemes for the recoupment of 'unearned increment', each of them in fact rather more radical than the 1947 Act. But this is exactly the point I would make—that these schemes, partly *because* they were so radical, evoked extreme political reactions, were enormously watered down before being put into effect, and were in any case extremely short-lived, hardly having got off the ground before being repealed. Nevertheless, it seems necessary in order to complete the story that we examine these two subsequent pieces of legislation very briefly.

In 1967, in the Land Commission Act, the Labour government introduced a 40 per cent tax on betterment, but this Act had hardly come into operation before it was repealed by the incoming Conservative government in 1971. In 1976, under the Development Land Tax Act, betterment exceeding £10,000 was to be taxed variously at rates of 80 per cent and 66.6 per cent, though in a scheme notable for its complexity, and incorporating many 'exemptions' and 'exceptions'. In 1980, the Conservative government raised the level of liability to £50,000 and reduced the rate to a single one of 60 per cent and, in 1985, it finally abolished this tax all together.[42]

Both the 1967 and the 1976 Labour attempts to deal with the problem of betterment, it should be added, were associated with ambitious legislative arrangements for the reform of the planning system more generally. These wider provisions will be briefly outlined in Section 5 of this chapter. The repeal of the 1967 and 1976 schemes for the taxation of betterment, in 1971 and 1985 respectively, left the country each time with the '1953 system', as described above, which is notable mainly for its crudity and unfairness. Most comparable countries have been far less racked by ideological battles. They have attempted rather less, more slowly and more carefully, and as a consequence have achieved far more.

The main conclusion to be drawn from this section, then, concerns the inherent contradiction in the British system, produced by the attempt to operate land-use planning in the absence of an effective tax on betterment. This illogical combination seems guaranteed to lead to pseudo-planning, the appearance of planning without the reality. It seems likely that in such a system it will often be the market rather than planning which decides.

## 5.   Is the British planning system 'negative'? And what might make it positive?

So far, I have stuck to a 'narrow' interpretation of 'planning'. By this, I mean that I have restricted myself to discussing those things which planners have the power to do, and to considering how these actual powers might be explained and justified. Planners themselves, however, often tend to regard these existing powers as too limited. Their powers are purely 'negative', they suggest, in the sense that while they can prevent that development which is 'undesirable', they cannot promote that which is 'desirable'. The existing planning system, they argue, is thus totally dependent on the development industry, and should be replaced by a system of 'positive planning'. In trying to understand what they mean by this, we are helped by two things. First, though the British planning system has no positive powers, periodic attempts have been made to give it such powers, and we can look at these. Secondly, the planning systems of other countries embody positive planning powers to varying degrees.

What types of power, then, would constitute 'positive planning'? Broadly there are two, *public land purchase* and *programmes of public development*.[43] To understand why these might constitute 'positive planning', we must go back to the typology of kinds of governmental influence on patterns of environmental change, set out at the beginning of Section 1 of this chapter. All governments carry out public development, it was pointed out, in order to build schools, hospitals, roads, and so on, and without necessarily thereby making any claim to be planning their countries' overall pattern of land use. And since they thus carry out development, all governments purchase land, to put it on. What, then, might be special about 'public land purchase' and 'programmes of public development', and how do they differ from the types of governmental intervention so far identified?

The answer to this lies in the *intention* and in the *scale* of such public land acquisition and development programmes. They can be understood as positive planning if they aim at influencing the *overall* pattern of land use and property development. And to do this, obviously, they must not only be carried out on a sufficiently large scale, but must also be conceived as part of some overall 'plan'. Public development as normally carried out in Britain, and as identified in Section 1 of this chapter, arises out of statutory obligations to provide specific things, such as education or medical care. In purchasing land to make these things available, government does not normally have much effect on the land and property market. Rather, it must act within the market, taking the price levels and the spatial pattern which the market produces very largely as 'given'. Under the 1947 Town and Country Planning Act, public bodies carrying out these specific and 'piecemeal' statutory obligations were in fact able to purchase the land they needed at existing use values. Since 1959, however, it has been necessary for them to pay market value.[44] This means, broadly speaking, that they must pay the existing use value *plus* the development value, the two together being the price which due to its location in relation to other development the land in question *would* have fetched, if sold to a profit-seeking developer. Given these terms, clearly, such public developers could hardly hope to influence either the overall spatial pattern, or the workings of the land market.[45]

By 'public land-acquisition', then, is meant a programme of land purchase carried out on such a scale that it does affect, if it does not determine, the overall pattern of land use, and which does significantly affect, even if it does not completely determine, the workings of the land and property market. Indeed, it may be on such a scale that the land purchased is sufficient to accommodate all development, both public and private. On this scale, however, it is of course only possible where the law provides for it to take place at existing use value; otherwise no government could afford it.

If a programme of public development, similarly, is to be capable of being regarded as constituting 'positive planning', then it too must clearly have wider aims than the provision of specific facilities. It must seek to determine the overall pattern of development, and to structure the whole financial framework within which the land and property markets and the construction industries operate. When 'positive planning' is urged in Britain, it is often suggested that the development programmes in question be carried out by the state (in this case usually the local authority) and the private sector acting 'in partnership'. The former has the powers, the argument runs (or should have), while the latter has the 'know-how' concerning the economics of property development.[46]

What arguments are advanced, then, for such 'positive planning'? First, there are arguments focusing on the inefficiency and wastefulness of the existing system. Because planning controls concentrate all development value on a relatively restricted area of land, such arguments suggest, they unavoidably produce property speculation, inflated land and property prices, the tying-up of too great a proportion of the nation's investment capital in land and buildings rather than in manufacturing industry, and (possibly) corruption. Such a system of regulation, the argument suggests, also perpetuates the existence of a fairly large army of lawyers, surveyors and valuers, busily engaged in enabling developers to find loopholes in a constantly expanding and highly complex body of law, and another fairly large army of publicly-employed lawyers and planners, busily engaged in trying to stop them. Such arguments have force, but it does not necessarily follow that what they imply is either public land acquisition or a programme of public development. Equally, they might be seen as pointing simply to the need for effective recoupment of betterment.

A second type of argument for 'positive planning', however, goes further, and constitutes in effect a critique of the existing system in terms of social values. It focuses not so much on efficiency, but rather on an evaluation of *what* the capitalist market produces. So far, in attempting to analyse the activity of 'planning' as it exists, I have suggested that it attempts *neither* to increase or decrease the amount of private or public investment devoted to particular types of 'development', *nor* to change the proportion of the nation's resources which is devoted to 'development' as a whole. On the contrary, I suggested, planning merely 'rearranges' this development spatially; both the total amount, and the division of this total into development of various kinds, it takes as 'given'.[47] This existing system of regulation, then, is 'negative' only in this specific sense, that it cannot provide society either with types of development, or with a level of development, which it would not otherwise have had.

In thus suggesting that the present system of planning is 'negative' because it cannot promote those *kinds* of development which they see as socially desirable, then, planners seem to be saying that there should be shifts in the way in which the national income is spent. First, there might be shifts *within* the category 'physical development'; more, for example, might be spent on housing which ordinary people could afford, and less on expensive luxury housing. Second, there might be shifts as between physical development and the rest of the economy; more might be spent on physical development and less, for example, on defence, or for that matter on any item of private consumption, such as alcohol or cars. They cannot, logically, be saying that development ought to be diverted to less privileged *places*, for powers to achieve this already exist, under the 'negative' system of planning which we already have. (Though admittedly, the regional planning powers which enable central government to divert new industrial development from one part of the country to another are used rather sparingly, and admittedly, again, success in this area is arguably more likely to result from investment programmes than from regulation).

What can we say of this second type of argument for 'positive planning'? To urge that government should control the economy in such a way as to change the 'mix' of goods produced is of course a perfectly legitimate thing to do. It seems better, however, to argue it as an objective in its own right, rather than to present it as a necessary part of a system of land-use planning. Its main implications seem to lie not in the particular sphere of land-values, land ownership or land use, but in the wider sphere of the economy more generally. But let us try to throw some further light on this idea of 'positive planning' by briefly looking at some ways in which both public land-acquisition and public development programmes have in fact been used. Excellent examples of the first of these two things are provided by the 1967 Land Commission Act and the 1975 Community Land Act, two pieces of legislation already discussed above.

I have discussed the 1967 Act above as a means for the collection of a tax on betterment. This was not, however, its main purpose. *Provisionally*, to be sure, it provided for betterment to be recouped in this way, in the form of a tax imposed when development occurred or land changed hands. But in parallel with this, the Act also established a second method for recouping betterment. And this second method, it was intended, would progressively become the norm, ultimately replacing the first method altogether. This second method lay in public land acquisition. The Act established a central government body, the Land Commission, which would trade in land, acquiring it either by agreement, or using compulsory purchase powers. In thus acquiring land, the Commission would pay a price net of the 40 per cent tax mentioned above. In disposing of it again, to a developer, however, the Commission would charge a price which included this 40 per cent tax.[48] At the same time, it was intended that this method of compulsory purchase and resale would fulfil a second objective, that of ensuring that the supposed shortcomings of the market would be overcome, and that land would be available for development in the 'right' places and at the 'right' times. The Commission would, therefore, working in conjunction with the local planning authorities, literally bring about that pattern of development which was thought socially desirable. Eventually, it was intended, as the Commission steadily extended its operations, it would slowly take over the entire land market; *all* land would eventually pass through its hands before being developed, and no development would be permitted to be carried out either by public authorities or by the private sector other than on those sites which the Commission made available. The Conservatives, however, who returned to office in 1970, saw this legislation as incompatible with democratic institutions, and secured its repeal in 1971.

The 1976 Development Land Tax Act, I have similarly discussed above simply as the device for the taxation of betterment. It too, however, was part of a wider programme, just as the 1967 Act had been, the accompanying land acquisition powers this time being in a separate piece of legislation, the Community Land Act of 1976. Just as in the 1967 legislation, however, the Community Land Scheme provided for the recoupment of betterment through the mechanism of acquisition at a price net of tax and disposal to developers at a price including the tax.[49] The only significant difference was that this time it was to be the local authorities themselves, and not a specially created central government body, which would carry out the acquisitions and disposals. Like its predecessor, however, the scheme of 1967, this second attempt to institute positive planning through public land-acquisition was repealed by a subsequent Conservative administration, in 1979.

Municipal land acquisition and 'land banking', however, is by no means a novel policy. In certain countries, the most obvious examples being West Germany, the Netherlands and Sweden, it has been traditional since the nineteenth century.[50] In Sweden, where it is perhaps most strongly developed, it seems almost to be taken for granted that most private and public development will take place on land made available out of the municipal 'land banks'; there is often no other land available. Land for these 'banks' is acquired compulsorily, at prices representing the existing use value ten years before the date of acquisition. In such a system, clearly, land-use planning becomes something very different from the ideas and practices discussed in the present book.

In Britain, too, certain cities have attempted to build up land banks as a way of controlling their patterns of physical development. This has, however, never been encouraged by central government, nor has it become traditional, or 'normal'. Though some local authorities have apparently practised it on a fairly large scale, little is known about this, and it is difficult to research, for there is no obligation to make ownership public, and the councils concerned have been rather secretive. It has apparently, however, rarely been done in the Scandinavian or German way, on a long-term basis, and as a considered part of the municipal planning policy. On the contrary, it has generally been subject to short-term political changes and to expediency; councils have simply disposed of land when they were short of cash.

What of the other instrument of 'positive planning', public development programmes? In Britain, an obvious example is the new towns programme. This was without doubt intended to modify the national settlement pattern, though it was perhaps not, at least after the return of the Conservatives to power in 1951, seen as an instrument for changing the financial framework within which the entire land and property market worked. The new town development corporations however, and right down to the winding-down of the programme around 1980, were absolved from the normal public sector obligation introduced in 1959, and mentioned above, to buy the land they needed at market prices; they bought compulsorily at existing use (usually agricultural) value. A minor example of public development programmes in Britain might be the 'advance factories' built in declared 'development areas' (depressed parts of the country) as a part of the government's regional policy. Currently, one might say that the urban development corporations established in the London Docklands and in Liverpool might be seen as examples of such planning-directed public development programmes, since they too are potentially capable of stimulating investment and influencing the spatial pattern of development over relatively wide areas. In Scotland, the Scottish Development Agency, and in Wales the Welsh Development Agency and the Land Authority for Wales[51] are all bodies with a similar overall 'planning' approach. Abroad, one of the most obvious examples lies in the Tennessee Valley Authority, set up in the United States during the Depression to revitalize the economy of an entire river-basin region. Other examples would include the planned reclamation and settlement of land from the sea in Holland or the large-scale state-organized industrialization and planned economic development of certain regions in France.

What conclusions can we draw, from the above brief discussion of 'positive' and 'negative' plannning? In its more ambitious forms, involving not only public land-acquisition but also large-scale programmes of publicly financed or publicly promoted construction activity, 'positive planning' clearly has a capacity to modify the entire national settlement pattern. But even restricted to a programme of public land-acquisition, positive planning could have quite radical implications. Once established, for example, the schemes of 1967 and 1976 would eventually have largely destroyed the market in land, for the state would have become in effect the only 'trader'. Since its disposals of land would then have been either leasehold or subject to legally enforcable conditions, government could then certainly have ensured that all development took place in those locations and took those physical forms which seemed best to promote its conception of the 'public interest'. It could, for example, just as any other large-scale landowner, have maximized the margin of positive externalities over negative ones by ensuring good spatial relationships between various land uses; just like any large-scale land owner, too, it could have 'cross-subsidized', for example securing the preservation of culturally valued landscapes or historic buildings by being freed from the necessity to ensure that each bit of land is put to its most immediately profitable use. Consideration of such possibilities, however, merely returns us to the question posed in Section 2, above: *Can* there be a pattern of land use which meets social needs, as opposed to that pattern which maximizes profits?

Finally, however, and leaving this question aside for the moment, it can be pointed out that even the relatively 'modest' measure of the recoupment of betterment, and even in the absence of any programme of public land-acquisition, could in principle probably achieve almost as much as such 'positive planning'. If, for example, this recoupment were to take the form of an annual levy on site value, and if all site values were determined by the existence of plans, showing exactly how all land could be used, this would seem likely both to remove virtually all incentive to land speculation, and indeed all incentive to hold land at all, other than for its use value.

## 6. Summary: developing the themes

Chapter 1 has concentrated on identifying what it is that 'planners' do, and asking how it might be justified. No clear explanation is offered by the planners themselves, and my own attempt, above, is tentative. Perhaps the core of the problem lies in the fact that while it is claimed that the planning system determines all land use, the whole of the development value accrues to the developer. In this self-contradictory situation, it seems likely that in many cases, or to a large extent, it is not planning which determines the pattern of development at all, but that on the contrary it is the market. But we do not know in which cases, or to what extent. And since we thus do not even know *what* is happening, it may seem a little premature to ask *why* it is happening, let alone to try to *justify* it, in terms of any theory or social philosophy.

If, however, the market were in fact to be rendered largely inoperative, as would have occurred if the 1947 Act's 100 per cent recoupment of betterment had continued in force, and as would have occurred if either the 1967 or the 1976 attempts to secure 'positive planning' through large-scale public land-acquisition had been successful, we would then be brought up sharply against what is probably the central intellectual weakness of the planning profession; in this situation the pattern of land use would *have* to be determined administratively, but 'planning' as a body of knowledge seems to offer no theoretically grounded technical criteria on the basis of which this might be done. While most scholars would probably be able to agree broadly as to how the national land-use pattern would tend to evolve if all governmental intervention were suspended and profitability were to become the sole criterion, it seems much less likely that all would agree on the pattern which would be implied by a resolve instead to base land-use decisions on 'social' considerations, or on considerations of 'human need', or on 'planning' criteria.

We can, of course, adopt the pragmatic answer to this question. This means accepting that in practice the outcome would be determined by bureaucratic infighting between a host of public bodies, all holding varying and conflicting conceptions of the public interest, and all having varying degrees of resolve either to promote their own particular conception of this public interest, or, indeed, to promote their own organizational interests. This, however, seems unlikely to be what the advocates of planning have in mind. They tend to believe in a higher rationality. And whether they would settle for such a 'pragmatic' interpretation or not, the fact is that such a conversion of economic processes into political ones has high costs. Whether such politicization were to mean smoothly conducted private bargaining between powerful elite interest groups, or whether by contrast it were to mean noisy populist 'participation', by community groups, its resource costs are high as compared with those of the market, whether in terms of time, energy, manpower, or indeed money.

In reality, of course, such social institutions as land-use planning do not exist because their existence has been accepted by the book-writing classes as rational, reasonable and logical in terms of ends and means. On the contrary, they exist because specific interest groups were powerful enough to get them instituted. They continue to exist, presumably, because their existence is in some way useful to those with power, or perhaps because it appears to them to be so. In Chapter 2, therefore, I ask how the perceived legitimacy of planning was in fact established, and how it is maintained.

In Chapter 3, however, I return to the (arguably regrettably 'idealistic') argument broached in this introductory chapter. It would seem to be a precondition not merely of an open and democratic society but even of a moderately efficient one, I shall argue, that the consequences of public policy should be known—or at least, that attempts should be made to discover them. The very first question to ask about the planning system, then, is: what effects does it have? In what ways is the national land-use pattern other than it would have been? And what are the further material consequences, in economic and social terms, of this 'planned' physical pattern? That these are *not* the questions at the centre of the stage in planning circles, however, should perhaps come as no surprise to those familiar with the literature either on bureaucracy, or on professions.

Chapter 4, then, may be seen as the nub of the argument. If (as seems to be the case) it is true that bureaucratic-professional groups tend to use such power as they have in such a way as to 'mystify' their activity (albeit unconciously, and with the most idealistic intentions), then an alternative model must be found. In Chapter 4, therefore, I attempt to identify a more open, more liberal and more critical approach to intervention, based on 'institutionalized scepticism' rather than on professional judgment, an approach in which researchers would be more likely to challenge policy in terms of its effectiveness and politicians more ready to challenge it in terms of the interests it promotes. A precondition of this more critical climate, however, is obviously that such challenges should be rewarded, or at least, not penalized. In the two following chapters, therefore, Chapters 5 and 6, I ask why it is that in the case of British town and country planning, these 'preconditions of institutionalized scepticism' are not found. Chapter 5 attempts to explain why the theoretical basis of 'town and country planning' is so poorly developed, and Chapter 6 attempts to explain why it is that the implications of this planning are so poorly understood in political terms. In Chapter 7, I try to summarize the argument, and to show what institutional changes are implied by it.

# 2 The legitimation and consolidation of the planning system

'Oh! What beautiful material!' cried the Emperor. 'I really *do* like that!' And the Emperor nodded, in a sage way, towards the loom, and looked at it, long, and rather thoughtfully. He certainly wasn't going to say that he couldn't see any material at all on the loom. And all the courtiers, who were with the Emperor, also looked and looked at the loom, but however much they looked, they couldn't see any material on it either, any more than the Emperor could. So just like the Emperor, they cried out 'Oh! What beautiful material!' . . . And everybody felt very very relieved.

– Hans Christian Andersen, free translation

## 1 Introduction

The problem addressed in this chapter is to explain why town and country planning has become accepted as a legitimate activity of government. Histories written from the viewpoint of the planning profession rarely pose this question. Instead, they tend to see it as self-evident that planning ought to be accepted. They assume that in a 'complex' modern society it is a technical imperative, and that it is obviously desirable, and concentrate on showing how over time a better understanding of these things has gradually become more widespread. Such accounts also generally take it for granted that town and country planning legislation was simply a natural extension of legislation on public health and housing, and that it has been part of a wider process of social reform leading to the creation of the 'welfare state'. On this interpretation, demands for planning have been acceded to because their justice became obvious.[1]

31

The approach adopted here rests on rather different presuppositions. Its main assumption is that there are various groups in society, each having a fairly readily identifiable interest in the matter, and all of them able to varying degrees to secure or prevent the adoption of particular powers or policies. It assumes that as the balance of power between these various interest groups has shifted over time, so will the perceived purposes and importance accorded to the planning system be found to have shifted accordingly. The central and local government bureaucracies, for example, the political parties, the development and construction industries, landed property and financial interests, the agricultural lobby, manufacturing industry, propagandist bodies, and not least professional bodies[2] could all be reasonably expected to have played some part, and therefore to have helped to shape the planning system as it now exists.[3]

In writing this book, I have concentrated on the part played by just one of these interests, the planning profession itself. In particular, I have concentrated on the way in which this profession has used ideology as a means of securing a role for itself. It must be said, therefore, that my account is certainly open to challenge, not only in terms of its being thought factually incomplete, but also because even those facts which I do take into account are inevitably capable of being interpreted in quite other ways.

One point on which I do broadly accept the professional view, however, is that the present-day planning system to a large extent constitutes the residue of a much more ambitious system, set up in the 1940s. At that time, it is generally agreed, there was a considerable degree of consensus in official and elite circles, not only concerning the form which the system should take but more especially concerning the aims which it should pursue. This wartime and immediate post-war consensus, it is however also generally agreed, was short-lived, and had either collapsed completely or had become at least very attenuated by the 1960s.[4] While accepting this interpretation broadly, I would however modify it somewhat. Official and elite consensus on planning has continued, I would suggest, right down to the present day. But a *new* consensus (or a new 'truce situation', reflecting the balance of conflicting forces,[5] and incorporating a *new* interpretation of the legitimate scope and purpose of planning), has been negotiated from time to time. This thesis, of a 'shifting consensus', implies a historical treatment based on fairly well-defined periodization, while in terms of political theory it suggests an interpretation relying fairly strongly on the concept of corporatism.[6]

In seeking to explain legitimation, it seems useful to distinguish three types of factor. First, there are those means by which the planning lobby has itself made its proposals attractive, not only to government but also to other interest groups whose support it required. Second, there may be factors causing governments or political parties themselves to encourage 'planning', because they have seen in it something or other which could be used as a political or ideological resource. Third, there is a tendency for the process of legitimation to continue, even in the absence of factors of the above two types. Once established, any bureaucracy tends to consolidate itself, and to enhance its status and perceived legitimacy. The longer anything is done, the more natural it seems that it should be done, and the more those who do it develop a material interest in its continuing to be done.

As to factors of the first type, it will be argued that the chief means by which the planning lobby has made its proposals politically acceptable is by portraying them as non-political. This ploy is by no means restricted to planners. All experts tend to use it. Indeed, it is often used by politicians themselves. By obtaining agreement that a matter is 'non-political', and by thus obtaining a mandate to deal with it on the basis of 'the facts', or as a supposedly objective technical imperative, we gain the power to deal with it in the way which best promotes our own interests. As to factors of the second type, clear historical evidence is lacking. It seems possible, however, as I shall show, that from the turn of the century to the present day, encouragement for the enlargement of the scope of planning has indeed come from time to time from political quarters. This is especially so in the case of the financial basis of the planning system.

Factors of the third type, relating to the tendency of the planning bureaucracy itself to enhance and consolidate its position, probably need little explanation. What does seem to require further explanation, by contrast, is the above suggestion that the planning lobby achieved the political legitimation of planning by portraying it as non-political. In order to promote the idea that planning is a technical imperative, the suggestion is, the planning lobby has used a distinctive ideology. This can be seen as consisting of four interlinked strands, here termed *physicalism, holism, technicism* and *role confusion.*

By *physicalism*, I mean a set of vague ideas which emphasize the importance of the physical environment. But what is interesting is that these ideas have been used in two quite contradictory ways. In the first way, planners have asserted a simple and uncontroversially beneficial connection between the planned physical environment and human welfare.[7] Especially in the 1940s, for example, they sought to legitimate planning by suggesting that a good physical environment could induce a 'sense of community', a 'sense of belonging', or other similar kinds of psychological or social wellbeing. By linking planning with such objectives, they often obtained the support of all kinds of interests, both official and voluntary, which themselves had vaguely 'social' objectives.

When, however, observers have suggested that the production of such beneficial effects might be doubted, and especially when they have suggested that physical planning may indeed have *un*desirable social effects, then the planners have used the quite opposite variety of physicalism. This asserts the importance of the physical environment as an end in itself, and quite apart from any social effects it may have. In recent decades, for example, social scientists have suggested that planning often brings about regressive redistribution of property values and real incomes. Faced with this, planners have often sought legitimation by identifying planning with architectural, ecological or 'heritage' interests. They have then argued that if the pursuit of good environment or aesthetic excellence has undesirable social or economic costs or consequences, this is a problem for politicians, and not for planners. Or they have suggested that social and economic factors are merely among the *many* 'factors' which planners must take into account, and that they must be 'balanced against' physical and visual objectives.

*Holism* is a set of vague ideas which centre on the assertion that planning is all-embracing and comprehensive, and provides benefits for all interest groups in society. Like physicalism, it also works in two ways. On the one hand, this doctrine has enabled the planning lobby to enlist the interest, and often the active support, of an amazingly wide range of other interest groups. Indeed, this diversity of support is so wide that one suspects that in objective terms, the various groups which supported planning must often in fact have had conflicting interests in it.[8] But this is where the other half of the doctrine of holism comes into play. Planners often tend to the view that in reality, interests in society are not in conflict, but only appear to be. The planning process, since it is based on a comprehensive understanding, is the means by which these apparent conflicts can be resolved, and the inherent consensus of interest made clear. Thus, it leads to the production of a plan, which is in the interests of all. This doctrine, which portrays the planners as generalists, with 'synoptic' vision, and which uses such words as 'comprehensiveness', 'co-ordination', 'balance' and 'integration', was developed, as we shall see, in certain circles to a marked degree in the 1960s and early 1970s, while in the 1940s an earlier version of it served equally to legitimate planning by portraying all its various ideas as a web of supposedly interdependent strategies.

By *technicism*, I mean a set of vague ideas which portray planning as not only technical, but also in some sense objective, and therefore 'beyond' politics. And here, of course, we see how technicism interacts with holism. Interestingly, however, this ideology of technicism gains its power by being used in a highly inconsistent way. The planners' techniques are virtually always applied to the production of new plans or policies. They are rarely if ever, by contrast, applied to the assessment of the effects of past plans or policies. Why techniques are so very much more necessary in the one sphere than in the other is unexplained, but this asymmetry certainly seems to work to the planners' advantage. It distracts attention away from the politically sensitive matters of the purposes of planning, and its consequences, and instead focuses interest upon the *methods* of planning. And methods, clearly, are an 'internal', 'professional' matter. In subsequent chapters, it will be argued that this 'asymmetrical' approach has enabled the planners to impose their own view of their research needs upon the funding bodies, with the result that the evaluation of planning has become neglected. For the moment, however, my interest is in technicism as a legitimating ploy. It can be used, as we shall see, to make planning seem almost 'scientific', and certainly rather impressive, and it thus worked extremely well in the managerialist and technocratic climate of the 1960s and early 1970s. In political science terms, both holism and technicism reflect the planners' assumption that society rests on consensus.

*Role confusion* describes the tendency of the planning lobby and profession to define the planners' task broadly or narrowly, as seems expedient. Its boundaries are left indeterminate, so that they can now be said to be in one place, now in another, according to the susceptibilities of the audience and the political climate of the times. When this climate has been conservative, as in the 1950s, planning has by tacit understanding been defined narrowly, as a matter of land use. When governments have shown more readiness to 'plan' in the economic and social spheres, by contrast, as in the 1960s and 1970s, town and country planners have portrayed themselves as 'planners', fully competent to integrate physical, social and economic objectives into a comprehensive strategy. Here, however, we see another interesting contradiction, and another illustration of the way in which the various strands of the planners' ideology reinforce each other. Even when they *do* thus take advantage of the political climate to portray their activity as having economic and social objectives, planners contrive nevertheless at the same time to make these objectives 'safe', by 'technicizing' them. As portrayed by planners, social and economic objectives can be at one and the same time excitingly radical and progressive, and yet totally innocent of politics; they become 'the goals of society', necessitated by progress itself, and on which all are therefore assumed to be agreed. 'Role confusion' is clearly a useful ploy. It ensures that 'planning' can mean virtually anything the hearer wants it to mean, from good architecture, to the restructuring of society, to the protection of a rare breed of goose.

All of the above four strands of planning thought are vague. In order to make their ideas politically acceptable, planners have portrayed planning as non controversial, and as no more than an obviously and objectively necessary technical response to the problems of a supposedly increasingly 'complex' society, while at the same time contriving to be extremely vague as to what planning in fact does and does not concern itself with. Planning, we might say, has made itself all things to all men.

One of the dangers of being all things to all men, however, is that one becomes nothing in particular. And this, it will be argued, is very much what has happened. Ruth Glass, in 1959, argued that the legitimation of town and country planning in Britain had come too easily, and too soon.[9] The planning profession, she suggested, had concentrated on making itself congenial and uncontroversial, rather than on developing a sound theoretical basis for its practice. Interestingly, this thesis of 'premature legitimation' seems still valid, nearly thirty years later. The disadvantage of achieving legitimation before developing an intellectually credible knowledge base is that those concerned experience no *subsequent* need to develop this knowledge base. They find themselves permitted to do whatever it is they do, even while the intellectual muddle which surrounds the doing of it gets worse and worse.

What follows, then, is an interpretation of the history of town and county planning in Britain, based on the necessarily brief explanatory framework set out above. An objection to this type of explanation is that it overemphasizes the role of ideology, and correspondingly neglects that of material interest. There is little published evidence available, however, concerning the ways in which material interests have influenced the development of British planning policies. If it were available, such evidence might show that many of the economic interest groups identified above have indeed had their aims promoted by planning. This, in fact, might help to explain their relative silence. We simply do not know. As for the planners, it may be that unlike the economic interest groups involved, they have nothing *other* than their ideology, with which to promote *their* interests.

## 2  1900–1914: Edwardian radicalism and the 'land question'

The town planning movement[10] which developed in Britain around the turn of the century has been well documented, though most of the contributions have been either of the 'professionally orientated' type mentioned above, or have been written from the viewpoint of architectural history.[11] Though this movement embraced many diverse strands, and though many of its adherents were no doubt motivated primarily by artistic, architectural or philanthropic concerns, it does also seem to have had a firm basis (though one not often discussed) in what is in fact one of the most important schools of late Victorian social and economic theory, the 'attack on the landed classes'.[12] This 'attack' was given intellectual credibility by the fact that it was inspired to a large extent by the writings of eminent economists and social theorists, such as J.S. Mill, Alfred Marshall, Nassau Senior, Sir Henry Maine and Herbert Spencer. In its more radical form, as exemplified in the work of the American writer Henry George,[13] this school of thought had a singular attraction for the British Liberal Party; it suggested that the fundamental division in society was not between capital and labour, but between on the one hand the two 'industrious classes', industrial capital and labour, and on the other hand the 'parasitic' and economically unproductive landlord class, which derived its income from the 'unearned increment' in land values. By this last was meant not only increase in value due to land acquiring a potential for change of use, but also increase in value due to its becoming more sought-after in its *existing* use. *Both* were seen as 'unearned', since both resulted from the enterprise of the 'community', rather than from any expenditure of money or effort by the owner.[14]

The Radical–Liberal attack on the landed interest was at times intense, was generally consistent, and extended from the late 1880s until the Liberal Party itself began to disintegrate, in the 1920s. What is difficult, however, is to know to what extent this 'attack' reflected a valid analysis of the structure of power, and to what extent on the other hand it was mere political window-dressing, focusing popular resentment against a class which was rapidly losing its power anyway. In support of the first of these two interpretations, it is usually pointed out that it was not until the Corrupt Practices Act of 1883 that commercial and manufacturing men began to be well represented in the Commons, that it was not until 1906 that they actually predominated, and so on.[15] What the second interpretation usually suggests is not, of course, that landowning became unimportant, but that landowners lost their distinctiveness as a dominant *class*, and became increasingly integrated with and indistinguishable from the owners of industrial and financial capital more generally. The socialist movements, and also the Labour Party, seem at first to have accepted the first interpretation. Indeed the Labour Party even competed for a time with the Liberals for possession of the land as an issue.[16] Later, however, Labour gave relatively little prominence to the land question in its programmes, a fact which seems to reflect its growing conviction that the analysis put forward by Henry George's followers was mistaken, and that both landed interests and industrial and financial capital should *together* be understood as constituting the 'common enemy'.[17]

Nevertheless, the fact is that the Liberal government of 1906 was very much influenced by what had become by that time a major political movement, and was itself strongly committed to an attack on the landed interest. Ten out of the fifteen demands of the 'Radical Programme' of 1885 had been concerned with land[18] and from this time on, there developed a whole range of propagandist bodies and pressure groups, all devoted to reducing the economic power of the landed classes to varying degrees, not only by taxation or public acquisition, but also through the adoption of site value taxation, and through changes in the laws of inheritance. In the 1906 Parliament, no fewer than 400 Liberal and Labour members were signatories to a memorial calling for taxation of land values[19], 280 were members of the 'Land Value Group', 130 were supporters of the Land Nationalization Society, an obviously more radical branch of the movement,[20] and 47 were members or stockholders in First Garden City Ltd, the company set up to build garden cities along the lines advocated by Ebenezer Howard.[21] Asa Briggs provides an apt summary: after its landslide victory in 1906, he suggests, the Liberal Party saw itself as 'sweeping away the last relics of feudalism'.[22]

As an example of the kind of social thinker associated with this 'attack on the landed interest', it seems useful to look at Ebenezer Howard. There were, of course, quite a number of other propagandist writers, many of them equally influential in the development of the planning movement and profession,[23] but Howard's case seems particularly instructive. His influence was at its height at precisely the time, when, due to the Liberal election victory, town planning legislation became for the first time a real possibility. His book has been republished recently and is easily accessible. Thirdly, Howard's idea of new towns has formed a particularly important strand in the ideology of the planning movement and profession.

What Howard proposed was the gradual development of clusters of 'garden cities', within which the land would be entirely municipally owned, to take population away from the overcrowded and unhealthy existing urban centres. As these new and spaciously planned clusters of towns developed, he suggested, they would become increasingly attractive to all those seeking sites for industry, commerce and residential development. The local authorities in these new garden cities, having bought the freehold of the land in their areas at agricultural value, would be able to charge ever-increasing rents, as their populations grew, and would devote this rent income to the provision of public services and social welfare. In the big cities, by contrast, the existing congestion, combined with the increasing availability of these better prospects elsewhere, would produce a corresponding *downward* spiral of property values and rents. Thus, the economic power of the landlord classes would be slowly but inevitably reduced; there would be a massive transfer of wealth and incomes in society, away from the property-owning classes, and into the hands of the new garden city local authorities, which would use these revenues to increase the living standards of their immigrant populations. It is important to note that these revenues, which Howard calls 'rents', are in fact *betterment*, as identified in Chapter 1, above. Land values, as Howard saw it, would be shifted from the existing cities to his new settlements, and then collected in the form of a periodic levy, 'rent'.[24]

Howard himself describes his scheme as a 'unique combination of proposals'[25], and says that he has 'taken a leaf out of the books of each type of reformer and bound them together by a thread of practicability'.[26] These claims are not exaggerated. In one single proposal, he succeeded in providing a remedy for an amazingly large proportion of all the various problems to which late Victorian social critics and reformers had addressed themselves. Rural depopulation, agricultural depression, and the consequent increasing concentration of land values in urban areas, haphazard and unregulated suburban growth, urban poverty, and the congested and unhealthy living conditions in the working-class districts of the cities, social and economic inequality in society generally—all these problems, apparently, would be ameliorated. His scheme must also have held out the promise of professional gratification to a wide range of rapidly growing occupational groups, with technical and aesthetic as well as social concerns—engineers, architects, surveyors, housing managers, and so on.[27] Above all, it had an attractive financial simplicity. All this could be paid for by taking wealth away, albeit slowly, from precisely that class in society against which the government of the day, with widespread support from industrial interests, intellectuals, and the Labour movement alike, was directing the main thrust of its rhetoric. Given that Howard's scheme was so politically well judged, and that it was so well attuned to so many of the contemporary currents in the society in which it was launched, it might seem that our major problem is to explain why it was not received more enthusiastically than it was.[28] Perhaps the answer lies partly in the disposal of the revenues which it would produce. Howard would take their away wealth from the landlords, and put it into the hands of the local authorities in his 'garden cities'. The Liberal government wished to be seen as taking away that same wealth, but needed it itself, for such things as old-age pensions, education, sickness and unemployment insurance—and ultimately, of course, for battleships.

In fact, Howard did not appeal to the government to back his scheme. Instead, he sought support first from the Bellamy-inspired Nationalization of Labour Society, and then from the Land Nationalization Society. Neither of these organizations was able to give him more than moral support, however. And though the national leadership of the Co-operative movement urged its membership to give financial support, its annual conference was unfortunately less enthusiastic. It was then that R. Neville, a well-known London lawyer, introduced Howard to such wealthy Liberal industrialists as G. Cadbury and W.H. Lever. From that point on, there was no problem in commencing the construction of the first garden city, at Letchworth, for these captains of industry provided generous financial backing.[29] Fishman suggests that this was because they saw in it quite other prospects than those envisaged by Howard himself. By reducing the existing concentration of the working classes in the big cities, they thought, population dispersal would *defuse* the prevailing popular demands for greater social and economic equality. As Fishman puts it, 'For Howard, the Garden City was an environment in which capitalism could be peacefully superseded. Most of his supporters, however, looked to the Garden City as the place where capitalism could be most easily preserved'.[30] And the price of this financial support was that Howard was required to abandon the entire financial *raison d'etre* of his scheme. Finance was to be on the basis of ordinary commercial shareholding, and leases were to be for ninety-nine years, rendering it impossible for the municipality and the residents to reap the benefits of rising land values in the way he had envisaged. But Howard seems to have accepted all this as the necessary price to be paid. He seems rather quickly to have allowed means to become ends. The objective seems rather readily to have been redefined, not as that of achieving social redistribution by building garden cities, but simply as that of building garden cities. He appears to have contented himself with the hope that if *one* could be built, others would surely follow—and that the subsequent ones *would*, somehow, be in accordance with his financial prescription.

This apparent tendency to allow means to become ends is understandable, of course. It also presages much subsequent planning history. The fact is, however, that Howard had already toned down the political content of his scheme, even before the first edition of his book was published; the published edition is apparently far milder than the drafts.[31] What seems significant, however, is that in thus toning down his socialism he did not tone down his attacks on the 'landed interest'; these still remain, even in the second edition.[32]

Having set out Howard's scheme, it should be noted that neither it nor the new towns programme which ultimately developed out of it, is town and county planning, as 'narrowly' defined in Chapter 1, above. Such schemes are development, rather than the regulation and 'planning' of development.[33] The history of the new towns programme is conventionally included in any account of town and county planning in Britain, however, and this history plays an important part in the ideology of the profession, even though relatively few planners have generally worked in the new towns. The explanation seems to lie in the aspirations of the profession; the creation of new towns, their ideology appears to suggest, is one of the things which planners *ought* to doing, and *would* do, if they were given the role in society which is properly theirs.

If no very positive political support was forthcoming for garden cities, what of the wider objectives of the town planning movement? This brings us to a consideration of the 1909 Housing and Town Planning Act. Why did the Liberal government of 1906 support this legislation? The Bill proposed a 100 per cent tax on the betterment created by the setting-up of a town planning scheme. Could this be interpreted as a potentially significant contribution to the 'attack on the landed interest', and thus explain the government's support? The thesis seems unlikely, for the revenues collected would have been small. The government was in any case preparing to impose taxation on rising land values in the country generally, and not just in the obviously limited areas in which town planning schemes might be drawn up.[34] If this proposed tax on planning-created betterment had any appeal to the Liberal government, that appeal might have been mainly symbolic rather than material, no more than a step in the right direction.

When we examine certain other aspects of this legislation, however, we can perhaps see more clearly the Liberal government's interest in it. The planning schemes proposed under the Act related only to undeveloped land. The measure was, in this sense, no more than a means of ensuring that henceforth, suburban expansion should be neat, orderly, economic and well integrated with provision of public services, instead of continuing to be often rather haphazard. What the framers of this legislation proposed, however, was that these planning schemes could in fact relate to land in the area of a local authority other than that drawing up the scheme, and in this case, the land in question would, after development had been carried out, be administered by the authority which had promoted the scheme. This possibly rather surprising provision would have enabled the urban municipalities, the larger of which, at least, tended to be politically radical, to build working class municipal housing within the areas controlled by neighbouring county councils.[35] It is not surprising, then, to learn that the Bill was promoted by the Association of Municipal Governments, and opposed by the County Councils Association. As is clear from McDougall's account, the Act reflected political conflicts in the three dimensions urban–rural, Radical–Conservative and industry–landed property.[36]

What happened in the event? In the Act as finally approved, the tax on betterment was reduced from 100 to 50 per cent. Powers which would have enabled the government to carry out a national valuation of all land, on which both the proposed general land taxes and the proposed tax on planning betterment depended, were included in the 1909 budget. Lloyd George, however, seems to have been more concerned to provoke the Lords into rejecting this budget, in order to bring about the constitutional crisis in which the power of the Lords was ultimately to be curtailed, than he was to ensure that this valuation was carried out.[37] It was finally effected, but only slowly, and in the face of much opposition, and in the case of assessments of betterment value made under the 1909 Act, these were viewed as being impossible to 'prove', and no betterment was in fact collected.[38] As regards the planning schemes carried out under the Act, these were used mainly to control the layout of privately built suburban housing for owner-occupation, and not to secure the construction of municipal housing estates. That the Act was not used to promote the provision of working-class housing is specifically attributed by a number of observers to the lack of enthusiasm of the President of the Local Government Board, John Burns.[39]

What can we conclude, from this brief examination of the events surrounding the introduction into Britain of statutory town planning? It seems possible that this legislation, since it provided for a tax on betterment, had some symbolic value to the Liberal government, concerned as it was to be seen to be attacking the privileges of the landed classes. The government may well have also been very sympathetic, of course, to the reformist ideals of all the many different groups which saw in town planning the possibility of improving the lot of the working classes. It seems difficult to believe that in practice, however, working-class housing conditions could have been much improved simply by ensuring that new suburban housing was laid out more attractively. As McDougall points out, it is significant that the labour movement has always actively supported demands for legislation which would ensure the provision of local authority housing, but it has not normally had any similarly strong connection with the town planning movement.[40] McDougall does however see the 1909 Act as constituting an attack on the landed interest, albeit in part a symbolic one, concealing the fact that the landowning classes were rapidly becoming overwhelmed by or assimilated into the capital-owning classes more generally:

> [T]he land clauses in the Town Planning Act and in the Finance Bill were intended to destroy the remaining economic advantages attached to landownership . . . These clauses were particularly aimed at preventing landowners benefiting from the development activities of industrial, commercial and public capital in urban areas . . . Intervention in the land marked was motivated by the desire to establish the hegemony of industrial and commercial capital rather than the desire to achieve social welfare ends.[41]

When we read the 'professionally orientated' accounts of the introduction of statutory town planning into Britain, however, we find little evidence of interest in these questions, either among those advocates of town planning who were involved at the time, or on the part of subsequent researchers. Whether as a ploy to make their demands politically acceptable, or in the fear that they might themselves otherwise lose professional opportunities, or out of a genuine but mistaken intellectual conviction, the professional people and social reformers involved in urging the adoption of town planning seem to have shown little regard for its social and economic significance. One searches in vain, for example, for any evidence of attempts to revive interest in the social questions which motivated Ebenezer Howard and other early protagonists of town planning. Equally, there is little evidence of attempts among the advocates of town planning to ensure that the betterment provisions of the 1909 Act were enforced, and made workable. Had such matters been taken up, the entire history of town and country planning in Britain might have been very different.

On one interpretation, this lack of interest in the economic and social significance of town planning came about in part as a result of the breaking of personal links. Until about 1907, apparently, some of the leading members of the town planning movement had also been prominent in the Sociological Society, but thereafter, these contacts were lost.[42] Insistence on professionalism among practitioners probably also played an important part, however, causing some of those who had earlier been politically active, like Unwin, later to deny the political implications of their work.[43] In many more cases, though, it seems likely that those who were active as professional planners had always had interests which were largely artistic and technical rather than political, and in some cases, these early planners were in fact avowedly *anti*-political.[44] Osborn, who was not a professional planner but who became very influential in shaping the non-political stance of the Garden Cities and Town Planning Association in the 1930s and 1940s, seems later to have doubted, at least to some extent, the wisdom of this.[45]

## 3. The inter-war period: mass suburbanization and mass unemployment

The legislative developments of the inter-war period can be dealt with very briefly, for they made little difference to the situation created by the 1909 Act. Successive inter-war planning acts reaffirmed the principle that the betterment created by the preparation of planning schemes should be recouped, the level of tax being confirmed at 50 per cent in 1919 and 1925, and even raised to 75 per cent in 1932.[46] But no betterment was collected. The Uthwatt Committee, reporting in 1942, was to find that up to the outbreak of war in 1939, three instances had occurred in which local authorities had actually succeeded in getting developers to pay this tax.[47] At the same time, however, it *was* accepted that compensation be paid, where owners claimed that planning restrictions depreciated the development value of their land. As shown in Chapter 1, these impossible financial arrangements made town and country planning in the inter-war period largely ineffective. In practice, it meant little more than the securing of adequate standards of layout and design; the geographical pattern of development continued to be shaped largely by market forces.

But if town planning as an *activity* was of relatively little significance, the *idea* of town and country planning developed apace, at least towards the end of the period. Two main sources contributed to this, but they were the products of two distinct intellectual currents, and they did not really come together until the mid-1930s. The first of these is the school of thought already briefly described in the preceding section of this chapter, centred, on the one hand, on the propagandist bodies such as Howard's Garden Cities and Town Planning Association,[48] and on the other hand on the design and land use professions.[49] The preoccupations of this school of thought were, as noted above, largely aesthetic and technical, but they perhaps centred mainly on what might be called a form of simple physical determinism; they reflected a strong conviction that improved physical surroundings would improve the health and well-being of the working classes. In these same circles, however, and in reaction against the rapid residential and industrial suburban growth so characteristic of the period, there developed a strong concern to protect the countryside against development.[50] It was on this issue above all, perhaps, that our two schools of thought were eventually to find some common ground.

The second source of planning ideas in the inter-war period was among those economists, politicians and influential business men and industrialists who concerned themselves with the problems of the depressed regions in the North and West, and with the nation's apparent failure to make the best use of its economic resources more generally. We can say something about each of these two main sources of ideas in turn. First, however, it may be useful to remind ourselves briefly of some of the main trends in Britain's social geography over this period, for these provide the background against which both sets of ideas can best be understood.

The twin phenomena of mass suburbanization in the fortunate regions and mass unemployment in the depressed areas are, of course, merely two sides of the same coin. As home markets increasingly became more important to industry than export markets, and as the basic industries which had facilitated the first stages of industralization began their long decline, the geographical centre of gravity of the nation's economic life was returning to the South, where it had been before the onset of the industrial revolution. Aided by a cheap money policy,[51] suburbaniza-tion in the inter-war period proceeded on a scale and at a pace which before 1914 would have seemed quite unbelievable. Electrification and development of road transport are, of course, two of the underlying factors behind this urban growth, but without much exaggeration one might almost say that one of the major industries of the period was residential development. Despite widespread hopes of social reform immediately after 1918, it seems that after the economic crisis of 1922 it became rapidly and widely accepted that the best hope of improving living conditions lay in the enlargement of house building.[52] If governments were relatively slow to act in other areas, their actions here were without doubt decisive. By 1939, about 4 million houses had been built. Of these, about 2.5 million were built by private enterprise, 0.4 million by private enterprise with government subsidy, and 1.1 million were council houses. About one-third of all the houses in the country in 1939 had been built since 1918. The built-up area of London in 1939 was five times what it had been in 1918.[53] Much of this rapid suburban growth was largely unplanned. It was not very well coordinatd with the provision of employment, schools, transport, shopping or other social facilities, and perhaps surprisingly, it was often the large-scale council housing estates of which this was most true, even though in their design and layout they embodied the ideals of the garden city ideal to a marked degree. Examples include the London County Council's Watling and Becontree.[54] Where provision of commercial facilities to serve new owner-occupied suburbs was profitable, however, it was often provided very promptly.[55]

We now can return to say a little more about each of our two main sources of planning ideas over this period. The first of them, of course, represents the 'mainstream', and to a large extent, as we shall see both in this chapter and in the following one, it continued to do so even until long after the Second World War. Indeed, it may do so to the present day. It reflects an assumption that big cities are almost of necessity unhealthy and undesirable. Secondly, it reflects an equally unexamined assumption that the countryside and small towns are the source of much that is good and wholesome in our national life. Third, it reflects an aesthetic aversion to semi-detached mass suburbia. Clearly, such attitudes reflect the values and interests of the privileged upper and upper-middle classes, often themselves living in the countryside, and given to 'appreciating' it. They may be widely shared, however. Certainly, they seem often to have been enthusiastically taken up by the professionals in our field, and especially, perhaps, by many leading architect-planners. Newby[56] cites the case of Patrick Abercrombie as a typical influential exponent of these attitudes and values. Later to become a leading member of the Barlow Commission,[57] and main architect of the first Greater London Plan, Abercrombie was a founder member, in 1926, of the Council for the

Preservation of Rural England, and one of the first and most outspoken advocates of the 'green belt' idea. Newby points out how strongly these rural preservationist values were to influence planning in Britain after the Second World War. But, he also points out, they are romantic ideas, based not on any real understanding of the nature of country life, but on an 'arcadian vision'. So strong was this assumption that rural England must at all costs be preserved, Newby suggests, that those who espoused it never really asked themselves exactly what it was that was being preserved. Essentially, however, their concerns were visual. They were interested in the countryside as scenery, not in such things as the structure of rural society, or job opportunities, or provision of public transport and social services. Indeed, they were not even very interested in agriculture, despite their taken-for-granted conviction that nothing but agriculture, and perhaps their own rural retreats, had any right to be in the countryside. Newby demonstrates the superficiality of these attitudes by quoting from Abercrombie's textbook *Town and Country Planning:* 'The essence of the aesthetic of town and country planning consists in the frank recognition of these two elements, *town* and *country* . . . the town should indeed be frankly artificial, urban; the country natural, 'rural'.[58]

One of the strongest influences on what I have called this 'mainstream' source of inter-war planning ideas was the Garden Cities and Town Planning Association. Though the Association did not generally place its main stress on aesthetic considerations, preferring a common-sense 'public health' emphasis on the need for improved housing conditions, it displayed relatively little interest in Ebenezer Howard's conception of garden cities as a mechanism for the redistribution of land values. The Association does, however, appear in the inter-war period to have completely overcome its founder's misgivings concerning the dangers of relying on the power of the state, and to have increasingly regarded governmental initiatives as indeed constituting the *only* way to get new towns built. In general (though see below) the Association seems to have concentrated its attention on the physical problems of the big cities, and especially London, as manifested on the one hand in overcrowding and congestion and on the other hand in the large part of their day spent by the new suburbanites as 'straphangers'. The Association's unswerving answer to all such problems was, of course, new towns. The Town Planning Institute, which over this period was slowly beginning to establish itself as the main professional body in the field, was careful to avoid too close a contact with the Association, however, seeing the latter as a propagandist body, and thus 'political'.[59] The irony of this was that the Association itself continued to stress that the policies which it urged had no political significance, and reflected only common sense. The sources of this widely-shared tendency to deny that town and country planning has any political and economic implications, as we saw, go back to the turn of the century. They were certainly strengthened between the wars.

It can convincingly be argued, of course, that the Association's concentration on questions of public health was very justified. As Aldridge[60] points out, 'we simply forget that rickets and tuberculosis were still major urban scourges, and that today, too, many people's health would be drastically improved by a better house in a better climate'. Equally, and especially in the light of the later experience of high-density council housing, it can be argued that the Garden Cities and Town Planning Association's single-minded advocacy of houses with gardens was also very well judged. The Association's tendency to deny that its programmes had political and economic implications stood it in good stead, too, as we shall see, in the relatively politically uncontentious climate of the mid-1940s, when it was able to gather together an amazingly diverse collection of interests in support of its policies.

The rural preservationists, the architect-planners, and the Garden Cities and Town Planning Association, of course, cannot by any means be said to constitute the whole of what I have termed the 'mainstream' of inter-war planning thought. There were also many other professional interests involved, municipal engineers and surveyors anxious to build model council house estates, highway engineers who produced 'regional plans' consisting largely of 'radial' and 'orbital' dual-carriageway tree-lined highways, housing reformers, and so on. Above all, perhaps, there was the Town Planning Institute, carefully avoiding committing itself to any identifiable cause, maintaining that town and country planning was technical and non-political, and yet itself very much engaged in the highly political task of trying to invent a new profession, with a distinctive and defined sphere of competence. But perhaps the general flavour has been sketched out. It is essentially physical, visual, anti-metropolitan and anti-political. It assumes, rather than demonstrates, a simple deterministic relationship between its espoused physical patterns and the enhancement of social welfare. It shows little interest in economics in general, and arguably even less in the economics of property development. Such sociology as it embraces is strictly amateur.[61]

The second source of influences on the development of planning thought in the inter-war period has very different roots. The movement for economic planning as a response to mass unemployment and industrial decline has its origins in the First World War, when it was seen that only 'planning', in the sense of central direction of the economy, could secure the necessary redeployment of resources and manpower. From about 1930 onwards, there developed the idea that the same remedy, 'planning', could combat the problems of the peripheral regions hit by the Depression. This idea was ultimately to form one of the more important strands in the ideology of British land-use planning, but in the inter-war period, even up to the late 1930s, the town planning profession as a whole seems to have shown relatively little awareness of it.[62] This was despite the fact that the example of the Tennessee Valley Authority, in the United States, provided a striking model for the integration of physical with social and economic planning.[63] From the early 1930s onwards, however, as it became known that what were in effect Keynesian public spending programmes were proving successful in combating unemployment in Sweden and in the American 'New Deal', this British movement for economic planning gathered force. Clearly, it embraced groups of politicians, intellectuals and industrialists with a wide variety of political viewpoints. But common to most of them was a degree of belief in expertise, and a certain impatience with politics *per se;* to a greater or lesser degree its adherents tended to believe that at least the extremes of party political posturing should be avoided, and that policies should instead be based on objective enquiry and rational decision-making. By such means, it was thought, economic recovery could be made compatible with democracy; it need not be the prerogative of dictators such as Mussolini, Hitler or Stalin.[64]

From the mid-1930s onwards, the town and country planning movement and this movement for economic planning began to grow increasingly closer together. Perhaps one of the things which facilitated this was the realization that each had a spatial dimension; the 'urban sprawl' which was threatening the prized rural landscapes of Southern England could be their very lifeblood, if it could somehow be diverted back to the declining industrial regions of Wales, the North and Scotland. F. J. Osborn, who became the Town and Country Planning Association's very committed and energetic Honorary Secretary in 1936, was apparently among those who were particularly instrumental in demonstrating to these two already very influential interest groups that they shared a common cause. Partly in response to the very different matter of the threat of bombing from the air, but also as a result of these growing pressures for national economic and spatial planning, a Royal Commission was established in 1937 to enquire into the 'distribution of the industrial population'. When 'Barlow' reported, in 1940, it came down very firmly in favour of strong governmental action to achieve a more 'balanced' distribution of the country's economic activity:

> It is not in the national interest, economically, socially or strategically, that a quarter, or even a larger, proportion of the population of Great Britain should be concentrated within 20 to 30 miles or so of Central London. On the other hand, a policy:
>
> (i)   of balanced distribution of industry and the industrial population so far as possible throughout the different areas or regions in Great Britain;
> (ii)  of appropriate diversification of industries in those areas or regions;
>
> would tend to make the best national use of the resources of the country, and at the same time would go far to secure for each region or area, though diversification of industry, and variety of employment, some safeguard against severe and persistent depression, such as attacks on areas dependent mainly on one industry when that industry is struck by bad times.[65]

Resulting from the very widespread support for this kind of thinking which developed in influential circles in the early years of the War, further governmental committees of enquiry were set up, 'Reith' on the need for new towns, 'Dower' on national parks, 'Scott' on land utilization in rural areas and 'Uthwatt' on the financial problems which would be faced if strict planning of land use were in fact to be introduced. Among these various reports, 'Scott' was to prove even more influential than was 'Barlow' itself. 'Uthwatt', by contrast, was to become largely ignored, when the post-war legislation was being formulated.

## 4.  The 1940s: town and country planning as promoter of socialism

In the 1947 Town and Country Planning Act, we see for the first time in Britain a
piece of legislation which (albeit temporarily) affected a profound shift in the
balance of power obtaining between the mass of the people on the one hand and
the owners of land and property on the other. As noted above[66] the Act not only
took away from all owners the *legal* right to develop their property. It also, in
effect, confiscated the development value in all land. It was likely to make many
people much poorer, for it was designed to eliminate totally the profit to be made
out of buying and selling land for development (as opposed to that to be made out
of organizing the construction process). How could such a statutorily-imposed
shift in the distribution of wealth and power have become possible?

The usual answer given to this question is that which is used to explain the
egalitarian social legislation of the mid-1940s more generally; it was necessary for
government to promise post war reform, it is suggested, in order to sustain
wartime morale. Thus, the promise of town and country planning after the war
was· in effect the promise of a vastly increased output of good housing, of the
provision of a wider variety of employment opportunities, of the revitalization of
the depressed regions, of a chance to move to a bright new garden city in the
countryside, and so on. Such promises, according to this explanation, take their
place alongside the promises of social security in the Beveridge Report, of better
and more equal educational opportunities in the debates leading up to the 1944
Education Act, of a National Health Service, and so on. The argument is not only
generally accepted, but persuasive, and there seems little reason to reject it. The
fact is that the wartime coalition government deliberately fostered public
discussion, especially within the armed forces, of the reforms which would
become possible once the war was won.[67] It also promoted material equality. As it
became increasingly necessary to divert resources from private consumption into
the war effort, it achieved this by taking relatively more from the affluent, thereby
bringing about a significant reduction in material class differences.[68] Both these
policies, apparently, were officially seen as necessary, if wartime morale was to be
sustained. But according to certain writers, at least, both also had 'snowball'
effects; they generated widespread demands that egalitarian reforms should go
even *further* than the coalition government had envisaged, and thus virtually
guaranteed the return of Labour in 1945.[69]

The sheer size of Labour's parliamentary majority in 1945, however, proved
greater than even they had dared hoped. Given this, and given the widespread
public mood of idealism, egalitarianism and hope of radical social reform, it must
have seemed to many Labour politicians that the creation of a new kind of society
had actually become a practical possibility.

For radical social change to occur, however, it is not enough that there is such a
public mood, and such a reforming party in office, eager to harness it. There must
also be expert lobbies, capable of working with officials to show how at the
technical level the reforms can be effected. But this, too, was abundantly present.
The Town and Country Planning Association has been described as 'one of the

most effective pressure groups operating openly in this country'.[70] Even all these things together, however, may not seem quite adequate to explain why the 1947 Act went as far as it did in taking wealth and income away from property owners and developers. Let us therefore look at another, complementary, explanation.

Backwell and Dickens[71] suggest that in part this confiscation of property values had become politically possible because by the middle years of the war many property owners had become so financially weak that they 'actively desired' their property to be taken over by the state, provided they were compensated for it. In the cities, much of their property had been destroyed by bombing. Ultimately, of course, they would receive war damage compensation for this, but in the meantime, their livelihoods were destroyed: they got no rents. Property and land values, even in the heart of London and the other big cities, fell to very low levels, therefore, during the war. Of course, it was well known that other operators, who could afford to wait for their financial returns until the end of the war, were at the same time and even at the height of the 'blitz' taking their chance to buy up these same destroyed properties.[72] For this group, however, there was no sympathy, whether from Right or Left; in the idealistic climate produced by the war they were regarded as rather contemptible. Backwell and Dickens's argument is, then, that the war greatly strengthened one fraction of capital, manufacturing industry, at the expense of another, the land and property interest and the finance capital which supported it. The prosecution of the war, they point out, *demanded* a vast expansion of industrial capacity, and thus increased not only the political power but also the profitability and the capital-accumulation propensities of the manufacturing sector; it clearly had quite an opposite effect on property interests.

But as well as having these contradictory effects on various 'capitals', Backwell and Dickens point out, the war also affected class relationships. Since it produced a shortage of labour, both the political and the economic power of the working class was improved; the demands of labour had to be met, and wages rose quickly relative to other incomes. All this does indeed seem to go quite a long way towards explaining why the 'promises' were made, and why, when the end of the war made this possible, they were kept.

In addition to the above arguments, however, Backwell and Dickens also attempt to analyse the balance of class forces as these are reflected in the Scott Report; this, as we shall see, is a crucial question, for most observers see this report as having been extremely influential when it came to the *interpretation*, in practice, of the legislation of the 1940s. Most commentators see this report and the policies which flowed from it as highly favourable to the rural landed interest, and especially to the big landowners, and Backwell and Dickens agree. They see this fraction of capital as having suffered less from the war than their urban counterparts.

Where Backwell and Dickens differ a little from this general interpretation, however, is in their analysis of the way in which the demands of manufacturing industry are reflected in the Report. Industry wanted to move into rural areas, they suggest, for this was the easiest way in which it could expand quickly. The rural landed interest wished to prevent this, in part because it would drive up agricultural wages. The bargain struck was that this outward movement of industry was in fact permitted to proceed, but subject to the proviso that the working-class population involved in this exodus was in general very strictly 'contained' within specific localities, and especially the new towns.[73]

Newby[74] also sees the Scott Report as having promoted the interest of the big rural landowners and rural preservationists, and goes on to suggest that by regarding agriculture as sacrosanct and promoting the view that the countryside should be preserved for agriculture alone, the Report in fact helped to create many of the problems with which we are familiar in the countryside today. By restricting industrial development in the countryside, he suggests, the planning policies derived from the Scott Report have kept down rural wage-levels, exacerbated the migration of working-class people from the country to the towns (to be replaced, of course, by middle-class commuters and retired people), and have made the provision of rural public services of all kinds uneconomic.

Hall *et al.*, too, express the view that the policies which have flowed from the Scott Report have been based on a romantic, aesthetic view of rural life, rather than on any realistic appreciation of social costs and benefits:

> It is hard to resist the conclusion that the objectives were not rational in a strict sense. They were mystical. In the special circumstances of a major war, that is perhaps understandable. But the effects were felt long after the war was over. The most important was to give the new planning system a pronounced preservationist bias. Those who operated the system in the counties accepted, in effect, the value judgements of the Scott Committee.[75]

Whatever the real explanation of the fact that the Attlee government was able to go as far as it did in taking wealth away from the land and property owners, and whatever the truth concerning the way in which the legislation of the mid-1940s reflects struggles for power between various 'fractions of capital', the fact is that there was in the 1940s a high degree of consensus, both on the need for 'planning', and on the actual objectives which this 'planning' should seek to achieve.

What, then, was the substantive content of this planning programme, and why were its protagonists so very successful in securing for it such a wide measure of political and public support? The thesis I would advance is that it was in large measure the *holism* of this programme which accounts for its widespread acceptance. I have already suggested that the policies emerging towards the end of the 1930s brought together two very different strands of thought, traditional design-based town planning on the one hand, and the movement for national economic planning on the other. In the 1940s, however, ideas deriving from these two main sources were linked with other social ideas, and elaborated into a veritable web of interlocking and interdependent analyses and prescriptions. The resulting seamless web of remedies embraced many different concerns, and many different fields of specialist knowledge. But it was so put together that virtually any interest group could see in it whatever it wished to see, or found most agreeable. What did this 'package' consist of, and why did virtually everyone 'buy' it?[76]

To solve the housing problem, made acute by six years of war, new towns would be created, separated from the big cities by wide green belts, the latter having obvious appeal to rural preservationists. Eventually, the growth of these new towns would permit reduction of excessively high residential densities in the poorer quarters of the big cities, which could then be rebuilt to far higher standards, with more open space.[77] Curbing the growth of the cities by means of the green belts would oblige any industries within them which sought to expand to relocate either in the new towns or in the depressed regions. As for the latter, these peripheral areas of the country would be aided by vigorous central government action. Mainly, this would derive from the power to control the location of all new industrial development, given to the Board of Trade under the 1945 Distribution of Industry Act, but in addition, there would be large-scale public investment in infrastructure. As for the countryside, its character would be zealously protected, and wherever possible, towns would have clean-cut sharp edges. Rural life would be revitalized, but any industry permitted in the countryside itself would be small-scale, linked with agriculture so far as possible, and appropriate to the rural scene. The truly remote or 'wild' areas would be preserved as national parks; these, however, tended to be seen by their protagonists as intended mainly for healthy fell-walkers, rather as venues for masses of car-borne day trippers.[78] Transport facilities of all kinds would be improved, but the need for travel would be reduced anyway, for as a more rational land-use pattern emerged, more people would be enabled to live closer to their work. Existing differences in the quality of the surroundings in which the various social classes lived would be reduced. But at the same time, the object would always be to counteract the growing tendency to 'sameness', by emphasizing the unique character of every village and town, and each particular quarter of the city. To meet the expectations of those who worried about 'amorphous suburbia', and who wanted 'community', both new and existing urban areas would be divided up into distinct 'neighbourhoods', or urban villages, in which local cultural activities would flourish. Most new housing would be council housing, and this would be built for people of all social classes.[79]

Clearly, there was something here for everyone—politician and professional, broad mass and socially-concerned elite, Left and Right, urban and rural, preservationist and modernist, layman and expert. But in such an all-embracing programme, there was obviously much scope for ambiguity. Even the most central items in the 'package', consisting essentially of the limitation of urban growth by green belts, the siphoning-off of population to the new towns and the economic revival of the depressed regions, had implications which in reality could only be properly understood by experts, specialists in industrial location, agricultural economics, and so on. Yet in fact this whole web seems to have been woven by amateurs and 'generalists'—civil servants, enthusiasts, propagandists, and especially, 'architect-planners' as they were called, visionaries who saw the future society in largely visual terms.[80]

And it was presented as a *whole*. Both the definition of the situation, and the proposed remedies for that situation, were deftly interwoven into a seamless web of ideas and arguments. This made it difficult to question any *one* policy or argument, for to question one, apparently, was to question them all. And to question the whole idea of 'town and country planning' was to go against the wisdom of the prevailing consensus. It meant to question policies in such disparate and specialized areas as housing, industry, agriculture and transport. It implied an understanding of economic viability, social acceptability, functional efficiency, administrative practicability, and even aesthetics. Who would lay claim to such a multiplicity of areas of knowledge, and such a variety of disciplines? That the planners themselves claimed to comprehend all these 'factors', that they claimed to be able to find the best 'balance' between them on the basis of technical expertise rather than political judgement, and that the claim went unchallenged, seems explicable only in terms of their high standing at the time. The contemporary enthusiasm for building a new and better Britain, delivered from the miseries of the depression and the war alike, had made them into important people, even popular heroes.

So far as mobilizing political support is concerned, then, the *holism* of this programme was its greatest strength. So far as the development of an intellectually credible knowledge base for public policy is concerned, by contrast, this same holism was an enormous handicap. A virtually new profession, with little tradition of learning, and which required its members to acquire some understanding of such a vast range of knowledge, was unlikely to produce among them any great taste or predilection for painstaking and detailed research into any one of all these many subject areas. And as the post-war planning machine continued on its course, it was precisely this lack of research capacity which proved to be its greatest weakness. This was pointed out early.[81] But it is a feature which still persists, even today.

At the time it was presented, however, this planning programme not only had the advantage of being a 'whole'. It also had the advantage of being virtually the *only* set of prescriptive ideas on offer. There were groups with other ideas, of course. Certain architectural lobbies, for example, urged quite opposite policies, not of decentralization, low densities, and new towns, but of rebuilding the bombed cities 'as cities', at high densities.[82] The Town and Country Planning Association, however, had developed during its long campaign a very sure feel for all those ideas which really did have wide appeal in Britain, and had concentrated on these alone. It had also, in a classically Fabian way, cultivated and infiltrated the administrative elite.[83] Though it had within its membership those who saw the purpose of town planning as the equalization and collectivization of living conditions, as in the Soviet Union,[84] the Association itself had carefully distanced itself from any overt political commitment. In this way, it had both secured the support of the professional town planners, and insured both them and itself against the possible return to power of the Conservatives.

Cullingworth[85] has argued that the content of the post-war planning legislation would have been much the same, irrespective of which party had been returned to power in 1945. There seems much plausibility in this thesis, especially when we consider the extent to which the consensus on planning, both in the 1940s and subsequently, was an 'official' consensus, arrived at on the basis of interaction between higher civil servants and the professional lobby. Nevertheless, Cullingworth's thesis seems to overlook certain facts. Michael Foot, for example, has suggested that planning, and especially the question of land ownership. was 'the real rock on which the wartime coalition was broken'[86] Secondly, it can be pointed out that the 1947 Act was in fact bitterly contested in Parliament.[87] Thirdly, as we shall see, the Conservatives took the very first opportunity, after returning to power in 1951, to render the 1947 Act ineffective, by removing from it its financial provisions.

## 5.  The 1950s: the eclipse of planning

In the 1950s, then, a very different political interpretation of the planning system was to emerge. Far from being seen as an integral part of a wider programme of social reconstruction, with broadly egalitarian objectives, planning became instead once again defined as a purely technical activity, and as largely devoid of political implications. The planning lobby and profession, however, seem to have fairly readily accepted this;[88] after all, many among them had always held to this view, even when more politically-minded people had wanted to make planning into an instrument for promoting socialism. In terms of the explanatory model set out at the opening of this chapter, then, we can say that a new consensus concerning the purposes and the scope of planning was quite quickly arrived at, even though this meant a considerable reduction in the perceived importance of the social role of the planners themselves. Some insight into the planning profession's willingness to have its role redefined in this way may be obtained by looking at the events surrounding a contemporary government report on the education of planners.

In 1948 Lewis Silkin had as Minister of Town and Country Planning in the post-war Labour government set up the Schuster Committee, to enquire into the 'qualifications of planners'. His motives, apparently, had been on the one hand a concern that there should be an adequate supply of people to man the by now greatly expanded planning system,[89] and on the other hand a conscious desire to widen the training of planners, and especially, to widen the disciplinary backgrounds from which they were drawn. The report of this Committee[90] accepted Silkin's case. In particular, it argued the need for more planners with backgrounds in public administration and the social sciences.

In the evidence which it had itself presented to the Schuster Committee, however, the Town Planning Institute had strongly opposed these arguments, suggesting by contrast that planning was essentially a matter of design, that it could not be done by a team of people from various different disciplines, and that it could on the contrary only be done by 'planners', members of a distinct profession with unique skills. Finding the Schuster Report not to its liking, therefore, the Institute largely ignored its recommendations.

In thus rejecting 'Schuster', the planning profession seems to have lost a valuable opportunity. What the Committee were really arguing for, was an approach which would have led to a much more rigorous examination of 'planning', in terms of its intentions and its effects; this implied a need, as the Committee pointed out, for well-educated people, with analytical abilities. As Hague notes, the Committee were in affect urging the need for people who embodied 'the traditions of the administrative civil service and the aura of Oxbridge'.[91] The likely effect, if people of this kind had in fact entered the field in significant numbers, would probably have been to raise the status of all who advise in this field of policy, for such people would have led planners to see themselves more as independent experts than as ordinary local government officials. Since the profession was at this time still relatively small in number, a progressive transformation of it along these lines would probably still have been possible. But as noted, the chance was not taken. As a result of its insistence that planning was a set of technical skills rather than a matter of policy analysis, the Town Planning Institute in fact ensured that the planning profession would continue to develop as an occupation for local government officials, and that its members would continue to be engaged in putting the law into effect (albeit with some 'discretion'), rather than in researching the intentions and the effects of that law. And in fact, one might comment, it seems very difficult indeed to 'plan' in any real sense, from this position of self-imposed inferiority.

For the moment however, the task is to identify the ways in which the new consensus of the 1950s, in which town and country planning was assigned a reduced role, was actually arrived at. What, then, were the political events which led to planning being defined anew as non-political?

In an enormous reversal of public mood, Labour was returned with a much reduced parliamentary majority in 1950, and finally lost office in 1951.[92] So great was the new Churchill government's aversion to 'planning', in any sense, that even the very word had to be eradicated; one of its first actions was to remove this word from the title of the central government department which administered the system of land use control.[93] In opposition, the Conservatives had been able to create resentment against the Labour government by pointing to the way in which, as a means of securing its political objectives, it had clung to regulations which in reality had been intended only as temporary wartime measures.[94] The extent to which Labour had in fact pushed 'planning' and reduced the private sector are sometimes forgotten. By 1951, for example, only 12 per cent of all new houses in England and Wales were being built by the private sector, and 59 per cent of all *other* development was public sector, too.[95] Once back in office, the Conservatives lost relatively little time in destroying the whole structure of the land-use planning system introduced by the 1947 Act, simply by removing its essential financial basis. The development charge was abolished by an Act of 1953, meaning that all development value, in a phrase characteristic of the period, was 'denationalized'.[96] Owners of land and developers, therefore, once more had the legal right to retain the whole of the 'unearned increment', or bettermenet value, which could be realized through development. This meant, of course, that there was once again a free market in land, that land prices would be determined by demand, and that logically and in equity public authorities should *also* pay the market price, when *they* bought land compulsorily. In fact, however, this last change was not effected, or at least not for some time. From 1953 to 1959, when this anomaly was rectified, local authorities and public development agencies continued to be able to buy land compulsorily at existing use value. This meant, of course, that there was a 'dual market', owners who had to sell to public developers being unfairly treated relative to those who sold to private developers. This seems explicable only in terms of expediency. Over the 1950s, the Conservatives built council housing at a rate and on a scale far greater than any previous British government had achieved. If they had been obliged to pay the market price for all the land required for this vast public housing programme, the cost to the Exchequer would have been very much increased, while at the same time they would have had to increase council rents considerably, thus creating wage demands. Merrett[97] suggests that in this situation, the Conservatives simply sacrificed the interests of land owners to the interest of those who paid wages.

In the wider sphere of regional policy, the Conservatives showed equal distaste for 'planning'. The 1945 Distribution of Industry Act was kept in force, but in practice the powers which it gave were far less stringently operated.[98] Despite clear evidence that in the South-East, at least, the pattern of development was now being determined far more by the growth of office employment in London than by the growth of manufacturing industry,[99] the government steadfastly refused to control office development. From 1951 to 1961 (when as we shall see, their policy changed abruptly) the Conservatives established only one new town, Cumbernauld, intended to take 'overspill' population from Glasgow. Labour, broadly one might say in line with Howard's ideas, had intended that as each new town was completed, its housing stock should be handed over by the development corporation to the local authority. The Conservatives, however, and arguably with reason, saw it as undesirable that these local authorities should have the power which would flow from their being landlords to the greater part of their electorates,[100] and therefore established in 1959 a central Commission for the New Towns, to administer the housing stock in all fifteen new towns jointly.

It would be wrong, however, to assume that the Conservatives abandoned in the 1950s *all* of the ideas promoted so successfully by the planning movement in the 1940s. Slum clearance, for example, they pursued with considerable enthusiasm, especially from the mid-1950s onwards. And in a circular of 1955 they gave very clear encouragement to local planning authorities to designate green belts around all the country's major urban areas. What one *can* say, is that the social purposes served by such policies, and indeed, by the planning system generally, became obscured or denied. As one observer puts it, land-use controls came to stand on their own rather than as part of a strategy for social policy'.[101] This, of course, is significant, for it is precisely by such means that the purposes and consequences of the use of planning powers are 'mystified'. The planning profession, however, seems regrettably to have accepted this 'mystification', and the neglect of research which is its inevitable corollary. The *technicism* which I have identified as characteristic of planning ideology enabled the planners to believe that it was more important to develop planning techniques than to research the efforts produced by the use of these techniques. The planner's tendency to *physicalism,* in the same way, enabled the profession to continue to believe that the physical and spatial patterns produced by planning controls were beneficial to society, rather than to seek to find out. One of the few voices to be raised against these tendencies at the time warned the planners that by neglecting to research the purposes and the effects of their activity they were in fact weakening their own position: '[If] objectives are divested of their true political content, less and less interest is likely to be taken in them by the public, by the political parties, and by the government'.[102] Such advice, however, was not heeded. On the contrary, we shall see that in the 1960s, and in a political climate which had once again become favourable to planning, the profession continued to maintain exactly the same aversion to the clarification of its activity. In the 1960s and 1970s, just as around the turn of the century and during the Second World War, there was to emerge a climate of opinion in which the control of land use became a live political issue. From the side of government and the political parties, as we shall see, repeated attempts were made to put the planning system on a sound financial basis, and from the side of the public there was almost continuous and very lively challenge and criticism. Yet as in the case of its response to the Schuster Report, the planning profession rejected all these opportunities for the clarification of its activity.

### 6. 1960 to the present day: the triumph of bureaucratic professionalism

It may seem odd, even in such a brief historical sketch as this, to regard the years from 1960 to the present day as a single period, for they have seen striking changes of fortune in the world of property development, as well as equally striking changes in the economic and political climate more generally. As Conservative and Labour governments with strongly entrenched and polarized views on the matter have alternated in office, these years have also seen striking reversals of policy on land and property values. But this is precisely the point I wish to make—that over this long period, and indeed right down to the present day, the planners' professional preoccupations have remained in essence much the same, and have remained in many ways isolated from economic and political realities. In the phrase 'triumph of bureaucratic professionalism', I refer to the fact that over this period the planning profession has been able to enhance its numbers very considerably,[103] to firmly consolidate its position within the governmental apparatus, and to maintain its perceived legitimacy, and yet all this without making any real progress towards the intellectual clarification of its work.

The main way in which this period differs from the 1950s is that it has been one in which in general governments have been positive in their attitudes to planning. In the latter part of this period, since 1979, this has been less true, but even here, a new consensus on the definition of planning seems to have been fairly readily achieved. *This* time, we might say in summary, it has become redefined as a form of governmental assistance to industry. At other times over this period, however, and especially after 1964 and 1974, the climate has seemed very propitious indeed for those who would define planning much more ambitiously, as part of a wider economic and social programme for the modernization of society. Yet despite these marked shifts in the political environment, real increase in our knowledge is slight; we still know relatively little about the effects which 'planning' is in fact producing, and could produce. One suspects, in fact, that despite these *apparently* very profound changes, the *actual* effects of the planning system have been much the same throughout.

And there is a further paradox. Over this period too, there has developed a widespread public debate, not only concerning environmental problems in general, but at times focusing precisely on the ethics of the social and economic effects produced by the property development industry. Yet the planners have failed, by and large, to engage in this debate. Rather, they have attempted to transform it into 'public participation', a process in which the public are consulted only as relatively powerless individuals, and only in order that their 'needs' and 'wants' can be planned for. In the face of this public challenge in plain words, the planners have tended also to retreat even further into technicism, and to seek, as one observer puts it, 'a more abstract definition' of their activity.[104]

The period opens with a political volte-face. In 1961, with Macmillan as prime minister, the Conservatives suddenly reversed their previous attitudes completely, and adopted both economic and physical planning with apparent enthusiasm. In the economic sphere, this is usually attributed to the example of France. The neo-Keynesian policies pursued in Britain in the late 1950s were seen as having failed, and France's far faster rate of growth was attributed to Monnet-style 'indicative planning'. So far as physical planning is concerned, this reversal of policy seems in part to have been due to the government's realization that despite all previous policy initiatives, both the poverty of the peripheral regions and the drift to the South-East still continued.[105] There were, however, even stronger imperatives compelling the government to act. The country was at last beginning to recover from the war, and economic growth was becoming relatively fast, and reflected in increasing pressures for development.

These pressures, however, both for commercial development in the city centres and for residential development on the peripheries of the more prosperous urban regions, interacted in an unfortunate way with two mutually incompatible planning policies. On the one hand, there was a free market in land values, as a result of the repeal in 1953 of the development charge imposed by the 1947 Act. On the other hand, the planning authorities were in fact operating quite stringent policies of urban 'containment', and in general allocating only as much land for development as was thought to be objectively needed, thus forcing up land and property values to far higher levels than any free market could have achieved unaided. The county planning authorities on the peripheries of the expanding cities, in particular, had generally placed a very enthusiastic interpretation on the 1955 directive, encouraging them to establish green belts around the cities. At the same time, central government had itself been urging the cities to build as much of their council housing as possible at higher densities, and in the form of multi-storey flats, and had indeed been paying them special subsidies to encourage this. Despite these increases of density, however, the cities were still clearly short of land.

Faced with the plight of the city housing authorities, and coupled with the fact that the birth-rate, the rate of economic growth and the pressures for development were all far in excess of what had been assumed in drawing up the statutory plans, the Conservative government was obliged to act. First, it completely reversed its previous attitude to the new towns programme, and began its own programme of designations. Second, it commissioned a series of regional planning studies, beginning with one for South-East England, designed to discover where the greatly enhanced amount of urban growth now anticipated could best be accommodated. So far as this search for physical solutions was concerned, the government showed considerable enthusiasm. Between 1946 and 1950, the Attlee government had designated fourteen new towns, with an aggregate 'target' population of 622,000[106] Between 1961 and 1964, when they lost office, the Conservatives designated six more, but these six had an aggregate 'target' population of 500,000.[107] In its deliberations on the South-East Regional Study, too, the government showed an equal enthusiasm for large-scale government-promoted urbanization, generally favouring the channelling of growth to the existing larger towns on the periphery of the region.

In its response to the financial problems posed by the high level of pressure for commercial property development, on the other hand, the Conservative government was far less decisive. The obviously illogical combination of strict policies of 'containment' with a free market in land, exacerbated by rapid economic growth, led to an even more rapid rise in land and property values, with much speculative dealing. Widespread public concern developed over the way in which enormous unearned profits were being made by developers, and especially those building offices in Central London. Despite mounting pressure for taxation of the 'unearned increment' in land and property values, however, the government was slow to act, generally suggesting that a better answer to the problem was simply to make more land available, as described above. It did, nevertheless, introduce a speculative gains tax in 1962, and by 1964, when it finally lost office, it was itself seriously considering the reintroduction of some kind of tax on betterment, so clamant and persuasive had the pressures become.

We can regard the policies of the Wilson government, which came into office in October 1964, under two heads. So far as the outgoing Conservative government's encouragement of planning for national population distribution was concerned, the new government continued these initiatives, and greatly enlarged their scope. So far as the financial basis of the planning system was concerned, the new Labour government took a diametrically opposed line to its predecessor, however. Broadly in accordance with a Labour Party policy document prepared in 1961, the new government put forward a scheme which went far beyond even the 1947 Act, to be supervised by a new Ministry of Land and National Resources. One of the main objectives of this scheme, as set out in the Labour 1964 election manifesto, was to reduce the cost of housing, by reducing the price of land. The scheme centred, however, as described above,[108] on the creation of the Land Commission, a central government body whose main function would be to acquire land and make it available to developers.

What can we say of the Land Commission Act in practice? It was certainly a radical approach, even 'positive planning',[109] but it seems to have been put into effect in a very half-hearted way, amidst many doubts in Cabinet and much inter-Department rivalry. To have succeeded, it would have had to meet three preconditions. First, the Commission would have had to be exceptionally well funded. Second, it would have had to be seen to be a powerful and permanent institution, whose continued existence was generally accepted. Third, the whole scheme would have had to be well integrated with the pre-existing machinery of planning administration. In the event, none of these preconditions was met. The kitty with which the Commission started its trading operations was so meagre that it could not afford to buy land in the cities, where the real problems were, but had to content itself instead with relatively innocuous trading in 'green-field' sites on the urban fringe. The necessary processes of research, prior consultation and mutual accommodation, essential if any propsed legislation is to be acceptable to all interest groups, had been skimped, with the result that the Conservatives announced their intention to repeal the Act completely as soon as they were returned to power. Thirdly, and perhaps most interestingly, the Commission appears not to have seen itself as a part of the planning system at all, but as an alternative planning system. Concentrating its efforts as it did in the urban fringe areas, it soon came into conflict with the county councils. As pointed out above, the latter had for many years, and with active government encouragement, been pursuing policies of strict 'containment', using their planning powers in such a way as to maintain the privileged environments of their predominantly middle-class populations, and depriving the cities of land for council housing. The Commission, however, appears to have had quite other ideas. In its first annual report it noted that 'the shortage of land for immediate development is due to insufficient land being allocated in local authority development plans'.[110] In its second report, the Commission was even more outspoken, stating that the prevailing shortage of land for development was 'largely due to planning policies which are directed to the containment of urban growth and the preservation of open country'.[111]

Probably the greatest problem with the Land Commission, however, and as the Labour Minister of Housing and Local Government, Richard Crossman, had himself predicted would be the case, was that land prices did not fall, but rose instead.[112] It was claimed that in the case of the vast bulk of land which was developed, and which did not pass through the Commission's hands, the owners were not selling, but were waiting for a Conservative election victory, and the repeal of the betterment levy. Developers, on the other hand, *had* to get land, in order to keep up their land banks, and were thus bidding up prices. And in reality the Commission acquired very little land indeed. By the time of repeal, in 1971, it had acquired 2,800 acres in all, of which only a very small proportion was in the Midlands or South-East. It did, however, in the short period of its existence, collect a gross betterment levy of £71 million. The Commission had been empowered either to buy land which was already the subject of a planning permission, or to buy land and then itself apply for permission. The local planning authorities had been requested by central government to co-operate with the Commission. Clearly, they did not do so.

Exactly why the Commission came in this way to promote urban interests against the rural counties is not clear. Whether in so doing it reflected significant class interests, in the way suggested by McDougall concerning the Liberals and the 1909 Act, or by Backwell and Dickens concealing the legislation of the mid-1940s, is something which clearly could only be revealed by historical research. The Commission may, by contrast, have been merely acting in a way characteristic of any bureaucratic organization, maximizing its power by concentrating its efforts in what were, due to its lack of funds, virtually the only places open to it. What *is* clear, is that it became politically easy for the enemies of this legislation to portray it as a 'failure', to suggest that it simply 'did not work'. Thus, they escaped any obligation to discuss it in terms of its purposes, or in terms of social justice.[113] By an Act of 1971, the incoming Conservative government of 1970 fulfilled its promises, and repealed the Land Commission Act. Once again, the country was in the illogical situation of having a system of land-use planning together with a free market in land; the '1953 system' was back.

If the Labour governments of 1964–70 thus failed in their attempts to provide the planning system with a sound financial basis, what of their planning policies more generally? The whole logic of the present book would suggest that without this sound financial basis, the planning system could hardly be expected to succeed, and I would suggest that this was indeed the case. The planning system was at no time during the 1960s and 1970s particularly successful in determining the national land-use pattern, while in the face of the property booms of the early 1960s and 1970s it failed completely to come to grips with these.

Yet if one looks at the *apparent* level of planning activity, one sees a strange paradox. Especially from 1964 onwards, this period witnessed a veritable flood of planning studies, planning reports, planning research, and especially, perhaps, talk about planning. Courses for intending planners in the universities and polytechnics multiplied rapidly in number,[114] and the profession entered into a second phase of rapid expansion, similar to that in the mid-1940s. If the Macmillan government had looked to 'planning' to solve its problems, the Wilson governments from 1964 onwards did so to an even more marked degree.

These Labour administrations, with their strong commitment to the idea that 'modernization' could be achieved through technology, expertise, and management, were markedly sympathetic to technocratically-inclined 'planners', of all kinds. Given that the British economy was buoyant and expanding, that both the local government system in general and the planning system in particular were being given strong encouragement to reorganize and restructure themselves, and were consequently offering rapidly expanding opportunities of employment, the future must have seemed bright indeed in the 1960s and early 1970s to any who could call themselves 'planners', in any sense of this notoriously vague word. To make sense of the ensuing flurry of talk and activity, in which the professional town and country planners took a leading role, is not easy, but one thing which can be said is that relatively little of it was concerned with making clear the social, economic or political implications of governmental intervention in the land and property development process. Rather, it all tended to be conducted at a highly abstract level, centred more on the notion of 'planning' itself than on what all this 'planning' was meant to achieve. In so far as it *does* seem possible to say what it was all about, one can point to four activities in which town and country planners sought to become involved.

First, there was 'economic planning'. In 1965, in connection with the creation of a new Department of Economic Affairs and the preparation of a National Plan, Britain was divided up into ten 'economic planning regions', each with a regional board of civil servants and a regional council composed of industrialists, trade union representatives, local politicians, academics and so on. Generally along the lines of the South East Study, referred to above, there was to be prepared for each region a regional survey, and eventually a regional plan. These plans were to be primarily economic in character, but were to be given a clear spatial dimension. Senior members of the town planning profession served on these regional councils, and the profession as a whole seems to have regarded this regional planning as something in which it should be involved, or at least, with which it should be closely associated.[115]

Second, there was so-called 'social planning'. From 1965 onwards, successive governments embarked on a long series of *ad hoc* policy interventions, most of which were said to be 'experimental' and to be designed to discover ways of helping to solve the problems associated with 'urban deprivation'. Certain of these initiatives aroused great interest among physical planners, and especially among those responsible for 'social aspects' of statutory plans, and those who taught about such things in the planning schools. This seems to have been partly because these initiatives were related to specific localities, defined in physical terms, and because they often used techniques for mapping the geographical incidence of social deprivation, in ways similar to those used in planning surveys. Thus, particular interest was taken in the twelve local schemes embarked upon by the Home Office, for example, in its Community Development Project launched in 1969. The greatest degree of integration of physical with socio-economic analysis, however, is considered by a number of observers to have been achieved in the three 'Inner City Studies' conducted in parts of Birmingham, Lambeth and Liverpool over the mid-1970s under the direction of the Department of the Environment.

Given that some versions of the theory of planning as 'rational decision-making' saw it as a kind of 'societal guidance', it became difficult at times to know where some town planners thought their own activity ended, and this 'social planning' began—or which subsumed the other. All tended to become submerged beneath a mass of talk about the need for ever more planning, and the need for ever greater integration of all these various kinds of planning. Those social scientists and social workers who actually worked on these central government poverty initiatives, however, or who studied them, generally took a very different and much more down-to-earth view. Rather than supposing that poverty was a problem best tackled by mapping exercises, statistical techniques, better organization of local government, or 'planning', they pointed out that poverty was simply a matter of economic and social inequality.[116]

The third area in which the new managerialist and technocratic climate of the 1960s and the 1970s appeared to offer opportunities for town and country planners to extend their sphere of influence was in local government organization and management. From the mid-1960s onwards, both the geographical division of the country into local authority areas and the introduction of new techniques of 'management' into local government became live issues, as it became clear that in both spheres, radical change was in fact politically possible. Planners, both individually and through the Royal Town Planning Institute, took an active part in the debate on local government boundaries, generally arguing for the kind of single-tier system of authorities centred on cities and larger towns which Redcliffe–Maud ultimately recommended.

In the area of local government 'management', the new ideas emerging in the 1960s had a fatal attraction for town planners, for they were extremely similar, in their abstract nature, in their technocratic assumptions, and in their anti-political bias, to similar ideas being evolved over the same period within their own field. Since it was being increasingly urged that the town and country planners' statutory development plans should have social and economic objectives, it became difficult to know whether the local authority's 'corporate plan' ought to subsume this statutory 'development plan', or whether it should be the other way round. Though all this abstract discussion of 'goals' and 'objectives' and 'corporate planning' seemed to most outside observers utterly divorced from reality, it was apparently taken quite seriously by many professionals, who saw it as a means of making local government more 'rational', and was even advocated by some academics.[117] With the adoption of the idea in many local authorities that all of the authority's departments should be subordinated to the control of a central policy-making unit, under a chief executive, many senior town planners saw their own understanding of 'planning' as a 'generic' approach as uniquely fitting them for these appointments.

The fourth way in which town planners attempted to extend their power and influence over the 1960s and 1970s, then, relates to this notion of planning as a generic approach, as a set of techniques for rational decision-making, applicable in principle to any subject-matter. It was on the basis of this claim, of course, that the town planners made their bid to move into the three areas already identified, 'economic planning', 'social planning', and local government 'corporate planning'. But it was *also* on the basis of their supposed mastery of this generic planning method, ironically, that they based their claim to competence within their *own* field, that of the control of land use. In the planning schools, relatively little was taught or researched either about land and property development, or about the governmental control of property development, but increasing emphasis was instead given to what became known as 'procedural planning theory'. In so far as the practice of town planning had any theoretical rationale at all, this came to be seen as consisting of a mixture of these abstract ideas of 'rational decision-making' with systems theory and with almost equally abstract theories of locational behaviour taken from geography. Within the almost impossibly broad and extremely vague framework thus established, we saw over the 1960s and 1970s an almost endless succession of fashionable new 'concepts' and 'approaches', each hailed in its turn as clothing the Emperor's nakedness by providing planning with a scientific basis.

The above four sets of ideas are all clearly ideological. Each of them, 'economic planning', 'social planning', 'corporate planning' and 'generic planning' is in effect a slogan, and encapsulates a web of ideas used by various professional groups in their attempts to secure for themselves better exmployment opportunities and enhanced status.

But as well as being ideological, in this precise sense of justifying bids for professional power, all of these sets of ideas are highly abstract, and rather divorced from reality. They reflect the approach of those who would take over a field without getting involved in its earthiness. I have already contrasted the abstract 'social planners'' approach to poverty with that of the social scientists and social workers, who actually study the reality of poverty. It is highly significant, I think, that in attempting to take over other people's fields, town planners pitched their bids at this abstract level. For this is precisely the level at which they operate in their own field. Governmental intervention in the property development industry, the activity in which town and country planners are in fact engaged in their everyday working lives, they *also* discuss at a rather abstract level, as a matter of 'balancing', of 'ensuring that all land is put to its best use', and so on. They do not look at it fairly and squarely, and straightforwardly admit that town planning is inevitably a matter of taking from some and giving to others, in the name of a political opinion.

Such developments in this field of policy since the 1960s as *are* worth noting, therefore, have originated not with the professional planners, but with those who *are* rather more prepared to look at the reality of town planning, such as academic social scientists, the media, and environmental pressure groups. I shall say more about these developments in later chapters, but first it is necessary to complete my account of the historical development of town and country planning legislation.

With the repeal by the Conservatives of the Land Commission legislation, in 1971, the way was obviously clear once again for a speculative boom in property and land, and as anticipated, this duly occurred. With the market in land once more a 'free' one, and with those owners who received planning permissions once more legally entitled to retain the whole of the betterment value in their property, values again rose to unprecedented levels. Just as last time, in the early 1960s, public knowledge of the vast unearned profits being made by developers became quite widespread.[118] Just as last time, too, public disapproval grew to such an extent that the government was obliged to appear to be doing something about the problem. At first, it did little more than exhort local authorities to allocate more land for development, just as it had done in the early 1960s. This, however, was hardly likely to help in the case of commercial development in the city centres, where the problem of land values was most acute. Eventually, in December 1973, the government acted, introducing a capital gains tax on land and property transactions at a rate of 32 per cent. This, however, did not succeed in holding down the level of inflation and speculation, and just before they lost office, in 1974, the Conservatives were once again contemplating the introduction of a tax on betterment, a so-called development gains tax.

The Labour government of 1974 took office on a programme apparently far more socialist than at any time since the mid-1940s. As McKay and Cox put it, 'The Community Land Act, together with the 1975 Industry Act which created the National Enterprise Board and the Planning Agreements System, seemed to signal a new era of state planning in economy and society'.[119] In the event, however, the international economic situation meant that the government simply could not find the money for its social programmes; this was as true of the Community Land Act as the rest. This legislation, it will be remembered, like the earlier Land Commission Act of 1967, was briefly discussed in Chapter 1. As in the case of the Land Commission, the attack was again two-pronged. On the one hand, there would during a 'transitional period' be a tax on realized development value, levied this time at rates of up to 80 per cent.[120] On the other hand, it was provided that all land to be developed should ultimately pass through public hands. This time, however, to avoid antagonizing the local authorities, it was to be the local authorities themselves who would have this power of acquisition. As in 1967, acquisition would be at prices net of tax, and resale to developers would be at development value, leaving up to 80 per cent of the 'uncarned increment' to be shared between the Exchequer and the local planning authority. In this way, development control would eventually be transformed into the promotion of development, or 'positive planning', while at the same time being the means by which the unearned increment was recouped; the control of land values and the control of land use were to be combined into a single operation.

What happened in the case of this third, and most recent, post-war attempt to get town and country planning in Britain on a sound financial basis? The long 'transitional period', and the many exemptions and exceptions to the development land tax, gave the legislation a gradualist flavour, reducing its credibility as a determined attack on the problem. It got onto the statute book at precisely the point in time at which, for quite extraneous reasons, there was a slump in the property market, so that it unfortunately appeared at the time of its inception almost irrelevant. Most local authorities at the time were Conservative-controlled, and made little attempt to operate the legislation at all, regarding it with scepticism and indifference. Those which did attempt to use the Community Land Act, just like the Land Commission before them, concentrated on 'green-field' sites rather than on the central areas, where the real planning problems were to be found. And they did so, again, for exactly the same reason, an inadequate level of funding for the scheme. All these factors led to a general dissatisfaction with the Community Land Act, and once again, therefore, it proved relatively easy and uncontroversial for the Conservatives, returning to office in 1979, to announce their intention to repeal it; this was duly accomplished in 1980.[121] In the case of the taxation of betterment value, however, the position of the Thatcher government was more ambiguous. At first, this government amended the 1976 Development Land Tax Act in such a way that the whole of the tax revenue went to the Exchequer instead of being shared with the local authority; later it reduced the rate of tax, and only in 1985 did it finally abolish this tax altogether.

It is not altogether easy, as yet, to assess the significance of governmental policies since 1979 for the land-use planning system. To some extent, the changed climate has economic rather than political causes, and the changes therefore predate the accession of the Thatcher government in 1979. For several years before 1979 the effects of economic recession had meant that, especially outside the South-East, there was quite simply less development to 'plan', while cuts in local government expenditure meant that job opportunities for planners were no longer increasing at the very rapid rate which had been produced by the 1974 reorganization of local government.

Often since 1979, planners have appeared to suggest that the government's policies constitute a very thoroughgoing 'attack on planning', but this interpretation may well be due, at least in part, to the way in which, as shown above, planners tend to confuse planning with other activities. In the case of all those functions of local government which involve significant levels of expenditure, such as education, housing, social services and capital investment in general, the climate has indeed changed, and changed very markedly. The whole balance of power between central and local government has also become the focus of bitter conflict, as the Thatcher government has attempted to shift power from the periphery to the centre. But in the case of a purely regulatory activity such as town and country planning, there seems relatively little to be gained politically by dismantling the system of regulation. Such a system of regulation, after all, can be used just as well to secure one political objective as another. And in practice, it would seem that whatever the political complexion of the party in power at Westminster, the planning system has tended to promote interests with which the Conservatives strongly identify, or from which they draw their support. It has been used, for example, to keep up market values in expensive residential areas, to keep working-class housing and other undesirable development out of 'commuter country' and prized rural villages, and so on.[122] Thus much of the post-1979 Conservative governments' 'attack on planning' may be at the purely symbolic level; it is the *word* 'planning' which is above all attacked, for it has the capacity to evoke images of red tape, bureaucracy, and the inefficiencies of socialist state control.[123]

Perhaps the most significant question we might ask, therefore, is whether the policies of Conservative governments since 1979 have in fact weakened the planning system or strengthened it. Abolition of the 'Community Land' scheme and Development Land Tax, after all, have little practical significance if, as seems likely, these two potentially radical pieces of legislation were having very little effect anyway.

The Community Land Act, it could be argued, was destroyed not by repeal, but by the failure of those who framed it to obtain support for it from all relevant interests at the time that it was drafted, and by the fact that many Conservative-controlled local authorities would probably have operated it with very little enthusiasm anyway.

As for Development Land Tax, this had apparently been rendered ineffective long before 1979, as a result of the ingenuity of the property developers' financial advisers in devising means of tax avoidance.[124]

If, then, we interpret the planning system as a mechanism of social redistribution, we see that in this role it tends to be ineffective whatever party is in control at Westminster. There are other ways of interpreting it, however. Since 1979, it has become increasingly clear that the planning system may be used not to strengthen the hands of consumers, wage-earners and environmentalists against the tendency of developers and producers to overlook the environmental costs which they impose, but for the quite opposite purpose, of strengthening the economic and political power of the development industry and producers themselves. Government may in fact be using the DoE and the planning system to do for the property industry what political scientists have long seen the Ministry of Agriculture as doing for the farming interest—that is, to strengthen its hand, to provide the conditions in which it can operate profitably.[125] Indeed, the new, present-day, consensus seems to suggest that the purpose and scope of planning *ought* to be defined very much in these terms.

Finally, however, in this brief historical sketch, we can note what may at first sign appear to be a profound paradox. The massive migration of population and of economic activity from the big cities, as proposed by Ebenezer Howard, has in fact occurred. It has occurred not only because government put into effect a modified version of Howard's new towns programme, but also because central and local government have used their powers to facilitate the outward migration of working-class populations to peripheral council estates, and above all, it has occurred as a result of the efforts of the private sector, and of 'voluntary' migration. Indeed, Howard's prescription has been followed to such an extent that by the late 1960s it had become obvious that the big cities had lost not only much of their population, but also much of their economic vitality.

This process had not, however, as Howard envisaged it would, led to a significant reduction in the economic and political power of the 'landed classes'. On the contrary, the power of property interests seems as great as ever, while the real cost of this massive exodus has instead fallen on the poorest sections of society, and in particular on those left behind in the inner-city areas.[126]

And yet, we may note, all this is by no means as paradoxical as it might appear. If the development values created in the peripheries of the urban regions had been recouped for the public purse, as Howard proposed, this considerable migration would probably *not* have benefited the property development industry to the extent it has. What *other* interests might have benefited from it, and therefore whether the incentives necessary to the achievement of this outward migration of population might have existed at all, are questions which I clearly cannot address within the scope of this book. What I must instead do at this point is to attempt to sum up the argument of this chapter.

## 7.  Conclusions

The legitimation and consolidation of the planning system, I have suggested, might be analysed in terms of three factors: first, the efforts of the planners themselves, second, the fact that governments might have their own reasons to encourage 'planning'; and third, the fact that once established, any governmental bureaucracy tends to grow under its own momentum.

Taking the first of these three factors, I identified four styles of thought which planners have used in order to portray their activity as a technical imperative and as non-political; these I have termed *physicalism, holism, technicism* and *role-confusion*. Physicalism in its first, determinist, form, was successfully used as a legitimating device especially in the 1940s. As a value in its own right, stress on the physical environment has ,been used more in recent decades, however, when 'ecological' and 'heritage' currents have given it a new credibility. *Holism,* or the tendency of the planning lobby both to wrap up all its prescriptive ideas into a single readily-comprehended 'package' and to assert a consensus of interest among all groups in society in pursuing that 'package' of policies, was also used with particular success in the 1940s. It re-emerged strongly in the 1960s and 1970s, however, this time as an ideology which suggested the planners' ability to discern and promote the public interest by using such techniques as mathematical modelling and rational planning method. *Technicism,* which leads to a stress on planning as a 'process', and which correspondingly distracts attention away from the question of the political purposes which planning serves, has also been used as a legitimating device throughout. Its use also reached a peak in the 1960s and 1970s, but it too, like the other styles of thought identified, is still strongly reflected in planning thought, even in the late 1980s. *Role confusion* enabled planning to be seen in the 1940s as part of a wider political programme for the creation of a more equal society, in the 1950s as a purely technical matter of land use, in the 1960s and 1970s as an integral part of a wider technocratic movement for the modernization of Britain, and in the 1980s as a means of encouraging private entrepreneurship.

Next, we can turn to the ways in which governments themselves may have encouraged the idea or used the reality of 'planning'. Though it is the Liberal government of 1906 which is responsible for the introduction of statutory town planning into Britain, it seems doubtful whether town planning played more than a minor and symbolic role in that government's political strategy. The Labour government of 1929–31, by contrast, would clearly have wished to promote 'town and country planning', but obviously had no chance. In the post-war Attlee administration, however, we see evidence both of a real commitment to physical planning, and of a conception of the way in which this physical planning could form part of a wider programme of social reconstruction; the 1947 Act, had it not in effect been virtually repeated in 1953, would have contributed to a significant redistribution of power and wealth in society.

When we turn to consider the Conservative governments of 1951–64 and 1970–4 and the Labour governments of 1964–70 and 1974–9, however, the picture becomes far less clear. From the 1950s onwards, we see a strangely dichotomized approach to policy-making; planning policies and land-values policies are kept apart, by both Labour and Conservatives alike. Indeed, so wide does this gulf become that we can with truth say that while planning has been underpoliticized, land-values policy has been overpoliticized. By 'overpoliticized' I mean a state of affairs in which there occur almost violent reversals of policy, mainly reflecting party ideology, and largely untempered and uninformed by research and expertise. Both the Labour attempts to institute radical solutions to the land-value problem, in 1967 and in 1975–6, and the Conservative decisions to overturn these attempts, seem to have been without exception insufficiently researched, hastily conceived, and put into effect without sufficient regard to those processes of consultation and mutual accommodation which are essential if legislation is to have credibility and to achieve public acceptance.

So strongly-marked has this separation of 'planning' policy from land-values policy become, in fact, that one is tempted to hypothesize that this separation serves a political purpose. So long as 'planning' is not discussed and understood as an integral part of this highly political matter of property speculation and land values, it is possible to maintain the illusion that this 'planning' succeeds in curbing any possible anti-social excesses on the part of the less scrupulous operators. 'Planning' can thus be officially portrayed as successfully promoting the public interest. If the market alone were to decide, this official view suggests, all manner of economically weak and yet socially valuable interests and viewpoints would get overlooked. 'Planning', therefore, holds the ring, and redresses the balance, reconciling all the conflicting pressures and demands on land in a small overcrowded island.

As soon as we do in fact analyse this 'planning' in relation to the operations of the development industry and in the light of the highly politicized matter of land values, however, it becomes immediately more difficult to maintain this official (and professional) facade. In reality, as I have shown, the existence and nature of planning controls is a very important part of the explanation both of the level of property values, and of the way in which the property developers make their profits. To bring together land-values policy with land-use policy (or 'planning'), therefore, though it would be logical and rational, would be to destroy the credibility and the legitimacy of this 'planning'. And this, in fact, brings me to one of the main conclusions of this chapter. The purpose of this chapter, I explained, was to analyse the way in which the legitimacy of planning has been established and maintained. It might have been more perspicacious, however, to have instead asked how the legitimacy of the property development industry and its associated financial institutions is maintained, the answer being that this is achieved by having a 'planning system'.

There is, then, a further, and related, conclusion. Governments may portray planning for their own political purposes as having a certain set of effects, while its actual effects may be quite otherwise. A right-wing government, for example, might conceivably portray the planning system along the lines sketched out above, as curbing the potential excesses of powerful developers, who might otherwise pay insufficient regard to the environmentally and socially harmful effects of their activities, while in reality using the powers given by the planning system to strengthen the economic and political power of those same developers. A left-wing government, conversely, might encourage the belief that 'planning' is in some way connected with its efforts to promote greater social and economic equality, in order to help conceal the fact that, in reality, its professed egalitarian aims are thwarted by international monetary pressures and other political realities. To throw light on such matters, however, we need to look not at the ideology of planning, but at the evidence concerning its concrete effects. And such evidence is very sparse. Such evidence as there is, I shall consider in the next chapter.

# 3 The effects of the planning system

The proof of the pudding is in the eating.

English proverb, Seventeenth-century

## 1. Introduction

The structure of this chapter is quite simple. First, in this Introduction, I set out the model of policy-making which I have adopted, summed up as 'policy as hypothesis'. This explanation is very brief, and is placed here only in order to make clear the standpoint from which I approach the empirical evidence which follows. In the second section of the chapter, then, I review what is known about the effects of planning in Britain. Knowledge of these effects, as we shall see, is sparse, and I shall therefore ask why this is so, my conclusion being that the planners simply do not operate with a model of policy-making which *calls for* knowledge of effects. In the third and final section of the chapter, therefore, I ask how policy-making might be improved. I take up the 'model' set out in this Introduction, explain it a little more fully, and suggest that though its use is fraught with difficulties, it (or something rather like it) offers the best hope of improving policy-making.

My basic assumption is that the justification for governmental activity must be in terms of its effects. To discover these effects, however, is far from easy; causation is not easily established. The web of governmental activity is so wide and so dense, and is so intricately enmeshed with the economy and with social institutions more generally, that it must often seem difficult to believe that any outcome can be explained, other than in terms of virtually everything else. Nevertheless, I suggest, the attempt must be made. In principle, the object should be to discover 'what difference' is made by the policy in question. How broadly or how narrowly we thus define 'the policy in question', however, then becomes a crucial question. Some of the research reviewed below interprets 'the policy in question' as the totality of all the influences and controls exerted by the planning system. It might be easier, I shall argue, if we looked at more specific policies. But however broadly or narrowly we define 'the policy in question', we clearly cannot compare its effects with those which would supposedly have resulted in some hypothetical 'free market' situation. Rather, we must in principle compare its effects with the outcomes produced by the whole web of existing public sector and private sector activity *minus this one bit*, the 'policy in question'.[1]

How, in principle, should a policy be operated? Before putting it into effect, we should hypothesize its likely effects. After it has been in effect long enough to *have* effects, we should try to discover what these effects are, a process I shall term *monitoring*. The explanation of the differences between hypothesized effects and actual effects is *theory*, and it is this theoretical knowledge which enables us slowly but progressively, over the years, to reduce these differences. This model derives from Popper,[2] and has been explained as follows:

> All government policies, indeed all executive and administrative decisions, involve empirical predictions: If we do X, Y will follow; on the other hand, if we want to achieve B we must do A . . . A policy is a hypothesis which has to be tested against reality and corrected in the light of experience . . . The implementation of every policy needs to be tested, and this is done not by looking for evidence that one's efforts are having the desired effects, but by looking for evidence that they are not. Testing in this sense is usually cheap and easy in practice if only because minute accuracy is seldom necessary.[3]

In other words, public policy is in a real sense the social science equivalent of what physical scientists do in their laboratories. This has striking implications. First, those who make and implement public policy not only *need* theoretical knowledge; they also help to *produce* it. *Second*, the model implies that intelligent policy-making is literally impossible, unless ist is based on knowledge of its own past consequences. A *third* point was in fact mentioned in the extract from Magee above, but it should be emphasized: the knowledge produced by such 'policy research', and by the social sciences generally, is of necessity less accurate than that produced by the natural sciences. But this does not make it less useful. Approximate knowledge of how to achieve those things we think important is very much more useful than even the most precise understanding of how to achieve outcomes which we consider to add little to human welfare.

Those involved in public policy-making and administration, however, often have a tendency to resist such monitoring of the results of their actions. Few public policies achieve exactly the outcomes envisaged by those who urged them, and many produce results which are positively embarrassing, often because the context in which they are operated is complex and changing, and thus affects them in ways which cannot be foreseen. It is always more pleasant, therefore, for policy-makers and their expert advisers to concentrate on devising new policies, rather than on studying the consequences of previous or existing ones.[4] Planners, however, seem to yield to this temptation more than most. The reason, as we shall see, lies in the sheer breadth of their ambitions, or what, above, was termed their *holism*.[5] The more things you seek to influence all at once, the more difficult it becomes to assess the effects produced.

Having set out my preferred model of policy-making, I can now, in the light of it, turn to review what is known about the consequences of the existence of town and country planning in Britain.

## 2. The available evidence

Broadly, this is of two types. We can call these *intended* and *contingent*. 'Intended' evidence results from research specifically designed to discover the effects of planning. 'Contingent' evidence, by contrast, is a by-product of research primarily intended to discover something else. The main reason why I look at data of the second type, is that there is so little of the first. Let us look first at contingent evidence:

### 'Contingent' evidence

The main source of this lies in political scientists' and sociologists' studies of the planning process. Such researchers have not generally been interested in the consequences of planning decisions, so much as in the way those decisions were arrived at. Political scientists do not in principle presume to be experts in the 'substantive' policy areas which they investigate; they focus, rather, on the use of power as such. They therefore concentrate on such things as the ways in which the various protagonists in the decision-making process 'define the situation', the extent to which they are able to get others to accept this definition, the ways in which they mobilize support and make alliances, which interest groups in society they represent, and so on. Nevertheless, such studies do in practice often tell us something about the effects produced. This is because, while not claiming to be experts in the substantive matter at issue, the researchers cannot afford to be wholly naive about it, either. Though mainly interested in the decision-making process, they must also understand *why* the various protagonists pursue the outcomes they do.

This might be illustrated by the case of an imaginary coal-fired electricity generating station. A political scientist studying the decision-making processes involved would probably not claim the ability to discuss the matter of where it 'ought' to be situated, or even of the ways in which its going to various possible sites mights create costs or benefits for the various interest groups involved. To pronounce on such substantive matters one needs considerable knowledge of the economics of electricity generation, of the costs of transport of coal, of the construction costs of various kinds of power station and overhead transmission lines, and so on, as well as an ability to estimate the financial and physical negative externalities which such a generating station might impose on other land users, a sociological understanding of the ways in which all those affected might perceive such costs (and benefits), and react to them, and not least, a knowledge of the ways in which, by skilful siting, engineering, and landscape design, such negative externalities could in fact be minimized in the first place. Quite properly, political scientists would leave judgments about such things to those who are expert in them. They would, nevertheless, familiarize themselves sufficiently with the arguments put forward by such experts, and by the protagonists in the issue, to provide a summary of them, for *this* degree of understanding of substantive questions is essential to an understanding of the political behaviour of those involved.

Such studies of planning in practice arer usually restricted to a specific locality, and often to a specific issue. As such, and despite the fact that they are not intended to tell us the effects of planning, they do at least provide us with detailed and often very revealing information on the ways in which planning 'works'. It would clearly not be justified here, however, to devote too much space to these 'contingent sources', for what they can tell us about effects must be of necessity uncertain and fragmentary, and we should therefore be careful to avoid drawing unjustifiably generalized conclusions from them. A few examples can be given, however, mainly to make clear what kind of work is referred to, and thereby to permit consideration of what its value actually is.

Ferris,[6] for example, in a case study from Islington, shows how the creation of a residential precinct freed from through-traffic served to enhance the standards of quietness and seclusion enjoyed by middle-class residents, while subjecting working-class people living nearby to very much increased levels of traffic noise and danger. Typically for such political science-orientated studies, he investigates the issue in terms of the pressures brought to bear by the two groups, and by all the various agencies involved. He does not ask (and this of course would be the key question, from the planners' point of view) whether there might not have been a *design* solution, enabling *both* groups to achieve good environmental standards. Lee *et al.*[7] discuss town and country planning as one aspect of the political relationship between a big city (Manchester) and an adjoining suburbanized rural county (Cheshire). In this case, the result of the use of planning powers was that the county was able largely to prevent the city acquiring land outside its own boundaries for council housing, and to prevent it getting its own new town under the 1946 Act. Such dispersal of population as Manchester did achieve, the county managed by 'mutual agreement' to restrict to extensions of existing small industrial towns in Cheshire, thus safeguarding its more exclusive suburban areas against working-class incursions.

Muchnik[8] looked at slum clearance and rehousing policies in Liverpool, concluding that virtually alone of all the departments within the local authority, the planning department attempted to secure the integration of shopping and social facilities with the construction of new housing. The department, he found, did not however altogether succeed in this objective, largely due to financial constraints. Elkin[9] studied the respective roles of the Chelsea Borough Council and the Greater London Council town planning departments, first in the construction of a large council housing estate, and second in the negotiations preceding the construction of the notorious 'Centre Point' office block in central London. In this last case, he shows very clearly how the developers were able to extract enormous concessions from the local planning authority, eventually putting up a building far larger than it had intended to permit. Similar stories of developers extracting concessions from planning authorities, or of developers ensuring that local planning policies suit their own interests, are fairly common.[10]

Other sources of 'contingent' evidence concerning the effects of planning occur in the form of remarks made *en passant*, in the course of discussing rather different matters, but which in effect often constitute quite fundamental and even devastating criticisms of the planning system; it is perhaps remarkable that such comments have not attracted more attention than they have, and have not provoked attempts at more detailed research. Newby, for example, in the course of a study of social and economic change in the British countryside, writes:

> By directing new industrial development away from rural areas, conventional strategic planning policy has had two important consequences: it has restricted the role of economic growth in the countryside; and it has weakened the bargaining power of existing rural workers by reducing the number of competitors for local labour... As in the case of housing, a policy of preserving the rural *status quo* has thus turned out to be *redistributive*—and in a highly regressive manner. Occasionally rural planners have become aware of these tendencies, but the political will has been lacking to bring about a change of policy.[11]

Cullingworth, similarly, towards the end of a work devoted to a detailed exposition of the legislative and administrative arrangements under which the planning system operates, almost casually mentions a quite breathtaking list of outcomes which, he suggests, may or may not be the result of planning: 'high rise development "difficult to let" council housing schemes, urban motorways, inner city decline and the like'.[12] What mainly seems to be missing here, ironically, is a clear conceptualization of planning, and of its powers and competencies; in so far as such problems do seem to result specifically from the use of planning powers, there would seem to be a clear need for planners specifically to research them.

How, if at all, can we summarize the significance of such 'contingent' sources of evidence? It is difficult, partly because the case studies in question are relatively few. That some of them show us how powerful developers can extract concessions from planning authorities, that others show us how apparently powerless residents' and environmentalist protest groups can nevertheless sometimes get what they want, and that yet others of them concentrate on demonstrating the bumbling dilatoriness of officialdom, or the ways in which the planners collude with powerful private sector interests, really tells us relatively little. The choice of case to study, after all, is very much influenced by the researcher's interest in these various aspects of human behaviour, and the studies which exist, therefore, can hardly constitute a statistically valid sample. We might, however, say that such studies have at least promoted a more realistic awareness of certain 'facts of life'—for example, that large-scale developers are often more powerful than planning authorities, that it is material interests rather than 'rationality' which often determines the behaviour even of the planners themselves, and that the use of planning powers often has unintended consequences. (This last will be shown to be particularly significant, below). My main conclusion, however, is to record surprise that insights such as those mentioned above have not provoked more thorough and more wide-ranging research into the effects of the planning system, and especially, perhaps, into its effects on land and property markets.

### 'Intended' sources of evidence

There have, however, been *some* attempts specifically to investigate the effects of planning, and it is to these that I now turn. Before doing so, however, it seems useful to make a fairly obvious methodological point. The thing to do, it would seem, would be to divide the research into two stages. First, we would try to discover the effects which the planning system has had on the pattern of land use,. and on the physical form of development. Then we would go on to investigate the economic and social effects of these 'planned' spatial patterns and built forms. Clearly, the first stage is the simpler one. Researchers would probably broadly agree, one would suppose, on what this 'first stage' research showed. It would be in the second stage that the main problems of interpretation of evidence would arise.

In fact, of course, many of the intended effects of planning are in 'first stage' terms easily understood. Planning has sought to keep rural landscapes open, to avoid scattered evelopment, to keep industry out of residential areas, to protect 'heritage' buildings, to ensure that shops, schools, open spaces and other amenities are conveniently located close to people's homes, and so on. But problems of research method obviously arise, even in researching such apparently simple things as these. We simply do not know to what extent given physical patterns result from planning, and to what extent they reflect developers' intentions, or the play of market forces.

The studies which do exist can however be divided into two types, in accordance with the two 'stages' suggested above. Some stop short, restricting themselves to documenting the spatial and physical patterns which emerge, and not going on to consider their economic and social effects. Three studies of green belt policies, for example, can be mentioned as being of this type.[13] To stop at this point is at least to avoid making mistakes. The traditional planning approach to the 'problem of the second stage', of course, is to assume physical determinism, and simply to *assert* that the physical patterns produced (or intended) will (or would) have desirable social and economic effects.[14]

A researcher who takes such determinism seriously, however, and in fact attempts to demonstrate it, is Coleman.[15] Analyzing data from the National Land Utilization Survey, both for the country as a whole and in greater detail for a thousand-square-kilometre area on the south side of the Thames estuary, Coleman concludes that control has been very lax, permitting much scattered development instead of restricting it to the interstices and peripheries of existing built-up areas. She also shows that much good quality agricultural land has been taken for development, despite the fact that other land, often within or adjoining urban areas, remains unused. Thus, she argues, the dividing line between urban areas and farmland is needlessly long and involuted. Much agricultural land is therefore difficult to farm, due to trespass and vandalism. In urging that planning should strengthen its efforts to create more compact settlement patterns, Coleman explicitly postulates a number of benefits. Not only would this increase agricultural production, which in the light of ecological realities she sees as a moral duty, but by reducing the need for car travel, it would improve health. Enlightened planners, she suggests, would

> design environments in which walking is a real option, by locating a large range of destinations within walking distance. They recognize that walking improves physical health; oxygenates the brain and improves mental health also; helps to integrate social systems and improves social health as well; conserves scarce oil resources; cuts down pollution by lead and carbon monoxide from exhaust fumes; and so on.[16]

Citing as her evidence work by Newman[17] Coleman has elsewhere suggested that the securing of certain forms of residential layout by planning control could also reduce the crime rate. She argues her assumptions to their logical conclusions, suggesting that since it is *known* that certain spatial patterns and physical forms produce specific economic and social benefits, the law itself should require development to take these patterns and forms, rather than giving the planners the discretion to decide what is 'good planning' in particular cases:

> I believe that we now know enough about environment and about planning to bring a large part of good planning under the rule of law instead of leaving it to the individual decisions of planners . . . The public is entitled to a framework of specific knowledge on what is or is not acceptable in the planning context, and also why.[18]

Simmie[19] attempts to discover, rather than to assume, the economic and social effects of the pattern of development which emerges under planning, but, unlike Coleman, he concentrates entirely on distributional consequences. Simmie examined development control decisions in three socially-contrasted wards of the City of Oxford, from 1953 to 1973, in order to discover which social groups benefited most from the development which was permitted. He concludes that 'commercial and industrial organizations', the local authority itself and 'ancient landowners', such as the Oxford colleges, were most successful in obtaining planning permission to build what they wished, though less powerful interests, and even the working classes, gained increasingly over the years from the construction of such things as council housing and schools. Though Simmie's research provides a most detailed and invaluable account of the operations of the local authority, however, it is difficult to gain from it any real understanding of the effects of the planning system *per se*. The question with which we are concerned is that of the 'difference' made by planning specifically, and this Simmie does not really clarify. He provides a detailed account of what was built, but clearly, much of it would have been built in the same locations and in much the same forms anyway, even in the absence of planning. His study seems to have been handicapped by an inadequate conceptualization of 'planning', as opposed to the wider web of governmental and private sector institutions and practices in which the system of planning is set.

Hague[20], who studied planning in Edinburgh from the end of the Second World War until the 1980s, provides a particularly valuable study, since he is specifically concerned to trace the links between planning in practice and the development of the planners' professional ideology. He concludes that throughout this period, the patterns of development which emerged were virtually always such as to promote the interests of the more privileged sections of the local population rather than those of the working classes.

By far the most thorough investigation of the effects of the British planning system to date, however, was published in 1973, under the title *The Containment of Urban England*,[21] and the remainder of this section of the chapter will be devoted to this.

### 'The Containment of Urban England'

The task addressed in this research was to discover 'the principal impacts of the [planning] system, intended and unintended: on the house building programme, on the housing and land markets, on patterns of journey to work', and to determine 'what sort of judgement can be reached on the system in comparison with what might have existed without it'.[22] The study restricts itself to the axial belt running from London to the North-West, on the grounds that this region, being the major urbanized part of the country, would in the absence of planning probably have been transformed into an incipient megalopolis, and was therefore of particular interest.

Though the research method is not stated very explicitly, it rests broadly on the kind of strategy outlined above, first demonstrating the spatial and physical outcomes, and then analysing the social and economic consequences of these physical patterns. In their attempt to identify the effects of planning, the researchers have used a fairly long list of what might be called 'factors suggesting what to expect to find'. I use this clumsy phrase, rather than calling them simply 'hypotheses', because their exact methodological status seems a bit unclear. They are a mixed bag, in fact. Some of them are the taken-for-granted cultural assumptions on which the planning system was based, others are the physical outcomes urged by those who advised on the creation of the planning system, while others again relate to the way in which the system was operated.[23] Let us anyway go through these various factors, starting with those which relate to the wider political culture.

(i)   *A tendency in Britain to elite government, based on a 'unitary' model of society.* The authors suggest that the elite (which includes the professional planners) 'have an organismic view of the public interest; all other interests are subordinated to that of the social "organism" '.[24] Such an approach, they suggest, 'tends to an extremely lofty yet imprecise definition of the public good in terms of ends . . . which are ideologically derived, and are characteristically presented in terms of the absolute virtue of a concrete set of policy measures'.[25]

(ii)  *A concern, on the part of these governing elites, for 'social stability and harmony'.* These elites, the authors suggest, did not oppose social and economic change as such, but were guided by a desire to 'control the effects of change' and to direct it in ways which safeguarded such values as 'political stability' and 'historical continuity'.[26] To illustrate this, they cite the extensive British use of Royal Commissions and other advisory bodies, which, they suggest, afford all interst groups at least the *feeling* of having been heeded. In particular, they note the extensive consultations, over the entire post-war period, over the question of local government reform. Whether or not all the various parties with an interest in this matter did in fact feel that their representations had been taken into account, the fact is that the outcome (which under the period covered by this research was one of 'no change'), certainly promoted certain interests at the expense of others. The retention of the old counties, often largely controlled by rural and middle-class interests, meant that the suburbs of the larger cities were left outside the cities' jurisdictions. This enabled the suburban local authorities to portray their areas as independent 'towns', as places in their own right, and to deny their dependence on the cities of which economically and socially they were in fact integral parts. It also enabled them to use their planning powers in such a way as to preserve the suburban lifestyle of their relatively privileged residents, to keep up their property values by keeping out such undesirable things as council housing, and so on.

(iii) *A similar concern on the part of these elites for 'public economy'*. This value too, however, was in practice interpreted in a way which promoted class interests. By 'public economy', the authors mean, *first,* the idea that population movement from the poorer peripheral regions to the London and Birmingham areas should be discouraged. The argument here was that physical infrastructure already existed in the poorer regions and would be underused if migration continued, whereas in the prosperous South-East and Midlands, immigration continually necessitated *new* infrastructure. *Second,* 'public economy' refers to the idea that urban growth should be restricted, since it would otherwise lead to underuse of land, buildings and infrastructure in the inner areas of the cities. *Third,* it refers to the idea of conserving agricultural land wherever possible. These economic ideas, we may note, did not rest on any real research, but rather were taken-for-granted assumptions.

(iv) *A preference for small towns over large cities.* The authors note a general assumption in Britain, not only among planners and in the planning movement, but in elite circles generally, that the quality of life simply *is* superior in small settlements: 'The small, comprehensively-planned community is a neat and tidy unit of urban life when compared with the great sprawling, dirty, congested city, and would appeal in Britain on these grounds'.[27]

(v) *A concern for 'stewardship of the land'.* 'One of the strongest values of the planning movement was and is the preservation of rural England, and it is of course the basic value of the high-status pressure group represented by the Council for the Preservation of Rural England . . . county planners all over the country make the distinction between those villages which are as they say "worth saving" from new development and those which can be "let go" to new development because they are "not worth saving" '.[28] This too, it is fairly obvious, is an idea which lends itself admirably to the promotion of class interest.

To see the above factors as rather vague 'values' lying behind the use of planning controls, as the authors of 'The Containment . . .' do, seems valid. The planners had not subjected them to any intellectual analysis, or considered their economic or social implications. They had not put forward even the most rudimentary explanations as to *why* and *how* the pursuit of these values might increase welfare—or *whose* welfare. Other observers, however, have characterized the ideology of the British planning profession, and of the political culture in which it operated, in very similar terms.[29]

The remaining factors noted by the authors of *The Containment of Urban England* are more specific. They relate to ways in which the *actual* British planning system, as it evolved over the 1950s and 1960s, differed from the 'idealized system' which the 'founding fathers', in the mid-1940s, had struggled to establish:

(iv) 'The idealized system was clearly meant to be centralized or unitary in character.' In fact, however, it was decided that planning control would *not* be entrusted to a new central government agency, but operated through the local authorities.[30]

(vii) 'The idealized system bypassed the market altogether.' The Uthwatt recommendations would have completely abolished the market in land, by ensuring that all land on which development was permitted would first be acquired by the state and then leased to users. The 1947 Act, however, 'kept the market in being but . . . .did not allow the market to work'.[31] (One might comment that in the later part of the period covered by this research, after the abolition of the development charge in 1953, the continued anomalous coexistence of both the market and planning may have meant that it became *planning* which did not work).[32]

(viii) Howard had proposed new towns built in clusters ('social cities'), each individual town having a population of about 32,000, but with no limit on the population of the cluster as a whole. The new towns actually built, by contrast, were not clustered at all, but widely scattered. The 'social cities' which Howard proposed would have been capable *first*, of supporting big-city facilities and social and economic opportunities, and *second*, therefore, of becoming alternative centres of attraction, capable of competing with existing big cities such as London or Birmingham. The new towns actually built, by contrast, were capable of neither of these things.[33]

(ix) When the post-war planning system was in preparation, it was assumed that most building would in future be carried out by the public sector. In the case of the dispersal of population from London, for example, as proposed in the Abercrombie plan, it was envisaged that less than a quarter of those who moved would be housed by private enterprise. In the event, of course, the private sector played a much bigger role than this.[34]

(x) It had been urged by Howard and by the garden cities movement that ownership of all land and buildings in the new towns should be vested in their local authorities, so that their residents would reap the benefits of the increases in property values produced by their development. In the event,

however, all these assets were transferred to a central government agency, the
New Towns Commission. This removed the crucial economic mechanism,
which would have provided both the incentive and the means for social
redistribution.[35]

Having looked at the factors underlying the operation of the post-war planning
system as these are identified by Hall et al., we can now turn to the way in which
these researchers identify the consequences of the system. First, there are two
physical consequences, then three socio-economic ones.

The first of the two physical consequences is 'containment': 'the amount of land
converted from rural to urban use has been minimized and compacted'.[36]
'Containment' has been effected by the establishment of green belts around the
major conurbations, by concentrating development beyond the green belts in
'substantial pockets in towns and villages' rather than permitting it to take a
scattered form, and by raising residential densities over the whole range of
dwelling types and over the entire range of types of location. The authors point out
that a density of thirteen houses to the net acre, which had become typical for the
new estates in the counties by the 1960s, was high compared with the inter-war
period, when eight or ten was much commoner, and high as compared with 'some
other industrially advanced countries with similar housing traditions'. They name
here the United States, Canada and Australia. Also, they say, 'the densities of
urban redevelopment schemes in the cities—typically between 120 and 150 to the
net acre—are extraordinarily high compared with the twelve houses to the acre of
the typical inter-war peripheral city estates built to rehouse the same categories of
people'.[37] This 'containment', however, has not prevented outward dispersal of
population from the big cities and conurbations. Development has gone to free-
standing towns and villages, within and often beyond the green belts. This
movement of population, however, has been socially selective. With the
exception of the new towns and certain peripheral council estates, which together
represent only a small part of the total, it has involved almost entirely those able to
buy their own homes. This pattern of 'contained' development, the researchers
explain in terms of the following four factors. First, it results from 'the failure of
the planning system to react quickly enough to the persistently upward revisions of
population projections in the 1950s and the early 1960s'.[38] What the authors
appear to be saying here is that the average density of residential development
could have been lower, if, acting upon these revised estimates, the planners had
made more land available. Second, it reflects the power of the agricultural and
rural preservationist interst groups. Third, it occurred 'to some degree . . . because
of the reluctance of urban local authorities to lose population'.[39] The point was
that to lose population meant both to lose rateable value (since fewer households
mean fewer dwellings) and to lose mainly Labour voters (where council housing
was concerned).[40] Fourth, (and, according to the authors, 'the most important
single factor') 'containment' resulted from 'soaring land prices' (see below). This
factor is seen both as a cause and as a consequence of 'containment'.

The second physical consequence is suburbanization. Hall et al. do not use this

word in its everyday sense, but more precisely, to mean separation of home and
workplace:

> The planning system did not succeed in counteracting the inexorable forces which
> have led to the decentralization of population. But it did slow down the rate of
> decentralization of most other forms of urban activity ... There seems, then, to
> have been a sort of unspoken and unwritten compact in many areas that the central
> city could keep much of the additional employment both in white collar and blue
> collar jobs, while the county took suitable white collar residents.[41]

The authors suggest that for many of those concerned commuting was in fact
welcome, provided they could travel by car, since 'country' living is so highly
valued in Britain. But they note its functional inefficiency, in causing 'congestion
and increasingly expensive and controversial urban surgery' in the inner cities.[42]

The first of the socio-economic consequences is *rising land and property values*:
'The crucial weakness of the post-war planning system', Hall *et al.* write, 'has been
the failure to control the price of land'.[43] From the end of the 1930s to the late
1960s, they say, the increase in the general level of prices was fourfold. Yet the
increase in the price of land with development potential was between ten and
twentyfold.[44] They suggest that by determining which land could be developed
and which could not, the plans made under the 1947 Act concentrated all
development value onto a relatively restricted supply of land, and that this 'forced
builders to economize on land by raising densities'.[45] The rapid rise in house prices
over the post-war period, however, they attribute *not* to increased demand, but to
the fact that local authorities were failing to designate sufficient land for
development. One can note two things here. First, one can point out that these
inflated prices result from the continued coexistence of the market *and* planning,
rather than from the existence of planning *per se*. Second, however, one must note
that the charge that the planning system has designated insufficient land for
development and created rapid inflation of land values has been keenly contested,
both by planners and others.[46]

The second socio-economic consequence is that *the rate of economic growth has
'probably' been reduced*. Certain observers have suggested that the growth of the
British economy has been reduced, *inter alia*, because land and property prices
have generally risen far faster than the general rate of inflation of prices, and
because large investors (such as insurance companies and pension funds) have
therefore put their assets into property rather than into manufacturing industry.[47]
Hall *et al.*, however, do not explicitly make this connection. Rather, they suggest
that the physical imposition of planning controls in itself, has 'probably'[48] played a
part in inhibiting economic growth. Their argument is that if the economy were to
have developed more 'naturally', or in accordance with its true potential, this
would have necessitated the spread of manufacturing industry and other types of
space-craving enterprises and forms of employment into the suburbs and the
countryside, but that the privileged guardians of 'amenity' prevented this: 'The
preservation of a way of life counted heavily above any economic considerations.
Indeed, it might be said that the counties took a conscious decision to rank quality
of life aove economic growth—nearly a quarter of a century before this problem

of trade-off became a fashionable one.'[49] Hall *et al.* suggest that two attitudes existed to this 'trade-off': economists generally saw it as 'a scandal', while planners saw it 'as a price the nation should be willing to pay for the benefits of order and stability which they feel their work has brought the country':[50]

> As is so often the case in contemporary societies, the socialists have used planning to implement traditional values which are often in opposition to the free play of the capitalist market forces. The paternalism and social responsibility which the planners, and their sometimes allies in the various conservationist groups, have exercised over the past thirty years, has undoubtedly contributed to the maintenance of historical continuity and social stability in contemporary British society. The valued civility of English life, so envied byu the citizens of more chaotic modern nations, has been purchased at a price of some social and economic inefficiency which probably contributes to placing the country in a disadvantaged position among the other developed countries of the world.[51]

Here again a comment seems in order: *Does* the preservation of privileged suburban and ex-urban environments against industrial and working-class incursions contribute to 'social stability' and 'civility'? The very opposite might seem more likely, at least in the longer run. Indeed, the confinement of the least privileged to the inner areas of the cities seems in recent years to have contributed to urban riots, rather than to 'civility'. Preservation of 'heritage' buildings or countryside, similarly, would seem likely to promote social harmony, rather than the reverse, only if *all* classes in society were enabled to identify with, to live in, to work in, and to enjoy, if not to own, the properties and environments in question.

The third, and final, socio-economic consequence of the British planning system is *regressive social redistribution, both of physical-environmental advantages and disadvantages, and in more purely financial terms*. The impacts of the effects described above, Hall *et al.* suggest, were socially regressive. The costs, both in terms of environmental deterioration, and in such terms as increased housing and transport costs and lower rates of capital appreciation of property values, were borne mainly by the underprivileged. The corresponding benefits, on the other hand, both in physical-environmental terms and in such terms as value for money in housing and in faster-than-average capital appreciation of house values, accrued mainly to those who were already privileged. The authors document these regressive effects by identifying the impacts on four specific groups in society.

First, the *'ruralites'*. The authors do not discuss the rural working class. By the term 'ruralites', they mean, firstly, middle-class people who use the countryside 'as a way of life' rather than 'as a way of work', and secondly, rural landowners. The first group, they suggest, have probably gained more and lost less from planning policies than any other group in society, for planning has placed great stress on preservation of the rural landscape and way of life: 'By establishing a civilized British version of apartheid', they suggest, 'planning has preserved their privileges'.[52]

Second, the *'new suburbanites'*. These, the authors suggest, are mainly owner-occupiers. All in this category had gained from planning, in that they had been enabled to move into areas considered socially desirable. Public housing, by contrast, had continued to be concentrated in the cities. The authors use the same word—*apartheid*[53]—to describe the separation of the 'new suburbanites' from the working class, as they used, above, to describe the even greater separation of the 'ruralites' from *all* those less fortunate than themselves. But among these 'new suburbanites', the authors suggest, those buying the least expensive houses benefited least from planning. For the increasing cost of land becomes more and more significant, the lower the final selling price of the house; land represents a larger proportion of the cost of a smaller house than of a larger one. Thus at the lower end of the market the builders reduced the standards of the houses themselves. It is thus the less affluent among the 'new suburbanites' who paid the greatest price for 'containment'.

Third, *tenants in public housing*: Over most of the period studied, standards of space, fittings and design were higher in the case of council houses than in the case of the cheaper of the houses built for owner-occupation. Yet council tenants are seen as having lost as a result of planning policies *per se*; had the policy of containment not been pursued, more of them would have been able to move out to low-density peripheral estates, as happened in the inter-war years, rather than being housed in the inner-city. Tenants in public housing in the new towns, on the other hand, benefited from the planned proximity of homes and jobs, an advantage which as we have seen was increasingly denied to those moving into new private sector houses.

Finally, *tenants in privately rented property*. Without any doubt, the authors suggest, this is the group which is at the bottom of the housing market. Households in this tenure group are heavily concentrated in older property close to the centres of the larger cities and conurbations. They have 'simply been left out of the urban growth process to a very large degree'.[54] But as the authors say, this is only in part due to planning policies. Far more, it is the result of housing policies.

Having set out Hall *et al.*'s findings, what conclusions can we draw? *First*, it should be emphasized that these findings can only be seen as provisional, or tentative, for there are few, if any, other pieces of research with which to compare them. *Second*, however, and insofar as we do at least take their findings seriously, we must note the ironic fact that the results of planning in Britain, at least until the late 1960s, seem to have been virtually the opposite of those intended. These intentions, as I explained above, were never stated very explicitly, and are arguably open to varying interpretations. Nevertheless, it seems fairly clear that most of those who urged town and country planning did not want social 'apartheid'. On the contrary, they wanted 'balanced communities', in which the different classes in society would live side by side.[55] Nor did they want the separation of home and workplace. On the contrary, again, they regarded this as one of the evils of the suburbanization of the 1930s, which planning would overcome. Nor did they want any of the socially regressive redistributive effects described above; rather, they tended on the whole to see planning as a means of promoting a more equal society. Nor, of course, did they intend that planning should induce an escalation of land and property prices. And if, as the authors of '*The Containment . . .*' suggest, planners were prepared to see a reduced rate of national economic growth as a fair price to pay for an improved physical environment, it seems doubtful whether they intended that the desirable physical surroundings thus 'bought' should be monopolized by the affluent. Only 'containment', of all the effects identified in this research, can be seen as intended, and even this, it would appear, has occurred in forms other than those intended. More crucially, 'containment' seems to have occurred for *reasons* other than those intended. In practice, it seems, 'containment' has occurred because it suited the material interests of the privileged, and the political interests of the cities. It was *advocated*, however, largely on visual grounds.

*Third*, then, and in view of the fact that this research constitutes in effect a disturbing indictment of the British planning system, one must note the strange fact that it has attracted relatively little attention in planning circles, is seldom discussed, and in the fourteen years which have elapsed since its publication, has provoked few, if any, further attempts to assess the effects of planning in Britain. This neglect may of course be explained by the fact that its findings are embarrassing, both to the planning profession and to government. But it seems doubtful whether in any other area of public policy, such a well-researched and yet disturbing report could have been ignored quite so thoroughly. This seems explicable only in terms of the absence in this field of any tradition of intellectual curiosity.

Reviewing the evidence on the 'effects of planning' as a whole, it is clearly necessary to ask why this is so very sparse. One explanation would seem to lie in the way in which planners approach their work. To research the effects of policy is, as noted, always difficult, and often embarrassing. But planners have not faced up to these difficulties or embarrassments. Their models of 'planning' (or policy-making) are unrealistic, in that they assume that new policies can be formulated *without* knowledge of the consequences of previous ones.[56] But it is now time to go back to the model of 'policy as hypothesis', set out at the beginning of this chapter, and to consider the extent to which this model is in fact practicable.

### 3.   Is monitoring possible?

Before considering the practicability of monitoring, it seems useful to note three points concerning the evidence set out above. First, there is relatively little evidence available. Even taking into account the fact that in Britain funding for social science research is so meagre, it still seems remarkable that in all the years in which 'planning' has existed, only one major attempt has been made to research its effects.

Second, we can note that such evidence as *is* available has been produced neither by planners nor as a result of any official initiative, but by independent academic researchers. Indeed, it has not even been produced by planning academics, but by academics in far more 'academic' subjects.[57] In town and country planning in Britain, in fact, we see a very strange 'inversion'. Such down-to-earth factual and practical knowledge as we *do* have of it is produced by 'ivory tower' academics. The professional planners themselves, by contrast, who pride themselves on being 'practical', have produced virtually no such down-to-earth factual knowledge of it. What these 'practitioners' *do* produce, by contrast, is largely utopian, unrealistic and out of touch with reality. Their plans often prove incapable of being put into effect, and the way in which they *discuss* planning, in textbooks, journal articles, and in everyday conversation, tends often to be equally lacking in both in realism and in respect for empirical evidence. The *development control* decisions produced by practising planners are of course by contrast real enough, but planners show a marked disinclination to talk about these in realistic terms, examining their actual effects.[58]

Third, it has been noted that in so far as the consequences of planning in Britain *are* known, they seem to be very much out of line with those intended, and indeed to be to a large extent even the opposite of those intended.

The argument is that the three things noted above are interconnected. Planning in Britain is largely unsuccessful, it is suggested, *because* planners avoid confrontation with evidence of the effects of planning. Their verbal obscurity and pretentiousness, similarly, is a form of defence against the kind of evidence produced by social science researchers. Their predilection for studying the 'planning process', instead of studying the effects of past policies, is similarly a defence mechanism, and while this last is by no means confined to planners, it seems to be more marked among them than among policy-makers in other fields. Why should this be?

One reason, it was suggested above, lies in what was called the *holism* of planning thought. A crucial part of the argument of Popper, mentioned above, is that if their results are to be capable of being researched, policies must be formulated in limited terms. If too many policy changes are attempted simultaneously, he argues, it will be impossible to know which of the observed effects to ascribe to which of the policy changes. To make this point, Popper contrasts what he terms 'piecemeal' and 'utopian' social engineering. The former introduces policy changes cautiously, and in such a way that their effects can be monitored, and is therefore, he suggests, a rational approach to policy-making. The latter, by contrast, is fundamentally irrational: 'utopian social engineers' attempt too much at once. Realizing subsequently that they have not achieved their objectives, they are quite unable to discover *why* this is so, for they are faced with a multiplicity of 'effects', but no means of ascribing causation. In this situation, their characteristic response is to seek greater powers. Knowing that their plan has failed, they tend to blame this on the context in which it was put into effect, and seek to bring more and more of these contextual factors within the scope of planning. Thus, Popper suggests, there is likely to be a drift towards totalitarianism, for few people seek power so avidly, or with such sincere conviction, as those who believe that they need it in order to achieve desirable ends. In contrast to such utopianism, Popper gives us the 'piecemeal engineer', who will 'adopt the method of researching for, fighting against, the greatest and most urgent evils of society, rather than searching for, and fighting for, its greatest ultimate good'.[59] In a later work, Popper writes:

The piecemeal engineer knows, like Socrates, how little he knows. He knows that
we can only learn from our mistakes. Accordingly, he will make his way, step by
step, carefully comparing the results achieved, and always on the look-out for the
unavoidable unwanted consequences of any reform; and he will avoid undertaking
reforms of a complexity and scope which make it impossible for him to disentangle
causes and effects, and to know what he is really doing.[60]

The point made here seems to be a telling one, and yet it is unfortunately cast at a
rather general and philosophical level. Indeed, it seems not unfair to say that it
primarily reflects Popper's concern to promote his liberal political philosophy,
rather than to analyse public policy-making. How exactly could we distinguish in
practice between those policy initiatives which are sufficiently restricted in scope
to be capable of being monitored, and those which are not? And how could we
overcome the even greater problem posed by the fact that government *is* engaged
in a multiplicity of policies and initiatives? Even if *we* introduce a single, restricted,
carefully considered, and meticulously 'hypothesized' initiative, its effects will
surely be obscured by the simple fact that so many other things are constantly
changing, and that in modern society the polity, the economy and 'civil society'
form a seamless web of mutual interactions?

Though there seems to be no completely satisfactory solution to this problem,
it does seem possible to suggest, at least in principle, how a partial answer might be
found. This lies in the two linked factors of *incentives* and *specialization*. If those
concerned in a relatively modest or marginal change in public policy have
sufficient incentive to research its effects, then provided they can specialize (that
is, concentrate on it alone), they will probably at least find out *something* about its
effects. Almost certainly, one would think, they will at least find out a lot more
than is known in Britain about the effects of 'planning'. In society generally,
rewards are given to those who produce specialized knowledge. In practice,
researchers in other fields of public policy do go to considerable lengths to
establish the effects of such things as a marginal change in a specific tax, or a
relatively small innovation in the way a particular subject is taught to children in a
specific age-group, or the introduction of changed eligibility rules for a particular
kind of welfare benefit.

The subculture of planning, however, offers no such incentives or rewards for
researchers. Planners tend to see themselves neither as academics nor as policy-
analysts, but rather as 'professionals', as 'practical men'. In reality, their approach
could hardly be *less* practical, for it inhibits the growth of the very practical
knowledge which they themselves need.

Nor does the intellectual climate of planning encourage specialization; indeed,
it is quite antithetical to it. Planners are trained to think 'comprehensively', and to
take 'all relevant factors' into account. Characteristically, they assert that all these
various factors 'interact', but significantly, the stress in planning is not upon
discovering the nature or the magnitudes of such interactions. Rather, it is upon
'balancing' the various factors involved. Thus, a plan or a planning decision is not a
hypothesis. Rather, it is a claim *to have balanced* competing or conflicting 'needs' or
'demands', by supposedly promoting each one of them only to the extent that its

achievement is desirable, or compatible with each of the others.

Below I shall argue that this claim rests on an epistemological fallacy. For the moment, however, I am concerned rather to clarify this more limited problem as to how knowledge of 'effects' might be obtained.

Local planning authorities do, of course, sometimes carry out and publish specialized reports, documenting their progress in such specific matters as ensuring a supply of land for house building or for industry, safeguarding areas of high landscape value, improving facilities for outdoor recreation, and so on. I would suggest, however, that if anything of significance is to be learned about the effects of land use controls, research must be carried out on a geographical scale far wider than the individual county. It is in aggregate terms, and over the longer period, that the effects of policies can best be discerned, and even more importantly, it is only evidence on this larger scale which seems likely to provoke political debate. What Popper's argument suggests, by contrast, is that in terms of subject-matter, town and country planning needs to be broken down into discrete policies, aimed at particular objectives. These two arguments, however, pointing respectively to geographical aggregation and policy disaggregation, I shall develop in later chapters. For the moment, my interest lies in explaining monitoring, but before I can do this, some conceptual clarification is needed. The verbal confusion which at present surrounds this matter of monitoring seems, as we shall see, itself to be part of the planning profession's defence mechanisms, helping to ensure that despite much talk of monitoring, monitoring in reality is rarely attempted.

How, in practice, do planners interpret the term 'monitoring'? First, its meaning is confused by its having become part of a phrase, 'monitoring and review'. In the planning bureaucracy, this phrase is used almost as if it were a single word. Kingston, who carried out research on the way in which planning authorities understand monitoring, examined all the published monitoring documents of all the British structure planning authorities, *inter alia* attempting to discover how these documents distinguished between 'monitoring' and 'review'. He concluded that they didn't. They virtually *always* used the entire phrase, and even those planners whom he asked personally, in interviews, to explain the difference, were unable to do so very clearly.[61] This led him to ask why the two words exist.

The reason, it seemed, is that they had *originally* described two quite different things. 'Monitoring' originally meant discovering the effects of policies which had already been put into effect. 'Review' meant examining the emerging political and economic situation, with a view to deciding whether these existing policies ought to be changed. Two points can be made, concerning these two quite different activities. The first is that 'monitoring', thus understood, is in practice much more difficult than 'review'. Generally speaking, it is usually fairly easy to look at the emerging political and economic situation, and see in it some reason for drawing up a new plan. This will be especially so, of course, if the old plan is discredited, or seems old-fashioned in terms of professional ideas, or if we want to distract attention *away* from the effects (or lack of effects) which this old plan is having.

To discover the effects of existing policies, by contrast, is far less tempting. First, it is methodologically difficult, and second, it is likely to be politically embarrassing, for, as explained above, public policies nearly always have unintended effects. No wonder, then, that the two quite distinct activities, *monitoring* and *review*, are transformed into a supposedly single activity, and that this having been apparently accomplished, the difficult bit in the new composite activity gets conveniently overlooked. This 'sleight of hand' looks very much like a defence mechanism.

The *second* point which can be made about these two activities, monitoring and review, is that they are in a real sense mutually incompatible. Or at least, they cannot be done at the same time. If, as a result of 'reviewing' the situation, we *do* change our policy, it will be some time before we can start to monitor it again. A policy must be kept in force in unaltered form long enough for its effects to become observable, if we wish to observe those effects. We cannot observe the effects of a policy if that policy is itself being continually modified. What follows, then, is that a policy must be monitored *before* it is changed as a result of a review. At the present time, it is fashionable to suggest that planning is not the achievement of an 'end-state', but is a continuous ongoing process, in which policies are *continually* modified in the light of new information. If this is true, it clearly makes monitoring impossible. It also has a further rather devastating implication: it makes 'planning' *less rational* than ordinary old-fashioned unplanned public policy-making. Before the rise of this 'planning', public policies *were* generally kept unchanged long enough for researchers to investigate their effects.[62]

Another term used in the literature, and which is equally subject to semantic and methodological confusion, is 'evaluation'. This term is used in two quite distinct senses. Among town and country planners, 'evaluation' is used to describe the critical examination of a plan or policy *before* it is put into effect, and indeed, before it is even formally proposed. According to this usage, we prepare a series of *alternative* plans or policies, and then 'evaluate' them in terms of a list of criteria, to see which of them scores most highly. Among policy analysts more generally, however, 'evaluation' is used to mean the application of the same type of criteria to the *consequences* produced by a plan or policy. In this second usage, evaluation means much the same as monitoring. In both uses, however, there is a further ambiguity. 'Evaluation' appears to mean that we should examine the plan in question not in terms of its objective consequences, but on the basis of our subjective evaluation of those consequences. Few planning writers who use the term seem altogether clear as to whether they do mean this, or not, however, and for this reason, the term seems best avoided.[63]

Finally, we need to look at the very special way in which planners use the word 'research'. This will clarify not only the specific question of monitoring, but also many of the confusions in planning thought more generally. When planners speak of their research needs, they nearly always seem to have in mind something very similar to what, above, was termed 'review': they are usually referring to their supposed need for such things as prognoses, extrapolations and projections of incomes and aspirations, lifestyles and values, social and economic conditions, and so on. In other words, they want *data*, on which to base plans and policies. In the way in which planners use the word 'research', it is also virtually indistinguishable from what they call 'forecasting'. All three words, 'research', 'review' and 'forecasting', refer to data on the context in which plans will be put into effect. By apparently basing their plans on such data, planners demonstrate that they have taken these contextual factors into account, and that the plans are therefore 'relevant'. This suggests that the real function of such 'research' is not so much to provide explanation, but rather to provide legitimation.[64]

In the present book, by contrast, 'research' is used to mean *explanation;* specifically, it is used to mean *explanation as to why planning has had the effects it has had.* 'Monitoring' is used to describe the discovering of those effects. Nothing other than such investigation of effects, and such explanation of them, I would suggest, can provide the means of *improving* planning, in the sense of improving its theory and thus enhancing the planners' capacity to achieve their objectives.

What I have suggested, then, is that any given policy must be kept in operation in unaltered form long enough for its effects to be monitored, and that it must be theorized. By the latter, I mean simply that researchers identify the policy in question as clearly and unambiguously as possible, and that they hypothesize its probable consequences.

This is not, however, to say that policy must rest on any statement of its 'objectives'. Politics, after all, often requires ambiguity in the way policy objectives are publicly stated, and any statement of 'goals', 'objectives' or 'aims', whether made by politicians or planners, is therefore both suspect and of little use in research or policy-making.

To talk in terms of *anticipated effects,* rather than objectives, has clear advantages. First, it means that different researchers can hypothesize quite different, conflicting, and even mutually exclusive consequences as likely to flow from one and the same policy initiative.

Second, it means we can hypothesize 'unrespectable' consequences from a given policy, desired outcomes which those who urged it would never dare to utter publicly; examples will readily suggest themselves if we consider the research on *The Containment of Urban England*, discussed above. The essential point, however, is that planners can only reduce the gap between the effects they intend to achieve and the effects they actually achieve by studying the effects of their past actions.

Planners themselves, however, tend to dismiss such research into the effects of past policies as irrelevant. Eversley and Moody, for example,[65] dismiss it as 'socio-political critiques of existing practices' and suggest that though it is 'helpful in showing the negative effects of past policies', it is 'not directly useful for the formulation of new ones'. Nothing, I would suggest, could be further from the truth. It is because the planning profession has dismissed the kind of work described earlier in this chapter as irrelevant, I suggest, that planning in practice is so unsuccessful.

So far as they *do* show an awareness of discrepancies between their intentions and the actual consequences of planning, planners tend to ascribe these to extraneous factors rather than to their own actions. Often, they suggest that these contextual factors be brought into the ambit of planning, in just the way which Popper, in the extract quoted above, identifies as characteristic of 'utopian social engineers'. On other occasions, they claim that the need is for better public education concerning the need for planning. If only their proposals had been better understood, they tend to suggest, or if they had received fuller support, or if only the politicians had refrained from ideological debate, and understood their common interest in putting into effect the policies which the planners had shown to be objectively necessary, then all would have been well.

All of these various ways of denying the need for research into the actual effects of planning, I regard as mistaken in terms of epismology. But further, I would agree with Popper that they reflect a cast of mind which is incipiently (albeit mildly, benignly and unconsciously) totalitarian. In the remainder of this book, therefore, I urge an alternative model of public policy-making, in which investigation of the consequences of past policies is not only seen as relevant, but plays the central role. The first step towards this is to set out a little more fully the concept of 'policy as hypothesis'.

Platt[66] suggests that any public policy-making rests on the analysis of three elements. First, there is the *existing state of affairs*. When any policy initiative is contemplated, this is because the existing state of affairs is compared unfavourably with a visualized *desired state of affairs*, believed to be empirically capable of achievement. Thirdly, there are the *mechanisms of change*, which get us from the one to the other. At all three stages, Platt points out, facts, theories and value judgments are needed. We can therefore set out the whole process in the form of a 3 × 3 schema:

|  | Existing state of affairs | Mechanisms of change | Desired state of affairs |
|---|---|---|---|
| Facts | A | D | G |
| Theories | B | E | H |
| Value judgments | C | F | I |

We can clarify the use of the above schema by going through its various 'boxes'. There is no reason to think, however, that the process of policy-making necessarily starts in any particular 'box'. We may have a descriptive vision of the state of affairs in our particular policy field as we think it 'ought' to be (G), but this is hardly possible unless we also have values, which lead us to perceive the existing state of affairs as unsatisfactory (C), and our desired state of affairs as ethically superior (I). We may even start with a 'pet theory' about what would work as a means of changing things (D), and why it would work (E). Unless we are totally ruthless, however, we usually find that certain means of realizing our ends are ruled out by our values. One way of putting an end to land and property speculation, for example, would be by ensuring that those responsible were convicted of 'economic crime', and either shot, at the very least sent into internal exile. In Western societies, however, such methods are ruled out by the prevailing value system (F).

One of the differences between conservatives and radicals hinges not so much on the 'value' boxes, (C), (F) and (I), but rather on the 'theory' boxes, (B), (E) and (H). It is often because conservatives think the desired state of affairs 'would not work' (H) that they are reluctant to attempt to promote it. Similarly, conservatives often believe that it is because they do not understand the *causal necessity* for the existing state of affairs to function in the way it does (B), that radicals condemn it so readily. Clearly we could go on, but the general line of argument, and the way in which the schema can be used, have hopefully been made clear. In all nine 'boxes', improvement of knowledge and understanding is possible. This may come about by more careful survey, or by more careful specification and description (boxes (A), (D) and (G)), or by more rigorous theoretical reasoning (boxes (B), (E) and (H)). Even our values can be 'improved' (or in more neutral language rendered less crude and categorical, more complex and qualified), as our theoretical understanding of *why* things work as they do itself improves. But above all, perhaps, it is the converse effect, of values upon theoretical understanding, which is of crucial importance. It is *because* we are dissatisfied, that we seek knowledge about how to change things.

What it is now desired to do is to combine the above approach, derived from the paper by Platt, with Popper's conception of policy-making as described at the beginning of this chapter, and with the concept of *monitoring*. To do this implies only one change in the way in which we use Platt's schema; we must learn to use it 'backwards', as well as 'forwards'. The concept of monitoring implies that we *have* brought about some change. Whether this change is that which we anticipated, of course, is another matter, but this is what monitoring is all about. We might set out a 'backwards looking' version of Platt's schema, to set alongside her 'forwards looking' one. Its headings can be labelled as follows:

| *Pre-existing state of affairs* | *Mechanisms of change* | *Existing state of affairs* |
|---|---|---|
| (which was judged unsatisfactory, and which we therefore attempted to change) | | (which may or may not be the same as that judged desirable, and which we attempted to bring about) |

That the central column has the same name, in both the 'forwards looking' and the 'backwards looking' schemas, is by no means accidental. The mechanisms of change which work in the past also work in the future. Laws of causation are not peculiar to time or place. Other things being equal, the same action generally has the same effect. Of course, other things never are equal. But this is the whole point, to refine our knowledge of cause and effect, by discovering the ways in which causal mechanisms are *modified* by various complicating contextual factors. Knowledge is cumulative, but it is only obtained by constant and painstaking efforts. Despite the prevailing fashion for methodological pessimism, knowledge of causation is not *entirely* impossible in the social sciences.

The same 'cause', for example, the removal of a pre-existing tax on betterment, played some part in helping to bring about property booms, first in the early 1960s, and again in the early 1970s. If the removal of such a tax for the third time, in 1985, is not followed by a similar property boom, this may be because the pre-existing level of Development Land Tax was in fact too low to have had much effect on property development, because prospective speculators in the 1980s are unable to borrow money as easily or on the same scale as they were on the two previous occasions, or for any combination of these possible factors with other factors. While *exact* attribution of cause is impossible, it is often possible nevertheless to get *some* understanding. Without even approximate knowledge of cause and effect, however, we have no theory, and thus, no capacity to *cause* any effects.

One of the main arguments against this model, however, lies in its apparently resting on a certain sociological naivete. One aspect of this naivete lies in the model's inability to take account of a multiplicity of causal factors and effects, as discussed above. Another aspect of this apparent naiveté, however, lies in the social mechanisms and practices whereby, in reality, policies or decisions are actually evolved, and given effect. Planners, it can be shown, simply do not in reality (and whatever their ideology says on the matter) rationally formulate decisions and policies, and then get them 'implemented'. In reality, such decisions are the outcome of an intricate process of social interaction, in which the planners themselves and their political colleagues, against a constantly shifting background of more or less informed political direction and professional debate, constantly negotiate and renegotiate their conceptions of what it is *reasonable* to demand of developers. Healey, in commenting on the work of Kingston[67], expresses this by pointing out that 'it is not necessarily the case that policies in structure plans are those that are actually being implemented'.[68] And of course, one must accept the truth of this. There are clearly many possible reasons why, in practice, planners may be confused, vacillating, or even devious, unclear about their objectives, or, most significantly, susceptible to the suggestion that those objectives be modified 'as they go along'. But if those who formulate administrative decisions *are* in fact allowed to modify their objectives as they go along, clear dangers arise; one way of showing this is by looking at the practice of 'bargaining' in development control, and in particular at the phenomenon of 'planning by agreement'.

'Planning by agreement' has become increasingly common since the property boom of the early 1970s. What it means, is a system of control in which *discretion* has been taken virtually to its ultimate. In 'planning by agreement', planners do not merely impose preordained standards or policies. Rather, they negotiate and bargain with developers 'privately', in an effort to ensure that in return for the granting of planning permission, the developers provide or meet the costs of providing such things as landscaped public amenity areas, roads and services, or even residential and other development which was not the subject of the original application. Such additional or alternative development as is extracted from developers in this way is known as 'planning gain'.[69]

The planners' rationale for extracting 'planning gain' is very much tied up with their notion of 'positive planning'.[70] By thus getting something built which the developers had never intended, the planners are able to feel that they are *initiating* development, and not merely applying rules to planning applications in a bureaucratic way, as any ordinary public officials might do. But given that there is such a lack of clarity anyway concerning the theory and the objectives of land use control, and given the fact that the planners themselves, especially in a period of economic recession, apparently derive considerable psychological satisfaction from operating as 'fixers', 'getting things done', and 'making things happen' by working behind the schemes in this way, there is obvious scope, if not for outright corruption, then at least for (let us call it) mutual adjustment.[71] In sociological terms, developers and planners will come to develop a shared subculture. They will be likely to develop shared attitudes and values, shared perceptions of what is economically possible and socially desirable, and most significantly, shared beliefs as to what kind of development best promotes the 'public interest'. They will be constantly working out between themselves, in private, what seems best for the 'community', rather than following standards and objectives imposed upon them as a result of open political debate and formal decisions reached by democratically elected representatives.

If this is indeed typical of the nature of land-use regulation in present-day Britain, one must of course concede that the Popper–Platt conception of the nature of public policy-making as consisting of the adoption and subsequent monitoring of specific and clearly identifiable measures does indeed seem somewhat naive. All one can *then* say, is that from the point of view of those who believe in a society which is reasonably open, such practices as 'planning by agreement' are disturbing. If, as Healey suggests, the decisions actually being arrived at are not in accordance with the structure plans, then we can ask what the structure plans are for. Indeed, we can ask the purpose of *any* attempt to control public policy through democratically elected representatives.

There is a further point, however. Researchers themselves, unfortunately, may develop a vested interest in the institutionalized complexity of administrative decision-making processes, for they make a living by investigating and explaining them. The modes of operating referred to above must be viewed against the fact that there are in reality usually many organizations and agencies involved, and not just 'planners' and 'developers'. The committee chairman and vice-chairman (if not the 'Council' as a democratically elected body), the unknown DoE officials whose possible subsequent involvement and anticipated reactions in the event of an 'appeal' are always a factor to be taken into account, colleagues in the planning profession at large, the financial department of the local authority, developers' own professional federations, which monitor current land-release policies and exert pressure in Whitehall accordingly, as well as amenity organizations and environmental pressure groups of various kinds, are all either participants or interested parties, at least in the more significant instances of control of development. Given such complexity, it is evident that researchers may develop a very real vested interest in their own intellectual capacity for conceptualizing, comprehending and describing this complexity, and even an intellectual taste for the sheer elegance of the explanatory models which they, and their colleagues, evolve. Thus, there is a strong temptation on such researchers to dismiss models such as that which I have set out above as 'simplistic'.

Again, however, one can only point out that an intellectual vested interest has no more merit than has a more obviously economic one. If one believes that a more open and more easily comprehended way of making public policies and putting them into effect would serve democracy better, even though it has the disadvantage that it can be understood by those of mean intelligence, then perhaps one's duty is to say so. 'Mystification' can serve the material interests not only of planners, but also of those who research planners. Researchers themselves, just like the planners they research, have an obvious vested interest in concentrating on the 'private', 'internal' matter of the interactions between the various actors in the 'planning process', rather than on the purposes which this 'planning process' is meant to serve, or the consequences which it has. Just like the planners, too, these researchers have an obvious vested interested in *not* raising the question of exactly what kind of political philosophy might justify all this 'planning'. For to raise such questions would be to imperil their good working relationship with those whose behaviour they research.

I would however suggest that the model I have set out above, though it is perhaps deplorably 'simplistic', would in fact get us quite a long way towards explaining and improving the effectiveness of any governmental policy, provided that policy were open to public and political scrutiny. But to be open to scrutiny, a policy must be capable of being comprehended. And to be capable of being comprehended it must relate to a specific matter. The very broad and extremely vague objectives pursued by planners, by contrast, cannot be understood by either politicians or the public, for they are far too wide-ranging, too ambitious, diffuse, poorly conceptualized and indeed varying, or as they themselves put it, 'flexible'.

I conclude that the test of the viability of any public policy is that it is comprehensible, widely understood, and publicly debated. Only if it meets these criteria can it be politicized. Its politicization encourages its being researched, and the findings of researchers, conversely, encourage informed political debate about it; the result is a kind of 'virtuous spiral'.

The difficulties involved in such policy research however, are certainly not to be underestimated, and in suggesting above that the issues involved can be fairly easily comprehended at the conceptual level, I am certainly not suggesting that they are capable of being so easily solved at the level of practicalities.[77] Not the least of these practical problems results from the fact that those in official or political positions may feel themselves to be criticized by such research, and thus find it difficult to accept its findings. The reason both for the 'conspiracy of silence' in the planning profession concerning the kind of research findings set out in Section 2 of this chapter, and for Eversley's dismissal of such research as irrelevant, is presumably that psychologically, the planners simply cannot 'face' this evidence.

And much of the policy research literature, in fact, is concerned with just this issue, on which there appear to be two broad views. On the one hand, there is the view which stresses the healthy and salutory value of vigorous public criticism, while on the other hand there is a large body of work explaining in detail exactly why it is that if the policy analyst wants his findings to be accepted he must cultivate a good working relationship with his 'client', see things from the client's point of view, and so. As Wildavsky puts it: '[A]cceptance of evaluation requires a community of shared values.'[73] Or as Rossi puts it, stressing the penalities of *not* having the 'client' on one's side: 'no good evaluation goes unpunished'.[74]

Which of these two views or approaches one prefers, clearly depends both upon the particular circumstances and upon one's values. While in principle I prefer the first, it is obviously only possible either where open competitive politics already exists, or where the research style itself can help to force such openness into existence; bureaucratic and professional norms, at least as they exist in British planning, tend to suppress such critical challenge.

That the professional planners do in fact nearly always react in this defensive manner may derive in large measure from the way in which they define their role. They tend *to take responsibility* for the outcomes of planning, and to 'identify' with the planning system, rather than seeing their task as that of *analysing* the way in which the system works. But this matter, of the way in which planners identify their role, I shall return to later in this book.[75]

In this chapter, I have sketched out a model of how theory is obtained. In the next chapter, I shall return to and develop the argument that planning in fact rests on no such theory, but on a somewhat confused and rather misleading professional ideology. The best hope of constructing a theory of land use planning, I shall argue, lies in developing the kind of research which Eversley and Moody, and most planners, dismiss as irrelevant.

# 4 'Belief' and 'scepticism': two approaches to policy-making

If a man will begin with certainties, he shall end in doubts, but if he will be content to begin with doubts, he shall end in certainties.

Bacon, *The Advancement of Learning*

## 1. Introduction

In Chapter 1, I suggested that the planning profession has developed no very credible theoretical explanation of planning. In Chapter 2, however, I showed that it has succeeded in establishing itself firmly within the governmental power structure, apparently unhindered by this lack. In Chapter 3, I asked how, in such a situation, we could hope for improved theoretical understanding. This, I argued, could only be obtained through monitoring, the comparison of actual with anticipated effects. And such monitoring, I pointed out, is conspicuous in British town and country planning largely by its absence.

In this present chapter, I enquire into the *social preconditions* of such improved understanding of policy. To try to make clear what kind of institutional arrangements might best promote the more open-minded and critical climate in which monitoring would in fact take place, I contrast two sets of social, political and intellectual attitudes and practices, summed up respectively as 'belief' and 'scepticism'. 'Belief' describes the situation in which the politicians and the public entrust decision-making largely to the professionals and experts who staff the public bureaucracies, and in which those professionals and experts themselves also possess a considerable measure of belief in their own capacity to find the best

95

solution; the 'belief' is two-sided. The reason *why* so much is entrusted to these elites, is that these are the people whom, we might say, 'society' has duly authorized as competent within their given subject-areas. The credibility of the solutions they arrive at, therefore, and the reason why these solutions are themselves accorded 'belief', lies in the accredited competence of the advisers concerned, more than in the intellectual credibility of the solution which they propose.

The contrasted ideal type, 'scepticism', it will be obvious, describes that complex of institutionalized attitudes and policy-making practices in which the credibility of the solutions arrived at does, by contrast, hinge on the critical public appraisal of the solutions themselves. In this contrasted situation, there is little emphasis upon credentialism, and nobody is 'licensed'; no one set of people, whether public officials or any others, have undisputed control or even influence over policy-making in any given area, and there is instead free challenge, by politicians, the public, and researchers alike. What is important here, and indeed, what is an obvious precondition of such a situation of 'institutionalized scepticism', is that its material basis must be secure; the financial resources on which independent critical research depends must be in some way institutionally guaranteed, and the 'challenge' itself must be socially perceived as useful.

The practice of town and country planning in Britain, it will be argued, lies rather close to the first of these two ideal types. From the 1960s onwards, the ideas on which planners based their claims to legitimacy underwent what most writers see as a profound change. The profession no longer relied upon the publicly accepted 'package' of physical solutions orchestrated by the planning movement during the war, but instead developed an apparently very different set of justificatory ideas, which can be summed up as the 'new planning'. It is these 'new planning' ideas which I take still to constitute the main legitimating ideology of the planning profession, even in the late 1980s, and it is these ideas, therefore, which I shall criticize below. Many, and possibly most, observers would disagree with my interpretation, instead arguing that the 'systems planning' and 'rational planning method' of the 1960s and early 1970s had by 1980 given way to an entirely new approach, characterized as less ambitious and more pragmatic. My reasons for adopting the interpretation I do are that while certainly agreeing that these 'new planning' ideas have for many years now been expressed in much more muted tones, more circumspectly, more tentatively, and often, indeed, not even referred to at all, they nevertheless remain important, and are still implicitly relied upon. Certainly, I would suggest, they have not been replaced by any newer and more intellectually credible explanation of what it is that planners do. They have not, for example, been replaced by an explanation of planning of the kind put forward in the present book, one which sees it as a politically motivated attempt to redistribute the costs and benefits produced by property development, and which analyzes in explicitly economic terms the specific types of redistribution which planning might thus seek.

Furthermore, my interpretation of the 'new planning' rests on a belief that most changes in planning thought are in any case more apparent than real. Though the 'new planning' ideas of the 1960s *appeared* to talk about quite different things than the advocates of town and country planning had urged in the 1940s, I shall argue, these apparently new ideas were in reality not so new at all, but based on the same fundamentally mistaken social and political presuppositions. And by the same token, I would therefore argue, the supposedly more realistic and more pragmatic planning ideas of the late 1980s are not new either, but are again merely new ways of rationalizing old fallacies.

Before contrasting 'belief' with 'scepticism', it seems useful to clarify several further points. First, it is emphasized that these two *are* used only as ideal types, as analytical devices rather than descriptive categories. There is no suggestion that all planners tend to think and behave in one way, and all their critics in another. There are many varieties and gradations, both of 'belief' and of 'scepticism'. Nevertheless, I would suggest, each of these two contrasted syndromes of behaviour and accompanying mental attitudes does, to a greater or lesser degree, tend to be more or less firmly based in the two social groups identified, the planners and their critics. And in the case of the planners at least, there seems little doubt that their material interests are involved, the planners' belief in planning serves both to sustain professional morale, and to secure legitimation. But elements of both ideal types are of course often combined or juxtaposed, in the actions or attitudes of particular individuals. Planners can certainly experience misgivings about what they do, and social scientists, conversely, excited by the idea of making a 'practical' contribution, may often forget the tradition of careful academic scepticism in which they were trained, and come to share enthusiastically in the planners' beliefs. Belief in the ideology of planning, then, is only characteristic of planners *to a greater or lesser extent.* Those in or near government, for example, whether senior civil servants explaining policy in circulars, politicians making statements in the House, or those influential members of the corps of the 'great and the good' who happen from time to time to interest themselves in the matter, will obviously tend to explain the idea of planning in more muted tones than, let us say, certain kinds of teachers in the planning schools. In particular, they will usually tend to stress the idea of planning as the co-ordination of land use, and will avoid the more ambitious of the professional planners' notions of planning as a set of techniques for rational decision-making.

Second, it may be objected that the treatment of 'belief' and 'scepticism' below is unequal. But this must be so, for I am concerned to criticize the one, and to recommend the other. In discussing the planners' 'belief', my main concern is to point to the fallacies on which it rests. In discussing 'scepticism', by contrast, my main concern is to urge it. I see the two syndromes of attitudes, too, as having unequal epistemological status. Whereas the first is fundamentally ideological, the second is concerned essentially with social scientific explanation. In saying this, there is no intention to make excessive claims for the objectivity of the social sciences. Social scientists' analyses of planning, however, as of anything else, and unlike planners' explanations of it, are produced in a fairly critical climate, and are judged in terms of their intellectual credibility rather than in terms of the extent to which they vindicate or criticize the actions of those they discuss.

## 2. 'Belief'

Since I have described the professional and official view of planning as an ideology, I must first say what I mean by this. *First,* an ideology is a body of thought which has been evolved to serve an interest, and most of its other features can be understood in terms of this. *Second,* ideological thought relies heavily on unstated and often unconscious basic assumptions. These concern such 'big questions' as whether society rests 'fundamentally' on conflict or on consensus, or whether man is 'by nature' emotional or rational. However many deductions and inferences flow from a given presupposition, and however logically they flow, we do not need to accept a single one of them, if we do not accept the validity of the presupposition. But ideological thought often leaves its presuppositions unclear, and thereby deprives us of the opportunity to consider them. *Third,* ideological thought is prescriptive. It does not merely tell us that various alternative lines of action are likely to promote various alternative states of affairs. It also suggests which of these states of affairs we 'ought' to prefer, and therefore to seek to bring about. But again, it is less than frank with us. It frequently omits to mention that the states of affairs which it regards as self-evidently desirable can only be justified in terms of values, and instead seems to suggest that they have been shown objectively or scientifically to be inevitable or desirable. *Fourth,* ideological thought tells us *how* to bring about the states of affairs which it urges. In principle, this is theoretical knowledge, knowledge of cause and effect, or 'science'. The connections asserted or implied in ideological thought, however, are often questionable. We might accept them if (for example) we had a strong psychological *need* to believe that our efforts were succeeding; more dispassionate observers, however, might well show us that these asserted causal connections do not stand up to scrutiny. *Fifth,* ideological thought appeals both to our emotions and to our intellect, but confuses us as to which is which. The potency of this mixture is obviously strong. *Sixth,* then, and finally, ideological thought succeeds at one and the same time in being both very confused, and yet apparently forming a psychologically satisfying, coherent, interlocking system of explanations, providing a clear and understandable view of the world. It weaves together all its unstated assumptions, its exhortations, its true theories and its doubtful theories, its true factual statements and its untrue ones, into an impenetrable web of mutually supportive arguments. Confronted by it, one has difficulty in knowing what is supposed to be 'fact', what is 'value', and what is 'theory'. Discrimination is difficult, and people often, therefore, feel that if they accept any of it, they must accept all of it. If they subsequently find that they can no longer believe in it, they may experience both emotional loss and intellectual disillusionment, for as noted, it has provided them with a psychologically satisfying explanation both of the world, and of their own place within it. Typically, ideologies justify the social position of those who hold them, and justify them in what they do and are.

In Chapter 2, I looked at the development of the ideology of planning over time, and at its capacity to elicit political support. Here, by contrast, I am concerned only with the 'new' ideology of planning, as this developed from the 1960s onwards, and I focus specifically on its intellectual credibility. The following characterization of it is based both on published material[1] and on personal knowledge of planning education. It is generally accepted by sociologists that professional education is crucial in shaping subsequent attitudes and behaviour, in any profession. In the particular case of planning in Britain, the profession and the planning schools are especially close. With the exception of the social scientists among their ranks, the most significant reference group for planning teachers tends to be not the wider academic community, but the local government planning profession.[2] Thus the ideology of the planning schools *is* the ideology of the profession, to a large degree. But it is always necessary to look at its professional schools, if one wants to understand any particular profession. It is here if anywhere, after all, that its knowledge base is researched, discussed, analysed, and made explicit in published work, as well as being rendered into a form in which it can be transmitted to new recruits.

Two points seem particularly helpful, when it comes to making sense of the 'new planning' ideas which developed over the 1960s and 1970s. First, we can best understand these 'new' ideas as constituting a transference of the planners' characteristically rather utopian mode of thought from the 'substantive' to the 'procedural' sphere. This can be explained in terms set out in Section 1 of Chapter 1, above, where it was pointed out that as well as describing the drawing-up of physical plans, with such things as land uses and roads upon them, 'planning' is also seen as a particular approach to the making of decisions.

What happened in the 1960s, then, was that town and country planners started to say much less about their ability to discern the ideal settlement pattern, and instead began to talk of their ability to use analytical techniques which would supposedly help them in arriving at optimal solutions—concerning land use patterns or, in principle, anything else.

The second point which helps us to make sense of these 'new planning' ideas is that as already noted they were in a very real sense not new at all. Despite this transference of planners' interest from the substantive to the procedural sphere, and despite the fact that the 'new planning' appeared to be far more 'scientific' than the 'package' of substantive ideas put forward during the war, these new planning ideas nevertheless reflected the same fallacious social assumptions as those which had underlain the planning ideas of the 1940s. These included, for example, the assumption that society rests fundamentally on consensus, and the assumption that public policies can be justified in terms of objective analysis rather than resting of necessity on political opinion.

But what does this 'new planning' ideology consist of? At the heart of it are systems theory and the notion of planning as a method of rational decision-making.[3] Secondly, and not quite so centrally, but both supporting and supported by these two central ideas, there is a shifting collection of apparently more specific techniques or approaches, 'land-use transportation studies', cost–benefit analysis, corporate management, and so on. Thirdly, and forming a kind of penumbra, can be seen an even wider collection of even more vague, 'optional' or ephemeral ideas.

These last are perhaps especially interesting, for in many cases they might seem to constitute a questioning of the central ideas of the 'new planning', rather than being an integral part of it. They often appear, in fact, to bring its essentially technocratic assumptions more into line with political realities, or to give it a 'social conscience' or a 'human face'.

In fact, however, these peripheral ideas reinforce and support the 'new planning' far more than they throw doubt upon it. They *appear* to modify, refine, or qualify its central assumptions, but in reality it is these peripheral ideas themselves which are modified, technicized, and stripped of their true political content and potency.

What are these 'third-level', constitutive ideas in the 'new planning'? One could mention such things as 'social planning', 'public participation', 'planning aid' and 'environmental education'. Technicized by planners, and thus rendered into means of extending their own professional power while simultaneously appearing to modify that power, each of these potentially critical or liberating ideas is rendered safe, and made into a way of preserving the status quo. 'Social planning', for example, transforms social policy into a mere technology, by assuming that the objectives of public policy are uncontroversial, and that there exists near-universal consensus upon them. 'Public participation' similarly, ceases to be an end in itself, valued as an essential feature of a democratic society, and becomes merely a means towards 'better' decisions, thus enhancing the power of planners and the perceived legitimacy of planning. 'Planning aid', originally a programme for enabling those affected by planning proposals to challenge them, and to put forward alternative proposals of their own, loses sight of the truth that any specific planning solution must inevitably promote specific material interests, and instead becomes merely a way of educating the public into the way in which the planning system works. 'Environmental education', potentially a way of helping young people to understand that human exploitation can also be effected through the manipulation of spatial arrangements, becomes merely a way of indoctrinating them into a belief in the need for planning and planners.

This mass of shifting and sometimes apparently conflicting conceptions, however, consisting as it does of a central core of technocratic assumptions, a varying collection of apparently 'hard' techniques and an equally shifting penumbra of 'soft', vaguely 'social' ideas, certainly did not arise overnight, and is still developing, even in the late 1980s. There has been no return to a belief in the 'simple' physical objectives on the basis of which the planning system was accorded legitimacy in the 1940s.

Nor indeed has the planning system adopted any *new* set of prescriptive ideas for the national settlement pattern. Instead, 'belief' has continued to focus on the notion of planning itself, as an 'approach' or a 'process', rather than on the 'thing planned'. Though at the time of writing planners like to portray themselves as 'industrial development officers', therefore, promoting national economic recovery by encouraging business enterprise, this should not be taken to imply that the planning schools have started to provide specialized courses in the economics of industrial location, or in the ways in which by manipulating the fiscal system or offering other financial incentives government can influence the decision-making processes of private firms. Rather, planners base their claim to operate in this area as in all others on their supposed possession of the same traditional planning approach, a uniquely broad perspective, enabling them to coordinate the efforts of many different actors towards a common goal. Such an approach, presumably, while it is currently invaluable in solving problems of business confidence, could equally be used to solve any *other* pressing social problems which might arise. To understand planning ideology as it has developed from the 1960s to the 1980s, however, it seems best to analyse it in terms of the same four traits as were identified in Chapter 2, above, *physicalism, holism, technicism* and *role-confusion*.

Physicalism in the 'deterministic' sense, of assuming that social behaviour can be influenced by physical design, has not played much part in recent decades. Bemused, apparently, by sociologists' criticisms of their naive determinism, architects and planners have transmuted their traditional faith in the social potency of design, so that it has re-emerged as a twin pair of legitimating ploys: *either* the role of the social scientist is to show 'what people want', thus providing legitimation for the plan in the name of democracy, or it is to discover 'human needs', thus providing similar legitimation in the name of science. This 'new naivete', however, seems no better than the old. To assume in this simple way that wants and needs are given facts, waiting to be discovered, is a neat administrative convenience, obliging others to shoulder the responsibility for one's actions. The private sector, which lives by selling goods and services for profit, does not think in this way. On the contrary, it operates on the sociologically sounder assumption that before things can be sold, it is necessary to *create* the belief that they are necessary or desirable. If planners and architects were to accept this sociological truth—that wants, neds and preferences are socially caused—they would then have to take part of the responsibility (as one group of influential opinion formers among others), for causing them.[4]

Generally speaking, however, the effects of the physical milieu on our perceptions, our behaviour, our subjective sense of well-being and even on our objective welfare are not direct. Rather, they are mediated by the symbolic social 'meaning' which we, and significant others, attach to the physical milieu.[5] And what usually in any case gets conveniently forgotten, in the sometimes rather jesuitical debates about the supposed effects of relatively minor differences in design, are the more gross environmental differences which exist in the real world, in which the various classes live in surroundings which the *generally accepted* symbolic meaning system calls better and worse ('nice places', and 'not so nice places').[6]

The 'new physicialism', it can thus be noted, tends to avoid all such common-sense (and sociologically sound) knowledge. It 'proceduralizes' physical determinism; it asserts that there are technical procedures for discovering 'wants' and 'preferences', and that there are experts (sociologists) whose task it is to legitimate planning by showing it to be based as the use of these procedures.

Physicalism in the second sense, which asserts the importance of the physical environment as an end in itself, and which suggests that aesthetic, 'heritage', 'ecological' or other physical considerations must be 'weighed against' social considerations in 'planning', I find difficult to assess in terms of its intellectual validity. It seems to me metaphysical to suggest that such things can have value apart from the human purposes they serve, and I pass rapidly on.

In going on to look both at 'holism' and at 'technicism', it seems useful to bear in mind what, above, was described as the planners' transference of their utopianism from the substantive to the procedural sphere. Planners have ceased to urge the use of planning to secure particular objectives, and have instead simply urged 'planning'. They have ceased to tell us what constitutes an ideal settlement pattern, and have instead claimed that rational planning method would enable them to *find out* what would be the optimal pattern, in any particular case. The old (substantive) ideology of planning was expressed in plain English, and could therefore be understood by politicians and by the public. The new (procedural) ideology is expressed in (supposedly) highly technical language, and is therefore inaccessible to non-planners. I would argue, however, that it is in fact largely devoid of intellectual content, and was evolved because it looked and sounded impressive, rather than because it actually explained anything about the control of land use. The 'techniques' on which this new ideology of planning is supposedly based, I would suggest, are almost without exception misapplied, and are in any case misunderstood. Systems theory, for example, was devised by physical scientists to analyze the behaviour of physical phenomena, and simply cannot explain human behaviour, whether spatial or political. The notion of rational decision-making, too, is mechanistic. It tells us, perhaps, how decisions might be made concerning non-human phenomena, but it can hardly tell us how social decisions can be made. This notion, in fact, seems best understood as a technocratic attempt to supplant politics. Analytically, its subject of concern is that which has occupied political philosophers from Plato onwards, the problem of government. Yet planners largely ignore this body of inherited knowledge, putting forward their abstract schemes as if intended for a new world brought into existence only at the time they were written. And fundamentally the same point can be made to a greater or lesser extent concerning all the various techniques associated with the 'new planning'. All of them are profoundly ideological. *If* they could be used to explain human behaviour, then those who used them would have great power. The very claim that such techniques are usable, therefore, even though it is false, and a kind of scientism, serves to enhance the perceived power of the planning profession.[7]

In the 1940s, planners had used 'holism' as an ideological ploy in a simple physical sense. Slum clearance and rehousing, control of urban growth, industrial location policy, new towns, the safeguarding of agricultural land—all these things, and many more, they had suggested, must be co-ordinated one with another, but only they, the planners, had the breadth of vision to secure this necessary co-ordination. While thus mobilizing support from a wide range of interest groups, by apparently offering something to each of them, planners by this means acquired a leading role for themselves. From the 1960s onwards, it became clear that this programme, largely inspired by the garden cities movement, was not working as intended. The planners' initial response was not to analyze the effects of the policies themselves, but to put the 'blame' on unanticipated demographic changes, and even on the technicalities of the ways in which their plans were formulated.[8] Their *main* response, however, was at the ideological level, and might be best described as a kind of 'avoidance mechanism'; it consisted as noted of increasingly portraying planning as a set of techniques rather than as having any particular objectives. Abandoning the simple certainties of the garden city movement, they asserted that planning could still be relied upon to secure the best possible pattern of land use, but increasingly avoided stating what this best possible pattern might be.

A 'muted' example of this 'newer holism', which asserts that planners have the techniques required to enable them to find the 'right' pattern of land use, incorporating the best possible balance between conflicting demands, is to be found in the report of the Skeffington Committee, which described the purpose of planning as being 'to set the framework within which houses, roads and community services can be provided at the right time and in the right place'.[9] The fallacy in this last is clearly shown in the following extract from the diaries of Richard Crossman, ironically enough Minister of Housing and Local Government, and therefore himself responsible for the national planning system at the time he wrote it:

> I find the job of a Minister relatively easy. It suits my temperament. When I sit at my desk here at Prescote and pull out a mass of papers from the red box and see that I have to decide on the boundaries of Coventry or on where to let Birmingham have its new housing land, I find these decisions easy, pleasant, and I take them in a fairly light-hearted way.[10]

In other words, there is no 'right' time or 'right' place. There is only a pattern of physical development which will suit *some* interests, and a pattern which will suit *others*. Crossman has no difficulty in knowing which pattern he prefers, because he knows where his political sympathies lie. The extent to which government should accede to various conflicting demands, and therefore the point at which it should 'balance' them, can never be shown by any science, and therefore the question cannot hinge on techniques, or be the concern of any profession. It is a matter which can only be determined by power, or in the light of our political sympathies or values. (Though skilful design and layout *can*, of course, minimize the negative effects which land uses impose upon each other, or maximize the positive locational benefits which they confer upon each other, and skillful management, as for example in 'countryside access agreements', can even enable conflicting uses to share the same spaces).

Exactly the same point as that made by Crossman was expressed by Buchanan, in his famous Memorandum of Dissent written as a member of the Commission of Enquiry into the siting of the third London airport. But it would be mistaken to suppose that Buchanan was here placing 'environmental' considerations before 'economic' ones. On the contrary, he was in effect making a political statement, a statement in terms of values, which asserted the view that certain artefacts and certain types of surroundings make a greater contribution to human welfare than do others. Though ironically enough being himself a professional planner, therefore, he too was demonstrating that the best use of land simply cannot be determined by 'planning', in the sense of objective technical expertise, but must inevitably be a matter of opinion.[11]

This fallacious notion of an objectively best balance between conflicting demands, however, is very much tied up with another central concept in planning thought, that of rationality. It is *by means of* 'rational planning method', supposedly, that planners *arrive at* the 'optimal balance'. This, however, merely shows us that planners' use of the word 'rationality' is peculiar to themselves. In the social sciences, and in philosophy, 'rationality' is normally understood as the use of those means which we have reason to believe most likely to achieve our ends. In this usage, it is assumed that objectives reflect values, but that means, in principle, do not; whether a given action will or will not tend to have certain consequences is after all not a matter of opinion, but of fact.

Planners do not use the word 'rational' in this way, however. By putting their own, quite different, meaning on it, they purport to give objective validity to their own proposals. Since the objectively best balance between competing demands has been arrived by rational planning method, they appear to believe, these proposals are themselves rational. In other words, rationality can, according to planners, show us *what* objectives to pursue, and not merely how best to achieve them. This puts their recommendations, apparently, beyond political debate. The demands made by all *other* interest groups, they assert, are selfish, partial, sectional, and political. Their own proposals, by contrast, are objective, technical and politically neutral. They alone see the whole, where others see only the parts. They alone, therefore, can discern and promote the public interest.[12] This question, as to whether rationality can relate to 'ends' or only to 'means', it should be emphasized, is no esoteric matter, of interest only to 'planning theorists'.[13] On the contrary, it is a practical question, lying at the very heart of planning as it is in fact done. According to the answer we give to this question, two matters of central practical importance inevitably flow. First, it governs the answer we give to the question of what should be the proper relationship between planning and politics. Second, it governs the answer we give to the question of what type of advice planners should in fact give to the elected representatives. It is because they misunderstand the meaning of the word 'rationality', I shall argue, that planners misconstrue their proper role in society. They attempt to influence the choice of objectives, when in fact they should advise only on the means of promoting those objectives.[14]

The planners' holist mentality, however, is applied not only to land use, to finding the supposedly objectively best possible plan. It is also applied to *people*. From the 1960s onwards, people from a whole range of disciplines were increasingly interesting themselves in and researching environmental questions or working in planning. Just as planners claimed to be able to co-ordinate all land uses into the best possible pattern, then, they also claimed to be able to co-ordinate the work of all these specialists, defined by the planners themselves as 'contributors to the planning process'. This claim, however, went beyond a conception of themselves as 'leaders', able to get all these various experts to work together. What the planners in effect claimed, rather, was to be able *to judge the importance* of the recommendations of each of these 'contributors'. Such specialists, the planners' ideology suggests, have each their own way of seeing environmental questions, and all their contributions are of course extremely valuable. But each of them tends to have a relatively restricted view, and each tends to think that the matters on which he is expert are more important than they in fact are. Only the planners themselves, who unlike all these people have been trained as synthesizers, or generalists, have the 'synoptic vision' required to assess the true importance of all these various kinds of 'special pleading' and to find the objectively best balance between them.

Such a view of things is not only fallacious in terms of epistemology (though this is my main concern in this chapter). In terms of government, it constitutes an attempt to usurp the politician's role, and to replace politics with 'science'. At the level of personal working relationships it places all these specialists in a position of predetermined inferiority, as is evidenced by their own accounts.[15]

In the sphere of planning education, this holist ideology has been particularly well developed, and strongly expressed.[16] Typically, the curriculum is organized in accordance with it. On the one hand, there is a variety of specialist 'inputs' from lecturers in such varied subjects as law, architecture, economics, surveying, political science, landscape architecture, sociology, engineering, public administration, ecology, psychology and philosophy. On the other hand, there is a dominant central element, known as the 'practical work' or 'project work', around which all these contributions are supposedly organized. In the 'practical work', the student learns what is seen as the central element in the planners' professional skills, the preparation of policies or plans. In the preparation of these plans, the ideology suggests, the things learned in all the specialist courses are taken into account, and given their due weight.

In reality, of course, the 'due weight' of some of them proves small. This tends to be especially true of the social science subjects. What most social science lecturers typically do, is to get their students to look at analyses of planning in practice, and thus to get some understanding of what the governmental control of land use does and could actually achieve. And this kind of real understanding is obviously very difficult to incorporate into the rather utopian plans which the 'practical work' teachers demand. That these social science subjects are in the curriculum at all, seems best understood in terms of the profession's need for academic respectability; some so-called 'theoretical' subjects must be seen to be in the syllabus, if planning degrees are to appear to be comparable with academic degrees in other fields. There seems little doubt, however, that from the point of view of the professional planners who control the syllabus, these social science subjects are an embarrassment. As for the student, his position is unenviable. It is difficult for him to resolve the tension between the 'practical work', which seeks to imbue him with an abstract belief in the mission of the profession, and these so-called 'theoretical' subjects, which encourage him to look at planning in reality.

These problems, of course, are not peculiar to planning. All professions experience them.[17] They may be expected to be particularly severe, however, where a profession attempts to harness knowledge from more than one discipline, where the disciplines in question are remote from the knowledge of the professionals who control the syllabus, where the profession in question is intellectually insecure, and where it espouses an ambitious conception of its social role, which strikes the teachers of the so-called 'theoretical' 'contributory disciplines' as inflated or unrealistic. All four of these conditions are found, and to a marked degree, in the case of town planning.

In terms of educational theory, this attempt to ensure that academic disciplines are taught in such a way as to promote the interests of a profession may be seen as a form of 'curriculum integration'. And as Musgrove for example notes, what is really at isue here is power: 'Only one man wins when you integrate subjects—the man at the top.[18] (One observer, interestingly, advocates integration not around the 'practical work', but around theory.[19] This might seem more reasonable, until one notes that the theory he has in mind is *not* the explanation of governmental control of land use, but the by now familiar abstract notion of 'rational decision-making'). As Hague[20] notes, this claim to see the wholeness of things has served as the basis of the planners' claim to professional status throughout their history. Other, pre-existing, local government professions could each claim to know more than planners did about each of the things planners interested themselves in. The *only* course of action open to this new profession, he therefore suggests, was to claim to comprehend *all* of them, and to 'co-ordinate' them.

In the 'old' ideology of planning, which talked about the injurious effects of big cities, the need to divide them up into neighbourhoods, the desirability of new towns, the evils of commuting, and so on, the planners' claims to technical expertise were related to physical objectives which, if ambitious, were at least comprehensible. The professions of architecture, surveying and municipal engineering, out of which the new profession grew, were all themselves clearly technical, in the sense that they concerned themselves with the design of buildings, roads, sewers and so on, and town planning simply retained this technical image.

With the emergence of the 'new' planning, however, planners' technicism grew to quite astonishing proportions. And much of it, as we have also seen, was transferred into the 'procedural' sphere; they misapplied technicist ideas to the age-old 'political science' question of how social decisions might be made. Planners drew increasingly complicated diagrams, consisting of neatly labelled boxes connected by fiercely determined-looking arrows, and they told us that government and administration would all work much better if we carried it out in accordance with these diagrams, instead of continuing to entrust it to selfish and irrational politicians.

But what of the 'substantive' subject area—that of spatial patterns—in which planners' ideas might reasonably be expected to be rather more sober and more authoritative? Quantitative geography and regional economic analysis made considerable progress from the 1960s onwards, and planning theory and practice might reasonably be expected to reflect these advances. Certainly, we can say that the formulation of plans and policies has been based since the 1960s on increasingly sophisticatd quantitative knowledge of spatial and socio-economic processes. The test of the quality of these plans, however, must surely be whether they have made possible any improvement in development control. Plans, after all, can have little practical function, other than to provide a basis for the control of development.[21]

Can we discern, then, any improvement in development control, facilitated by better plans? It is difficult to answer this question, for as was shown in Chapter 3 research is sparse. One way to try to answer it, however, lies in seting out what we think *would* constitute a technically informed system of land use control, and comparing the reality with it. In principle, there seem to be two possible models.

In the first model, the criteria used in assessing development proposals would be clearly stated, publicly, and at national level. The regulations, then, would be uniform, and automatic, and there would be no 'discretion'. In this model, there would be relatively little need for qualified professional planners at the local authority level, but rather for officials, who would merely carry out such routine tasks as comparing the proposals with the regulations, informing applicants whether or not their proposals conformed, and preventing infringements. At the national or overall level, however, at least if it were to be rationally implemented, this first model implies a considerable research element. Monitoring would be needed in order to discover the effects of each policy. If it were to be constantly improved, and indeed if it were not to lose sight of its objectives and allow means to become ends, this approach would also depend on the existence of informed public and political debate. In summary, its success would demand exactly the same combination of technical research on the one hand and political assessment on the other as are the essential prerequisites of any *other* policy initiative, such as, for example, adding a year to the period of compulsory education, or increasing or reducing tariffs on specific categories of imports.

The second possible model is very much in accordance with the existing British system, with a high level of 'discretion' at the local level; there would need to be one important difference, however. If local authorities *are* to have this discretionary power to permit or to prevent development, I would suggest, it follows logically that in an open society they should be required to explain their reasons publicly, and in terms of cause and effect. What this second model implies, therefore, is that the research element be brought down to the level at which development control decisions are made, and indeed, that it should become the rationale for the individual decision. This implies that applicants, and indeed any member of the public, should have the right to what might be called 'anticipated impact statements', or 'planning balance sheets'.[22] These would set out all the anticipated economic and social effects and implications of granting and of not granting permission, including such things as the anticipated betterment tax, the anticipated rate revenue, the number of jobs, homes, and other facilities likely to be lost and gained, the effects on neighbouring land values, the negative and positive externality effects both in physical terms and in terms of estimated money values, the wider effects on the local employment and housing markets, and so on. Arguably, too, such things as the method of financing, and the developers' profits, would be relevant considerations.

There is little point in making such 'impact statements', however, unless they are made as hypotheses, and monitored. Without this, there is no growth in knowledge, and consequently, relatively little technical capacity to *make* such impact statements.[23] The politicians, the media, and the public, therefore, should also have the right, subsequent to the carrying out of the development, to know the extent to which each of the anticipated impacts was anticipated accurately.

Either of these two models is rational and logical in principle. It is fairly obvious, however, that the second one is quite impracticable. To devote resources in this way to the investigation of each and every planning application, even if it were technically feasible, would be in economic terms morally indefensible. Yet such monitoring of the effects of decisions must be done *somewhere*, if the system is to be 'self-aware', and thus to make sense. The conclusion I would draw is that the land-use planning system is only worth preserving to the extent that it can be brought into line with the first model, and this implies a much greater degree of separation of policy-making from day-to-day administration than we have at present. The former requires a much higher level of expertise than currently exists. The latter, by contrast, does not seem to require the services of the highly trained professionals who at present carry it out. It could of course be argued that the policy research which I describe could be done at the local authority level even if not at the level of the individual decision, but this, to me, would seem to represent a poor compromise. Local authorities cannot legislate, and the extent to which policy *can* be peculiar to a given local authority is therefore relatively small. From the point of view of the public, too, it is difficult to understand why planning policies should differ from one local authority area to another, and it would seem socially inequitable that they should do so. They might of course logically differ between *types* of area, so that there would for example be policies for the inner cities, for outworn industrial areas, for designated types of countryside, for green belt areas, national parks and so on. But that is another thing, and a matter which again is easily understood by the public.

These points become clear, if we think about the British planning system as it was for the first time more or less consciously formulated at the end of the Second World War. The rationale behind the system was clearly socio-economic, derived as it was mainly from the Barlow and Scott Reports; these last, in effect, constituted 'policy hypotheses', postulating that certain economic and social benefits would result, if the national settlement pattern were modified in certain fairly clearly-defined ways. Yet the necessary research capacity, needed if these 'hypotheses' were to be tested and thus to add to our knowledge, was not established. Though the intention had been that this planning of the national settlement pattern should be the responsibility of a central government agency, it was in the event handed over to the local authorities; this geographical fragmentation, together with the intellectual fragmentation resulting from the fact that so many different professional and lay interest groups saw something of potential benefit to themselves in planning, meant that in effect, as we have seen, 'planning' became anything and nothing, 'all things to all men'. And after 1953, when the financial mechanism underlying this 'planning system' was removed, it becomes difficult to see why these powers of development control were kept in existence at all, for they could clearly no longer work as intended. Healey[24] suggests that they were kept for four reasons, none of them, I would suggest, having either very much 'respectability' or intellectual credibility:

(i) 'the strong lobby behind countryside preservation and the protection of agricultural land'. (This refers to the fact that, as shown in Chapter 3, the planning system had shown itself capable of being 'misused', to promote class interests, in a way its progenitors had probably never intended.)

(ii) 'the inertia built up within local authorities by the existence of a planning bureaucracy'. (This refers to the tendency for all bureaucracies to grow, irrespective of their usefulness to anyone other than themselves.)

(iii) 'the desire of local politicians to be in a position to exercise control over development—a sort of local fiefdom, or patronage'. (This, in plain English, means something very like corruption.)

(iv) 'Another reason . . .may be that while land value and ownership measures impinge clearly on specific property interests, the system of land-use regulation backed by development plans is open to manipulation by many interests. (This too, like Healey's first suggested reason, suggests that the planning system was kept in existence because it had been found capable of promoting sectional and private interests.)

Even if it be considered that Healey's analysis is too strong, the fact still remains that the clear 'policy hypotheses' implicit in 'Barlow' and 'Scott' were lost. They were lost largely because the central government bureaucracy and politicians at national level were content to allow planning to become a local responsibility. Central government has certainly subjected local planning to increasingly tight legal and administrative control, but it has not, by contrast, done much to clarify its *objectives*. These clear 'policy hypotheses' have also been lost because at the local level, planning has generally become publicly perceived as a matter of design, or at the most, as a physical matter. It seems doubtful whether any local authority could formulate socio-economic objectives capable of firing the public imagination as 'Barlow' and 'Scott' did, and even if it were to do so, such ambitions would very quickly be scotched by Whitehall, at least if formulated under town and country planning legislation.

Whatever one thinks about the possibility or the desirability of such local social and economic planning, therefore, the fact is that the monitoring of town and country planning in Britain is virtually non-existent. Central government regards it as a local responsibility (if, indeed, it is willing to accord it any encouragement at all) while local government, to put it quite simply, is just not geared up to the task of critically appraising public policy.

My question, then, was whether the new planning techniques of the 1960s and 1970s have led to any improvement in development control. The answer would seem to be that they have not. There has been no significant improvement, since 1960, in the planners' ability to assess the consequence of their actions. The 'new' planning techniques, even when of a 'substantive' rather than 'procedural' nature, have been applied almost entirely to plan-*making* rather than to discovery of the effects of planning, and as a result there has been very little, if any, growth in the knowledge-base of planning.

I would conclude that these new planning techniques have a largely ideological function. They consist of a *show* of supposed technical knowledge, rather than of technical knowledge itself.

The fourth, and final, strand in the ideology of planning was 'role confusion', the ploy of portraying the scope and objectives of planning in a changing way, according to the susceptibilities of the 'audience'. This, as I have shown, is a ploy which was used extensively in the 1960s and 1970s, when planning was portrayed as pursuing vaguely 'social' objectives, but it is equally strongly relied upon today, when it is portrayed on having the function of promoting business enterprise. As I have also shown, however, planners have in general made relatively little effort to study the detailed *content* of the various fields of knowledge in which they have in this way from time to time interested themselves.

Having considered the intellectual validity of the techniques of the 'new planning', and having concluded that they are in a very real sense more ideological and less intellectually credible than the 1940s planning ideas which they replaced, a number of questions arise. Who brought in these ideas? And why? Whose interests do they serve? And so on.

On the first of these questions, the conventional wisdom is that these ideas were brought in by 'social scientists'.[25] The 'old planning' of the 1940s, this conventional view suggests, had been largely dominated by architects, and was mainly visual and physical in its concerns. The 'new planning', by contrast, reflected the influx into the field from the 1960s onwards of social scientists.

There seem to be a number of grounds, however, on which this widely accepted view can be questioned. First, it seems doubtful whether there has, in fact occurred any such influx of social scientists. There has, by contrast, been an influx of geography graduates.[26] The latter, however, seem in general to the present writer to have mental orientations and taken-for-granted assumptions very different from those of most social scientists, and much closer to those traditional in planning itself. In particular, geographers' conceptions of 'theory', and of 'research' seem very different from the interpretations put on these concepts by social scientists; geographers seem, in summary terms, to be technically and physically orientated rather than to think in terms of social or political theory.[27]

*Second,* one can point out that those few social scientists who *did* find themselves in the planning schools over the 1960s and 1970s were in general very much engaged in questioning and arguing *against* the 'new planning'. Systems theory, notions of 'rational decision-making', mathematical modelling and all the rest seemed, to most sociologists at least, to be quite inappropriate to the explanation of governmental control of land and property development, and very often they said so, in no uncertain terms.[28] That they were not heard perhaps reflects the fact that they were indeed small in number.

*Thirdly,* one can point out that the most influential 'new planning' texts were not written by social scientists, but mainly by planners themselves.

Ravetz[29] confirms this impression that British planning was taken over by geographers rather than by social scientists. She points out that at just about the same time that planning turned to geography for its theories (around 1960), geography was itself 'invaded' by mathematical modelling, cybernetics and the 'systems approach', introduced through American-style transportation planning.[30] She also suggests that planners would in fact have 'preferred' to turn to sociology rather than to geography, but found the sociologists 'aloof'. She cites Eversley, as a typical example of what she calls the planners' 'pettish' reaction to this 'aloofness': '[Sociology] is not a science', Eversley wrote, 'it does not establish truths by which man may act'.[31]

In contrast to what Ravetz says on this point, I would suggest that sociologists were by no means aloof. The problem was not this. It was that the planners did not want to hear what the sociologists said. Essentially, what virtually all the sociologists involved were pointing at was that the social sciences cannot show what the objectives of public policy 'ought' to be, any more than the natural sciences can. They can only show *how* to achieve given objectives, or what the consequences of the pursuit of various objectives are likely to be. The uncomfortable 'message', therefore, which the planners apparently did not want to hear (and perhaps could not afford to hear, since it conflicted with their whole conception of planning) was that if planners wished to recommend that specific objectives be pursued, then they themselves must take responsibility for these recommendations; in effect of course, they would then be acting as politicians. It seems in any case a little unfair to suggest that the sociologists were 'aloof'. Over the 1960s and 1970s a small band of them tried hard to get this simple message across, not only in their published work, but also by visiting planning schools, giving talks at the invitation of planning students' societies, writing in student magazines, and so on.[32]

As to the purposes served by the introduction of the 'new planning techniques', there are probably few who would doubt that they were intended to enhance the status of planning, by giving it an aura of scientific objectivity. It may still seem difficult, however, to explain why *these particular ideas* were adopted. To the observer, it seems fairly obvious that if town and country planners wished to improve their intellectual standing as experts within their field, they would have done better to study the physical, economic, political and social implications of governmental intervention in the property development process. This, after all, is the activity in which they are engaged. Why, then, did they instead embrace idea systems which were so general, so contentless, and so abstract? In a real sense, their choice seems odd.

It ceases to seem odd, however, when we consider the point made above, that this 'new planning' was in a very real sense not new at all. Planning had always, traditionally, avoided any down-to-earth analysis of the political and economic processes in which it was involved. The planning movement and profession had always technicized matters which were in reality questions of economic redistribution, and had always asserted the existence of consensus in society, as a means of concealing the true political nature of planning. Systems theory, therefore, with its inbuilt conservative and anti-political assumption of social consensus, was in this sense a perfectly logical vehicle for the further consolidation of this traditional professional ideology. And so indeed was the notion of 'rational decision-making', with its inbuilt assumption that government policies can be justified by reference to objective truth, and politics thus dispensed with.

But if the 'new planning' is merely the old planning wrapped up in fancier dress, we still need to explain exactly *how* these particular Emperor's new clothes were flaunted and displayed. And here, we see the point of the transfer of interest from the substantive to the procedural sphere. To concentrate interest on the techniques of decision-making which planners use, and to distract attention as far as possible away from the substantive outcomes which planning is meant to achieve, is a political ploy (if an unconscious one) of some astuteness. Discussion of the outcomes which planning was meant to produce was sensed by the professional planners to be potentially dangerous, since politically contentious; better, then, to talk about the 'planning process'. What was wrong with the 'old' planning was *not,* as the conventional wisdom suggests, that it had naive physical objectives. What was wrong with it was that it had any objectives at all. The only way to overcome this weakness was to mystify 'planning' further, to concentrate attention on procedures rather than on purposes, and to redefine planning as a mystical 'process' rather than as concerned with 'blueprints'. And 'blueprint planners', in fact, became the term of disparagement used in the profession to castigate those who would not adopt the thought-styles of the 'new planning' quickly enough. The irony of this is fairly profound. To be concerned with 'blueprints', in this sense, is to concern oneself with the most important and the most neglected question in town and country planning, the question of the states of affairs which it seeks to promote.

To the extent that this analysis has validity, its most important implications probably lie in the sphere of planning education. No knowledge is 'pure', of course, and all knowledge can be used to serve some interest or other, but a field in which *so much* of what is taught seems to be of a markedly ideological nature may be thought to give grounds for particular concern. It would be misleading, of course, to suggest that the ideological notions criticized above are *all* that is taught to intending planners, but it seems fair to say that they constitute a significant part of it, in the specific sense that they pervade and infuse the whole curriculum. Conversely, one's concern is increased when one reflects how little of the work of the planning schools is by contrast devoted to gaining an understanding of the workings and consequences of the planning system in practice. The proper function of the planning schools, one might suggest, is to find out how land-use controls are and might be exercised. What this seems to mean is that they should be engaged in research on such matters as the operations and financing of the property-development industry, the various forms of taxation and regulation imposed upon this industry in various countries, and the economic and social impacts of such controls. This would seem to provide the obvious basis both for what they teach, and for the 'practice' of planning. But this is not, generally speaking, what they concern themselves with. What is known about such matters has been produced largely outside the planning schools, and is to a surprising extent ignored within them.

It is perhaps what tends to ensue when students *do* become familiar with the social scientists' research into planning in practice, which gives the greatest grounds for concern, however. To the students, most of whom are straight from school, and have relatively little knowledge of the realities of government and administration in general, such empirical studies are often disturbing; they suggest that the reality of planning is in fact very different from the rather utopian visions which they are taught in their 'practical work' and they frequently, as a consequence, raise serious questions concerning the capabilities of 'planning'. In my experience, however, such students are not, as one might expect in a university, encouraged in their intellectual curiosity. On the contrary, they tend to be labelled by staff as 'not having the right attitudes', and as being unlikely, perhaps, to make good reliable members of the 'profession', and this, inevitably, colours the way in which their work is seen.

There is probably nothing in this which marks planning off from other similar professions. On the contrary, it may well be the almost inevitable result of a form of training which is professional rather than academic. Yet it raises profound questions concerning the desirability of allowing would-be professions to use the institutions of higher education as a means of promoting their ambitions. Professions whose practice *does* rest on a more secure knowledge base, of course, such as medicine, are a totally different matter, but the universities should perhaps be more aware than they appear to be of the possibility that organizational loyalty and professional power may often be placed a long way before intellectual integrity.

In drawing this section of the chapter to a close, therefore, I list some of the ways in which planners, when their ideas are challenged at the intellectual level, tend to dispose of the criticism in quite inappropriate terms, and at a quite different level. There is arguably little in such ploys which is peculiar to planners, and indeed we may all be tempted to use such stratagems when hard pressed, yet I nevertheless believe that the list which follows does indeed tell us much about the dangers of entrusting public policy to professional judgment.

*First,* planners display a well-marked tendency to turn criticism aside by claiming to have already abandoned the ideas criticized. This, of course, misses the point. The point is to know *why* the ideas were abandoned (if indeed they have been), and to know *why* they were adopted in the first place. Often, planners seem almost too willing to abandon their ideas, almost as soon as sociologists even begin to question them; this reaction suggests an apparent desire both to avoid all intellectual discussion, and to be in fashion. Over the years, planners have donned one set of 'Emperor's new clothes' after another, now seeing themselves as designers of cities, now as 'systems analysts', now as 'allocators of scarce resources', now as 'urban managers', now as 'corporate planners', or 'social planners', or quantitative geographers, as analysts of 'social malaise', or even as 'bureaucratic guerillas, or 'planning aid' workers, intent on liberating oppressed minorities from official indifference. The guise most popular at the time of writing, as noted, is that of promoters of entrepreneurial initiative. The point is not that any of these role-conceptions is misleading. In reality they all are, for not one of them describes what planners actually do. The point, rather, is that this constant production of a shifting and faintly amazing series of self-images, and the slightly frantic search for new 'approaches' which accompany it, reflect something deeper. They reflect the fact that the 'profession' of planning has no real intellectual base, is profoundly insecure, and experiences, therefore, a fairly permanent identity crisis.

Second, planners often turn criticism aside by exaggerating the differences between various schools of thought or tendencies within the profession. The criticisms made, they suggest, are certainly true, regrettably, of others, but not of themselves. These others, they often imply, are unfortunately slow to change. They themselves, on the other hand, are far more progressive, and have already taken one's criticisms into account. What can we say in reply to this? There are differences, of course, between various schools of thought within the planning profession, and they are often experienced as very profound by those concerned, but they are small indeed, when compared with the differences between the characteristic thought styles of planners and those of social scientists. The first are rooted, whatever their particular nuances, in a sense of professional mission, the second in a tradition of intellectual scepticism. There is very little evidence indeed, either in published material or from personal observation, that there is any significant group in the planning profession, even those most critical of their 'diehard' colleagues, which has in reality shown any real understanding of the criticisms of planning made by social scientists, let alone taken those criticisms into account (though there are, of course, many individual planners who are made uneasy by these criticisms, and who sympathise with them in some sense or other). The 'Radical Institute Group' within the Royal Town Planning Institute, which probably comes closest to constituting such a tendency, seems to have been hampered both by too close an association with the Labour Party, and by an insufficient emphasis on the need for theoretical as opposed to political clarification of the issues.

Third, planners are apt to turn criticism aside by ad hominem attacks on the critic. There seems to be a particular reason for this, and it lies in the fact that the planners and their critics are socialized into totally different intellectual worlds, whose fundamental presuppositions are virtually incompatible. Quite literally, therefore, the criticisms are simply not understood. In such a situation, and given that planners are often busy and harassed people, with problems of their own, there is obviously a strong temptation upon them to avoid trying to think about the content of the criticism, and instead to concentrate on the critic. Thus, planners often turn criticism aside by ascribing it to 'clashes of personality', to the fact that the critic 'does not fit into the organization', and so on, and even, in a singular confusion of cause and effect, sometimes even go so far as to suggest that it is 'only to be expected' that the critic will try to find reasons for criticizing planning, since he 'does not believe in it'.

*Fourth,* planners often turn criticism aside by means of what might be described as a crude application of the 'sociology of knowledge'. Some groups, they suggest, will inevitably oppose planning, since they have a vested interest in those things which planning threatens. Davies[33] has analysed this particular defence mechanism with especial insight, showing how it enabled the planners he studied to dismiss all criticism on the grounds that it emananated from those who represented either privilege or ignorance. More recently, since 1979, planners have similarly rejected criticism on the grounds that it is part of the contemporary 'attack on planning', or that it serves to promote the interests of the 'New Right'. What, however, if the same criticisms are levelled at planners by the New Right and the Old Left alike? Will *this,* at last, convince them that the validity of an argument is not in fact dependent on the identity of the person who puts it forward?[34]

A *fifth* way in which the planning profession turns criticism aside is by what we might term licensing it. 'We need criticism', they say, 'it keeps us on our toes'. On the strength of such irreproachably liberal sentiments, sociologists are appointed to the staff of planning schools. With such public demonstration of their open-mindedness performed, however, planners regard their duty to the search for truth as very adequately discharged. To actually think about and to debate what their licensed critics say, apparently, would be to carry liberal principle to immoderate lengths.

In concluding, I should perhaps note the characteristic commitment and sincerity of planners, and above all, the sheer intensity of their belief in 'planning'. As a number of writers have noted, 'planning' is for many planners quite often a kind of a secular religion.[35] But this, again, does not make it any easier to reason with them. In summary, it seems fair to say that planners, and even those who teach in the planning schools, show a depressingly anti-intellectual tendency to think in terms of 'disloyalty', 'attacks' and 'enemies', rather than in terms of reasoned debate, and a tendency to 'close ranks' against the critic rather than to consider what he says.

This, then, concludes my attempt to characterize the 'institutions of belief', and to explain why I find them objectionable. If the formulation and interpretation of public policy is largely entrusted to a self-perpetuating occupational group, I conclude, and especially if that group regards itself as a 'profession', the result is likely to be the development of a closed intellectual climate, in which only those perceptions which further the interests of that group will be allowed to prevail.

## 3. 'Scepticism'

The only real attempts to challenge the 'planners' view of planning,' and to suggest alternative explanations, have come from social scientists, and especially, from sociologists. Kirk[36] divides up these critiques according to their ideological and theoretical presuppositions, identifying four more or less distinct schools. Since such 'labelling' is quite common, and because I find it unhelpful, I shall use Kirk's typology as a framework, to explain *why* I find the approach unhelpful.

What Kirk seems to have done is to have taken four social science perspectives, and, by exaggerating the ideological content in each, shown them to be capable either of providing differing degrees of vindication of the planning system as it exists, or of implying varying degrees of radical repudiation of it.

By the *pluralist* view, Kirk means a social science perspective which assumes power in society to be widely diffused in *general*, and which therefore assumes that equally in the specific case of land-use planning, no particular interest will be systematically promoted.[37] By the *managerialist*, or 'bureaucratic', perspective, she means one which assumes that power in society generally is very much in the hands of managers, experts and bureaucrats, and that in the specific case of land-use planning, therefore, power will similarly be exercised mainly by the professional planners, rather than (for example) by property developers, politicians, or the public.[38] By the *reformist* view, Kirk means a perspective which, starting out from the fact that material inequalities in society are very considerable, urges that land-use planning should be used as one of the means of social redistribution.[39] Kirk's fourth perspective is the Marxist one, and her purpose, in identifying and contrasting the four, is to urge that it has greater intellectual credibility than the other three. The main features of the Marxist view of planning, as Kirk identifies these, are that it pays particular attention to economic factors and that it explains urban development as part of a wider process of capital accumulation.[40]

Why is Kirk's attempt to distinguish these approaches unhelpful? *First,* the contrasts between the four rest on an exaggeration of their distinctiveness, both as social scientific perspectives in general, and as identifiable schools of thought on land-use planning in particular. They can indeed be recognized as four tendencies within the social sciences, but there has not, as yet, appeared a single thoroughgoing attempt to analyse British land-use planning in terms of even one of them. Most of the social scientists who have looked at planning have probably used insights and concepts from all four (and other) perspectives, as seemed appropriate to the particular phenomena they were examining—and this seems highly desirable. Kirk's anxiety to find four contrasted approaches leads her to exaggerate what in reality are merely tendencies, or even insights, and to present them as if they were almost incompatible. In reality, I would suggest, it would be difficult to find *any* sociologists who accept the tenets of pluralism, as Kirk describes them,[41] to find *any* sociologists who regard the hypothesis of professional power as any more than a hypothesis, to find *any* who would reject the basic assumption of Kirk's 'reformist' view, or to find any who do *not* find Marxist insights, concepts and theories useful.

*Second,* Kirk's contrasting of these four perspectives involves a conflation of social science with ideology. Any such 'perspective' can be seen either as a source of research hypotheses, or as an ideology. Pluralism, for example, if regarded as a source of hypotheses, is really no more than a reminder that we sould not *assume* all power to be concentrated in elite circles; relatively powerless groups may, on occasion, be able to ensure that decisions go the way they want. As an ideology, by contrast, pluralism means the assertion that power *is* widely diffused in society, that the political system *is* responsive to demands from any quarter, and even that we should consider ourselves fortunate to be living in such a highly desirable kind of society. As a hypothesis, pluralism suggests questions for research. As an ideology, one might say, pluralism provides us with the answers, but almost without the trouble of actually doing the research.

And exactly the same point can be made about each of the other three of Kirk's perspectives, or indeed, of any such perspective in the social sciences. In making what might to some seem a rather too simple distinction between social science and ideology, I am not unaware of the many complex, subtle and quite unavoidable ways in which the researcher's findings and his values interact. But we should try to distinguish between them precisely *because* it is so difficult to do so. Kirk is too pessimistic. She seems to assume that we are quite incapable of even considering the empirical truth of something which is uncongenial to us in terms of our values.

Third, Kirk's approach leads her to 'label' specific pieces of research, and thereby to do them injustice. She puts the work of Davies,[42] for example, and of Dennis[43] very firmly in the 'managerialist' camp, suggesting that their focus on the way the professional planners operate 'restricts [their] viewpoint, and does not incorporate more general questions concerning the relationship between land-use planning and the market, for example, or central government policies'.[44] Further, she calls their work 'an anti-bureaucracy-cum-profession diagnosis, in which the only structure recognized is an economically empty structure of authority'.[45] Yet in reality Dennis shows every awareness of wider economic processes, characterizing planning for example as a 'bureaucracy of consumption, having the function of keeping up demand for the products of the development industry'.[46] And Davies sees planning as 'a highly regressive form of indirect taxation ... giving most to those who already have a lot and giving least to those who need most',[47] criticizing planners for behaving 'as if economy, property, and society were somehow unconnected'.[48]

*Fourth,* Kirk confuses an ideology with an interest in a particular subject. It does not follow that if one studies managers, one is a 'managerialist'. It does not follow that if researchers focus on certain aspects of a problem, they thereby reveal themselves to consider other aspects unimportant, or not to have considered them at all. Nobody can study everything at once, and particular researchers are often especially well fitted to study particular things. A division of labour in academic work is normally accepted and understood, and to suggest that the researcher's focus of interest reveals his ideological bias is not only illogical, but unjust.

One could also note that Kirk's third 'perspective', the 'reformist' one, does not really 'belong' in her typology, having a different epistemological status from the other three. To urge that planning ought to be used to achieve social redistribution is not to engage in sociology, but in political persuasion.

The above, then, are specific criticisms of the 'labelling' approach as I have called it, and of which Kirk's work is an example. But there are more fundamental reasons for refraining from dividing up the work which has been done on a subject into distinct schools, at least in the case of such a very undeveloped subject as the sociological analysis of town planning. What the various critiques of planning have in common seems to me much more important than what divides them. What seems to have been the starting point, for most of them, is their realization that the ideology of planning, with its claim that planning secures those outcomes which are objectively best and in the public interest, simply *could not* accord with reality. This has usually provoked such researchers to go on to attempt to discover how the system *does* work in reality, and in whose interests. Though the various pieces of work on the subject focus often on quite different aspects of planning, and are indeed written from different philosophical and theoretical viewpoints, it seems better to regard them as complementary rather than competitive, and to see all of them as valuable contributions towards our knowledge of this subject area.[49]

So far, then, I have merely questioned the usefulness of 'labelling'. But what do thee various social science analyses of planning actually say? To speak of summarizing their findings seems rather premature, for they are, as noted, still quite fragmentary. Some of them, the more solid ones which rest on empirical evidence, I have looked at in Chapter 3. As for the rest, they are for the most part merely discussions (such as the present book), or comments on planning made *en passant*, in the course of investigating other things, or what we may call deductions about the functions of land-use planning derived from 'grand theory', and without the benefit of very much empirical evidence. What most of them agree on, therefore, is for the most part either rather general in nature, or less than fully unsubstantiated, and can be stated fairly quickly.

First, most observers agree that the body of ideas in terms of which planners justify what they do is mainly ideological rather than a body of technical or theoretical knowledge. Further, they note that such technical (or pseudo-technical) knowledge as planners *do* have is not, in the main, concerned with land use controls, but with other matters, apparently peripheral to their actual work. Second, most observers agree that both what planners do, and the consequences of their doing it, seem to differ significantly from what their ideology suggests. Third, as regards these 'consequences of planning', most observers agree that these are unclear, but in so far as they *are* known, they seem to differ significantly from the planners' intentions (in so far as *these* are known!). Fourth, some observers, mainly Marxist-inspired, have deduced from broader, over-arching social theories that the land-use planning system has certain 'functions', or brings about certain effects at the level of the economy as a whole. These include facilitating private sector capital accumulation, by creating monopoly or at least scarcity levels of land and property values, securing 'legitimation', by giving the *impression* that private sector development 'is controlled' in such a way as to increase social welfare, co-ordinating publicly-funded infrastructure with private development, again rendering it easier for the private sector to make profits, achieving regressive redistribution of environmental benefits and positive externalities, from 'have-nots' to 'haves', and similarly, redistributing environ-mentalcosts and negative externalities from 'haves to have-nots'.

*Fifth*, however, the extent to which these postulated 'functions' or effects have been empirically demonstrated is generally seen as insufficient. In addition, other observers (and sometimes the same observers) suggest that at least sometimes, the redistributive effects of planning are *progressive*. Consequently, therefore, (and *sixth*), most observers agree that further research is required. In view of the large and increasing part played by land and property investment in the economy, such research could even be seen as important. I would also personally add, as a research hypothesis well worth investigating, a final point: that among the main beneficiaries of the existence of planning are the planners themselves.

What I have emphasized, then, in looking at the alternative, 'sceptical' view of the planning system, is neither the supposedly conflicting ideological sympathies of the sceptics (as Kirk does), nor their substantive findings (which seem to me too fragmentary as yet to collate) but simply their scepticism. Social science analyses of planning approach the subject from an attitude of doubt. It is this that they have in common. And such doubt is to be commended. If planners had *also* doubted whether their activity produced the benefits claimed for it, and had tried to find out, they would probably have been much more successful than they are.

The intellectual incompatibility which poses a problem, then, is not, as Kirk suggests, between the various perspectives within sociology. Rather, it is between attitudes of 'belief' and 'scepticism', where the making of public policy is concerned. In the case of planning, there exists between the 'believers' and the 'sceptics' an almost complete mutual incomprehension, reflecting the fact that the two groups are socialized into different worlds, with contrasting taken-for-granted assumptions.

And *these* two conflicting views of the world, unlike those identified by Kirk, *do* rest on different material bases. The planners' interest in portraying planning in such a way as to justify its continued existence is obvious. It is their livelihood. Their social science critics, by contrast, inhabit an academic subculture in which they can obtain professional rewards by 'laying bare' the realities behind social institutions. 'Planning', with its over-ambitious and sometimes faintly ridiculous professional pretensions, provides a tempting target. It is perhaps surprising that it has attracted as little attention as it has.

I now turn to consider, in the final section of this chapter, how we might come out of this impasse.

## 4. Belief in professional judgment and the drift towards corporatism

At this point, then, one might logically try to 'win over' the planners, by attempting to persuade them that the control of land use would be both more popular and more successful if there were to emerge a very much freer competition of ideas about the matter. Informed public policy-making, one might urge, is most likely to emerge in a social climate in which criticism is not merely tolerated, but actively rewarded. And this, in turn, implies an institutional milieu in which power and influence are much more widely diffused than at present, in which no one set of people any longer has the ability to control channels of communication, to allocate research funds, or to influence policy-making. The institutional arrangements which one would thus be urging, however, are readily recognizable, to planners as to anyone else. They are recognizable, in fact, because they are the institutions which in all Western societies we assume or assert more or less to exist. They are the institutions of liberal democracy. 'Scepticism', or, as we might say, the assumption that nobody has a monopoly of truth or of wisdom, and that all have the right to challenge existing practices, lies at the very heart of liberal democracy. Rather than urge these values and institutions upon planners, therefore, a procedure which would be tedious because they are, as noted, generally assumed more or less to exist, it seems more useful to adopt the quite opposite tactic, and to demonstrate the extent to which these liberal values and institutions are in fact threatened. My argument will be that the syndrome of attitudes and practices which I have characterized as 'belief' in planning tends to lead to incipient corporatism, and that under such incipiently corporatist arrangements it becomes increasingly difficult for policies to be challenged, and thus improved.

What do I mean by 'corporatism'? The term was in fact introduced in Chapter 3, where I decribed certain ideas and practices centering on the extraction of 'planning gain' as incipiently corporatist.[50] To enable the argument to be taken a bit further, however, it seems useful at this point to look at the meaning of this term a little more closely. The following is one of the most-quoted explanations:

> Corporatism can be defined as a system of interest representation in which the constituent units are organized into a limited number of singular, compulsory, non-competitive, hierarchically ordered and functionally differentiated categories, recognized or licensed (if not created) by the State and granted a deliberate representational monopoly within their respective categories in exchange for observing certain controls on their selection of leaders and articulation of demands and supports.[51]

To make matters plain, it seems also worth quoting Schmitter's definition of his opposite ideal-type, 'pluralism': In the plural model, the constituent units

> are organized into an unspecified number of multiple, voluntary, competitive, non-hierarchically ordered, and self-determined (as to type or scope of interest) categories that are not specifically licensed, recognized, subsidized or otherwise controlled in leadership selection or interest articulation by the State and that do not exercise a monopoly of representational activity within their respective categories.[52]

To make things even more plain, it would involve no undue oversimplification to substitute 'parliamentary' for Schmitter's ideal-type 'pluralist' representation. For what we are really in ordinary language concerned with, when we talk of the tendency to corporatism in society, is the contrast between parliamentary, party, politics and institutionalized pressure group, administrative politics.[53] The latter, it is clear, must of necessity be conducted out of the public gaze, and it is this tendency to secrecy which will be emphasized below as one of the main features of corporatist arrangements in practice. In a constitutional democracy such as

Britain, as we know, political representation is ostensibly on the basis of geographical units, constituencies, and is effected through parties and through parliament. There is no formal provision for the representation of interests as such. In practice, however, and as we also know, there is a strongly developed tendency for representation of interests also to be effected on a 'functional', as opposed to a geographical, basis, and not through parliament at all, but 'direct', through Whitehall. This, we can say, is incipient corporatism. Functional pressure groups of all kinds, from the CBI and the TUC to the Royal Town Planning Institute and the Ramblers Association, all enjoy some measure of institutionalized rught of access to those officials who, on the one hand, draft legislation, and, on the other hand, decide how that legislation is to be interpreted in practice, once parliamentary approval has been obtained for it.

Once a government bureaucracy becomes involved in such working relationships, it evinces a strong tendency to promote the emergence of one 'licensed' body to speak for each recognized interest; this makes life much simpler.[54] The archetypal examples here, perhaps, are Austria and Sweden, sometimes regarded as being of all Western societies those which are furthest advanced towards corporatism. In Sweden, for example, *all* employers' organizations are represented by a single national body, and *all* employees, whether blue-collar, white-collar or highly educated professionals, are similarly brought together, and each represented by one single organization at national level.

It is very important to make clear, however, that corporatism is best regarded not as a descriptive category, but as an analytical one, or ideal type. Tendencies to corporatist institutional arrangements, therefore, always co-exist with other tendencies. The political parties are, after all, still functioning, as is Parliament, and as are the elected councils of local authoritis, and by no means all political pressure in Britain is brought to bear by 'backstairs' methods or converted into 'administration'. In the person of a Member of Parliament who is sponsored by a trades union, in fact, we see corporatist tendencies and those of constitutional parliamentary democracy strikingly 'co-existing'. The question as I see it, then, is not whether the planning system as a whole, or any part of it, is or is not becoming corporatist, but rather *the extent to which* specific policies, specific institutional arrangements and practices and even specific decisions are arrived at or implemented in ways identifiable as corporatist.[55]

Most writers on corporatism restrict their concern largely to economic issues, and tend to focus in particular on 'tripartite' institutionalized industrial bargaining between employers, unions, and government. This relatively narrow focus of interest is rejected here, however, for two reasons.[56] First, it seems misleading to study such industrial bargaining in isolation from the wider social structure, and in particular, in isolation from the wider structure of legitimating ideology and welfare provision which *sustains* the economic system. Those who tend to *advocate* what are in effect corporatist arrangements, in fact, often tend to assume or to assert that if they *are* 'brought together' in this way, the various interest groups involved can, and indeed ought, to be able fairly readily to accommodate to each other. This belief, in its turn, rests on the even more fundamental corporatist assumption that society is, or should be, a smoothly functioning organism, in which the various groups, though they occupy very different positions, have no true conflicts of interest. And such beliefs do not arise 'naturally'. They have to be created.[57]

The second reason for doubting the validity of restricting the study of corporatism to the economic sphere is that as a matter of historical fact corporatism is not a set of ideas restricted to the economy. On the contrary, it is a social and political philosophy which has its roots in a reaction against what its progenitors saw as the dangerously socially disintegrative consequences of the Enlightenment, and of the individualism and liberalism which flowed from it. Social theorists such as Saint-Simon, Comte and Durkheim urged the reorganization of society along corporatist lines in order to promote social cohesion, and to re-establish binding social norms. Saint-Simon, for example, advocated a society consisting of 'corporations', each based on a specific area of skill or knowledge.[58] Durkheim urged that society be reorganized on the basis of professionalized occupational groups.[59] He also saw the re-establishment of authority and hierarchy as a precondition of such an organic society: 'There must be centres of command: One must not imagine that the authority which has been indispensible to all known societies, can suddenly turn out to be useless.[60]

Corporatism, then, was in effect an attempt to re-establish the kind of order which had characterized medieval society or the continental *ständesstaat*, in which one's identity and one's status derived not from the fact that one was a citizen or a human being, but rather from the fact that one was a member of a specific organized occupational group. This same philosophy can be seen in twentieth-century corporatism, as put into effect in Portugal, as preached but hardly practiced by Mussolini, and as attempted by Pétain's Vichy regime in France, for example. Present-day use of incipiently corporatist administrative arrangements, I would therefore suggest, however limited in scope they appear to be, are best understood in terms of this wider background of fundamental social assumptions. And occupational groups whose function is a 'legitimating' one are quite as important to the smooth functioning of a society which employs corporatist mechanisms as are economic producer groups. In medieval society, which bears strong resemblances to a corporate society, it was of course priests who performed this legitimating function. In modern society, it is such groups as teachers, journalists and social workers which perform this same function of creating a perception of the existing system of power as reasonably equitable, and as therefore legitimate.

Such groups, of which 'planners' seem also to be a good example, are perhaps not surprisingly often employed by the state itself. In fact, planners can be seen to have a threefold relationship to the state. First, of course, they are a part of the state apparatus, implementing its policies. Secondly, however, they are themselves an interest group, with the institutionalized right of privileged access to Whitehall, and thus help to shape the very policies which they themselves administer. Thirdly, they are a 'client' group, in that they are almost entirely dependent upon the state for employment.

An obvious question which arises is *why* corporatist ideas have attraction in today's world. That there is a widespread longing to return to the highly structured and rigid medieval or *ständesstaat* type of society, in which each individual has his fixed place, may be doubted, though there are probably many, especially on the Right, who share Durkheim's fear of the breakdown of social order.

The main attraction of corporatist mechanisms, however, is not at the level of ideology at all, but at the purely pragmatic level; they have low political visibility and low political cost. If, as seems reasonable, we assume the state's legitimating function to consist of demonstrating that the excesses of private or sectional interest 'are' curbed, and that the public interest 'does' therefore prevail, it is clear that as means towards this end, both the nationalization of industry and unambiguous legal controls have high political costs. They are 'controversial', since open, and public. Corporatist strategies, by contrast, both leave economic activity in private hands, and avoid detailed legislation; they rely on general 'enabling' Acts, leaving the detail to be worked out through negotiation between officials and representatives of industry on a day-to-day basis in practice. They rest on the assertion or the assumption that the state can equally well promote the public interest by informal methods, by 'working with' the private sector, and indeed, by getting *all* possible interests to 'work with' each other. As Winkler[61] puts it, corporatism works by 'not recording publicly what the State is doing and by operating through personnel and organizations which are not nominally part of the State apparatus'. 'Corporatism', he continues, 'will tend towards indirect, unformalized, non-public and covert forms of administration'.

If by bureaucracy, then, we understand a system based on the impartial application of clear rules, corporatism is profoundly anti-bureaucratic.[62] On the contrary, it is pragmatic, opportunistic, informal and discretionary; those representing the state on the one hand and some sectional interest on the other, who have 'got together' supposedly in order to promote the public interest, will tend to make up the rules as they go along. Corporatism is a bargaining mode, not a bureaucratic mode: 'The most absurd thing any directive State can do is to make a plan and then follow it ... Flexibility is essential to all planning ... all rules are restraints; they bind the State as well as the subject.[63]

And because corporatist mechanisms adopt the low-cost and low-visibility tactics thus described, they have the added advantage that those controlled can both do the controlling themselves and yet feel themselves to be in charge:

> Once the State reaches 'voluntary' agreements with a few large or representative bodies, it then obliges them to enforce these bargains themselves ... Self-enforcement ... is commonly presented as an invitation to take part in the processes of decision making; that is, it is usually wrapped up in some ideological softening. Our contemporary word for this is 'participation' ... 'Participation' provides the legitimation for co-opting potential dissidents ... for defusing opposition and, if successful, for turning them into agents for implementing State policy.[64]

To Winkler's characterization, I would add just one reservation. It seems to me unjustified to assume that once such 'working relationships' are established, it will be the state's policy which will prevail. On the contrary, it seems sounder to assume that it will tend to be the interests of whichever party to the relationship has the greater power, and often, I would suggest, this will tend to be the interests of private sector capital.[65] Indeed, it is not clear that the state will necessarily have an interest in securing *any* particular substantive outcomes. Rather, one would think, its interest will generally lie in giving the *public impression* that all interests have been represented, and in creating the *belief* that the 'public interest' has therefore prevailed over powerful sectional interests.

Corporatist arrangements, in which the public is told that the various interests 'get together', but in which the public is not enabled to follow the arguments which they use on each other when they have thus 'got together', seems well suited to this kind of impression-management. In a society in which the forces of ideological persuasion are so successful in convincing us that objective conflicts of interest in society simply do not exist, however, it must be difficult for the weaker parties in such private negotiations, or those excluded from them, to express any intellectually challenging arguments, and even less likely that such challenges will prevail. Almost inevitably, one would guess, such intellectual opposition will be at least to some extent transferred to the personal and the psychological level; those who honestly disagree but who lack power will often be made to experience their disagreement as an 'inability to work with others'.

What I shall argue, then, is that tendencies to corporatism may be discerned in four aspects of the British planning system, in *development control*, in the *way in which statutory plans are produced*, in the *relationship of the planning profession to the state*, and at the *ideological level*.

The first of these, the tendency to corporatism in development control, has already been discussed, in Section 3 of Chapter 3. Corporatist tendencies may be hypothesized here, I suggested, to the extent that the system of control moves away from the 'pure rule of law' model, and towards 'discretion', 'planning by agreement', 'bargaining', 'partnership', and so on. We are not, however, concerned only with the fact that the local planners and those whose operations they 'plan' work together in such ways, and may thus come to develop a shared subculture and shared perceptions of what is economically feasible, socially desirable and in the 'public interest'. These things are clearly important, but the corporatist web may spread more widely than this. The developers' federations and their financial backers have institutionalized rights of access to the Whitehall bureaucracy, 'over the heads' of the local planners.[66] And indeed, when we consider the multiplicity of interest groups of all kinds which have this kind of access to Whitehall, from the local authority associations, to professional bodies, to the agricultural and rural protectionist lobby and others too numerous to mention, it becomes clear that the practice of development control at the local level can really only be understood as part of a far wider web of (possibly corporatist) interactions at the level of society as a whole.

The *second* sphere in which I suggested that corporatist assumptions and practices may make their appearance is in the production of plans. If developers or other powerful interest groups have a significant say in the formulation of plans, it seems reasonable to hypothesize that those plans will be likely to promote their aims. On this there is little evidence, but there are some suggestive 'leads'. Flynn, for example, who studied the process of formulating the structure plan in Kent, found that this plan was explicitly stated to be 'geared to wealth creation', and that the planners sought to work in close cooperation with industrialists and other major employers and business groups.[67] Though this was a county in which land-owning and agricultural interests had had great political power, ways were apparently found by the planners to enable the plan to accord greater weight to the demands of business and industry. Darke[68] describes the process of formulating the structure plan in South Yorkshire. In this case again, the professional planners were apparently more anxious to produce a plan which reflected the interests of industrialists, and which simply extrapolated existing economic trends, than were the politicians. The latter, by contrast, wanted the plan to seek social redistribution, 'by concentrating on the areas and groups which appeared to be in greatest need'.[69] The Secretary of State for the Environment, however, after the 'Examination in Public' of the plan thus produced in accordance with the elected members' intentions, required it to be modified in such a way that it 'would not include policies which would tend to inhibit the growth of major centres with the greatest potential for new industrial, commercial and office development'.[70] And, as Darke makes clear, this was by no means a decision reached *after* careful ministerial consideration of the evidence presented at the 'Examination'. On the contrary, he suggests, it was evident *during* the 'Examination' that the proceedings were being 'managed' in such a way as to discredit the local politicians' case: 'An overall conclusion from observation of the Examination and subsequent discussions is that the debate was carefully managed and controlled, with an intention of undermining the credibility of key policies in the Structure Plan'.[71]

Since it is held 'in public', this statutory 'Examination' of structure plans appears at first glance to constitute an interesting exception to the general tendency discussed in this book for political matters to be transformed into administrative ones, and resolved by experts.[72] In fact, however, it is nothing of the kind. The right to be heard at this type of public enquiry is by invitation only, and invitations are extended only to recognized interest groups. Even more crucially, the policies proposed are discussed purely at a supposedly 'technical' level, with no analysis of their true political, social or economic significance; as Bristow and Cross put it, the Examination is a 'formalized discussion between professionals'.[73] The Royal Town Planning Institute itself, however, and much to its credit, has suggested that this pattern be abolished, and that any citizen should have the right not merely to forward objections to structure plans before the 'Examination' (as at prsent), but to be heard at the Examination in Public itself.

The *third* sphere in which it was suggested that corporatist traits may be present in town and country planning is in the relationship of the planning profession itself to the state. By this, I refer not so much to the role of the planners as agents of the state, for this has already been mentioned, but rather to their 'converse' roles, both as the professional element within a propagandist-professional pressure group which urges 'planning', and as a client group, dependent upon the state for employment. Before we can go on to look at these matters, however, we first need to say something about planning as a profession.

The nature of what we might call the 'twentieth-century' bureaucratized public service professions, such as teaching, social work and town planning, is fundamentally different from that of what we might call the 'old' or 'traditional' professions, such as law or medicine. So great is this difference, in fact, that to use the same word, 'profession', to describe both groups, seems positively misleading. And of course, this usage was *intended* to mislead. It was in a bid to obtain for themselves the same kind of power and status in society as the older professions enjoyed that these newer occupational groups adopted this title of 'profession'. As virtually all commentators agree, however, the bid largely failed. The newer, bureaucratic, professions have not obtained the key privilege enjoyed by the traditional professions, that of controlling the terms upon which their services are performed. Because the traditional professions were already very powerful forces in society even before the emergence of the welfare state, governments intent on achieving social redistribution have been able to oblige them to serve their political ends only to a limited extent, and with difficulty, and most significantly, on those professions' own terms. Doctors, for example, have strongly and successfully resisted all attempts to make them mere employees of the state, and in effect remain private entrepreneurs, who will provide 'welfare' if they must, but then in effect send in their accounts in the traditional way.[74] The new bureaucratic professions, in stark contrast, do not resist the extension of state power in this way, for they have no choice but to be public employees. On the contrary, they generally welcome the extension of state power, for it is the only source of such power as they themselves possess; indeed, these occupational groups owe their very existence to the extension of the power of the state.

One writer sums up all this as it relates to planners by saying that planners are 'one of a number of groups which have attempted to emulate the trappings of professionalism, mistaking the control over education, credentials, codes of practice and so on for the substance of occupational self-control.[75]

It is this perception—that certain newer occupational groups have largely failed in their attempts to achieve for themselves power in society equivalent to that of the older professions—which seems to have been largely responsible for what is in effect a major reorientation within that branch of sociology which concerns itself with professions and occupations. Until comparatively recently, sociologists working in this area were apparently content to take the ideology of professionalism at face value. They thus explained the relatively high status of the professions both in terms of 'trait theory' (that is, their members' supposed possession of unique knowledge and qualities), and in terms of 'functional theory' (their supposedly carrying out key functions in society). More recently, however, sociologists have instead begun to concentrate far more on the *mechanisms* whereby certain occupational groups have been able to persuade the rest of society both that they had unique knowledge and that they performed key functions, and on the ways in which they *obtain* their monopolies over certain knowledge and certain positions.

Thus, they have identified these successful claims to high status simply as the achievement of monopoly over social and economic opportunities, and have used the concept of 'social closure' to explain the way in which such successful occupational groups have been able to deny such opportunities to others.[76]

If we adopt this latter approach, then, we see that *all* occupational groups achieve power, status and independence from outside control *to varying degrees,* and that they are able to operate 'social closure' against others, also, to varying degrees. The concept of professionalism is now seen to have relatively little utility, for there is nothing which in analytical terms distinguishes a so-called profession from other occupations. In thus concentrating on the use of power, however, it is important that we do not overlook the role of knowledge, for the thesis that government and administration 'ought' to rest on knowledge is at the heart of the argument of the present book.[77]

It is difficult, of course, for the observer to gauge the extent to which the claim of any occupational group to possess specialized knowledge or skills is in fact genuine. Certain writers, however, have noted that in practice, such claims refer variously to two rather dissimilar types of 'knowledge'. On the one hand, an occupational group may claim what we can term 'specific' knowledge, by which is meant factual knowledge of particular matters, and causal knowledge of how specific states of affairs can be produced. On the other hand, it is especially characteristic of relatively high-status groups, having or aspiring to 'professional' standing, to claim possession of what we may call 'diffuse' knowledge. By this is meant such things as the claim to have particular capacities of 'judgment', to have a particularly valuable and unique 'perspective' on things, to be uniquely fitted for certain high-status roles by virtue of 'wide experience', and so on.[78] One of the ironies of occupational stratification in modern society is that as knowledge in the first of these senses has been enlarged, claims to status have become increasingly based on the supposed possession of knowledge in the second, 'diffuse', sense. The reasons for what we may thus characterize as a 'retreat into vagueness' are, however, fairly obvious. In the modern world, knowledge cannot be property. Science is public, and if specific knowledge *is* obtained as to how particular states of affairs can be caused, it is public knowledge. To a perhaps surprisingly and arguably alarmingly great extent, therefore, claims to high status advanced by such occupational groups as planners are *not* based on demonstration of exact knowledge, but on supposed possession of certain rather vague capacities and qualities.

How, in a world supposedly the very embodiment of science and rationality, can 'social closure' be made to work when it is based on such vague claims? One possible answer is in sociological terms. As members of these 'new' professions, we are socialized in such a way that we can only apparently *see* these vague and yet supposedly crucial qualities in those who unmistakably share the presuppositions of our professional subculture, who speak its language, and who evince belief in its values. That others find our professional ideas intellectually woolly is not, as one might think, a problem. On the contrary, it is an advantage. It is one of the grounds on which we can exercise 'closure' against them, and thus maintain our monopoly.

And, moreover, with good conscience; the very fact that such outsiders criticize our way of thinking is evidence that they lack the qualities which have earned for us the positions which we enjoy.

For if these new bureaucratized professions have failed in their bid to achieve the same power and status as the older professions, the fact remains that they have nevertheless achieved power and status far in excess of (for example) the manual working class. In aggregate terms, too, they are a significant and increasingly large group in society; planners, it can be argued, form only a relatively small proportion of what is, in effect, a 'new class'. In thus identifying the bureaucratized salariat as a 'new class', however, we run up against the more dogmatic variants of Marxist theory, insisting as they do that it is only on the basis of the ownership or the non-ownership of the means of production that classes can be identified.[79] Fortunately, however, a certain theoretical convergence can be discerned. More sophisticated Marxists are now quite willing to accept that such clearly identifiable groups within the occupational structure do indeed merit analysis in their own right.[80] The non-Marxists, for their part, have as noted abandoned their acceptance of the professions' own ideological claim, that there is some intrinsic difference between the knowledge base and the social role of professions and those of other occupations.

Having now said a little about the way in which the newer, 'bureaucratic' professions are discussed in present-day sociology, we are ready to look at the relationship between the planning profession and the state, and to consider reasons for viewing this relationship as incipiently corporatist.

One writer who throws some light on these matters is Gould.[81] Gould suggests that in practice, the main benefits of the welfare state go not to the working class (for whom, arguably, they were originally primarily intended), but rather to the middle class in general and to the state-employed section of the middle class in particular. The latter, as we know, has grown rapidly in number, and as noted does indeed enjoy a degree of privilege and even of power. To justify its new-found position, it has evolved a legitimating ideology, and this, Gould suggests, rests to a large extent on portraying the power both of big business on the one hand, and of the trade unions on the other, as excessive:

> Working class organizers have reified capital as the enemy. The ruling class blame the workers for wage inflation, low productivity, welfare dependency and rising crime. Capital sees the salaried middle class as being in its service, the workers see them as parasitic pen pushers. The salaried middle class itself sees a world dominated by big business and manual trade unions.[82]

This ideology, Gould suggests, is used by the salaried middle class to justify on the one hand its claims to be allowed to regulate the excesses of the private sector, and on the other hand its demands that the growth of the supposedly already excessive privileges of the working class should be resisted:

> With the support of the working class on the one hand [the salaried middle class] has fought for the expansion of public expenditure and the growth of taxation. It has used State power to restrict, regulate and direct the private sector. With the support

of capital on the other, it has ensured that the benefits accruing to the working class have been minimal and subject to control and supervision. This has enabled the salaried middle class to distribute substantial benefits to its own members through fiscal and social policies and, most importantly, secure well-paid careers in State bureaucracies.[83]

Such attitudes towards the less privileged are, of course, well known from (for example) discussions of the way in which officials regard welfare claimants. But could they equally explain the behaviour of professional planners? Could they, for example, explain why planners can at one and the same time be reluctant to see planning as a means of achieving radical social redistribution, and yet, paradoxically, urge planning as a means of curbing the potentially socially irresponsible behaviour of powerful big developers?

The weakness in most characterizations of corporatism, Gould suggests[84] is that they fail to ask whose interests it serves; on this point he himself advances an unequivocal answer: 'The corporate State is based upon the values and pursues the goals and interests of the salaried middle class'[85] . . . 'I think there is a strong case for arguing that corporatism is an advanced industrial system in which the balance of power within the State shifts from capital to the salaried middle class'.[86] The first of these propositions seems credible, and I shall take it up and attempt to argue it in the particular case of 'planning'. The second, by contrast, seems to go beyond the available evidence. And elsewhere in the same paper, Gould appears to accept this. It is in fact not clear, he suggests, whether it is capital or the salaried middle class which has gained the most; all that *is* clear, is that it is not the working class which has gained from the trend towards corporatism.

Clear empirical evidence that planners are among the main beneficiaries of planning is arguably lacking, but in the related field of housing policy there is a recent and very thorough study by Dunleavy, which both investigates the part played by local government professionals as opposed to that played by other interest groups, and also goes some way towards explaining this in class terms.[87] One might add, however, that Dunleavy's research does not seem to lend much support to Gould's second propositions of a transfer of power from capital to the salaried middle class. On the contrary, Dunleavy's findings suggest that the large-scale production of high-rise council housing promoted the interests *both* of capital, and of the local government professionals, at the expense of the working class. The various local Labour Party establishments, it seems, were apparently rather powerless to prevent this high-rise housing, even though it was perfectly obvious to them that it did not reflect the preferences of the vast majority of their own supporters. Or perhaps, one might say, these Labour ruling groups had themselves been 'captured', or had otherwise become under the influence of, their professional advisers. As Rosenberg puts it, commenting on Dunleavy's findings, 'Paradoxically the decline of the traditional right-wing Labour Party machines in cities like Liverpool emphasizes the weakness of working class representation and the rise to Labour Party power of members of the State service class'.[88]

That planners benefit from the existence of the planning system and have a material interest in the enlargement of its scope is of course at a certain level of analysis no more than obvious. Until we have similar studies, however, analysing the operations of the planning system in the way in which Dunleavy has analysed those of the public housing system, we clearly do not know exactly how, or in what ways, or to what extent, the planning system promotes the interests and the values of planners. That it gives them work, for example, might need to be weighed against the fact that this work is frustrating, or undervalued, or that it serves to conceal more than it reveals. Plain accounts of what the members of any occupational group actually do, in their daily lives, of the internal politics of their occupation, and so on, tend always to be socially 'liberating', for they lead us to see the structure of society afresh, in a new light.[89]

The *fourth* way in which I suggested that a tendency to corporatism is apparent in planning, however, is at the level of values. And here, of course, we should remember that one of the functions of values is to promote material interests. There is a striking similarity, I would suggest, between the values of corporatism and those of the planning profession. Indeed, the philosophy of corporatism seems tailor-made to suit the interests of managers, experts, planners and technocrats of all kinds, who as a group tend almost instinctively to believe that the best way to run a society is that people of their own sort should get together and work out the objectively best or technically best way of doing things, without political interference. But what exactly are these similarities of value?

First, we can note, both corporatist thought and planning thought are *technicist*. Saint-Simon, generally regarded as one of the forerunners of corporatism, is equally one of the forerunners of technocracy, and indeed of 'planning'. Neither corporatist thought nor planning thought has much time for politics in general, and even less for discussion in terms of political values. Both tend, rather, to the positivist assumption that there is some objectively best possible way of doing things, and that experts can be relied upon to find it.

Secondly, both corporatist thought and planning thought are *holist*. The early advocates of corporatism, as we saw, urged it as an antidote to what they regarded as the dangerously excessive individualism and normlessness set afoot by the Enlightenment. To reinforce their view that society ought to be understood and indeed ought to become a smoothly functioning organic unity, they denied the significance and even the existence of divisions of interest based on class. Present-day corporatism, though it is based on expediency rather than on ideology, and makes little pretence to be a coherent social philosophy, nevertheless still reveals this unstated assumption that cooperation is normal, and conflict pathological. Planners, too, tend to these same consensus, holist and organicist assumptions, and tend to deny the value of conflicts of interest and ideas; often, just as in corporatist thought, they rely on organic analogy to explain both cities and society itself.[90] They, too, often tend to assume that where conflict *does* occur, it is pathological, and that it can be resolved by demonstrating this to those involved.

This mistrust of conflict is arguably the most fundamental idea in both corporatist thought and planning thought, and in itself goes a long way towards explaining the planners' failure to produce 'relevant knowledge'. Corporatist thought advocated that one professional body should represent all those who worked within any given field. Professionals in general seem to follow corporatist thought here, and planners are no exception. All who take professionalism as their occupational model tend to attempt to concentrate all power and influence within a single professional body, to attempt to demarcate for it as wide an area of competence as possible, to prevent others from entering it, to claim the right to sole authoritative pronouncement within this field, to attempt to ensure that all who work within the defined field become members of the designated professional body, and that they do not develop allegiances to other bodies, and so on.

This denial of the value of a plurality of competing centres of power and influence seems likely in itself to inhibit the growth of knowledge. Indeed, the intellectually stifling effect of this assumption that a single body can accredit and speak for all those who work in a given field seems too obvious to require elaboration. In a society based on such assumptions and such institutional arrangements, the validity of any idea derives from the fact that it is uttered by a duly licensed member of a duly licensed self-perpetuating monopolistic 'guild'. In a liberal society, by contrast, the validity of an idea derives from its perceived success, in open competition with other ideas.[91]

This mistrust of conflict, however, common to both corporatist thought and planning thought, can also be seen in the economic sphere. A corporatist society, quite obviously, is one in which economic competition is restricted, and economic activity subordinated to social and political considerations. Pahl and Winkler discuss this corporatist distaste for economic competition, ascribing it to a predilection for 'order'. 'Order', they suggest, implies 'elimination of the "anarchy" of the market in all its forms'.[92] Instead of the uncertainty and risks inherent in a free market, business and industry in a corporatist system would have the prices of materials and products guaranteed, and would have binding agreements with labour. (The 'social contract' is of course a corporatist idea). In the particular sphere of land and property development, this would seem to mean that the state should eliminate all uncertainties as to the uses to which other nearby land can be put, that it should similarly eliminate all uncertainties concerning such things as future population distribution, provision of services, and so on, thus eliminating developers' risks, and guaranteeing the profitability of their schemes. And these, of course, are exactly the kinds of things which planning attempts to do.

## 5.   Summary and conclusions

In this chapter I have contrasted the kind of public policy-making which arises out of what I have summed up as 'the institutions of belief' with the kind which seems possible under 'institutionalized scepticism'. If British town and country planning is to achieve either intellectual credibility or real political support, (as opposed to mere political acquiescence), then there must be a move towards the freer, more open and more pluralistic institutional and intellectual climate which I have characterized as 'institutionalized scepticism'; this is the argument I have advanced.

The problem is not merely however that the existing overreliance on and faith in professional judgment leads to insufficient public challenge and debate. It goes beyond this, in that the rather intellectually closed climate produced by the professionalization of planning has led to the emergence of ways of thinking and ways of formulating policies and of reaching day-to-day decisions which are recognizable as distinctively if incipiently corporatist in nature.

The forces conducive to the emergence of incipient corporatism seem very strong. On the one hand, government is almost inevitably tempted by its combination of low political cost and high political reward. By shifting the resolution of sensitive issues out of the glare of parliamentary and public debate, and allowing them instead to be resolved on a day-to-day basis at the expert level between the representatives of the property developers and the planning profession, government is able to claim that the public interest 'is' being safeguarded, though without the inconvenience of having to explain quite how this is being achieved. On the other hand, these corporatist ways of doing things have clear attractions both for the developers and for the planners who ostensibly control and regulate their activities. Such arrangements, clearly, both increase the ability of both these groups to order things to their mutual convenience without undue political interference, and increase their own power. As Wilding[93] puts it, summing up all these temptations and attractions and the bargains which flow out of them in a single neat phrase, 'Ruling interests want—and need—the world to see planners as important'.

In the economic sphere, what we might call 'the corporatist bargain' means that in exchange for controlling prices, wages and the potentially politically disruptive behaviour of their members, industry and the unions are given a share in government. In the ideological sphere, this 'corporatist bargain' means that in exchange for portraying existing social, political and economic arrangements as reasonably fair and equitable and as therefore legitimate, professions such as teaching, social work and town planning are given a modicum of perceived power and status. In the particular case of town planners, this means that in exchange for economic security and an official definition of their role as 'important', the planners are expected to create the impression that the property industry *is* regulated, that the worst of its potentially anti social excesses *are* kept in check, and that all land is put to its socially best use, rather than that which maximizes private profit or promotes sectional interests.

'Corporatist bargains', however, may impose costs on other groups in society, which are not so fortunate as to be 'incorporated' or accorded privileged access. On the one hand (though this is a matter not pursued in this book), they seem likely to lead to a shift in the balance of power in society, away from the political parties, Parliament, consumers, voters, employees and environmentalists, and towards producer interests and the private and public sector managerialist elite. On the other hand, they lead to an increasing lack of transparency and clarity in the formulation, presentation and implementation of public policy. The incipiently corporatist working relationships between officials and developers described above seem almost expressly designed to lead to a fudging of the issues, to the creation of an intellectually confused manageralist consensus, in which 'getting things done' comes to seem more important than the effects of doing them, and in which the planners in particular come to place more importance on the psychological rewards of being personally involved in the decision-making processes of the property development industry than on clarifying the purpose of that involvement. Both corporatist assumptions and the dominant value system of society deny the necessity and the desirability of conflict, both of material interests and in the sphere of political ideologies. In such a climate, it seems unlikely that those who ostensibly control the developers will have any great incentive to clarify either what is at stake in material terms or the political ideas which in fact lie behind their own opportunity to make a living out of supposedly exerting this 'control'. On the contrary, their primary concern seems likely to be that of demonstrating their ability to 'work with others', and to harmonize the activities of all those sectional interests which *do* have sufficient power to make successful demands for privileged access.

I have said that these incipiently corporatist taken-for-granted assumptions and institutional arrangements discourage clear thought about planning in general. In fact, however, they lead to the obscuring of thought about two quite distinct matters. On the one hand, they discourage clear thought about the *political values* which planning is meant to promote. On the other hand they discourage clear analysis of the *redistributive mechanisms* through which it might promote these political values. These two matters will be the concerns of the next two chapters.

# 5 How the growth of theoretical knowledge is inhibited

The insubstantial nature of planning utterances is in large measure the consequence of the fact that in many of the subjects (and they are legion) on which planners pronounce there is simply no such thing as an objective body of knowledge allied to a coherent theory which can be used as a basis for rational decision making
J.G. Davies, *The Evangelistic Bureaucrat*

## 1.  Introduction

This chapter is concerned with the theory of planning. By this is meant the attempt to explain why specific policies and decisions have the effects they have. Chapter 6 will be concerned with the philosophy of planning, by which is meant discussion of the desirability of these various effects, in terms of social and political values.[1] There is no 'right' order in which to place these two chapters. It is research into the causal links between policies and outcomes which, by pointing to inefficiences, inequities or other perceived problems, provides the best basis for informed political debate. It is political debate, conversely, which provides the best source of hypotheses for research.

The main aim of this chapter is to explain why it is that the theory of planning remains undeveloped. First, however, I try to give some idea as to what kind of knowledge *would* constitute an intellectually credible theoretical basis for the practice of planning; before one tries to explain why something is missing, after all, one must say *what* it is that one misses. My argument is that the obvious starting point, if we wish to explain planning in theoretical terms, lies in study of the physical environment itself. In the first part of the chapter, therefore, I try to identify those 'features in the scene' which might reasonably be seen as constituting problems for society, and as therefore justifying intervention. In the second part of the chapter, I set out a further list of 'justifications for intervention', this time in terms of economic theory. I shall not, however, attempt to construct a 'theory of town and country planning'. In part, this is because thought on the matter is so undeveloped, and the most one can do, therefore, is to suggest where such a theory might be found. But it is also because I do not believe there could be such a theory, but only theories explaining specific interventions. It is the third, and final, section of this chapter which I see as the most important, for in it, I try to suggest *why* it is that the theoretical understanding of this area of public policy is so poorly developed.

If we think the main purpose of the planning system is merely to create the public *impression* that the worst anti-social excesses of the property developers are being redressed, of course, then arguably we need no theory. All we then need is to show strong concern, and much 'busyness'.

## 2.  The logical starting point: 'problems in the scene'

The logical and obvious starting point, I would argue, if we *do* think theoretical understanding is necessary, is in the physical environment itself. 'Why are society's spatial arrangements are as they are', I would suggest, is the question with which we ought to begin, if we wish to think about ways in which governmental action might modify these things. And since 'planning' has presumably already played some part in shaping these spatial patterns, there is also another obvious question: How, and why, has planning already modified the processes whereby society's spatial arrangements are shaped? The available evidence, on this last, of course, was considered in Chapter 3.

Any attempt to identify those 'features in the scene' which justify the existence of planning powers must concentrate on those things which the writer thinks are *generally* seen as unsatisfactory. It will therefore probably focus upon whatever in our physical surroundings is widely perceived as squalid, inequitable, inefficient or wasteful—on dereliction and decay, pollution, gross environmental inequalities, 'private affluence and public squalor', and so on. What we see as being so intolerable as to merit the expenditure of public resources, however, in a world in which the calls on these resources are almost unlimited, must obviously be determined by our social and political values. I have therefore tried to identify those things which would probably be seen as problems by those who would give the physical environment a 'reasonable' degree of priority—the obvious things, we might say. I have also included in the list what I take to be among the main institutional forces, lying behind these perceived problems. But again, I have included only those institutional factors which are obvious, and well-known.

### (a)  Regional disparities
The fundamental problem here is that of knowing whether social welfare would be enhanced more by 'going with' migrations of profit-seeking capital, or by seeking a more even spread of economic activity over the national territory as a whole. Regional policy has not been discussed in this book, on the grounds that despite considering themselves to be competent in this field, members of the Royal Town

Planning Institute are not generally employed within it. Yet concern at the plight of the peripheral regions in the 1930s and 1940s was one of the mainsprings of the social movement out of which statutory town planning developed, and the problems caused by the similar migration of capital out of the inner areas of the big cities have recently attracted wide concern, even, for example, from the Church of England.[2] Whether we are actually any nearer than we were at the time of 'Barlow' to knowing whether in specific cases it is better to 'go along with' such migrations of capital or to seek to stem them, I do not know. The fact is, however, that since the Barlow Report, government has acted *as if* the answer to this question had been found; albeit often half-heartedly, it has sought to secure a geographically more even spread of economic activity. That the problems posed here go far beyond the competence of the planning profession, however, seems obvious.

### (b)  Spatial class segregation

Quite apart from all the other kinds of inequality in society, there is environmental inequality; the various social classes tend to live in isolation from each other, in areas of very different environmental standards. To those who believe in greater social equality, then, the reduction of spatial class segregation seems clearly desirable. But beyond this, there is the fact that this environmental segregation and inequality is both cause and consequence of other types of inequality. To live in a physically run-down area among people who tend mostly to be as deprived as oneself, for example, can in itself make it more likely that one will be educationally, socially and culturally underprivileged, and thus, for example, find it more difficult to find satisfactory employment.

One of the causes of spatial class segregation lies, as already noted, in the migration of profit-seeking capital. A second cause lies in status competition; both in the areas which capital finds attractive and in those which it deems less profitable, there are hierarchical systems of residential areas, of differing perceived desirability. A third cause of social segregation, however, at least in Britain, lies as we saw in Chapter 3 in the planning system itself. But whatever the relative importance of the various causes, the problems to which it gives rise are generally agreed. In addition to those already mentioned, there is the fact that in the poorer areas the fiscal base declines as the need for social expenditure increases.

At the bottom of this status hierarchy, the very poorest sections of society tend to be 'contained' within areas, usually of public housing, which can only be described as slums, sinks, or ghettos. Frequently, though by no means always, these consist of flats, sometimes system-built, and sometimes multi-storey, some of the worst areas consisting of the high-rise developments of the 1960s and early 1970s. Within some of the most deprived areas, the sense of hopelessness and alienation from society is apparently so great that it even expresses itself at times in the form of violence and rioting. As a 'policy phenomenon', it may be argued, the high-rise boom is no longer of crucial interest, for once the pressure mounted against it, the whole high-rise machine stopped dead in its tracks, socially perceived and officially defined simply as a 'mistake'. This view of things could, however, itself be mistaken. The main lesson to be learned, perhaps, is that the same combination of professional and political ambition, irrational subsidy and corporatist governmental facilitation of private profit could lead to *other* 'mistakes', to the production of *other* types of physical milieu which are out of line with popular aspirations. The physical form itself may be relatively unimportant. Stigma may be attached to housing of any physical form, simply *because* it is provided by the state to house the least fortunate.[3] The planners' usual response, when asked to discuss the high-rise estates, is instructive. They were created not by the local authority planning departments, they point out, but by the housing departments. Yet the planning system is officially explained as existing in order, first, to ensure that everything is built in the right place, and second, to ensure that development which would be socially undesirable is not built at all. And these two forms of control, supposedly, are exerted over development proposals of the public and private sectors alike.[4]

Beyond the relatively limited areas in which conditions are at their very worst, however, there are very extensive areas of urban Britain, and especially, perhaps, areas of council housing, in which such problems as unemployment, juvenile delinquency and petty crime are sufficiently widespread to be reflected in the physical fabric, in the form of decay, dereliction, vandalism and neglect.

The suburbanization of those who can afford to become owner-occupiers, meanwhile, both continues apace and thereby contributes to the problems of the areas already discussed. A particular form of suburbanization prevalent at the present time, that involving large-scale projects constructed by the self-styled 'volume builders', may usefully be taken as an example. There seems little doubt that the government is at present actively involved in encouraging this type of suburbanization, operating through markedly corporatist understandings with a relatively small number of large construction firms.[5] Often, apparently, these are the same firms which built the high-rise council estates discussed above. One of the disturbing things about such arrangements lies in the power of these large firms to determine the form and location of development in ways which suit their own purposes, just as they did in the case of the high-rise council housing; the 'privileged access' to Whitehall which is afforded them seems often to mean that other interests, such as those of consumers, environmentalists and even the local planning authorities themselves, concerned to safeguard green belt or to co-ordinate development with transport and other facilities, get scant attention. This encouragement of producer interests is effected by such means as involving them in 'land-availability studies', which then become the basis of central government policy, by encouraging the Department of the Environment to modify local planning authorities' structure plans, by allowing 'appeals' against these authorities' refusals of planning permission, and so on.

Though the construction of mass-produced suburbs may in quantitative terms be contributing very significantly to the progressive impoverishment of the inner cities and other areas of deprivation, however, such suburbs are themselves far from being the areas of greatest privilege. These latter, we may define as including extensive rural (or ex-urban) tracts preserved as national parks, 'areas of outstanding natural beauty', and green belts, as well as urban areas protected on 'townscape' or 'heritage' grounds because they contain buildings of architectural or cultural interest, and so on. It is overwhelmingly within such areas, whether 'rural' or urban, that the more affluent members of the middle classes seek to make their homes, or to find second homes, or places to which to retire. It is also within these areas, presumably, that domestic property values will rise most quickly. The faster the rate of spatial class segregation, the more likely it is that these values will be spatially concentrated. Properties in desirable areas will display faster than average rates of capital appreciation, while those in the less desirable areas will have lower than average, and in some cases even negative, ones. It is therefore probably significant that the Secretary of State for the Environment in the Conservative government of 1979 stated quite early in his term of office that he saw the protection of such privileged areas as one of the main objectives of planning.[6] As a proportion of the total land area of Britain, the rural areas in question are quite large. The similarly protected urban areas, of course, are relatively small, but it is likely that similar levels of planning protection are given to socially desirable urban areas in general, and not only to those with the benefit of special statutory designation.

Finally, in this brief review of the socio-spatial pattern, one might mention the new towns, for these constitute virtually the only significant exception to the general trend. They are arguably the only significant 'feature in the scene' which *does* reflect the ideals and aspirations of the planning movement. Though in the peripheral regions they have suffered unemployment, one could say that in the South-East at least (where most of them are situated) they stand as 'islands', reflecting in their physical form many of the ideals of the social democratic ethos of the early post-war years. Nor are these 'islands' insignificant in the quantitative sense. By 1980, when the new towns programme was wound down, they occupied only 103,616 hectares, but accommodated just over 2 million people, or about 4 per cent of the total population.[7] It is significant, however, that this was not achieved by planning powers. It results rather from the fact that as 'landlords', the development corporations could control the whole social and physical fabric of their towns, and that virtually alone among public sector developers they enjoyed the unusual privilege of being empowered to acquire land at existing use rather than market value.[8]

*(c)  Pollution, dereliction, vandalism, and general environmental degradation*
The most significant point about all these things, one might suggest, is that they tend to be the experience of the poor rather than of the affluent. Spatially, they are probably rather highly correlated with unemployment and other social problems. It would be quite unfair to suggest, however, that planners have shown any lack of concern for these problems, or indeed for any other of the problems discussed here. But they have not *theorized* them, and it is for this reason that we can doubt their practical capacity to deal with them.

*(d)   The anomaly of agriculture*

In principle, the whole surface area of the country is 'planned'. In reality, however, some 80 per cent of it is not subject to planning control at all. Yet while being free of planning *control*, agriculture certainly gets planning *protection*. Indeed, it would be no exaggeration to say that a very large proportion of the total effort put into planning since the end of the Second World War has been devoted to protecting agriculture against the encroachments of other land uses, on the mistaken assumption that the farmers themselves would be the best guardians of the traditional English landscape. The political power of the agricultural lobby is attested by the fact that despite over-production and growing surpluses on the one hand, and despite pressures from planners and others for more ecologically sensitive practices on the other, farmers still contrive to receive very considerable subsidies for increasing and intensifying production, bringing marginal land into cultivation, destroying hedgerows, copses, and other wildlife habitats, and so on. If the intensification of agriculture use of land were subject to planning control, and if the betterment value thus created were taxed even at relatively low rates, this might both discourage some of the more economically questionable and ecologically damaging forms of production, and at the same time provide funds out of which, for example, more adequate recreational facilities in the countryside could be provided. At present, the position seems, to put it as mildly as possible, rather biased. Dawson[9], for example, points out that the total aid given to agriculture in 1981 was forty times greater than the budget of all the government-funded and independent conservation agencies put together. Shoard[10] estimates on the basis of 1979 figures that each farmer in Britain was receiving on average a free handout from the state of about £8,400 per annum. This money might be better spent on helping to develop agriculture in hungry Third World countries.[11]

*(e)   Social competitiveness*

With this fifth factor, I move on from the major physical 'features in the scene' which seem to constitute problems for society, to the social and economic forces which seem to lie behind these physical patterns. Whether our social and political values cause us to emphasize the extent to which the market economy tends to produce status-striving, or whether by contrast we have values which lead us to believe that the market merely responds to 'human nature', the fact is that a very large proportion of all we see, when we examine our physical milieu, is a reflection of people's desire to give private or corporate expression to their status. 'Planners', who by tradition seek decent and even gracious surroundings for all, are faced with the problem that in such a socially competitive system it becomes literally impossible for all types of physical milieu to symbolize decency and graciousness. Some, however decent they may be in objective terms, must inevitably serve as social symbols of various degrees of relative failure, simply because the less successful live within them, and they will therefore tend to be neither valued nor treated with care.

Much environmental degradation and many types of economic inefficiency, therefore, are not caused by any failures of understanding or of organization, which might be remedied, but by the fundamentally competitive nature of society itself. Much of the housing stock, for example, and especially public sector and private rental housing, deteriorates far faster than it need do, as a result of the social stigmatization of areas as undesirable. Housing choice is unnecessarily curtailed, too, by status factors. In most provincial cities, for example, one is virtually limited to the suburbs if one wishes to buy a house, even though vacant land and residential areas capable of redevelopment or rehabilitation exist near the city centres. Or, if one does buy in the 'inner city', one risks one's capital, due to this social definition of these areas as undesirable. Again, private cars are used for commuting in ways which are generally accepted to be wasteful, dangerous and inefficient, and which impose significant negative externalities on inner-city residents, in large part because to travel by public transport is seen as socially stigmatizing. The resulting deterioration in the efficiency and economic viability of public transport has created a new class of 'transport poor'[12] 'Social competitiveness', I would suggest, is a phenomenon which any intellectually credible theory of planning would have to take into account.

*(f)  The commodification of environment*
Increasingly, the pattern of development reflects the financial institutions' search for inflation-proof investments, rather than the needs of users for homes, work-places or whatever. Until about the time of the Second World War, property development was generally carried out by a myriad of small entrepreneurs, or by the industrial and commercial firms which themselves needed the accommodation in question. Since the war, it has become increasingly the province of large-scale developers, backed by financial institutions operating at national level, and especially, of course, the pension funds and insurance funds. This means that to some extent at least, money goes into property development not so much in response to 'demand', but rather in response to relatively poor prospects of profit and capital appreciation elsewhere (and especially, of course, in manufacturing industry). Though this might conceivably result merely in property prices being higher than they would otherwise be, it seems likely that it also significantly affects the form, scale, timing and location of development, for the financial institutions not only have very considerable economic power, but also have 'preferences'. Their preferences, in fact, since they see property as something which can be 'quoted' and traded in, are for physical and thus visual standardization, for this means that any 'investment' can be readily compared in financial terms with any other.[13]

The creation of the physical environment, then, is increasingly a by-product of the financial institutions' search for profit, rather than being an economic activity in its own right. Nor is this true of the built environment alone. The agricultural landscape, too, is increasingly a reflection of the fact that it is used as a repository for finance capital, rather than being simply the workplace of farmers. The economic, social and political effects of these changes seem likely to be considerable.[14] And any intellectually credible theory of land-use planning, again, would have to take them into account. Such a theory, in fact, must start out from an analysis of the structure and operations of the property industry, for this is in a real sense the 'thing planned'.

(g)   *The instability of the property sector*
One of the main 'features in the scene', when we look at the physical environment in Britain, is the extent to which the pace and scale of development is determined by what might be considered rather primitive economic processes of 'boom and bust'. The extent to which these sharp fluctuations have been caused by the repeated imposition and abolition of taxation of betterment, the extent to which they are attributable to fluctuations in the relative attractiveness of other forms of investment, and the extent to which they are due to quite other factors, are questions clearly beyond the scope of a book such as this. Few observers, however, see this feature of the property industry as desirable. One refers to the property booms of the early 1960s and 1970s as 'the biggest misdirection of resources of modern times'.[15] Most others, while using more restrained language, seem broadly to agree. It seems important to remember that these things did not occur in a free market. Rather, they occurred in a 'distorted' market, set up within a planned system of restriction of supply of land. Any intellectually credible theory of land-use planning would clearly have to address itself to the problem of explaining this relationship between planning and market forces.

(h)   *The possibility of corruption*
Few writers suggest that corruption is common in the British planning system, though some do.[16] Many economists, however, would suggest that in a system which both purports to determine land use administratively and yet which also allows developers to retain all or most of the betterment value thus created, a tendency to corruption is virtually inevitable.[17] The possibility of corruption, then, might be seen as a 'feature in the scene', requiring to be taken into account in constructing any theoretical explanation of planning. What follows is not that planners should demonstrate that corruption is not occurring. Rather, the onus would seem to be upon them to devise institutional mechanisms which remove the *causes* of the tendency to corruption.

The above, then, are some of the main 'features in the scene', so far as society's spatial arrangements are concerned. Before looking at the 'justifications for intervention' which economists have suggested, it might be useful by way of summary to briefly consider the social significance of environment in more general terms. Sociologists have often criticized planners for exaggerating the social significance of physical milieu, but these criticisms have been much misunderstood. In the main, they arose out of the planners' tendency to suppose that relatively trivial variations in design or layout could produce significant changes in social attitude and behaviour. It was often suggested, for example, that if a particular part of a new town could be made to *look* distinctive, for example by separating it from other areas by open space, by giving it some architectural unity, or by laying out footpaths in such a way that they led to common meeting points and shared facilities, this would produce a 'sense of community'.

It is not in general at such a level, however, that the social significance of the physical environment in fact lies. Rather, I would suggest, it lies at the level of the kinds of phenomenon listed above. At this level, physical milieu is certainly of social significance. A large part of the energies of many people, for example, and over a significant portion of their lives, is devoted to finding ways of moving into a 'nicer' house, in a 'nicer' area; one of the main ways in which better-than-average financial resources are in fact used (or more accurately, perhaps, invested) is in acquiring better-than-average physical and social surrounding. Nor do those who move merely buy a house. On the contrary, they 'buy' a particular local authority, with a particular rate poundage reflecting the relationship between social needs and rateable values within its own borders. They 'buy' schools, neighbours, suitable friends for their children, and a whole set of other externalities, many of which are publicly created out of taxpayers' and ratepayers' money before being thus internalized in house prices.[18] In such ways, environmental advantages and disadvantages can help to create, reinforce and perpetuate social inequalities, for they are passed on from one generation to the next; much household migration reflects parents' desire to bring up their children in 'nice' surroundings.

That physical milieu is of social significance is of course also attested by the fact that it is one of the great themes of literature, though here again we see that this significance lies in a subtle interaction between physical features and social symbolism. Another aspect of the importance of physical surroundings is seen when we remember that much of people's leisure time, too, is spent in going to look at 'places', and that much of their energy when they *cannot* look forward to a move to a more desirable area is spent in improving and embellishing the milieu which they *have* achieved, in maintaining and improving their homes and gardens (though generally, it must be said, only where these are owned by those who live in them).

The social significance of the physical environment, however, lies not only in such objective facts as profit, capital appreciation, or social exclusivity. Many of its most socially significant consequences lie in the subjective psychological states produced by its very potent visual symbolism; in brief it signals success or failure in life. There seem, too, to be marked class differences in people's relationship to their physical surroundings. The higher one's social class, apparently, the easier it is to 'use' the physical environment, exploiting physical mobility to achieve social, cultural, psychological or visual variety. The poor, conversely, tend often to be more 'trapped' within the relatively depressing surroundings in which they live and work.

Given facts such as these, we understand why it is that though both the political parties and the professional planners define planning as non-political, environmental questions and development proposals raise such strong emotions and are the subject of so much popular protest. Indeed this largely extra-parliamentary environmental protest is itself one of the major 'features in the scene' when we look at society's spatial arrangements.

What we can conclude from all this, is that governmental intervention in the land and property development process, if it were well thought out, could make a significant difference to people's lives. But to be well thought out, it would need to be based on theoretical understanding. And this, I have argued, is largely conspicuous by its absence.

## 3. Justifications for intervention

The suggestion is, then, that we can look at major 'features in the environmental scene', such as those sketched out above, and ask how people's welfare, life chances or satisfactions might be improved by governmental intervention. Clearly, however, we are not going to get very far until we are a little more specific. We shall have to identify specific situations in which welfare, life chances or satisfactions are at risk, and discover specific mechanisms through which these states of affairs might be improved. To make this argument clear, we can look at the way in which 'planning' is at present conceptualized and attempted. The existing planning system is *not* conceptualized or organized in this way, as a collection of specific types of intervention. On the contrary, it purports to be an *overall* system of control. And precisely *because* is purports to control all development, it is very difficult to see what is happening under this system. To what extent, and in what types of situation, is it planning criteria which are determining environmental outcomes? And to what extent, and in which types of situation, is it other factors, such as profitability or bureaucratic power, which are determining the outcomes? The reason why we do not know, is that planners have not identified those types of case in which they intend that the criterion of profitability should be overridden. Instead, they simply purport to control all development. This claim is clearly false, but we do not know how false it is, or in which types of situation it is more false and less false. In the existing system then, there is a strong tendency to *pseudo-planning*. By this, I mean a pattern in which control is supposedly exercised over all, but in reality is exercised very selectively, probably according to the economic and political power of those controlled. Such a system could even be said to rest on a fundamental dishonesty. In a liberal constitional state, one might suggest, it should be plainly shown in which instances, and to what extent, profitability is overridden; intervention should not only be done, but should be seen to be done.

It is possible to hypothesize, however, that it is likely to be the planning system which determines the outcome to the extent that three types of situation are present. First, this is likely to be so where the planning system has powers going far beyond its normal regulatory function, and amounting, in fact, to some type of 'positive planning'.[19] This, for example, would explain the new towns. Second, it would seem likely that planning rather than market forces determines the outcome where the planning system offers something similar to what people seek in the market, but going beyond what they feel able to afford to pay for. In this case, they will effect a substitution, 'investing' by devoting time and energy to the support of planning, rather than needing to invest in their property in a purely financial sense. This would explain much about the 'areas of privilege', for example, discussed above. Thirdly, it seems likely that planning rather than market forces will tend to determine the outcome where the developers are economically or politically weak, unorganized, or unable to mobilize support. This would cover the case of much small-scale development, and probably most 'development' which consists of improvements to their own homes by householders.

In all other cases, one might hypothesize, it will tend to be market forces, and especially the power of developers, rather than 'planning', which will determine the form of our physical surroundings. And there is a further question arising: What of those situations in which profitability and planning criteria coincide? Due to the nature of the planning system we have, we do not know where, or to what extent, such cases occur. But what we *can* say, is that to the extent that they occur, the whole system of planning control is an expensive waste of resources. A more satisfactory approach than this purported 'blanket' system of control, therefore, which it seems likely is in many cases merely pseudo-control, lies in identifying specific perceived problems, and theorizing specific forms of amelioration for them.

For what reasons, then, might government wish to intervene in the property development industry? In thinking about the 'justifications for intervention' set out below, it may seem useful to analyse them as follows. First, they differ in the extent to which they are aimed at either aiding market processes or at replacing them. Second, they differ according to whether their concern is to improve efficiency or equity (the latter being usually equated nowadays with equality).

(i)   *It may be thought desirable to control the overall level of land values.* On the one hand, high land values are *created by* planning. On the other hand, these high land values *thwart* planning, for they make it extremely expensive, if not actually impossible, to buy land for such public purposes as government-sponsored working-class housing, public open spaces or social facilities.[20] *Very* high land values, apparently, cannot be simply 'destroyed' by placing planning restrictions on the sites in question. On the fringes of the cities, the planning system gets away with allocating certain agricultural land for development and preventing the development of other agricultural land, and without paying any compensation to the owners of the latter. In the case of city-centre land, on the other hand, (and quite inconsistently), it often seems to be accepted that simply to 'destroy' land values in this way would be illegitimate. The whole question of the desirability of either raising or of lowering land values by public action seems to be not only a neglected area, relatively seldom discussed, but also shrouded in mystery. Yet it is a matter which lies at the heart of the 'theory of planning'.

Though I have above accepted the validity of the 'Uthwatt' argument that in principle, the existence of planning must have the effect of concentrating value on specific areas, and though I have suggested that this must, in principle, also have the effect of raising land values in aggregate terms, economists seem divided on this. Foster, for example, assumes that this is indeed the case, and terms this planning-induced rise in values an 'indication of inefficiency'.[21] Other economists, however, have argued strongly that planning does *not* raise land values[22] or that the question of whether it does or not simply cannot be answered, since the processes involved are so complex. What would be very valuable, therefore, is research aimed at discovering the relationship between land values and the general level of prices of other commodities in various countries, and at explaining this in terms of such factors as their systems of land taxation, their systems of planning control, and the extent to which investment funds are channelled into property rather than industry.[23] Allied to the question of whether planning raises land values is the question of whether it 'ought' to do so; in contrst to Foster, quoted above, certain economists have suggested that a planning system is efficient to the extent that it *does* raise land values.[24] One thing which *is* clear, however, is that the taxation of betterment is likely to reduce land values, at least if this is achieved by a tax or levy on unrealized betterment rather than in the form of a charge imposed when development is carried out.[25]

*(ii)    It may be considered desirable to redistribute land values.* Usually, this is seen as an unfortunate *'side-effect'* of planning, rather than as an objective of it. Ebenezer Howard, however, urged the creation of his garden cities precisely in order to transfer wealth from the urban property owning classes to the populations of his 'garden cities'. This reminds us that the achievement of such transfers, while seldom discussed nowadays, is perfectly conceivable.

*(iii)    Problems arise from the fact that land and property are used as a 'store of value'.* The fact that land and buildings are bought not only in order to develop them or for the rents which they yield, but also, as a relatively inflation-proof form of investment means that owners are often unwilling to sell, even when offered high prices. This, apparently, is one of the factors explaining for example why so much land remains vacant in inner-city areas.[26] The only way to counteract this increasing 'commodification of the physical environment', clearly, lies in separating the profits to be made out of holding land from the profits to be made by using it, or constructing buildings upon it—and confiscating the former.

*(iv)    'Ordinary' development, which is profitable, must always be serviced by non-profit-making public services.* This is probably the simplest, the oldest and the most obvious of all justifications for governmental intervention in land and property develop-ment; *some* land must be taken out of the market, to provide the rest with non-profit-making physical infrastructure and social facilities. To control the pattern of growth spatially should, in principle, minimize the cost of such infrastructure. At the present time, however, discussion of the economics of infrastructure provision is very much tied up with discussion in terms of ethics, and law, due to the growth of the practice of securing infrastructure as 'planning gain'.[27]

(v)   *Developers may be unable to assemble land.* (Or, of course, they may be perfectly *able* to do this, but may find it cheaper or more convenient to allow government to do it for them.) Compulsory purchase for the purpose of resale or lease to developers is of course particularly justifiable where 'remaining' individual owners exploit their monopoly position to hold out for unreasonably high prices.[28]

(vi)   *It may be considered that there is likely to develop a shortage of land suitable for any particular purpose, either nationally or in some particular locality.* Hitherto, the most obvious example has been agricultural land. Now, by contrast, it is widely suggested that the need is to devise policies to encourage farmers to take a significant proportion of the nation's agricultural land *out* of production.[29] That there threatens to be a shortage of land for a particular purpose *within a particular area* has also of course been used in practice as a justification for the use of planning powers. The growth of urban areas has been curbed, for example, in part because it was argued that the land thus required to be kept in agricultural use, as green belt, was needed as a recreational area for the urban populations in question.

(vii)   *Diseconomies of scale.* Advocates of planning in Britain have often used the argument that diseconomies of scale of various kinds, both in the private sector and in the provision of public services, are likely to set in if urban areas are allowed to become too large. (Whether there is an economically optimal size of settlement—Within a given type of economy? From whose point of view?), or whether it is preferable on grounds of economic efficiency to encourage the development of a supposedly natural 'hierarchy' of settlements of graduated population-size, has been a recurrent topic of discussion and research among economic geogaphers and others for many decades, as well as having been one of the favourite topics of debate among the advocates of planning.[30] Unlike some of the other justifications for intervention set out in this list, this one has, however, been used in practice. But it has been used in combination with vague aesthetic and 'social' arguments (for example, that big cities are 'overwhelming', 'anonymous', lack 'sense of community', 'feeling of neighbourhood', and so on).

(viii)   *'Stewardship', 'posterity', 'heritage', etc.* The market can respond to present demands, but hardly to future ones. Since the latter are unknown, it is a central element in the philosophy of 'stewardship' that we must act for others in accordance with our own values; this means that we must identify those things which our descendents will demand or appreciate if they are enlightened, cultured, and so on, *as we understand these terms.* Some things, however, such as the biological conditions which make human life possible at all, our descendents might appreciate whether they are cultured or not. To conserve resources by consciously determining not to maximize present profits has been a form of management traditional in the big landed estates, both urban and rural, but which is difficult for those operating on small profit margins in competitive markets, especially small firms and owner-occupier farmers; planning, therefore, is often seen as performing a valuable function in taking over this tradition.[31] The research reviewed in Chapter 3, however,[32] suggests that it was largely *because* it was so heavily imbued with this 'stewardship' philosophy that the British planning system in fact brought about a fairly massive regressive redistribution of environmental benefits. Many writers have pointed out that those who espouse concern for generations yet unborn, or for 'the environment' as an abstract value, can thereby greatly protect and enhance their own material well-being, in the here-and-now.[33] What all this seems to suggest is an urgent need to subject 'stewardship' and 'posterity' arguments to careful analysis and research.

*(ix) The existence of (or the need to provide) public goods.* 'Heritage' landscapes preserved for us by previous generations of landed proprietors with 'stewardship' philosophies often become public goods so far as those now alive are concerned. Public goods are defined as those for which it is difficult to make a charge for use (at least to users individually, and at least at the time of use), but they have the compensating feature that once they *are* supplied, it does not cost any more to supply them to additional users. It is difficult to exclude people from using them, in fact, so that 'if supplied to one they are automatically supplied to all'. They are also said (in principle) to have the characteristic that any one person's enjoyment of them does not inhibit any other person's, but this last is subject to qualification, in accordance with *how* 'pure' they are. It is true, of course, of the lighthouse (the traditional economist's illustration), or even of the TV signal (its contemporary equivalent) but less true, perhaps, of the Lake District hills. Public goods are often, though not necessarily, provided by the public sector (if in fact they are produced at all; often, or at least from the point of view of those now living, they simply *exist*, as in the case of the 'heritage' landscapes mentioned above. In such cases, however, there are usually costs involved in *maintaining* them). But certainly, it is usually fairly difficult to make a living out of providing public goods. Examples relevant to our concerns include open spaces, roads, and indeed all public places, including even such areas as national parks, and in a very real sense 'the environment' as a whole. Birds, butterflies and wild flowers, however, or the sound of the waves on a beach, might perhaps more accurately simply be described as 'free goods'. The effects of town and country planning itself, therefore (provided they *are* goods, and do not by contrast constitute a *diminution* of welfare) are public goods.

The reason why 'public goods' figure so prominently in discussions of the case for governmental intervention, of course, is that government action is often needed to ensure that they are made available. Illustrations of this include education, health and welfare services, and so on. In planning, however, we seem usually to be more concerned with problems arising out of the *maintenance* of such goods, and especially, where they are not 'pure', with preventing their being over-used. It is not impossible, of course, to convert many public goods into private ones, as the examples of education, health services and so on, make clear. Where public authorities *do* provide them as public goods, it is however usually pointed out, they will often tend to be both under-provided and over-used. This is because if *asked* to state our level of use (for example in order to be taxed to help pay for the facility in question) we are tempted to underestimate, whereas in *reality*, and because it is 'free', we are tempted to use the facility in question more than we would if we had to pay for it.[34]

*(x)  Externalities.* Externalities overlap to a large extent with public goods. A pure public good, one might say, is *nothing but* an externality effect.[35] An externality, then, is a beneficial or a harmful effect for which no payment is made to or by the person *creating* the effect in question. This does *not*, of course, mean that such beneficial or harmful effects are not reflected in market prices. The proximity of a 'good' state school, for example, with 'good' teachers, will raise house prices in a middle-class suburb. Indeed, a very large proportion of *all* land value is created by externality effects. Betterment value, for example, is an externality, even though it is in a sense 'internalized' when a developer pays an owner a price which reflects it. It would be 'internalized' in a wider sense, however, to the extent that it was instead taxed away, and returned in the form of exchequer revenue to the community which created it. The proximity of the poor may constitute a negative externality to the rich,[36] and the proximity of the rich may constitute a positive externality for the poor (if, for example, it gives them access to environment of a standard they could not otherwise afford, or opportunities for work as domestic cleaners). 'Natural' social segregation, as brought about by a combination of social norms and market processes, often internalizes such effects.[37]

Since one of the main effects of planning is to reinforce such tendencies to 'natural' zoning, therefore (not only as regards rich and poor, but in separating industry from residential areas and so on), it is often seen as having the function of internalizing externalities. Market-orientated economists, by contrast, are often concerned to stress the extent to which people might instead use market processes to internalize their externalities for themselves.[38] If objectively harmful land uses, such as noisy or polluting industrial enterprises, were obliged by law to compensate all those on whom they impose such negative externality effects, they would presumably soon devise ways of reducing these effects, or would at the very least adopt 'natural zoning', moving to sites where the smallest possible number of such payments would arise. At present, planning keeps such industries out of the more exclusive residential areas without any resort to such payments for damages, but may be less successful in keeping them out of other, less prestigious places. Residents in exclusive areas often endeavour, however, to keep out not only such 'objectively' damaging uses, but also what may be called more 'subjectively' damaging ones, such as cheaper housing. If planning controls were no longer used to afford these exclusive areas such protection, it seems likely that many such potential intruders would be able to buy their way in, for example by building at rather higher densities than are normally found in such exclusive areas. Thus, the substitution of market mechanisms for planning controls would seem likely to reduce the level of class apartheid in society. If the residents in exclusive areas were to persist in regarding these intruders as constituting a negative externality, then one might argue that a preference for reliance on market mechanisms would imply that they themselves 'buy out' the potential intruders, for example by clubbing together to outbid them. The more such payments were made, however, the more easy it would clearly become, in aggregate terms at least, for the intruders to intrude.

What this example seems to illustrate is that there may often be element of subjectivity in the evaluation of externalities, but this does not imply that socially (and legally) acceptable definitions of what constitute negative externalities cannot be devised. Biologically valid assessments are also possible; it is not unusual, for example, that the biological sciences demonstrate the harmfulness to us not merely of conditions which we tolerate, but even of ones which we believe we enjoy. That simply declaring the production of specified negative environmental externality effects illegal may make better sense than taxing them, is also important to remember. We do not, after all, attempt to reduce the incidence of burglary, vandalism or violence against the person by simply placing taxes upon these activities.

It seems important to remember that the kinds of externality effect we are concerned with in planning are often neither from a single source, nor even from an identifiable source. The gradual deterioration of a neighbourhood, for example, is caused by the constant repetition of a myriad of externality effects, each of which in itself is quite small (an unrepaired broken window, a petty act of vandalism, a noisy party, an item of litter). Many externality effects, too, are both long-distance and highly diffused. Quite apart from such spectacular examples as the pollution from Poland, East Germany, West Germany and Britain, all of which falls as acid rain on Sweden, one might mention easy motorway access both to North Wales and to the Lake District, experienced as positive externality effects by those who live around Manchester or Liverpool. What all this means is that the justification of planning in terms of its externality effects seems to run up against considerable difficulties. But it does not make it impossible—in principle.

The textbooks also usually discuss problems resulting from so-called 'neighbourhood effects' (for example the fact that from the point of view of any one house-owner in a given neighbourhood, it is rational to spend as little as possible on maintenance, in the hope that all others will spend more, and thus keep up house prices in the area). Such problems, however, since they arise mainly in connection with development rather than in the control of development, seem of less direct relevance to our consideration of the justifications for land-use planning.

(xi)   *It may seem desirable to improve the level of information of those operating in any given market.* This 'justification', of course, lies firmly within that group of reasons for intervention which aims at aiding market processes rather than at supplanting them.[39] The argument is that since the markets for land, property, and accommodation are so complex, their functioning and hence their efficiency in allocating resources and satisfying demands could be fairly readily improved simply by helping those involved to 'find their way around' more effectively. Evans[40] cites the example of the Location of Offices Bureau, which from 1963 to 1977 engaged in a publicity campaign designed to demonstrate to London office employers that they could in fact substantially reduce their costs by moving out of the city. Pearce[41] suggests that 'planning aid', since it improves the knowledge which the 'planned' have of the choices actually available to them, is also an example of this form of 'intervention'. This, however, is not an example of a market in the usual sense, but of a political market. In the latter, it is not purchasing power which decides; the rewards tend rather to go to those who are most articulate, most persuasive, who are the best organisers, who have the widest network of contacts in key positions, who can mobilize the widest basis of support—and, of course, who have the most information. Any system of bureaucratic or administrative allocation is a political market in this sense, and as we know these tend to be more socially regressive in their distributive outcomes than are economic markets; the planning system itself is a good example.

(xii) *Overuse effects may necessitate intervention.* These are often discussed by economic writers under such names as 'the tragedy of the commons', 'the problem of the free rider', 'the problem of large numbers', 'the social trap', and so on; essentially, they seem to be all part of the problem of public goods.[42] If individuals share a given facility (the classic example is the grazing rights on a common,[43] it pays each one of them to increase his use of it far beyond the point at which the benefits which others derive from the facility are impaired, but *not* to offer to pay for the maintenance, improvement or regulation of use which would ameliorate the problem. This is because the inconvenience or loss involved in continuing to use the facility, even in its increasingly overused and degraded state, is less than would be his share of the cost of such improvements. The same phenomenon is seen with roads: to go on driving to and from work on an already congested route imposes such externalities as noise, air pollution, physical danger and increased journey times on many other people, but each individual continues to do it because the cost to him is less than the cost of his share of improving the road. It is also, despite its wastefulness, slowness and inefficiency, nevertheless still usually quicker, more convenient and more status-conferring than using public transport. Such problems seem to justify the increased use of public powers to achieve the public provision of needed facilities (and/or the increased use of pricing), but these matters go far beyond the scope of town and country planning understood as the regulation of land use. In reality, of course, town and country planners in Britain are not very much involved in the political and administrative processes which determine decisions about investment in infrastructure.

(xiii) *It may be desired to effect social redistribution.* Under (ii), above, I have raised the more specific question of the desire to redistribute land values. But what of redistribution of environmental costs and benefits more generally? In recent years, it has been increasingly pointed out that planning has redistributive consequences, though Foster[44] suggests that 'there are only limited ways in which redistribution can be achieved through town planning, and this raises the question as to whether redistribution might not be better achieved by other means'. Such redistribution as *is* brought about through planning is largely unintended and often denied, or at least, not spoken of. The fact that people have unequal incomes is one of the very strongest arguments for intervention in general, and not merely in town planning, but it is essential that the argument is put plainly in value terms, and not concealed behind a mass of pretentious verbiage, or disguised as a technical matter.

Purdom, writing in 1946, is one of the few people who have actually urged redistribution through town planning in plain terms;[45] more recently, those who urged this have nearly always wrapped up their arguments in pseudo-technical discussions of 'social factors', 'human needs', and so on, making it very difficult for us to know what they are in fact saying. What Purdom suggests is that if social redistribution were to be effected specifically through land-use planning, this would imply putting more low-status or 'damaging' development in exclusive areas, and more status-conferring development in poor areas. In London, for example, it would mean reducing the area of royal and other parks in the west of the city, by putting working-class housing on them, creating large new parks in the East End, putting all new middle-class residential development on cleared sites in slum districts, and so on. Presumably complete nationalization of all land would be a precondition of such a programme; it differs from Howard's scheme for social redistribution through planning in not employing the purchase of cheap rural land as the main redistributive mechanism. In the communist countries such things as Purdom suggests are indeed the stated objectives of town planning.

That those with the lowest incomes are 'doubly penalized' if they also live in *places* which are in effect vast working-class ghettos, and that the best hope of creating a more equal society therefore lies in enabling as many people as possible, of all classes, to live in socially and occupationally-diversified moderately-sized cities, is the traditional social democratic view, reflected in the hope that the new towns would become precisely this kind of place.[46] The Marxist view, by contrast, has been that the emergence of working-class demands for social redistribution depends on the development of class consciousness, and that this can best develop in homogeneous working-class districts; such reasoning in the early post-war years led to the conclusion that instead of new towns there should be relatively high-density construction of working-class flats in the traditional working-class quarters of the cities. Such clear statements and discussions of alternative policies, together with equally clear demonstrations of the differing environmental standards of the areas in which the various classes in society *actually* live, would seem to offer the best hope of clarifying planning policy.

*(xv) It may be thought desirable, or even necessary, to stimulate the economy.* This particular 'justification for intervention', unlike a number of the previous ones, has of course been highly actual in the 1970s and 1980s. Increasingly, the assumption seems to be that the best way to stimulate production is by assisting producers, rather than by encouraging demand. Perhaps one might suggest that a precondition of clear thought on this matter is some explanation as to *why* the market needs stimulation in this particular form. It seems to have become increasingly taken for granted, for example, that property developers and industrialists can hardly be expected to ply their trades at all, unless they are constantly 'encouraged' and 'assisted' by being offered sites, provided with

infrastructure, given information and advice, and so on. Indeed, one can say that in a striking reversal of thought, traditional planning ideology has been turned on its head, the planning system now being seen as having the function of promoting the very forces which it was set up to control. Here, then, we see a rare instance of agreement between planners and their Marxist critics. But whereas the Marxists have seen support of the capitalist system as a more or less 'hidden' function of the planning system, concealed behind a facade of rhetoric about 'community', 'public interest' and so on, the planners now disarmingly identify the producers' interests with their own quite openly, and without any apparent embarrassment at all. It is difficult to know what to make of this. Like every other rationale which has been called in aid to legitimate the existence of the planning profession over the years, it is untheorized, and indeed, largely unexplained. If assistance is given selectively rather than to all firms in a given category, this constitutes a kind of corporatism. Labour politicians often urge such arrangements, however, on the grounds that in exchange for the aid given, they can extract concessions in the form of extra jobs, better working conditions and so on. One might reasonably doubt the validity of such arguments, however; it seems likely that the state will tend to be normally the weaker partner in the negotiations, and thus unable usually to extract anything of any great significance.

(xvi)   It may be considered that certain goods simply ought not to be produced, whatever the public demand for them. In the wider sphere, the traditional examples here are of course such 'goods' as drugs, alcohol and pornography; people must be protected against themselves. A classic example within our own field of concern, however, is spatial class segregation; this was a 'good' undoubtedly produced by a combination of social norms and market forces, but which the planning movement and profession saw as socially undesirable.[47] Another example is the inter-war speculative builder's semi-detached house, and the mass-produced 'amorphous' suburb in which it stood. In the early post-war years it was confidently expected in planning circles that improved public education, coupled with building licensing and a massive output of public housing to serve all social classes, would rapidly lead to the disappearance of this particular kind of 'un-social' building form. A more recent example is provided by planners' ideas about what a city centre ought to look like. If left to the forces of the market, as we know, it tends increasingly to consist of office blocks and standardized 'package deal' covered shopping centres. Planners, however, argued that it should instead be 'lively', by day and by night, with an intimate mixture of land uses; in order to prevent the driving-out of those uses which Stretton[48] charmingly characterizes as 'artistic, intellectual, unofficial, scruffy, charitable and otherwise marginal', therefore, planners urged that the power of planning be used to override the power of the market.

In all three cases, of course, the 'justification' put forward would have to be that the reduction in welfare as measured in financial terms (as in GNP figures, or in terms of developers' profits) would be more than offset by a gain in 'real' welfare.

The fact is that we may simply *dissprove*, whether in terms of ethics, aesthetics, social ideals or whatever, of what the market produces. That commercialism tends to lead to the production of buildings and physical surroundings which we consider vulgar, trashy or tasteless, which pander to the lowest common denominator in public taste, provides even today the fundamental rationale for the existence of aesthetic control in town planning. And it is this control of the design and appearance of buildings, not the promotion of socio-economic objectives, which in reality constitutes probably the largest element in the work of development control officers, in practice.[49] There is after all a long tradition, going back at least as far as J.S. Mill, of arguing that certain things are simply so dreadful that they ought not to be permitted to be produced.

(xvii)   We may believe that producers have too much power to shape public tastes, or in other ways to create market conditions which suit their own interests rather than those of consumers. The argument here is less 'paternalistic'. It rests on the assertion (or the assumption) that the public would choose more 'wisely', even in a free market, if producers had rather less institutionalized capacity to shape perceptions and preferences. It is closely associated, of course, with the idea that there is an altogether too high degree of oligopoly or even monopoly among producers, and is a theme quite strongly developed in the work of Galbraith. In our field of concern, it leads for example to the idea that large developers operating at national level should not be permitted to construct shopping centres using similar designs from one end of the country to the other. It also, of course, relates to the tendency to monopoly in land ownership.[50]

At this point, having mentioned some of the 'justifications', it may be helpful to set out a summary of the argument thus far. The object, it will be remembered, is to explain why the practice of planning rests on no credible theoretical basis. First, however, it has seemed necessary to give some idea, at least, as to where such a theoretical basis might be found. In the first section of this chapter, therefore, I have looked at those features of the physical environment itself which are widely perceived as unsatisfactory, on the assumption that the first step in formulating a corrective measure lies in identifying the state of affairs which we wish to correct. In Section 2, I have gone on to look at the kinds of justification for intervention in this sphere which can be found in the literature of economics. The two lists stand in uneasy relationship to each other, however. The economists' 'justifications', quite obviously, themselves specify the states of affairs, perceived as unsatisfactory, which they offer to ameliorate. At the same time, however, there is often no very clear or obvious correspondence between the kind of environmental conditions identified in Section 1 as posing problems, and the 'market failures' as these are identified in economic theory. Putting all this rather differently, I can say that my attempt to provide some rough idea as to where the theory of planning might be found is indeed only very rough. It is also tentative, disputable and of course open to correction.

Nevertheless, it is difficult to refrain from drawing conclusions, even from such confused material. Perhaps the main conclusion which I would draw, is that there cannot be such a thing as a theory of land-use planning. The variety of situations and states of affairs capable of being perceived as environmental problems is so great that it would clearly be necessary to identify these on a piecemeal, one-by-one basis, and to research their possible remedies, equally, in this one-by-one way. This implies that if it is to become effective, 'planning' must be broken down into a series of disparate and separate types of intervention.

It also seems useful to say what is meant in insisting that the justification for such interventions in environmental processes must be in terms of economic theory. There is no intention to suggest, in saying this, that there could be any such thing as an economic theory as opposed to a social theory, or a political one. All that is meant, rather, is that any theory of intervention must be expressed in material terms, in terms of conceptions of what in fact is taken to constitute welfare or well-being, and *why*. Those who talk of 'social' considerations in planning as opposed to 'economic' ones, or who urge that planning be used to meet 'human needs'[51] usually prove on analysis not to be opposing themselves to analysis in economic terms (for in truth, this would be literally impossible), but to be objecting to the outcomes of specific market processes. They want different things to be produced, and/or they want them to be distributed differently. But those who seek to achieve these last things must solve specifically economic problems. They must devise ways of getting their preferred goods produced (whether by offering profit, by administrative decree or however) and they must devise ways of getting these goods to those people who they think should get them (again, whether by use of market mechanisms, by bureaucratic allocation, or whatever). A free market is a social and political phenomenon, then, just as a system of bureaucratic allocation or 'planning' is an economic phenomenon.

Another point to be made, and continuing the same line of argument, concerns an equally commonly encountered false dichotomy. Often, in discussion of planning issues, it is assumed or suggested that a choice must be made between 'economic' and 'environmental' considerations. Environmentalists do not pursue their aims as ends in themselves, however. They do so because they believe that their achievement would contribute to human welfare. The objectives of even the most 'idealistic' environmental pressure group, therefore, are quite as much economic objectives as are the objectives pursued by profit-making industrial enterprises. Environmental pressure groups do not attempt to keep lakes and forests alive, to preserve old buildings, or to secure that development goes to one place rather than another because they believe that an *uninhabited* globe would be better if their recommendations were followed. On the contrary, they urge these things because they believe that they would contribute to the material welfare of identifiable groups of people. Their aims, therefore, are far from being non-economic. As compared with those interests whose profits are at stake, environmentalists simply have a different conception of what *is* good economics, of what *does* constitute human material well-being, or of the way in which this material well-being ought to be socially distributed.[52]

Another point made clear by a consideration of the possible justifications for intervention in the processes which shape the physical environment is that just as the market has inherent weaknesses, so does intervention. Far from adding up to a coherent alternative way of ordering society's arrangements, called 'planning', the various kinds of intervention are likely to impede *each other*. Nor are interventions introduced into 'markets', in such a way that their effects can be clearly seen. Rather, they are introduced into complex situations consisting already of confused mixtures of 'distorted' markets and previous interventions, meaning that to identify their effects is extremely difficult.

And there are further problems with interventions. Any intervention must of necessity be based on a purely subjective judgment, or *opinion*, as to what states of affairs are desirable and undesirable. There can therefore be no acid test, as there is in the case of the market, as to whether this judgement results in the satisfaction of needs or demands; in the market, by contrast, misjudgments on such matters are reflected clearly and automatically, in loss of profits. And because any intervention is of necessity based on mere opinion in this way, those who make it are open to 'influence'; their judgments as to what is in the 'public interest' may be unclear, vacillating, or reflect mere expedience. Their judgments may for example be affected by such things as the wishes of those who have power or patronage over them, by considerations relating to their own career prospects, or perhaps simply because they become genuinely persuaded that they should use their powers differently.

A further difficulty, then, resulting from this previous one, is that the job of the 'planner' is quite simply far more difficult than the job of those who operate in the market; this alone suggests it may be less well done. Having no clear criteria of price or profitability, planners must instead make very delicate judgments between conflicting pressures and demands. Occasionally, they may misjudge the intellectual or moral force, or even the sheer political power, behind certain of these demands. In such a situation, it is not just that they themselves are in trouble. Rather, the perceived legitimacy of the planning enterprise itself is put at risk.

Another problem is that it is difficult to restrain the power of intervention, once established. Whereas the market provides an automatic restriction on power, in the form of financial loss, 'intervention' has no corresponding mechanism. Since all 'intervention', in every society known, is legitimated in terms of the 'public interest', those engaged in the intervention seem almost inevitably to develop an ideology which not only justifies the enlargement of their own power of intervention, but also invests this demand with a *moral* fervour.[53] Planners, for example, still continue to portray themselves in evangelical tones as the creators of a more equal society, even though research has for long suggested that their efforts are in fact producing a *less* equal one.

A further point is that the purely economic costs of intervention are higher than those of the market. Where resources are allocated administratively, we have the cost of administration; where they are allocated by the market, however, this cost is largely avoided. But beyond this, the cost of planning seems almost inevitably to rise, over time, for again there is no self-regulating economic mechanism, which 'rewards' the intervention only to the extent that it succeeds in fulfilling 'demands'. In addition, there is the financial cost of legitimation. The outcomes produced by the market tend to be accepted as 'natural', or at least as inevitable, whereas those produced by bureaucratic allocation must be explicitly justified. The cost of 'participation exercises' was such a legitimation cost.

Finally, there is the problem that interventions can be subverted, and tend to encourage corruption. Any system of bureaucratic allocation is prone to corruption, but this danger is very much exacerbated where, as in the case of British land-use planning, bureaucratic allocation coexists with the market, and has the very function of determining who shall and who shall not be allowed to operate in that market. In this situation, entrepreneurs are able to make profits far greater than they could ever achieve in any freely competitive market.

But despite all such weaknesses[54] there is nevertheless often a good case to be made for intervention, and this case is perhaps especially strong in the case of land and property markets. We reintroduce the market to correct the undesirable effects of intervention, and then reintroduce more interventions to correct the undesirable effects of the market, in a never-ending search for 'better' solutions. There seems to be no case on *a priori* grounds either for advocating *no* interventions in market processes, or for advocating that all, or even most, of the functions of the market be achieved instead by bureaucratic allocation.

'Planning', however, in the sense of the activity discussed in this book, can *only* be justified to the extent that a case is made for intervention. Why, then, has the case not been made? Why have the kinds of argument set out in the preceding sections of this chapter not been taken up by planners, and developed into coherent justifications for the various things they attempt to do? This question brings us to the final section of this chapter.

## 4.   Why has planning no theoretical basis?

Justifications of land-use planning using arguments such as those set out above are of course to be found. They remain, however, at the very broadest level of generality, unrelated to everyday practice. And in a very real sense, a theory is not a theory at all, until it has been used in practice, over a considerable period of time. Theoretical knowledge is simply not secure, until we know that we can rely upon it to produce the specific and detailed outcomes which we desire. The rudimentary 'justifications' set out above, therefore, have not benefited from the processes of refinement, elaboration and increasingly clear exposition which normally occur, when theoretical knowledge is tested in the pursuit of practical objectives. They remain at the level of generality and confusion, qualities which I have no doubt captured very accurately in my recital of them.

All this can be illustrated, for example, by reference to a recent report on the future of planning, published by the Nuffield Foundation.[55] This report, based largely on opinions expressed by leading members of the profession, does indeed set out the case for intervention in terms of economic theory, but only in the most vague and general terms, and without any attempt to relate these general ideas to concrete policies. In case after case, the planners consulted by the Nuffield enquirers express the belief that planning *can* do this or that, that it *ought* to be able to achieve this or that, or even that it *has* achieved certain desirable things, but in no case do they offer evidence. They refer to no generally accepted theories, explaining in terms of cause and effect *why* it is that specific actions can be expected to lead to specific outcomes. (Nor, for that matter, do they refer even to any factual data concerning the results of planning.) This Nuffield report, then, provides striking evidence of the fact that the planning profession in Britain still operates at the evangelical level, at the level of faith, or, as I called it in Chapter 3, the level of 'belief', rather than at the level of serarch for knowledge.

How, then, can we explain this failure to look for knowledge of cause and effect? One explanation, advanced in earlier chapters of this book, I summed up as 'premature legitimation'. Planners simply do not *need* to seek justifications of their activities in terms of cause and effect, I argued, for these activities have already been legitimated by portraying them as promoting widely held social and aesthetic values, supported in fact by some of the most influential groups in society.

A second reason, equally obvious from what has been said in earlier chapters, lies in what I termed planners' *technicism*, their lack of interest in the substantive nature of the 'thing planned', and their tendency instead to concentrate most of their efforts on inventing theories about the process of planning itself. Present-day planning, of course, does not stress the idea of planning as 'rational method', or as 'system guidance', to anything like the same degree as it did in the late 1960s and 1970s; the tone is much more muted. The failure to analyse *what* is done, however, and *why*, and the tendency to concentrate instead on how to achieve a 'planning' approach, is still quite as strongly marked as ever. Planners still reveal a remarkable lack of interest in analysing either the behaviour of landowners and the property development industry, or the effects of their own actions upon these economic interests. They still devote much time and energy to urging 'co-ordination', and to discussing possible changes in administrative arrangements, at the cost of neglecting the analysis of the purpose which planning is meant to achieve. The recent Nuffield report, mentioned immediately above, again provides a good example. In urging that the activities of virtually every interest group and organization in both the public and private sectors be co-ordinated one with another, the report maintains a noticeably confident tone. When it comes to the substantive outcomes which all this co-ordination is intended to achieve, by contrast, the tone becomes markedly less sure; planners no longer believe that they have *the* right answer, where the physical environment is concerned, the report suggests, and indeed the whole approach becomes that of commending diversity and variety. If diversity and variety are the objectives, however, it seems remarkably odd to urge planning and co-ordination to achieve them; the market provides these things far more effectively.

A third reason why the theoretical basis of 'planning' remains undeveloped lies in the fact that the possible 'justifications' do indeed each relate to specific perceived problems or market failures. This means that to use them, we must think very carefully about exactly what things we find objectionable, and why, specifying our reasons very carefully. Due to their tendency to *holism*, however, planners simply do not think in this way, and this in itself probably makes the 'justifications' uncongenial to them. For if they *did* approach things in this way, they would be no longer planners. The whole enterprise of planning, resting as it does on an explicit rejection of each subject specialist's plea for some particular intervention as too 'narrow', yet resting equally as it does on the planners' claim to be uniquely able to co-ordinate all these specialized piecemeal approaches into a co-ordinated programme, would collapse.

A fourth, related, reason, also lies in the nature of the possible 'justifications' themselves. Because they are formulated within the framework of the social sciences, these 'justifications' must be intellectually credible. This means that they cannot merely assert in some vague way that the public interest would be promoted, but must explain quite clearly *who* would gain and *who* would lose; no intervention is costless. This, too, probably makes them uncongenial to planners. So great is their fear of appearing 'political' that they confuse the analysis of redistribution with the advocacy of it.

A fifth reason why the 'justifications' remain so undeveloped and are so seldom used in practice lies apparently in the already noted antipathy on the part of many planners to economics in general. Ratcliffe,[56] for example, writes:

> It is no secret that there is a cadre of practising planners who are downright antipathetic towards the property development industry, and a significant proportion of the rest who remain culpably ignorant of its nature and operation. This may owe something to the predilections and perceptions of those attracted toward planning as a profession and it certainly results from an almost complete disregard, wilful or otherwise, on the part of planning schools in their lack of education in this direction.

This 'missing dimension' has been noted by a number of writers. Ravetz, for example, remarks on a 'remarkable insulation of professional and academic planners from economic realities'.[57] Drewett notes that '[d]espite the economic and social implications of the problem, there has been surprisingly little interest shown in academic or planning research into the value of land, and the utility of land as a factor of production'.[58]

This last, of course, was written some fifteen years ago, but it remains unfortunately almost as true today as when it was written. Nor should the planners' present-day enthusiasm for acting as 'industrial development officers', often cited by them as evidence that such critics are quite mistaken, and that the profession indeed takes a keen interest in economics, be taken too seriously. An economic understanding of the property development industry and its financial backers, the economic knowledge which planners *in fact* need, is hardly the same thing as the 'economic understanding' needed in order to persuade all manner of small firms to set up shop in one local authority area rather than another.

There is, however, an important point to be made concerning this failure on the part of the planners to study the economics of planning. Ratcliffe himself has been criticized, for giving the impression that economics can be equated with explanation of the workings of the market, and even with the defence of the market, and to a large extent the antipathy noted above seems rooted in this confusion.[59] This is unfortunate. As noted above, it is economists who must explain and even speak for the 'interventions', quite as much as for the market, and the kind of economic analysis which is needed in this area of policy thus goes far beyond the laws of demand and supply. What is called for is a 'wider economics', capable not only of examining alternative views of what makes economic sense, but also of analysing those things which cannot be reduced to monetary terms.

And here, the planning profession has shown no antipathy, but on the contrary has made a valuable contribution. Once it became accepted that the type of cost–benefit analysis which attempted to reduce everything to monetary terms was a scientistic delusion, the way became clear for the far more reasonable and rational tool of the 'planning balance sheet', in which all those impacts which *cannot* be expressed in monetary terms are nevertheless enumerated and quantified, as a guide for political decision-making.[60] The only criticism one would make here, then, is that this valuable and yet simple technique has not been developed further, and used more extensively. It could, after all, have been used to provide rational justification for planning policies which have instead been based on nothing more than ideological presupposition, or misleading pseudo-scientific analyses.

And there is a further criticism, unfortunately, which perhaps gets to the heart of the matter. Where planning decisions have almost blatantly significant redistributive impacts (as for example where large developments deprive local residents of social facilities or even of their homes, and put large sums of money into developers' pockets)—here, there is an extreme reluctance to use 'planning techniques', to quantify, to evaluate. Where, on the other hand the impacts are vague, diffuse and in any case problematic (as, for example, in some technically grandiose 'subregional study' or 'structure plan'), here, the enthusiasm for the identification and quantification of quantitative impacts runs riot. It is for this selective vision, especially, that the planning profession should be criticized. One of the themes of this book is that those decisions which can in fact rest only on values should not be disguised as technical matters. But decision-making can certainly be technicized *this* far, as far as the 'planning balance sheet'. Such a clear and precise statement of estimated impacts is after all no more than a precondition of wise political judgment. Indeed, it is a precondition of the rational exercise of political prejudice.

Sixth, in explaining the lack of any adequate theoretical basis for planning, we can note that the law gives planners little encouragement to consider the probable consequences of their decisions in economic terms, or to conceive of their activity as having economic objectives. In Chapter 1, I raised this matter of the extent to which planning statute has in fact been interpreted, whether by central government or by the courts on appeal, as empowering planners to pursue social and economic objectives, and it was shown that their powers in this direction are very circumscribed. This, then, is clearly an important factor. There is after all little incentive to develop knowledge, if one has little prospect of using it. One might, of course, argue that this lack of powers is itself a reflection of the planners' attitudes, but this might be to go too far. Rather, perhaps, one might say that the profession today is hindered by its past, and by its traditions, a victim of its founding fathers and of its own history. Nowhere is this lack of economic powers more apparent, of course, than in the matter of the taxation of betterment. Never, even under the very short period of operation of the 1947 Act, has the collection of this tax been very closely related in practice to the exercise of planning powers, and this separation probably constitutes the most serious weakness in the planning system. The fact that the planners themselves did not assess this betterment levy, and that they were not required in any way to make any connections between the nature of their decisions and the incidence or the amount of the levy, probably did as much as anything to divorce the planning system from economic realities. Later, of course, under the equally short-lived 1967 and 1976 systems, this divorce went in some ways even further. But if it is a technical fact that land-use planning simply cannot work when betterment is left totally in the hands of the developer, is it not reasonable to suggest that this fact should have been pointed out by the planners themselves? It is after all normal for experts to point out the fact, when the powers accorded to them simply do not enable them to do the job they are asked to do.

Seventh, however, in explaining why planning rests on no credible theory, we must look at the role of the political parties; it seems clear that much of the blame can be laid at their various doors. It has rarely suited them, apparently, to politicize planning by demanding clarification of its redistributive or other consequences, or to seek to invest it with any clear social purpose. Instead, they have preferred to go along with the planners' own definition of it, as non-political. Even in periods when questions of land and property speculation, 'unearned increment', and so on, have become very live issues, the political parties seem to have preferred to keep these matters as far as possible firmly insulated from 'planning', and to play down the links between economic forces and physical outcomes. Neither in office nor in opposition has any of the main political parties promoted any significant research into the fundamental economic problems posed by the existence of town and country planning. With some surprise, we can note that the most recent government-initiated inquiry into these matters was published as long ago as 1942, and that even at that time, it was regarded by most economists as somewhat amateurish, and as certainly constituting no advance on work done by academic economists in the early decades of this century.[61]

Eighth, one needs to ask about the role of the property developers themselves, and of their professional advisers. Lack of pressure from this quarter, it might be suggested, could perhaps go some way towards explaining why planning has continued to be officially portrayed as a purely technical matter, and why its economic implications have been so very well concealed; if such interests were profiting financially out of the situation created by the existence of planning controls, one might hypothesize, it certainly would not suit them that this fact be given much publicity. The present book has concentrated on the role of the planning profession, and to be in a position to discuss either the role of the political parties or that of the development industry and its professional advisers, one would have had to engage in quite other areas of research. One can, however, note that some academic observers suggest that developers and their professional advisers tend to be far less opposed to redistributive interventionist policies than one might imagine, and that, in particular, they have shown a far greater readiness to accept the ethical case for the effective taxation of betterment than governments have shown a willingness to impose such a tax upon them.[62]

Hallett[63] makes the further and very interesting point that the quality of the expert advice given to government by the surveyors and valuers has been very high, but that it has itself been undervalued, accorded less than its true worth, on the quite mistaken grounds that it has come from mere professional men rather than from academic economists. Though the surveyors and valuers may not have done a great deal to clarify the economic rationale for planning, it seems reasonable to conclude, they have not done much to mystify it, either.

Ninth, then, and finally, we must ask about the academic economists themselves. To what extent can we attribute the failure to develop the theoretical explanation of town and country planning to shortcomings on their part? Certainly it seems possible to say that land and property development are curiously unresearched areas in economics,[64] and this seems all the more difficult to understand when one remembers that the growth of the property industry and its associated financial institutions has been one of the most marked features of the British economy since the Second World War. For some reason, this particular area seems to have been left largely to neo-Marxist writers, and even they have produced very little empirical work. Where academic economists *have* interested themselves in this area of policy, they have usually limited themselves, unfortunately, to stating the case for planning 'in principle', in very general terms.

Part of the problem, it would seem, is that such economists have taken at face value the planners' own 'delusions of grandeur' concerning the scope of their activity; thus their discussions usually cover a quite bewildering range of subjects, including the economics of housing, of transport, of industrial location and of pollution, as well as urban economics, regional economics, models of local economies, and even discussions of the case for and against governmental interventions in the economy in general.[65] There has, by and large, been a failure to link economic analysis with the analysis of legal powers or administrative practices, and in general, the instutional context is given scant attention. In particular, such discussions, while looking at virtually everything else, seem to ignore the one thing which town and country planners in fact do; they say very little indeed as to how one might analyze the consequences of granting a planning permission or of refusing it. Even when it comes to the somewhat broader matter of the analysis of the economic implications of the production of the development plans themselves, the contributions from economists seem very sparse. Perhaps the newly-fashionable area of 'pollution' seems more attractive to economists than the decidedly dated matter of 'zoning'; the latter, they might feel, has received sufficient attention in the American literature. Whatever the reasons, this relative dearth of economic research into the workings of the planning system has had unfortunate effects. By failing to clarify the way in which the system works, it has not only served to perpetuate professional obscurantism among planners themselves, but has also contributed to the development of an obscure style of *public* debate about planning, in which the exchange of vague concepts like 'preservation of community', 'public participation', 'social factors', and so on, takes the place of honest debate about who gets what and who should get what.

In summarizing my attempt to answer the question addressed in this chapter, it seems reasonable to attribute the main blame to the planning profession itself. Though other groups with an interest in the matter, such as the political parties, academic economists and the professional advisers of the property industry seem also to have been surprisingly reluctant to press for clarification, the professional planners seem by contrast to have contributed *actively* to the mystification of planning, by constructing a professional ideology which conceals its true redistributive nature. Perhaps we might hazard the guess that planners have failed to develop any theoretical explanation of planning because, instinctively or intuitively, they felt safer without it. A theory of planning, since it would be an explanation of 'who gets what', would be dangerous knowledge. In the long run, however, it could be more dangerous to be *without* such knowledge.

# 6

# How political choices are obscured

The drawing of the line between the political and the non-political is itself a political act

B. Hindess, *The Decline of Working Class Politics.*

## 1. Introduction

In Chapter 5, I tried to explain why the theory of 'planning' is so poorly developed. In this chapter, I shall try to show why this area of public policy is equally poorly understood in political terms. The first step in my argument lies in distinguishing between *political clarification*, *political mobilization*, and the *construction of political philosophy*.

By *political clarification* I mean analysis of the impacts of policies or decisions, probably (though not necessarily) in terms of their effects on various identifiable interest groups. By *political mobilization* I mean the activity of generating political support for or against a given policy or decision, either in the sense of obtaining electoral support for it, or by securing commitment to it among influential elites. Political clarification, then, is a research task, and indeed is a part of the task of theoretical explanation. Political mobilization, by contrast, is clearly a political activity. Ideally, we might say, political mobilization should *rest on* political clarification, which is to say that those 'mobilized' ought ideally to be truly informed rather than misinformed. And here, I might add, I do not take the 'pessimistic' view that such improved public understanding of the probable distributional effects of policy will of necessity merely lead all concerned to pursue their own material interests all the more effectively; there is, after all, such a thing as a regard for the needs of others, and for what is *morally* right. Electors *do* consent to be taxed in order to provide such things as foreign aid and welfare services, even when it is perfectly obvious that they themselves will never benefit from these things. Without such 'informed altruism', in fact, the modern welfare state is impossible.

And this last, the consideration of the role of moral values in politics, brings us conveniently to the third of my three concepts, the *construction of a political philosophy*. The 'philosophy' of a field of public policy such as planning, we may say, consists of the statement of arguments, often of a moral kind, suggesting the extent to which the material interests of the various groups involved 'ought' to be promoted. An egalitarian 'philosophy of education', for example, is one which urges that policies should seek to ensure that in some sense or other all members of society achieve similar educational standards. An educational philosophy based on 'equality of opportunity', by contrast, urges that all members of society should have equal chances to compete for a range of rather *un*equal educational experiences, corresponding to the range of positions of unequal power, status and authority available in the wider society.

Any realistic political philosophy, it may be suggested, made more specific by being related to and intended to be applied within a particular area of public policy, must of course be designed in such a way that it can achieve political mobilization. Obviously it will attempt to show that in the cases of as wide a range of interest groups as possible, there is indeed 'something in it' for them. At the same time, however, it will base its appeal at least in part on ethical arguments, on conceptions of what is morally just or equitable. And any rational policy-making, we might suggest, should rest on such a conscious and coherent philosophy, whether it takes for example the 'modest' form of merely trying to find the point of balance between opposing interests as these *are* perceived by those concerned, or whether it takes the more 'ambitious' form, of an attempt to *change* public beliefs about what is an equitable solution. But before there can be such a political 'philosophy', of education, of planning policy, or whatever, there must be political clarification; policy demands knowledge.

In previous chapters, I have argued that theory and politics should reinforce each other, in what might be termed a virtuous spiral. If we think of the kind of research findings set out in Section 3 of Chapter 3, for example, it seems obvious that if they chose to do so, politicians could rather easily make 'political capital' out of these. That planning actually leads to regressive redistribution, in such a way that the rich tend to live in more exclusive physical surroundings and the poor in even poorer surroundings than they would do if we had no planning system at all, is a matter which could fairly readily be made into a 'political scandal'. A new and supposedly more egalitarian 'philosophy of planning' could be announced, and political support for it could probably fairly readily be mobilized. When these new policies had themselves been in operation long enough for their effects to be researched, however, we would reasonably expect this new research to lead to new criticisms. It is political interests and political conceptions of what is socially equitable which stimulate research, and conversely it is policy research, and in particular what I have called 'political clarification', which stimulates political debate as to what is socially desirable.

If, however, we consider the three activities I have identified, political clarification, political mobilization and the construction of political philosophy, in relation to town and country planning, one thing at least is absolutely and abundantly clear: none of these three things is done. This fact is, of course, well known. It is commonly expressed by saying that planning is not politicized. I have preferred, however, to 'break down' this fact that town and country planning is 'not politicized', suggesting instead that there are in reality *three* activities which are conspicuous by their absence. I hope my reasons will become clear below.

That the effects of this lack of politicization are harmful, is a point which has been made in earlier chapters of this book. In brief, these effects are that in the British planning system, democracy, too, is lacking. But what does this rather abstract notion of lack of democracy mean, translated into more concrete terms? It implies that policy-making and decision-making are technicized and professionalized, and that behind the facade of objective rationality thus created, powerful economic interests are probably able to ensure that the planning system serves their own interests.

An absolutely crucial question therefore, and one which will run through the remainder of this chapter, is how we might in fact get these tasks of political clarification, construction of political philosophies of planning, and political mobilization, carried out. In asking who 'ought' to do these necessary but apparently thankless jobs, we might be guided in principle by the traditional idea that there should be a division of labour between politicians and their expert advisers, corresponding roughly to the distinction between 'values' and 'facts'. This of course would imply that the task I have called 'political clarification' should be done by experts, and the other two of the three tasks identified by politicians. But it is unrealistic to be *too* bound by this principle. For one thing, the two groups have very unequal resources of power. Experts can, and almost inevitably do, even unconsciously, shape political perceptions in the widest sense. Politicians, by contrast, cannot possibly obtain all the technical information which is essential to informed political judgment. It is this imbalance of power, of course, which explains the whole modern phenomenon of the increasing domination of the government by experts, and which lies behind my own concern at the possibility of the growth of corporatist attitudes and policies. But if we cannot always succeed in determining *who* should deal in 'facts' and *who* in 'values', we can at least try to be a little more clear as to *when* the question we are dealing with is mainly a factual one, and *when* it is more a matter of political choice.

The problems involved in attempting to visualize the kind of institutional innovations which would lead to the politicization of planning are made painfully clear when we see the extent to which, at present, all the various interests concerned are so obviously ready to acquiesce in the portrayal of planning as *non-political*. To suppose that it is the professional planners alone who maintain this stance would be quite mistaken, and would be to underestimate the magnitude of the problem. And in fact, of course, we know that planning is far from alone in this respect. In the case of virtually *any* governmental activity, there are strong political temptations to ensure that the question of 'who gains and who loses' is not raised. If the comforting illusion can somehow be maintained that all sections in society gain, it seems most unlikely that any will choose to question this illusion. This is as likely to be true of politicians as it is of officials, for if the latter are provided with careers, the former get the benefit of being credited with 'running' the policy area in question—without the inconvenience of actually getting involved in any thorny political questions concerning it.

And ironically enough, this attitude of acquiescence is likely to be true even of supposedly independent researchers. If, after all, one has invested many years of one's life in becoming a specialist in a given area of public policy, one will not lightly throw away this hard-won advantage. To advocate that the distributional impacts of public policies be made more clear, when one has a vested interest in one's ability to grasp the byzantine complexities of law and administration which *prevent* these things from being clear, demands considerable public spirit.

All who have a stake in the continued existence of any given governmental activity, we may perhaps therefore conclude, however small this stake may seem to the outside observer to be, will probably tend not to question that activity in any fundamental way (though they will certainly wish to be seen as capable of criticizing it at the level of detail). And when, on top of all this, we remember that much governmental activity is engaged in for its symbolic value rather than because it actually achieves anything in particular, we begin to see just how great are the forces we are up against, when we advocate that the consequences of a given policy should be researched. Nevertheless, we may feel, such processes of 'acquiescence' do seem to go further and to have continued longer in certain policy areas than in others. And in the case of 'town and country planning', we may feel, they have perhaps gone far enough. As Denman puts it, we have simply 'lost all knowledge of why we plan the use of land'. Planning, he suggests, has become 'a process without a purpose'.[1]

In what circumstances, then, could we reasonably expect the fundamental questioning of public policy to occur? In principle, it would seem, this will tend to happen where the questioners tend to gain by it, and where they are protected against being penalized for it. Political parties out of office, for example, will often stand to gain by it. Independent academic researchers, provided they have tenured positions, cannot be penalized for it, or at least cannot be penalized too obviously. It would seem to be only in such quarters, however, consisting principally of opposition political groups and researchers whose livelihoods are guaranteed, that we could hope to find this demand for the critical analysis of public policy. And when we reflect how slender are the resources of such groups, we realize how insecure is the basis on which democracy stands, and how unsurprising it is that, as Denman notes, 'planning' simply continues to be done because it is done. It seems unlikely that planning is alone in this.

The only significant 'interest group' which *does* seem likely to gain from the fundamental questioning of public policy, we might conclude, is 'the public'. The problem, then, is to devise institutional arrangements which would oblige the political parties to demand such questioning on behalf of 'the public', and which would enable researchers to investigate the questions this posed. Or in the terms in which I put the matter in Chapter 4, the problem is to think out how we could promote the 'institutionalization of scepticism'.

So far, the argument suggests that it is hardly surprising that 'planning' has remained relatively immune from fundamental questioning, since the forces which have an obvious interest in preventing such questioning are so strong. In fact, however, I shall argue the very opposite. Since the 1960s, I shall suggest, there has arisen a whole series of changes in the wider political climate and in the ways in which questions of milieu and environment are conceptualized. So strong have been these shifts in mental orientations, that the problem, rather, is to explain why they have not led to the virtual disappearance of the planning profession, or at least to the breaking-down of this rather nebulous activity of 'planning' into a series of more concrete and more clearly defined types of governmental initiative. For these shifts in the wider political climate held out the promise of what I have called political clarification. In the remainder of this chapter, I try to explain why this promise has not been fulfilled.

## 2. The promise of political clarification

The argument is, then, that from the point of view of the public things would be better if 'planning' had been broken down into a number of specialisms, each addressing itself to a specific perceived problem. But the argument goes beyond this. The planners themselves would be better off, it suggests, and in particular they would be more secure. The intellectual currents to be identified below, and in particular the rapidly growing interest in society in both the man-made and the 'natural' environment, offered to planners the opportunity to acquire an enhanced role and a new importance, by clarifying in explicitly political and distributional terms the part which governmental regulation of the property development process could play in shaping environmental outcomes. The opportunity was not grasped, however, and I shall argue that the main reason for this is that planners saw the emerging tendency in society to discuss the physical environment in plain terms of 'who gets what' as a threat rather than an opportunity. To engage themselves in such plain speech, they seem to have believed, would have threatened their position as 'professional men'. On the contrary, I shall argue, it would have helped to free them from their unnecessarily narrow and self-imposed conception of their role. But before I try to develop this argument, I need to set out those currents in the wider society which I see as having presented the planners with this disregarded opportunity. The following list of factors is of course arbitrary, and debatable. Other factors, such as the emerging physical 'features in the scene' identified in Chapter 5, might equally be seen as offering the same challenge and the same opportunity. But this would not affect the structure of the argument.

### (i) Fresh attempts to impose taxation of betterment
Perhaps the most obvious of all these various sources of intellectual stimulus, positively inviting planners to rethink the whole nature of their activity in more theoretically credible and thus more down-to-earth terms, lies in the attempts of

Labour governments in 1967 and 1975–6 to reintroduce comprehensive planning-linked schemes for the taxation of betterment. There seems little need to say more about these pieces of legislation here, for they were discussed in Chapters 1 and 2. The political debates surrounding these schemes provided a more than adequate reminder of the essentially redistributive nature of planning, however, and that they did not lead to a reconceptualization of it in these terms is on the face of it difficult to understand.

### (ii) The rise of environmentalism

In Britain at least, the immediate roots of this seem to go back to such events as the great London fog of 1952, the publication of Rachel Carson's *Silent Spring* in 1962 and Frank Fraser-Darling's Reith Lectures of 1969. As the environmental movement gathered force it seemed often to be particularly susceptible to the same utopian and anti-political tendencies as the planning movement itself. Environmentalists, like planners, were impatient with politics, and tended to supose that there could be some objectively correct answer to human problems, derived from a higher rationality than that of which politicians were apparently capable. Later, however, the 'green wave' developed a much greater measure of social and political sophistication. By the late 1970s, it had become a widespread and many-faceted social and political movement, resting on a more open-minded popular scientific curiosity, and displaying a level of intellectual understanding going far beyond that of the earlier 'outdoor', 'rural preservationist' and 'town and country planning' movements of the 1930s. In suggesting that planners might have learned far more than they did from the environmentalist movement, I am not suggesting that they should have associated themselves more with its substantive concerns. Indeed, they often went too far in this direction, and I have described the result as 'role-confusion'. Rather, I am suggesting that they should have learned from its *approach,* and sought to apply this to their own much more specific area of concern. This is an approach in which physical milieu is analysed as a social product, serving specific interests, and conferring costs and benefits unequally. Planners could have been expected to apply this same kind of research-orientated, analytical and investigative approach to their own particular concern within the wider field of environment, that of the land and property development process. They could have been expected to question the social purposes served by the property development industry in the same critical and independent spirit that environmentalists were applying to other industries.

In many instances, of course, environmental arguments have been 'misused' in the planning context by privileged individuals and groups anxious to preserve their own surroundings, and many planners have been quick to develop an understanding of this as a political phenomenon. In many other cases, where questions of a specifically ecological nature have arisen in connection with proposed develop-ment, the planners concerned have shown an admirable readiness to call in environmentalist aid and support, and even to form alliances with such groups. But they rarely seem to have adopted the environmentalists' critical stance, or to have used it to free themselves from their identification with authority; it is this which seems most significant.

*(ii)   The rise of consumerism*
By 'consumerism' I mean the idea, increasingly prevalent in the West from the 1960s onwards, that consumers should determine the nature of goods and services rather than that producers should do so. I use this term to refer to goods and services produced by the public sector quite as much as to those produced by the private sector, and the term thus includes all kinds of local political protest, for example against slum clearance, against motorway construction, and so on. I also include under this heading all manner of propagandist and pressure-group activities, from that of national bodies like Shelter to a local campaign to force the provision of a school crossing. Often, challenge of this kind has used environmentalist, conservationist or 'heritage' arguments, but equally often it has used 'social' arguments, such as the idea that established communities should not be broken up, and especially, it has used the ideology of 'participation'. It also clearly exists along what we may call a selfish–unselfish continuum.[2] What is common to all these various kinds of protest, however, is that they challenge established authority. First, they challenge official decisions concerning the form which the environment should take. Second, they have sometimes also challenged authority at the more profound level popularized, for example, by the writings of Illich, questioning whether such decisions should be made by experts or professionals at all.

To some extent, of course, this movement has been supposedly promoted by authority itself, as in the form of the 'maximum feasible participation' of the American 'War on Poverty' programme under Johnson, the British Home Office's Community Development Programme of 1969, the British planning system's adoption of 'public participation'[3] or the adoption by both the Town and Country Planning Association and the Royal Town Planning Institute, from 1972 onwards, of 'planning aid'.[4] Such 'top-down' promotion of 'participation', however, seem best understood as a bid for legitimation. It is generally only used by those governmental agencies and those bureaucratic professions which are insecure, or feel threatened. The officials who administer the National Health Service, for example, do not ask us to 'participate' in their decision-making, as planners do. Nor do officials within the local authority educations departments, and for the same reason; unlike their colleagues in 'planning', they are perfectly professionally secure.[5]

At least two extremely important points seem to have emerged, however, from the experience of consumerism in the public sector. The first is that the British system of government appears to give insufficient opportunity for public and political debate about alternative ways of providing society with the things it needs. Instead, such issues seem wherever possible to be converted into local 'planning' issues, and thus depoliticized, and determined administratively. Such major matters as how the country might best supply its energy needs, for example, or how it might strike a balance between private and public transport provision, become redefined by government as questions of where to build a particular power station or a particular new road link. As such, they then become the subject of local administrative hearings, 'public local inquiries'. An important point to bear in mind concerning such an enquiry is that no matter how big the issue it concerns itself with, and no matter how much interest it attracts, even at national level, it is indeed an administrative procedure, and not a legal or political one. This means that though the inspector who presides over it may listen to a quite extraordinary amount of evidence, and may consider this evidence most carefully, he is in making his ultimate decision bound only by 'policy', and not, in principle, by the weight of the arguments presented to him.

The implication of this is quite clear. The more government succeeds in transforming the big issues in society into 'planning' matters in this way, the easier will government become. To show that many things officially defined as planning issues are not planning issues at all, therefore, but major questions of social choice, seems to be the first step towards getting them determined through normal parliamentary processes.[6]

The second important point emerging out of the rise of consumerist attitudes to the activities of government concerns the need for better information. Logically, one might think, it is no more than simply obvious that the various parties to any inquiry into the desirability of proposed public policies need equal access to information. In British government circles, however, the matter is not seen this way. British government at all levels is notoriously secretive, and we still seem to be very far away from the day when authorites will share all that they know with those for whom they supposedly act.

At a certain level, of course, planners have come to terms very successfully with consumerism; they have learned to live with it. What they have not done, however, is actually use the insights which it affords, in order to construct a more intellectually credible explanation of their own activity. Cherry, in a most telling phrase, brings out this contrast between the level at which the planning profession has in fact sought to cope with this 'illuminating force', and the more profound level at which it might have done so. Public officials, he suggests, in dealing with public protest of all kinds, 'have found it increasingly difficult to define the public interest'.[7] In other words, they have clung to their traditional belief that there *is* a public interest, and that 'planning' can discern it, by using techniques which point to the best way to find a balance between all the various 'selfish' sectional interests. What the planners have not done, is to draw the obvious intellectual conclusion—that the concept of 'public interest' has no real meaning.[8]

Though the rise of what I have summed up as 'consumerism' is in fact one of the most exciting developments in the West in the post-war period, and though it has directly challenged their own activity, planners have refused to be stimulated by it to look afresh at the idea of 'planning', to seek to relate it to political theory, and to find a better explanation of it. Instead, they have responded defensively, endlessly identifying themselves with the frightened and defensive reactions which government itself has adopted in response to 'consumerist' demand for freer flows of information and freer debate. And as shown above, planners have often borne the brunt of this challenge—by needlessly allowing central government to redefine all manner of public issues as 'planning' matters.

### (iv)   Theoretical support? The rise of the new urban sociology

The impacts of the kinds of questioning and protest identified above were real and tangible; planners encountered them in their everyday lives. But if this very immediate challenge at the practical level were not enough, there developed from the mid-1970s onwards an equally strong challenge at the level of theory. Until the 1960s, urban sociology had consisted of 'community studies', 'human ecology' and occasional studies of local government bureaucracies. By the 1980s, it had become an attempt to relate society's physical arrangements and their 'planning' to central questions in social theory, and in particular to the part played by the state in maintaining the economic and social structure. These contributions, however, most of which were written from a broadly neo-Marxist standpoint, have had no more impact on planning thought than have the social movements already referred to. One of the most surprising and altogether puzzling aspects of this is that according to planners' own accounts the profession has been increasingly taken over by social scientists. If this is so, why has no theoretical debate developed, within the profession, analysing the role of planning in society in terms of these new perspectives? The explanation of the state's intervention in the property development process is one of the questions at the heart of the new Marxist urban studies. It is also precisely what planners are engaged in. Yet by and large planners have tended to ignore this body of work.[9]

### (v)   Destabilization of the central–local government relationship

For many decades, and despite the fact that there has been since the Second World War a tendency to transfer responsibilities from local government to non-elected regional or 'area' authorities, the relationship between central government and local authorities in Britain was both stable and marked by mutual respect. From the mid-1970s onwards, however, and increasingly after 1979, this traditional pattern was subjected to severe strain, as a result of attempts by central government and the Whitehall bureaucracy to reduce the financial independence of local authorities. This, it is widely agreed, was not necessitated by any economic imperatives, but was motivated almost entirely by political objectives.[10] This phenomenon too, since it suggests that the whole status of public administration in Britain is now open to question, might be expected to have provoked more response than it has from the planning profession. Perhaps its main significance, however, lies in the response it has evoked among local politicians themselves:

### (vi)   Grassroots backlash: The enhanced politicization of local government

The politicization of local government in Britain is no new phenomenon, either, of course. It has been proceeding steadily since before the First World War, and increasingly since 1945. What is new about it from our point of view, however, is that in its present-day, 1980s form, it is often accompanied by attempts at 'local economic planning' sometimes linked with attempts at local 'positive planning' in the physical sense.[11] Such ambitions, clearly, are found mainly in Labour-controlled authorities. They are very much associated with a tendency in such areas for the elected representatives of the Labour party to be better educated, younger, more enterprising, and above all more ideologically motivated than has been the case in the past, tendencies especially marked in the London boroughs and in the former Greater London Council. Often, this new type of Labour member is himself or herself a local government employee, an academic, a social worker, teacher, or planner, perhaps, in a neighbouring local authority; otherwise, such people tend to be drawn from the professional middle classes rather than to be in working-class occupations.[12] Such attempts to impart firm political direction to the activities of a local authority, since they often imply to some extent at least the 'wresting back' of power from officials, constitute in effect a reversal of a very long-established trend in British local government.[13]

In other cases, however, and this may well be particularly true of the attempts at 'positive planning' and 'local economic planning' mentioned above, there is no question of wresting back power from officials, for the officials in question clearly share the ideological sympathies of the elected members. And here it is interesting to note the extent to which the emergence of such approaches was in fact encouraged and promoted both by the fashion for 'corporate planning'[14] and by the idea, equally strongly held in the 1970s, that the development plan prepared under town and country planning legislation should also seek to promote economic and social objectives. Where the professional town planners involved in such local political initiatives are themselves Labour supporters, they tend also to be supporters of the 'Radical Institute Group' within the Royal Town Planning Institute, of the Conference of Socialist Planners, or of the Labour Party's 'Alternative Economic Policy'.[15]

This group of professional planners, who tend to join with elected members of similar class background to themselves in order to promote a specifically socialist kind of local physical, social and economic planning, are of particular interest from the point of view of the argument of this book. Their existence, in fact, points to a strange paradox. Their professional colleagues, the great majority of the membership of the Royal Town Planning Institute, refuse even to engage in what I have termed the *political clarification* of planning (that is, the analysis of its distributional consequences), on the grounds that to do so would be too political. This small minority of socialist planners, by contrast, does not engage in this political clarification either, but in their case on the quite opposite grounds that to do so would be not political enough. Instead of *analysing* the redistributive effects of planning, these socialist planners seek to secure the adoption of policies which would *achieve* redistribution in favour of the less privileged. I would argue that both groups, both the vast majority of planners and the socialist ones, fundamentally misconstrue their role, and fail to perform what is in fact their proper task. This last, I would suggest, is to engage in political clarification, to engage in the analysis and the revelation of the distributional effects of those policies which are actually pursued, and to make clear the probable distributional effects of those policies which the politicians advocate.

(vii)   The central government's 'attack on planning'
Most observers, and certainly most planners, seem agreed that the Thatcher governments from 1979 onwards have evinced a certain antipathy to planning, and some have even suggested that these governments' actions reveal an apparent desire to 'abandon' planning in some sense. Like the six factors briefly discussed above, this 'attack' could have been used as a means of clarifying what is really at stake, where planning is concerned. It has not been, however; both the 'attack' and the planners' 'defence' against it have been conducted largely at what we might call the symbolic level, or the level of impression-management, and it is very difficult, therefore, to know what to make of them.

What the government seems mainly to have done from 1979 onwards, then, is to attack the *symbols* of 'planning', using this word to conjure up images of 'red tape', 'regulations', 'bureaucracy' and 'controls'; simultaneously, it has introduced measures which are clearly meant to serve as symbols of the spirit of free enterprise and private initiative. First of all, the government has attempted to speed up and to simplify both the production of statutory plans and the process of development control itself, using the argument that by taking an unnecessarily long time to deal with planning applications, and especially those for industrial and commercial development, the planners were holding up the provision of new jobs. There is nothing inherently wrong with this, of course (provided we are prepared to overlook the rhetorical suggestion that there is something inherently 'socialist' in dealing with planning applications slowly, and something inherently 'Conservative' in dealing with them quickly). And in fact the professional planners have joined enthusiastically in the exercise, co-operating in the production of 'league tables' showing the number of days taken by the various planning authorities to deal with development applications of various types. The whole exercise, however, provides a rather neat example of the way in which any Conservative administration is torn between on the one hand its need to be seen as stimulating qualities of initiative and entrepreneurship, and on the other hand its need to preserve the privilege on which its power is based. Many of the Conservative Party's most solid supporters, as reflected in statements made by local amenity societies and so on, have expressed fears that if there is to be this presumption in favour of the developer, and if such emphasis is to be placed on giving developers the go-ahead as quickly as possible, insufficient attention may be paid to safeguarding what are in effect privileged and exclusive environments against undesirable development.

And the Conservatives face a second dilemma. Whereas they are ostensibly committed to the market, they find themselves in practice in control of an administrative apparatus which can be used to give advantages to chosen interests going far beyond what those interests could hope to achieve for themselves in any competitive market situation. Nor have the Conservatives resisted this temptation;

as was shown above they have for example used corporatist stratagems to shift the balance of power in favour of certain sections of the property development industry.[16]

These dilemmas can be seen running through virtually all the initiatives of post-1979 governments in this sphere of policy. Following their 1979 election pledges to ensure that bureaucratic controls are prevented from discouraging entrepreneurial initiative, the Conservative government has issued a series of circulars,[17] ministerial pronouncements[18] and legislative measures (notably the Local Government, Planning and Land Act 1980), all of which appear to contribute to the stimulation of the market and to the supposed freeing of the development industry from the constraints imposed by the planning system. And outside the planning system narrowly defined, there have been measures reflecting apparently very similar motives, from the abolition of the Regional Economic Planning Councils in 1979 and the subsequent running-down of regional economic policy, the sales of new town assets and the winding-down of the new towns programme from 1980 onwards, to the abolition of the Greater London Council and the Metropolitan County Councils, portrayed as empires of bureaucratic wastefulness and inefficiency, in 1986.

Within the planning system itself, the establishment of 'Enterprise Zones' provides an excellent illustration of the ambiguity of the Conservative government's policies. These were intended to produce a 'demonstration effect' within the inner cities, supposedly stimulating economic growth by reducing planning controls to a minimum, rescinding local rate payments and offering other special financial incentives. Thus, as Lloyd and Botham observe, Enterprise Zones were 'presented as a radical free market alternative to conventional interventionist policies'.[19]

In the event, however, as these same observers point out, such success as these Zones have achieved 'owes more to public sector intervention, expenditure and subsidies than to the relaxation of regulations and controls'.[20] Consultants appointed to monitor the scheme reported that the relaxation of planning controls in fact played little part in inducing firms to locate within the Zones.[21] Rescinding rate payments, by contrast, clearly may play quite a large part, but it is fairly obvious that industry cannot everywhere be freed from the obligation to pay rates; in many cases, apparently, firms have merely moved into these Zones from other nearby sites. Whether the removal or the simplification of planning controls generally rather than in these defined 'Zones' would in fact make any great difference to the level of economic activity is another question, though the Conservatives certainly seem to think so. As opposed to most academic observers, the government judged its Enterprise Zones to be a great success, and proposed a wider application of the same kind of approach: so called 'Simplified Planning Zones' were to be introduced, in which the normal British system of requiring specific planning permission to be obtained for each particular development proposal would no longer apply, and in which the designation of the 'Zone' itself would constitute permission for all conforming types of development. This proposal, however, met with strong resistance from the professional planners and the RTPI, and at the time of writing the government has still not succeeded in putting it into effect.

Another radical initiative in the inner-city areas has been the establishment of two Urban Development Corporations, in the London Docklands and in an area of inner Liverpool respectively. This might be seen as a logical extension of the reversal of the new towns policy, and the concentration instead on the needs of the inner cities, announced by Peter Shore for the then Labour government in 1976. Again, however, the implications are ambiguous. The Corporations are of course presented by the Conservative government as promoting entrepreneurial attitudes and private initiative, and they do, as a matter of fact, work in close partnership with the private sector. From another point of view, however, they can be seen as examples of strong state enterprise; they are modelled on the new town development corporations, and they have rather all-embracing powers, overriding virtually all of the powers of local government within their respective areas. That only two have been set up perhaps reflects the government's own ambivalence concerning them.[22]

The argument is, then, that the initiatives of central government in this field of policy since 1979 have consisted to a large extent of political window-dressing, and that their actual effects are unclear. What the professional planners should have been doing since 1979, therefore (and indeed, at any other time) is researching the effects of planning policies. If the planning policies imposed by central government since 1979 have led to a changed distribution of environmental costs and benefits, it is the planners' job, as the experts in this particular field, to point this out. If, for example, these post-1979 policies have caused the environmental privileges of the already privileged to be even further enhanced, and if, conversely, these policies have brought about a further deterioration in the environmental conditions in which the poorest groups in society are living, then the planners should not only know the facts concerning these matters, but should also be able to explain the causal mechanisms involved.

If the debate is not conducted in terms of such outcomes, indeed, what is it all about? If the planners do not point to changes in the *effects* of planning, what are we to make of their complaint that the government is engaged in an 'attack' upon it? If it is not the effects on which they concentrate their interest, there is a strong suspicion that their real concern is to preserve their own right to engage in the 'planning process', to operate certain administrative procedures, almost irrespective of their effects. This, for example, might explain their reaction to the proposed 'simplified planning zones', as described above. And indeed, it seems fair to say that in general the planners' response has in fact been at this level. Their 'defence' has been largely at the same level of generality, impression management and symbolism as the Conservatives' 'attack'. What the planners are defending above all, it seems, is their right to '*do*' planning, rather than any specific outcomes which this 'planning' produces.

And in thus urging 'planning', they are caught in an unfortunate semantic trap, again of their own making. To urge 'planning', since the term has clear political connotations and is associated with at least some measure of movement away from the market and towards a 'command economy', is to make onself, as a supposed technical expert, politically suspect.[23] The position of these experts would be far stronger if they could avoid this title, and this rhetoric, and get on with the technical task of discovering the distributional effects of policies and decisions. Whether the effects of planning have actually changed since 1979 is a question on which it would be most interesting to have some information. One suspects, however, that despite all the professional and political 'window dressing', the *actual* effects of the planning system have not changed much over the eighty years of its existence; these actual effects have probably been mainly to maintain class privilege, throughout.

### 3.   How political clarification is prevented

The freer and franker attitudes emerging in the wider political culture from the 1960s onwards, it has been argued, held out the promise of a better understanding of the real nature and potential of government control of land use. If they had been accepted as intellectual challenges, the developments listed above could all have been used by planners as means of thinking about and clarifying their own activity. The 'political clarification' of planning would have been promoted, by which I mean that its tendency to promote particular interests would have been 'laid bare', and this, in its turn, would have obliged the political parties to analyse it afresh, in terms of conceptions of social justice, and to make clear *their* beliefs as to the ways in which planning powers 'ought' to be used.

Yet in the event, this promise was not fulfilled. In the event, planning remained as narrowly technical, as avowedly non-political and as obscure in its purposes and its effects as it had ever been. Why was this? In trying to identify the factors which thus prevent 'clarification', I shall concentrate on the reactions of the planners themselves. This is not because the onus for the clarification of planning lies *only* with them, but because it might be seen as lying *mainly* with them. To explain the attitudes and the reactions of the political parties, the other obvious potential source of this 'clarification' of the issues, would in any case have involved quite another kind of research. I shall put forward two explanations, though there are no doubt a number of other contributory factors. Those which I suggest are both manifestations and consequences of the ideology which was evolved historically to secure the legitimation of planning, as analysed in Chapters 2 and 4. These suggested explanations of continued obscurity can equally be seen as 'defence mechanisms', but in saying this, there is no suggestion of conscious intent. Rather, the planners' responses are simply reflections of the fact that due to its history and its ideology, their profession was intellectually unprepared for challenges of the kind I have discussed. The two suggested explanations can be termed 'rejection by affirmation' and 'role muddle'.

#### (a)   Rejection by affirmation
'Rejection by affirmation' means preventing something from happening by

asserting not only that it has already happened, but indeed that one welcomed it. In this case, it will be remembered, the event in question can be conveniently summed up as the political clarification of planning. We might equally call this ploy 'keeping politics out by claiming to have already let politics in'. To work, of course, it depends upon misunderstanding, misrepresenting, and above all on oversimplifying whatever it is that one is 'defending' oneself against. But this, it should be added, is no machiavellian or even conscious ploy. It is merely the misunderstanding, misrepresentation or oversimplification of which we are all only too capable, in relation to things in which we have no great interest (or perhaps, which we fear).

It is very convenient, after all, not to understand the full implications of things which are themselves inconvenient to us. 'Rejection by affirmation', then, works on the purely semantic level. Using it, we claim to have done what our critics criticize for not having done—by misunderstanding what they are asking us to do. 'Rejection by affirmation', then, centres on the statement 'planning is political'. When social scientists said this, it was a 'shorthand' way of summing up the need for all manner of empirical investigations and philosophical analyses; it constituted a programme, a statement of the need for a reorientation. Planners, however, took to repeating it as if it summed up the fact that this reorientation had already been achieved. For about a quarter of a century now, it has been *de rigeur* among them to repeat this statement, but in all this time, they have not even begun to grasp its meaning. Indeed, they seem often to use it as an incantation, to ward of evil; by constantly repeating it, they reassure themselves and each other that they have 'seen the light', but they avoid the necessity of explaining what this enlightment consists of. Allison puts all this particularly well:

> Environmental planning, the processes and patterns of action through which the use of land is controlled in a nation-state, is political. In the last few years this truth has become a kind of trivialized orthodoxy. By this I mean that the statement is made or admitted without its meaning being made clear or its implications realized     the statement is a sort of semantic dignified element formally stated but playing no real part in the argument. People say it, but then argue as if it were not the case. This is reflected in a great deal of writing about planning'.[24]

In so far as planners *do* put any clear meaning on this slogan, they seem usually to take it to mean that 'planning' (still seen as a more or less 'rational' and technical way of ordering things) is *constrained by* political realities, and must work within a political context. But this is a complete misunderstanding. What the statement really means is that the idea of planning is itself a political idea.[25] One can only logically propose that land use be determined by planning rather than by the market, if *first*, one has committed oneself to some specific political philosophy, which urges some specific redistribution of the costs and benefits which the land and property market would otherwise produce.

And because this 'planning' is thus a political idea, it is clear that planning ought not to be urged by planners. As the technical advisers in this particular area, their task is to analyse the feasibility and the probable effects of planning. It is the *politicians'* job to urge it.

A second example of the way in which 'rejection by affirmation' works is provided by the debate (or rather, non-debate) over 'disjointed incrementalism'. Political scientists, sceptical of the claims of planning, have suggested that in practice, the rationality, comprehensiveness and farsightednesss implied by planning are not possible; in reality, they have suggested, most public policy-making is short-term, incremental, uncoordinated, and so on.[26] This could have led to fruitful empirical research, designed to discover the exact circumstances in which policy is likely to be more rational and less rational, more comprehensive and less comprehensive, and so on. If the planners and their critics had been prepared to clarify their terms to their mutual satisfaction, to agree on what counts as evidence, and so on, a valuable discourse could have been built up, in which eventually, no doubt, we could have arrived at a better understanding of the feasibility of those methods of decision making which planners urge.

This, however, was not the planners' reaction. Sensing that the theory of 'disjointed incrementalism' was an 'attack', and a 'threat', but at the same time sensing that it was an insight which, like the slogan 'planning is political' reflected a formidable realism, they adopted the same defensive technique, of taking over the phrase without understanding it. Instead of studying the *theory* of 'disjointed incrementalism', planners simply took over the phrase itself. 'Disjointed incrementalism', they announced, is merely one kind of planning. It is one of the most up-to-date, sophisticated types of planning, evolved to cope with the very much enhanced levels of political and social complexity and uncertainty now prevailing. Like the assertion that 'planning is political', the assertion that planners are using disjointed incrementalism as a planning technique is intended to demonstrate both their realism and their intellectual sophistication. In reality, it is vacuous, anti-intellectual and, indeed, ludicrous.

Both of the examples discussed reflect a tendency which is particularly strongly developed among planners, and especially in planning education, a tendency to pick up words and phrases and to use them because they sound impressive, rather than to seek to understand the things which these concepts describe.

### (b)   Role muddle

I am calling this 'role muddle' so that it is not confused (or muddled) with 'role confusion'. 'Role confusion', introduced in Chapter 1, is the tendency of planners to confuse their own task with that of other experts. 'Role muddle', by contrast, describes their failure to clarify the distinction between their own role and that of the politicians.

At the formal level, or when explaining their role 'officially', planners tend of course to place considerable stress on the traditional and formal distinction between 'officers' and 'members' in British local government. They tend to stress that it is the politicians who ultimately decide what is to be done, and that they themselves can only advise. In reality, I would however suggest, the professional planners tend themselves to identify rather strongly, in a psychological sense, with what is done, if not literally to take responsibility for it. Certainly, they do not restrict themselves to analysis, to discovering and to making clear the probable consequences, if this or that is done. And this, of course, is because they make 'recommendations', and because normally, as a result of the 'law of anticipated reactions'[27] these recommendations are accepted.

Thus, planners recommend what should be done. They do not, by contrast, analyse the probable consequences of doing various things. They do not, for example, see their task a that of analysing the probable outcomes of the various suggestions put forward by the various political parties. Nor do they take the objectives of the controlling party group as 'given', and see their role as that of devising technical means for achieving these political objectives Nor, for that matter, do planners even analyse the probable consequences of acting on *their own* recommendations.

All this we can trace back to the meaning which planners place on the concept of 'rationality'. They are mistaken in this interpretation, as I argued in Section 2 of Chapter 4, for unlike virtually everyone else, planners appear to believe that rationality can refer to 'ends' as well as to 'means'. Planners tend to think that it can be more rational to pursue certain objectives rather than others. Philosophers and social scientists, by contrast, suggest that our objectives can be justified only in terms of our values, and that rationality can refer only to the effectiveness with which we pursue those objectives.

And yet, it is clear, planners had no choice in this. They had always recommended what should be done, from the very earliest days of the planning movement, and had certainly not seen their role as that of researchers, analysing the probable effects of doing this, or of doing that. When, therefore, they attempted to give their professional activity more weight by suggesting that it was based on rationality, they had no choice but to commit this philosophical fallacy, to relate rationality to 'ends'; planners did not advise on 'means', after all.

The role conception which planners embrace, then, and which centres upon this belief that expertise can suggest what should be done in relation to any development proposal, is much older than the planners' claim to rationality. This role conception, which is, of course, traditional, unremarked and taken-for-granted among professional planners, is in reality illogical and confused, for quite obviously it cannot be the role of expertise to tell us what social or political values we should pursue. The only explanation of it seems to be that it is a consequence of the original assumption or assertion, adopted early in the history of the profession as an expedient way of making planning politically acceptable, that this 'planning' was a technical and non-political activity.

This, quite obviously, led inevitably to the planners in effect usurping the politicians' role. If advising on what should be done was an activity which could be based on professional, technical, and objective considerations, then clearly it is obvious that this activity would in practice, and despite the formal division of powers, pass fairly rapidly into the control of the professional planners. The politicians, therefore, would be superfluous, except of course, as 'rubber stamps', taking formal responsibility for what was done in their name,

All this, of course, explains why the technical analysis of the *effects* of planning has become almost totally neglected: if professional judgment indicates what is the objectively best solution, it is clearly unnecessary to discover the effects of adopting that solution; these effects are *by definition* the best that could be achieved.

The politicians for their part, however, and for their own good reasons, accept all this. In effect, there is an implicit bargain. The planners get the right to make what are in reality political decisions, on the understanding that they portray them as non-political, and on condition that they give the impression that these decisions could hardly be other than they are.

This 'bargain' is not inevitable, however. The planners could renounce it, by insisting that their proper role, as experts, is to analyse the probable consequences of doing various things rather than recommending which of them should be done. And if they had in fact insisted on changing their role-definition along these lines, the professional planners would certainly not have been so troubled by all the various challenges to authority which developed during the 1960s and 1970s. Rather than feeling it necessary to defend themselves against all this questioning and criticism, they could by contrast have joined with the critics, and helped to make their criticisms more technically informed. Putting all this slightly differently, we could say that despite all their rhetoric about professionalism and all their claims to professional status, planners do not behave like professionals at all. Rather, they behave like bureaucrats. They do not display that disinterestedness or that independence of spirit or of judgment which is the hallmark of an expert who has his own, *technical*, means of assessing the feasibility and the probable consequences of whatever it is that politicians or others attempt or propose.

The argument is, then, that professional planners are in a trap of their own making. Their status in society is reduced, their professional frustrations are increased, and, most important of all, they are unable to make the social contribution of which they are capable, by providing the technical understanding of cause and effect which would make our available political choices clear to us. And all this, I am suggesting, is because they have adopted and clung to a muddled conception of their own role. On the one hand, this mistaken role conception is too arrogant, for it gives them the power which ought to belong to the politicians, the power to make policy. On the other hand, it is too modest, for it deprives them of the power which they ought to have, the power to subject policy to critical technical analysis.

If planners are thus unnecessarily in a trap of their own making, however, this is certainly not to say that they could very easily come out of it. The process would probably take considerable time and considerable effort, for as shown in Chapter 2, the attitudes and values traditional in planning since the early days of the profession are by now extremely firmly entrenched and securely institutionalized. Nevertheless, it seems possible that changes could in fact occur, if advantage were taken of such opportunities as are afforded from time to time by shifts in the general political and social climate.

One such opportunity, for example, was offered by the publication in 1950 of the 'Schuster' report, which invited planners to redefine their role more in terms of the 'policy analyst' model (see Section 5 of Chapter 2). Another came in 1964, as a result of an initiative taken within the Royal Town Planning Institute itself to broaden its membership and to take on rather more the character of a learned society rather than a professional body.[28] A third such opportunity came in 1971, when again efforts were made to broaden the qualifications for membership and to render the Institute into a meeting-point for people interested in various types of 'planning'.[29] All three occasions, though in a sense internal to the Institute, might in fact be seen as reflecting shifts in the wider intellectual climate; other similar opportunities, as has been argued above, were offered by the various challenges to planning discussed in Section 2 of this present chapter.

But all of these three 'internal' Institute initiatives were rejected. On each occasion, the planners expressed a preference for a continuation of their self-imposed and narrow conception of themselves as local government bureaucrats.

To the question as to how planning might become politicized, then, the answer would seem to be that above all, planners themselves must free themselves from this bureaucratic self-conception, and from the narrow patterns of professional education which support it. They would have to claim, in effect, the status of researchers, demonstrating to the public and to the politicians the *effects* of planning policies and decisions. This would oblige the politicians to shoulder at last what is in fact their proper task, that of devising planning policies in the light of their political values, and mobilizing public support for them. The real nature of governmental intervention in the property development process would thereby be made far clearer than it is today. And the professional planners' role would thereby become what they themselves quite falsely claim it already to be—technical and non-political.

## 4.   Summary and discussion

Social protests and challenges to authority as these have developed from the 1960s onwards, focusing as they often have upon the physical environment, and especially because they have been backed up by clear and challenging academic and journalistic re-examinations of existing political institutions, have sometimes reached such a pitch of intensity that we might reasonably expect them to have led to the laying bare of the distributional effects of even the most firmly entrenched and powerful of bureaucratic machines. But this has not happened. In this chapter, as in previous ones, we have seen how authority both defends itself, and preserves obscurity. Such defensive attitudes, however, at least in the long run, seem hardly to be in the best interests even of the defenders themselves. Thus we might summarize the argument of this chapter.

To make some of the implications of this argument a little clearer, I can contrast it with a very different interpretation of the same events, put forward by Cooke.[30] Cooke's thesis is particularly relevant, for it may be seen as a sophisticated version of the planners' own view. He suggests that though having been hostile to politics in the past, the planning profession has more recently come round to a perfectly adequate understanding of the necessity for political struggle and ideological conflict over land use, an understanding which is reflected in a fundamental reorientation of planning practice. Cooke does not however ascribe this improved understanding and practice to any change of heart on the planners' part, or to any effort on their part to 're-educate' themselves, or even, apparently, to any significant extent to any influx of social scientists into their ranks. Rather, he sees it as an apparently more or less automatic reflection of social forces and consequent intellectual currents in the wider society. In the early post-war period, he suggests, the *general* intellectual climate was one of 'consensus', reflecting in effect a denial of the necessity or the desirability of conflict in society, and this view of things was shared even by social scientists. When the climate changed, however, the climate within the planning profession changed accordingly. Cooke therefore criticizes sociologists for seeking to explain the practice of planning in terms of planning ideology, and for seeing this ideology as peculiar to planners. Rather, he suggests, we should seek to explain it in terms of structural factors and social forces.

Though I think it contains some truth, I would put forward the following arguments against Cooke's thesis. First, it seems to me that he greatly exaggerates the extent of 'paradigm change' among social scientists, and among opinion formers generally. Rather, I would suggest, there was a wide diversity of theoretical viewpoints among them both *before* the rise of the environmentalist movement and protest movements generally, and *after*.[31]

Secondly, however, and even if one does admit a certain and perhaps significant degree of 'paradigm change' in such circles, it seems to me rather unlikely that planners would be greatly affected by it, or even aware of it. Planners are as a profession not notably interested in social and political theory. Their 'social theory' is of the unconscious, amateur, kind; they would in general tend stoutly to deny that it is social theory at all, but would tell us that it is merely common sense.

Thirdly, I would suggest that the implicit and largely unconscious ideological presuppositions of any group in society will tend to reflect that group's material interests and social situation, rather than any change of theoretical fashion among social scientists or other supposedly influential intellectuals. And the social situation of planners has *not* changed. They were local government officers at the end of the war, and they are still local government officers.

Fourthly, I have argued in this book that the whole function of town and country planning in society is not so much to produce any clearly specified physical outcomes but rather to provide legitimation; the social function of the planning profession, I have suggested, is to provide an ideology which portrays the operations of the property development industry as sufficiently promoting the public interest as to be socially acceptable. And to the extent that this analysis is valid, it would seem very relevant indeed to study the ideology itself, in order to understand how it performs this legitimating function.

Unlike Cooke, then, I would suggest that the analysis of planners' taken-for-granted social and political presuppositions *is* of value, and indeed that it provides one of the best ways, though not of course the only way, of explaining the nature and the physical outcomes of 'planning' in practice. That planners have in the main been unable to respond at the intellectual level to the various intellectual challenges mentioned in this chapter, seems to me also to be best explained in terms of their implicit social assumptions and their professional ideology. They have been unable to use these 'challenges', to fashion out of them a more intellectually credible and therefore useful and effective explanation of what they themselves are engaged in doing, precisely because their professional ideology and their taken-for-granted social and political assumptions rendered them incapable of doing this. Specifically, it is their *innocence of social theory* which renders planners incapable of harnessing these 'challenges' to their own advantage. It is this lack of interest in social theory which also explains their failure to work out any intellectually convincing explanation of the nature and status of the advice they give, and of their role relative to that of the politicians.

In trying to explain why the operations of and the effects produced by the planning system remain as obscure as they are, however, it would seem a mistake to attribute *all* the responsibility to the professional planners alone. In the opening part of this chapter I suggested that all involved in a given area of government, and not merely the officials within it, will tend to have a vested interest in ensuring that its usefulness to society is not questioned, and it is therefore necessary in this connection to look in particular at the behaviour of the political parties. And indeed, when we begin to reflect on the sheer extent of the parties' neglect of this area we begin to wonder if it is not here after all that the *main* blame lies. A very large population of all 'grassroots protest', from the 1960s onwards, has been about matters of physical environment or property development. Something like one-third of all complaints to the 'local ombudsman', the Commissioner for Local Administration, concern planning matters.

Yet the political parties have failed to bring planning matters within the sphere of politics. They have failed to 'theorize' such issues, to analyse them in terms of political philosophy, and to relate them to wider political ideas. They have failed to analyse in the light of any coherent conception of social justice the rapid growth in the power of the property development industry and its financial backers. They have failed to demonstrate the connections between the 'consumption' politics of the home neighbourhood and the 'production' politics of the workplace. They have with certain exceptions fairly consistently declined to acknowledge that environmental questions are political matters at all, and they have failed to acknowledge the political relevance of local environmental protest to such an extent that one might almost suspect them of *wanting* to compel the emergence in this area of extra-parliamentary politics. In strongly politicizing the question of land values while failing to demonstrate its relationship to town planning, they have made it even more difficult for the electorate to understand either of these things. In failing to take up the fact that planning has redistributive consequences, and in failing to give the electorate the chance of deciding whether it wants these particular kinds of social redistribution, the political parties have further obscured the real nature of planning.

All this, however, is perhaps too easily said. The problem, after all, lies in knowing where the 'institutionalization of scepticism' might begin. The political parties need the stimulus provided by research findings, before they are able to examine these in the light of their political philosophies and to politicize the issues. The potential researchers, for their part, are unable to engage in any very searching enquiries until such work is both demanded and given material support. The professional planners, who as I have argued are the people who ought, logically, to be providing this policy research input into the political system, simply do not see this as their job. Indeed, they seem almost to see their job as that of loyally defending authority *against* such research findings as independent academic researchers manage to publish. The situation, then, is one of stasis and stalemate, in which each of the main actors in the system prevents the others from making their much-needed contributions.

To the extent that we *do* have some knowledge of the workings of the planning system, in fact, this must in very large measure be attributed to the media.[32] The 'environmental correspondents' of the 'quality' newspapers, the makers of documentary television programmes and those journalists who have attempted to publicize questions of environment and property development in book form must surely all be seen as having made very valuable contributions. The extent to which such contributions can be and are ignored, however, both by the politicians and by the professional planners, is remarkable. Free and open public debate, in which the politicians, the professional planners and their critics treat each other as equals and with mutual respect, has been rare in this area of policy in Britain, and a large part of the explanation for this, it would seem, lies in the professional planners' implicit belief that the whole subject is highly 'technical', and therefore beyond the grasp of laymen.

In large measure, however, as I have tried to show in previous chapters of this book, the planners' supposed technical knowledge is not technical knowledge at all, but rests on a false portrayal of political questions as technical ones. And this, in its turn, results in the elaboration of a pretentious and intellectually inflated pseudo-technical jargon. To one who has taught in a planning school, it seems clear that the professional planners' *own* powers of clear thought and analysis are seriously impaired, as a result of being professionally socialized into these habits of expression.

So obscure are the characteristic thought processes and speech habits of planners, in fact, that one is obliged to take very seriously the Marxist suggestion that the entire function of the planning system is to provide 'mystification'—to conceal the way in which 'planning' in fact promotes the interests of private sector capital against those of the poor, the powerless, the consumers, the environmentalists and the working class. And nowhere, perhaps, is the need for clearer expression more apparent than in the way in which such interest groups are themselves discussed. What I have called 'political clarification' is quite obviously impossible, until we can bring ourselves to speak more clearly and frankly, and to identify the groups affected by policies in plain terms. There seems no indecency in this. It is in fact far *less* offensive than is the existing practice, of talking in a mealy-mouthed way of 'social factors', 'social considerations', 'the needs of the local community', 'the public interest', and so on. Analysis in class terms might in fact be a good first step towards true 'technical' understanding of planning.

Hall and his colleagues, it will be remembered, in their study of the effects of the planning system (see Section 3 of Chapter 3) distinguished the effects of policy on 'ruralites', 'new suburbanites', 'tenants in public housing' and 'tenants in privately rented property' among the 'consumers' of planning, while among those interest groups most influential in shaping the pattern of development they identified the developers, the local authorities (of various class compositions), the agricultural lobby and of course the planning movement and the planning profession themselves. This list is obviously not complete, nor was it claimed to be. Some interest groups will be both influential in shaping environmental outcomes and in 'consuming' them. We often belong to groups with conflicting interests, as for example when we take advantage of cheap air travel but wish to be protected against aircraft noise. Above all, of course, the identification of the class and other material interests involved in 'planning' will vary from issue to issue, from time to time, and from place to place. It is an empirical question.

Nevertheless, I would suggest, the germ of a clearer understanding of planning, or of what I have called 'political clarification' of it, is here, in the method adopted in Hall's research.

Healey,[33] like Hall looking at the planning system at the national level, identifies four main interest groups, manufacturing industry, the property development industry, consumer interests and conservationist interests. Her purpose is not political analysis as such, but rather to provide a broad characterization of past and possible future planning policies. Whereas most observers had identified changes over time in the *vigour* with which various governments have promoted land use planning in Britain, Healey suggests by contrast that perhaps what is of greater significance is that government has from time to time used the planning system as a means of promoting different *interests*. In the late 1970s and 1980s, she suggests, the planning system has been used very much as a device for aiding the property development industry. Previously, by contrast, it had been used rather as a means of promoting consumer and conservationist interests. The reason for this change, she suggests, is simply that the property industry has become more powerful, and is thus *able* to bend the planning system to its purposes. In the future, she however suggests, it may well be widely accepted that the need is rather to use the planning system in a third way, this time as a means of promoting the interests of manufacturing industry. And Healey traces out the implications of each such shift in emphasis, showing what powers and instutional arrangements are implied by it.

I am concerned here neither to comment on the validity of Healey's analysis of the interests which the planning system *has* promoted, nor to express any opinion as to the interests which it *should* promote, but merely to commend her mode of analysis. Such analysis in terms of interests, I have termed in this chapter the *political clarification of planning*, and I have argued that it is the most important of the technical tasks on which professional planners should be engaged.

# 7 Summary and Conclusions

The *customer* is always right: he can choose, criticize, and reject. The *client*, on the other hand, gives up these privileges and accepts the superior judgement of the professional. It is one of the aims of the would-be profession to convert its customers into clients and in so doing to stake out an exclusive area of discourse in which those persons trained in the skills and inducted into the 'mysteries' of the trade can claim a monopoly of wisdom and proficiency. A group of men becomes a profession by elaborating a language intelligible only to itself, and it is the sheer unintelligibility which persuades other men to take them seriously and to defer to them.

J.G. Davies, *The Evangelistic Bureaucrat*

## 1. Deprofessionalization?

Summarizing arguments put forward in this book, we can identify three reasons why we would be better off if planners ceased to regard themselves as a 'profession', and if the problems addressed by the planning system were instead to become the province of a variety of more specialized researchers and policy-makers. We may call these three reasons 'practical', 'epistemological' and 'democratic'.

### (i) 'Practical' reasons
The 'practical' arguments against the existence of the planning profession centre on the wide-ranging nature of all those perceived problems in society which have a spatial or land-use component; the case rests quite simply on the fact that there is too much here for any one kind of expert to comprehend. In Section 1 of Chapter 5, and on the basis of the argument that the logical and obvious starting point for the construction of a theory of land-use planning lies in looking at the physical environment itself, I identified a number of perceived social problems. Each had a

clear spatial dimension, in the sense that it could be observed in the form of such things as blatant environmental inequality, dereliction and decay, obvious physical inefficiency, pollution, and so on. By the end of that chapter, however, I had come to a rather different conclusion; each of these environmental problems, it was clear, is part of a far wider set of problems and interactions, which are not themselves peculiarly physical or spatial at all. I therefore argued for specialization; there cannot be 'environmental planning', I suggested, but only *specific* interventions in the economic and social forces which shape our surroundings, each designed to ameliorate a specific physical, economic or social problem. And each such specific intervention must be researched and formulated in relation to *other* areas of public policy, which are not physical or spatial at all.

To illustrate this 'practical' argument against the planning approach, let us again look at an area of public policy with an obvious spatial or environmental component, that of food policy. It is on the face of it odd that large sums of public money are devoted to agricultural research, and handed over to farmers to encourage ever-increasing levels of output, when in fact one of society's major problems is agricultural overproduction. The result of this policy, the intensification of rural land use, is arguably one of Britain's major environmental problems: first, it produces serious, ecological hazards; second, it renders increasingly difficult the coexistence of agriculture with any other activities or land uses, and in particular, of course, outdoor recreation; third, it leads to the destruction of the rural landscape which we have come to regard as a cultural heritage; fourth, by causing rural depopulation, it leads to problems in providing rural public transport and other physical services.

Already, each of these four 'environmental' problems can be seen to be quite obviously linked with wider, economic and social, questions of various kinds. But beyond these four 'environmental' problems, there are many other questions raised by this intensification of agriculture. And these too, if we are to understand food policy in relaion to land use, we must also clearly consider. Among these 'other' questions might be mentioned the desirability of producing surpluses of such things as cereals and dried milk, in order to give direct aid 'in kind' to countries subject to periodic famine, the desirability of a high level of self-sufficiency in food on 'strategic' grounds, the desirability of maintaining a class of owner-occupier 'family-type' farmers on 'social' grounds, and problems caused by the fact that agricultural land and property is increasingly being used by finance capital as a repository for funds which might otherwise stimulate the economy by being put into the modernization of manufacturing industry. The nation's increasingly economically important tourist industry is also directly threatened by this intensification of agriculture, the provision of social (as opposed to physical) services in rural areas is being made increasingly difficult, and above all, perhaps, every single one of these problems must be considered in relation to the fact that the country's food policies and economic and social policies generally are constrained by the requirements imposed by Britain's continued membership of the EEC.

Nobody, it is fairly clear, could be expert in all the various problems involved in national food policy. Yet politicians (or more accurately, perhaps, 'the political process') must arrive at some sort of 'answer' to it, and in arriving at any such answer it is clearly important that the political debate is informed by the arguments put forward by all manner of experts; often, these will speak for specific material interests.

Any food policy adopted, however, if its effectiveness is not to be be threatened *from this quarter in particular*, implies a complementary *land-use* policy. But this can now be seen to be a relatively specific and specialized matter, involving such things as possible legal limitations on the eligibility of persons or corporate bodies to acquire farmland, questions of land taxation, legal controls over the intensification of agricultural land use, and quite possibly, once overproduction is in fact acknowledged as a problem, various forms of financial encouragement for the transfer of land out of agriculture.

We thus see how *specifically land-use policies* could contribute to the achievement of a broad set of objectives, arrived at through the political process of negotiating and balancing competing claims. Each specific aim of any national food policy implies in principle a specific set of fiscal and legal constraints or incentives in the particular area of land ownership and land use.

Planners, however, tend not to operate on the basis of such a specialized role-conception. Rather, they seek *themselves* to arrive at the political balance. This is why in concerning themselves with 'rural planning problems' they involve themselves in all manner of economic and social questions, such as those mentioned above, and in none of which, of course, they could ever hope to be expert. At the same time, they neglect the very thing in which they could be expected to make a specialist contribution, analysis of the effects of specific forms of control over land use and land ownership.

The same argument could be put forward in the case of all the other areas of public policy with which town and country planning is involved. It could be put forward in relation to housing, transport, industrial location, and so on. If we look, for example, at energy policy, we see that the perceived problems here centre on the relative costs of various types of 'fuel' (including, of course, sunlight, wind power, tide power and the heat which can be extracted from the earth or from the sea), and on the dangers to life and health involved in the use of certain of these fuels (especially nuclear energy). Clearly, these are problems for society as a whole, and even for co-operation between nations, and the expertise required to illuminate them centres on the one hand on science and technology, and on the other hand on economics. Their land-use component, though clearly significant, is limited. Yet they are often quite misleadingly portrayed as 'planning' problems. It is assumed that 'planning', by which is meant a balancing of the claims made on land in particular places, can help us to decide whether or not a particular development proposal, arising out of the need to produce energy, should or should not go ahead.

Considering the above examples, of food policy and energy policy, we see how misguided it is to abstract out the purely spatial, environmental, or land-use aspect of every public issue, and to suppose that the resulting collection of abstracted spatial components can be the subject-matter of a discipline or a profession. What the town and country planners have done is abstract out in this way the purely spatial components of a range of problems or subject areas, and insist that these abstracted spatial components be studied and planned 'comprehensively'. In addition to the purely spatial component of agriculture, they have got hold of the purely spatial element of social inequality ('the inner-cities problem'), the purely spatial element in economic policy ('the regional problem'), the purely spatial elements of housing policy, the purely spatial elements in transport policy, and so on—each made more-or-less incomprehensible by being removed from its context.

The conclusion which I would draw from the above analysis, however, is *not* that the 'boundaries' are drawn in the wrong places. I would *not*, for example, suggest that the need is to draw the line around 'agriculture and all its public policy implications', instead of around 'the land-use implications of all areas of public policy'. On the contrary, I would draw two separate conclusions, one relating to the political matter of the formulation of public policy, the other relating to the social scientific matter of policy research. So far as politics and policy formulation are concerned, I would suggest, there simply cannot be any boundaries. Since political objectives are all in competition for the same finite resources, their relative importance must 'by definition' be weighed by the political process (even if this 'weighing', in practice, consists of ignoring some of them!), and this must inevitably be done in terms of values (even when those who do it tell us [or even themselves believe]that they do so on the basis of facts!).

Where knowledge is concerned, on the other hand, there *must* be boundaries, and these must be drawn quite narrowly if we are ever going to be able to study anything in sufficient depth actually to know anything about it.

### (ii)  'Epistemological' arguments

I have emphasized these, for this book has been very much concerned with the knowledge base of planning. On the one hand, these 'epistemological' arguments against the existence of a planning profession overlap with and help to explain the 'practical' reasons. On the other hand, they similarly overlap with and help to explain the 'democratic' reasons.

That a profession of 'planning' could reasonably exist is a belief only possible if we commit a fundamental philosophical fallacy; this is, to put it simply, the fallacy of believing that 'ought' can be derived from 'is'.[1] It is because they subscribe to this fallacy that planners can see the advice which they give as technical rather than political. Without this fallacy, the whole edifice of planning thought and practice would collapse. Planners would no longer be able to recommend *what* should be done, and instead would have to content themselves with researching the preconditions and consequences of doing it. The professional socialization of planners, then, rests on a crudely positivistic creed, which inhibits their capacity to distinguish questions of fact from matters of opinion. There are obvious dangers in this, even when it relates to a single, specific, and narrowly defined matter; it conceals from us the choices which we in fact have. These dangers are very much compounded, however, when we do *not* thus limit ourselves, and this is why I have looked first at the 'practical' case against the existence of planning. At the heart of the notion of planning is the belief that the planners can look at a range of different claims and arguments and arrive at the best balance between them. I have discussed this epistemological fallacy at some length above, and in this final chapter I will therefore limit myself to drawing out its implications for planning education.

To show the harmful effects of this fallacy in the educational sphere, we can compare the teaching of planning with other fields of knowledge and of practice, which, we might say, rest on rather more secure intellectual foundations. At the heart of the difference between planning and such other fields, is what might be called 'distancing'. The 'normal' relationship between knowledge and practice, as we see it in such intellectually more secure fields, is one in which a clear conceptual separation is maintained between *knowledge*, and *the uses to which knowledge is put*.

Indeed, this 'distancing' is often reflected also in an institutional separation, and it is this, perhaps, which helps us to see their epistemological separateness. This, in fact, might help to explain why it is that quite ordinary people can usually distinguish fairly readily between 'facts' and 'values', or between 'science' and 'politics'. Thus, knowledge produced by the biological sciences may be used in medicine, but equally it may be used in warfare. Knowledge of psychological processes may be used in education, but equally it may be used to sell cigarettes or cars. No doubt planners too can readily see this distinction, in fields other than their own. But how exactly do we make it in the case of town and country planning? What is the 'relevant knowledge', which could be used by governments wishing to intervene in the processes whereby society's spatial arrangements are determined? Whatever this knowledge is, the previous examples suggest it would be equally capable of being used by quite other actors, not, for example, to achieve social redistribution, but to maximize their own profits. For as the examples show, true knowledge is relatively neutral; this, one might say, is almost its hallmark, distinguishing it from ideology. And on *this* analysis, which is the one put forward in Chapter 5, 'planners' should be trained in the same places as are land economists, surveyors, valuers, and other professional advisers of the property development industry. The 'relevant knowledge' in both cases, is fundamentally the same. It is simply used in pursuit of different 'ends'.

If, then, planners were to be trained and to have their intellectual points of reference in independent academic departments of the universities, institutions concerned with producing knowledge of the development process, and not seeing it as any of their business to concern themselves with the uses to which this knowledge is put, this would clearly enhance the intellectual independence of the planners themselves. Research, in any subject, means critically investigating the way in which things work. The reason for the oft-cited fact that the planning schools produce so very little research, then, is very largely that it simply *does not occur* to planners to investigate critically the way in which planning works. In large measure, this is because they 'identify' so closely with it, and therefore seek, rather, to defend it. By developing an image of planning as highly technical and complex, and as demanding of its practitioners qualities of judgment of a high order, they seek to enhance its perceived status. By portraying it as a rewarding career, and in 'bad times' when jobs are fewer even by asserting that a training in planning is an excellent general education, fitting one for virtually any *other* occupation,[2] they seek to attract students. Thirdly, they sustain morale, that of their colleagues in local government, that of their students, and their own alike, by emphasizing the 'mission' of the profession, and the rightness of its cause. The whole of this evangelistic ideology, it is important to remember, is built up around what I have termed the fundamental epistemological fallacy in planning, which suggests that it can arrive at more objectively valid resolutions of situations of conflicting and competing demands than can the political process.

The result of this evangelical approach, I have argued, is to produce tension and frustration; the 'image' and the reality of planning stand in sharp mutual contradiction. Planners often seem to attempt to reduce this tension by living in hope; they sustain themselves with the belief that eventually, and however slowly, planning in practice must inevitably come more closely into line with the 'rational' model in which they have been taught to believe. In particular, hope seems often to be maintained by placing the blame for the continuing gap between the ideal and the reality upon external factors—on the 'irrationality' of the encapsulating political system, on the fact that the public has not been educated into an understanding of the need for planning, and so on.

The tension, then, is not between the planning schools and planning practice. Much of what is done in local government planning departments is quite as out of touch with reality as what is taught in the planning schools. Rather, the tension reflects the fact that while the planning schools and the practitioners alike want to believe that planning improves the physical surroundings of the less privileged sections of society, the available evidence fails to support this belief.

Planners not only tend to believe that there is a technically based way of arriving at the objectively best solution to any problem. They also, quite naturally, believe that that solution *ought* to be 'implemented'. If it is not, then the blame must attach to those who cannot or will not understand the need for it. To a considerable extent, it seems likely that processes of self-selection are of importance here. Those who are attracted to planning as a career tend often to be interested in design, in technical matters and in 'things', rather than in ideas, human behaviour, or social questions. They tend to low 'tolerance of ambiguity', to think that there is a 'right' answer to most questions, sometimes even to be somewhat authoritarian, and to assume that in ordering human affairs, just as in the world of cybernetics and physical systems, there is an objectively and technically best possible solution, the 'right balance'.

To such students, of course, the syllabus of the planning schools presents few problems. It confirms their taken-for-granted assumptions, and provides psychological support and reassurance. Not all students are of this type, however. Some, especially among those who were attracted to planning in the late 1960s and 1970s, when opportunities were expanding, were very gifted; such students often tended to find the syllabus intellectually stultifying, and reacted rather strongly against it. But sooner or later, it would seem, whether it occurs while still in planning school or subsequently, and whether it results in active intellectual opposition or is reflected simply in the resentful acceptance of a mortgaged life of dull frustration, the contradiction between the image and the reality seems to be experienced by most planners. Often, the final realization that the rational planning promised by the image cannot be found anywhere in the real world produces a fairly severe personal crisis. As Ravetz puts it: 'The indoctrination provided by professional training provides a powerful motivation that can dominate a person through a lifetime and which may carry the individual, if challenged, to the brink of destruction.'[3]

Those members of the staff of the planning schools who are not themselves planners, however, are also placed in an unenviable situation. To them, it seems clear that the planning schools are being used not for their proper task of achieving knowledge of the ways in which government could modify environmental processes, but rather as places in which belief and commitment are inculcated, and in which the power of a would-be profession is enhanced by creating an inflated conception of what its members do. To such 'non-planner' staff, it seems wrong, and in conflict with the whole idea of a university, that its institutions should be used in such ways. To those members of staff who *are* planners, by contrast, it seems quite obvious that such 'doubters' simply have no right to continue to hold their posts, since they do not 'believe' in planning.

There are, of course, important questions of intellectual integrity and of academic freedom posed here, and I would myself draw the conclusion that it should be carefully considered whether planning should continue to be taught in the universities and polytechnics at all. This conclusion does not reflect an exaggerated or naive belief in the supposed intellectual purity of true academic disciplines as opposed to the venality of professions. All academic disciplines are to some extent simultaneously networks of power and patronage; this is probably unavoidably so. The difference between such other fields and planning is not this. Rather, it is that these other fields, and despite their being as subject to human frailty as any other human institutions, *also* produce usable knowledge. The planning schools, by and large, do not, for quite literally, those who control them do not see this as their primary purpose.

### (iii) 'Democratic' reasons

The moral seems clear: if a 'planning' system exists, and if there also exists a profession whose members are socialized into a belief in their own ability to resolve on the basis of expertise matters which in truth can only be resolved in the light of political interests or values, then politicians will be tempted to *use* these institutions. They can be used to conceal the fact that political interests are in reality being promoted. In order to avoid the public exposure which is the source of all political success but also of all political ruin, and thus to make their careers more secure if less exciting, politicians will be tempted to redefine as many as possible of the potentially sensitive issues in society as 'planning' matters. By this means, such issues can be shifted from Westminster to Whitehall, from the national level to the local, from the ideological sphere to the technical, and from the political to the administrative. Also, they will become redefined as questions of 'land use', an apparently innocuous, and, from the point of view of the population at large, possibly rather boring category.

This, then, is what I have described as the implicit corporatist bargain; in exchange for some involvement in the decision-making processes of developers, and thus, a feeling of having some importance, the planning profession is expected to create for public consumption an ideology which persuades us that these matters are indeed local, physical, technical, highly complex and altogether best left to the judgment of those who are expert in them.

Instead of a national debate about food policy, therefore, we have requests that Ministry of Agriculture and Department of Environment officials should get together to iron out certain supposedly relatively minor matters arising out of a failure sufficiently to coordinate the needs of farmers in particular areas with the needs of visitors to the countryside. Instead of a national debate on the growing power of the roads lobby and the effects of ever-increasing levels of motorization on those without cars, we have administrative hearings at local level into the precise alignment of particular stretches of new road. Instead of a national debate about various possible alternative energy policies, we have again local inquiries into the pros and cons of enlarging particular power stations or of burying radioactive material in particular places. And so on. This is not policymaking. It is the triumph of inertia. It is achieved by allowing the less powerful only to request administrative reconsideration, and never to advance political arguments. And above, I have shown how it can be traced back to the central epistemological fallacy on which the whole idea of 'planning' is based.

As well as thus being cause and consequence of certin of our governmental institutions, however, the fact of official support for the ideology of planning also affects the planners' own behaviour at the personal level. Specifically, this official support encourages them in the belief that they are under little obligation to respond to criticisms in intellectual terms. When challenged at the intellectual level, planners tend to respond not at the intellectual level at all, but at the level of power. Their tendency is to 'close ranks', and to seek to isolate or silence the critic rather than to answer the criticism. Where the critic is within the planning field, as for example in the planning schools, their tendency is to treat the matter as one of loyalty; as noted above, they often suggest that those who choose to question or critically to examine planning ideas or practice have thereby demonstrated that they do not 'believe' in planning, and that they therefore really have no right to hold the positions they do. When, on the other hand, criticism comes from outside the profession, it tends to be discounted on the grounds that the critic, not being a planner, can hardly be expected to understand the complexities of the matter which he presumes to discuss.

## 2. Possible futures, with or without the planning profession

Further erosion of the occupational monopoly held by planners, however, is likely to be slow, and in the meantime there is a need to think about the rather different matter of the evolution of policy, and of the planning machinery itself. The three possible futures outlined below are intended only as ideal types, and certainly not as attempts at empirical description. The actual course of development, therefore, may embody any or all of them, in any possible proportions. Equally, it may embody quite other tendencies, which I have failed to identify. The first two of the trends I identify below, however, are ones which seem to be already clearly discernible, albeit in incipient form. The third, by contrast, seems to me rather unlikely. It is, however, the direction of change which seems to me most desirable, and I therefore concentrate upon it.

### (a) *Positive planning at the local level, or municipal corporatism*
The likelihood of this first tendency I see as in part dependent upon the extent to which the contemporary struggle for power between central and local government is resolved in favour of the local level; alternatively, it may develop within those local authorities which adopt more aggressive stances on this matter. The sources of this tendency lie not only in the attitudes generated by the conflict over local government, however. It also has its roots in the marked drift towards 'bargaining' in development control, in the urging of 'positive planning', in the increasingly prevalent idea that planning should be a matter of cooperation between the local authority and the developer, in the 'corporate planning' movement, and in the idea that land-use planning should be linked with an attempt on the part of the local authority to engage in local economic and social planning. Usually, though perhaps not always, the approach which I am identifying here will be most marked within those authorities which tend to 'local socialism'.

In Section 2 of Chapter 4 it was argued that if the main thrust of land-use planning in Britain were to continue to be at the local level, this would logically imply that the necessary 'research' input (in so far as there *is* any such input) would have to be focused on the individual planning application. The various sets of ideas mentioned above, all of them encouraging the emergence of the approach which I have characterized as 'local corporatism', and implying as they do a tendency to evaluate planning applications in terms of their effects on the local economy, on the local labour market, on rate yields, and so on, seem in fact to imply a situation in which development control in practice would become increasingly discretionary, operated on the basis of informal negotiation between the planners themselves and other functionaries and representatives of business interests, trade unions, the Labour Party, and other local pressure groups.

The problem of what I have termed the research element or knowledge base of this approach to planning, therefore, reduces itself to the question of whether there could in fact be found reasonably objective and consistent criteria for assessing development proposals in terms of the kind of welfare criteria which 'local socialism' assumes. Given the fact that to elucidate the social and economic impacts of even one development proposal *is* in a very real sense a significant piece of research, however, and bearing in mind both the relatively small numbers of people competent to do such work and the fact that the politicians within the local authorities in question will probably have their own ideas about such social and economic evaluation, it is difficult to believe that any very uniform or reliable system of evaluation could emerge. The result, I would suggest, is therefore likely to be something which, if we should be wary of calling it corruption, might be best described as a state of affairs in which conceptions of what is legitimate and of what is in the public interest will be fluid and negotiable.

Since I see this approach to land-use planning as very much tied up with the growth of the idea that a local authority should engage in social and economic planning, and since I view this last with some misgivings, it seems necessary to set out my reasons. First, it is widely accepted that these initiatives are unlikely to make any great impact on economic and social conditions within the areas in question, and that they seem to have largely symbolic or ideological value.[4] Second, these attempts by local authorities to attract employment to their areas are wasteful, for they involve competitive spending, among the various local authorities, to 'sell' their attractions.[5] Third, therefore, we may ask *why* they are engaged in, and here it seems likely that all this activity mainly promotes the interests of the local government bureaucracy itself. In particular, it seems to provide employment opportunities for a small army of 'employment planners' and 'employment researchers', and for what might be called the 'local government research and promotion industry', centred in such places as the Institute for Local Government Studies at Birmingham and the School for Advanced Urban Studies at Bristol. It has been noted above that many of the left-wing Labour councillors who urge these approaches are themselves either academics or professional officers in other local authorities.[6] It seems unlikely that these activities reflect the attitudes of the majority of the electorates in the areas in question, who probably in general realize that the possibility of local economic recovery depends rather on decisions made at national level. Having expressed these reservations, one should perhaps add that such initiatives might help, marginally, while nevertheless doubting the value of all the 'planning' which seems to be associated with them.

(b) *Whitehall corporatism: a Ministry for the Development Industries?*
Like 'local corporatism', this is a tendency which is, as noted already, apparent. Increasingly, the Department of the Environment seems to prefer to control the pattern of development by dealing with major developers or their national associations 'direct', rather than by going through the cumbersome statutory procedures of local planning. As mentioned in Chapter 6, these emerging patterns hinge on such means as enabling developers to take part in joint 'land availability studies', the outcomes of which the local authorities are expected to accept, and requiring alterations to be made in structure plans submitted by local authorities to the DoE for approval. In a sense, it is perhaps surprising that the property development industry has until now *not* had a ministry of its own. It has been one

of the fastest-growing sectors of the economy, and the pension and insurance funds on which it is dependent have themselves played an increasingly important part in the structure of finance capital. Again, this industry has suffered instability and fluctuations in its fortunes, to a degree which, because it has attracted public criticism and disquiet, has almost *invited* 'regulation by mutual understanding'. The Property Advisory Group within the Department of the Environment has however apparently constituted in embryonic form the beginnings of such as 'Ministry of Property Development', and is presumably capable of being expanded.[7]

As well as being apparent in incipient form, however, this tendency to central government direct control by informal means seems to be in fact virtually advocated, at least by certain writers. Healey,[8] for example, in urging that government should use its land-use planning powers in such a way as to facilitate the operations of manufacturing industry rather than those of the property industry, would seem to be in fact advocating such informal 'bending' of existing statutory powers, albeit to aid rather different economic interests.

In fact, however, one would think that manufacturing industry is already 'well-connected' in this sense, not only in Whitehall, but also at Cabinet level. On those occasions when major industrial enterprises *have* wanted to develop in green belts, national parks, or generally in the 'wrong' places, they have often been able to obtain governmental interventions overriding the Department of the Environment's 'planning' criteria. And if industry in Britain *does* require governmental encouragement, one would think that in general there are more obvious ways to provide this; lack of land, of suitable sites for expansion, or even of infrastructure, are surely not in general among British industry's major problems.

One's reasons for viewing this tendency with misgiving are much the same as those set out in the case of 'local corporatism'. The interests of consumers and environmentalists, which I would assume it should be the main purpose of any intervention in the property development process to safeguard, seem on the whole to be better served by public campaigns, open political debate and the parliamentary process than by direct access to Whitehall, where their economic and political insignificance seem usually to be seen as grounds for according them little beyond politeness. Though such weaker interests and the proponents of progressive redistribution may be admitted into corporatist decision-making processes ostensibly as 'equal partners', therefore, they seem unlikely to be accorded equal treatment. It is arguable, for example, that the reason why the 1947 planning system 'lost its way' is precisely that it was so very much the result of Fabian consensus-style infiltration of the Whitehall bureaucracy, by the Town and Country Planning Asociation; it is precisely *because* the proponents of redistribution were 'inside', and incorporated, the suggestion is, that their arguments failed to get the widespread public airing on which politicization of their case depended. This, for example, might explain the relative lack of concern displayed in 1953, when the whole economic basis of the 1947 Town and Country Planning Act was destroyed.

Above all, it is from a belief that the purpose of public policy should be publicly comprehensible, that one has misgivings concerning this tendency to 'Whitehall corporatism'. When one considers how obscure are the purposes and how mysterious are the operations of the British planning system even now, under what is still, nominally at least, a statutory and regulative approach, one realizes how very much more opaque this system might become, if it became accepted as legitimate that the Department of the Environment should by direct and informal means manipulate the planning system in such a way as to promote the wider political objectives of the government of the day.

Since what I would identify as implicit and taken-for-granted corporatist assumptions seem fairly widespread, and indeed to be the dominant ideology among those who discuss land-use planning in Britain, it seems useful at this point to explain a little more fully why I find this approach questionable, whether it is applied to the local level or the national.

First, these writers[9] say too little about the *purposes* of governmental intervention (or participation) in the property development process. Before one has a case for such intervention, or 'planning', I would suggest, one must identify those features of the property industry or of the pattern of development which one finds objectionable. These writers, however, do not say very much for example concerning the fact that the different social classes in Britain tend to live in surroundings of very different standards. Nor do they take any very clear stand one way or the other concerning the rapid growth in the economic and political power of the property industry and its associated financial institutions. Nor do they usually devote much space to the absolutely central question of whether increases in land and property values should in law belong to the property owners and developers or to the state. What, then, is the *purpose* of the complex negotiatory processes which they explore in such detail, and which they urge? One almost suspects, to adapt a well-known phrase, that in planning, it is the process which is becoming the purpose.

Second, then, we may note that these writers say very little about *the need for political direction.* Yet this, as we have seen from the history of 'planning' so far, is crucial. What the system of control is able to achieve will depend quite obviously upon the way in which the issues are clarified in open and public political debate. Without such political direction, the system of control simply gets lost within its own intricacies.

Third, and as an obvious corollary of the two previous points, we can note that such writers tend to assume that in so far as there *are* any clear policies or rationales for intervention, *these will evolve, in practice, out of the process of intervention itself.* Since this seems almost inevitably to mean that they will evolve largely out of the process of interaction between the planners and those whose activities they plan, in a style which I have identified in this book as incipiently corporatist, I regard this confusion of policy-making and policy-implementation with particular misgiving.

Fourth, these writers appear largely to assume that the priorities and the political objectives of recent governments are valid in an almost objective sense, as indisputable, self-evidently correct, and as hardly therefore requiring any analysis or vindication. In so far as they *do* ascribe any clear purpose to the land-use planning system, they assume its role to be *that of stimulating economic recovery in general and the operations of the property developers and industrialists in particular.* But no very convincing explanation is offered as to *why* it is that these particular interests find it so difficult to operate without 'encouragement', or why it is that they, rather than other interests in society, should be 'encouraged'. If to stimulate the economy is the aim, there would seem many more appropriate ways to achieve this than through 'land policy'.

What this school of thought seems in fact to reflect, I would therefore conclude, is an attempt to find a role for planners, and, moreover, a 'non-controversial' one. Land policy as the promoter of economic recovery, I would suggest, is merely the latest in a long line of 'Emperor's new clothes' donned by the planning profession. The strong emphasis placed by this school of thought on the complexity of decision-making processes, both within the public bureaucracy and on the part of developers and their professional advisers, and the equally strong emphasis which it places on the need to subject these decision-making processes to academic research and analysis, coupled with its equally marked neglect of analysis of the *purposes* of intervention, reveals this school to be firmly in the mainstream of traditional planning thought, concerned with the 'planning process' itself rather than with the political intentions which lie behind it or the social outcomes which it produces.

What researchers and advisers should on the contrary be primarily concerned with, I would suggest, is analysis of the feasibility of political objectives in technical terms, as well as the clarification of them, and with advising on the means of their achievement. Clearly, I would suggest, this school of writing constitutes a managerialist philosophy. It is an attempt to demonstrate the need for planners, while at the same time allaying 'Establishment' fears by suggesting that what planners do has no political implications but rather is an obvious technical necessity.

As regards the probable outcomes, however, should this approach gain ground, it seems to me doubtful that these would greatly contribute to economic growth. Rather, I would suggest, this approach is likely to result primarily in a transfer of economic and political power in society, away from consumers, workers and environmentalists, and towards producers, management, 'experts', industrialists and capital.

In reality, one might suggest, economic growth might be better promoted by the very opposite tactic, of *reducing* the economic power of the development industry and its associated finance capital. If, for example, developers were deprived through taxation of the development value in land, this would enforce modernization and increased productivity in the construction industry, by obliging them instead to make their profits out of the construction process itself. It seems to me very odd indeed to suppose that the planning system should facilitate the operations of the property development industry, or even of industry in general. For these are the forces in society which, through their power socially to define certain areas as outworn, and as poor investment risks, and thus to shift prosperity elsewhere, have created the very problems of 'induced obsolescence' to which planning addresses itself. As a result of the operations of these forces, visitors to Britain have the impression of travelling through a semi-derelict land.

### (iii)   An alternative approach

In this final section of the book, then, and summarizing arguments advanced in earlier chapters, I put forward an alternative approach, characterized in terms of seven features.

First, this alternative approach has as its central feature and as its major aim the recoupment of increases in land values, not only on grounds of equity and economic efficiency, but above all as the obvious source of the money required to repair environmental damage. Second, this alternative approach is firmly piecemeal, and based on a rejection of the whole idea of 'planning'. As regards any objectives other than this central one of recoupment of rises in land value, I would suggest, these should arise out of political debate and specialized social and economic research. Thus, policies might be evolved with such objectives as improving working-class housing conditions, improving accessibility without reliance upon cars, reducing traffic noise levels, conserving wildlife habitats, bringing derelict land into use, or whatever. Each, I would suggest, is best researched by specialists, not planners. Each does, however, imply specfic controls (or perhaps relaxation of controls) over the ownership and use of land. (Many non-physical public policies equally require such land-use controls for their effectuation, for that matter.) Third, the suggested approach is firmly backward-looking. Instead of attempting to justify policies in terms of supposed future economic and social trends, policy-makers would base them on research into the effects of past policies. Fourth, the suggested approach rests on a separation of policy-making from implementation, the former being seen as essentially a matter of politically-motivated research and the latter as routine public administration. Fifth, and as an obvious corollary of the previous point, this suggested approach is based on rule of law, and reflects an attempt to reduce 'discretion' to a minimum. The routine putting into effect of policies would rest on clear rules, comprehensible to all. Sixth, the approach assumes that in principle policies should be formulated at the level of central government, and rejects the right of local authorities to make their own policies. Seventh, and finally, this alternative approach suggests a need for a much higher level of politicization. At the same time, however, it suggests that the proper role of experts in the public service is to subject policies to analysis, in principle, in purely technical terms. Having set out these seven points, I will discuss them a little more fully one by one.

*First*, then, we can look at the economic basis of the system. A 'national environmental protection service', if it is to be effective, requires an income. Many of those parts of the country whose populations suffer the worst environmental conditions, and in which intervention is therefore most urgent, are those from which both economic activity and households seeking more attractive surroundings have fled. Older industrial regions and the inner cities are of course the main examples of such areas. If it be considered that the 'narrow' economic calculations which lead to such private locational decisions are in some sense mistaken, or 'antisocial', and that on a wider interpretation of economics there is a case for reviving areas, milieux, artefacts, landscapes, and perhaps even lifestyles labelled as declining or uneconomic, then it seems reasonable that the finance required to achieve such revival should be obtained from recoupment of the betterment value thus produced in the more favoured areas.

It is after all manufacturing industry and the private sector generally, we might reasonably point out, which has the power to 'socially define' certain places as areas of opportunity and others as areas of hopelessness. Households, too, remove themselves to the suburbs from the areas thus socially defined as undesirable. In doing so, they help to accentuate their stigmatization further, and the dereliction and decline of property values within them. They also compound the damage they have already inflicted, by requiring pollution-creating radial motorways to be constructed through the neighbourhoods they have thus stigmatized. And it is out of the migration of population and capital, produced by this power of the private sector to label and to stigmatize, that the property development industry is enabled to make much of its profits. It is by inducing premature obsolescence in *one* place that economic demand is created for new development in *another*.

The suggestion is, then, that all these are negative externality effects, and should be compensated. Recoupment of the development value thus created in the areas defined as desirable is the obvious and logical source of the resources required to repair the damage which the migration of capital and population has caused. For without this power to socially define areas as outworn, outdated, unfashionable, even as dangerous, and certainly as best avoided, the property industry would lose much of its momentum, and many of its business opportunities. To regard this creation of the perception that an area lacks development potential as a negative externality effect is merely the converse of the statement that all development value in land is socially created.

The unearned profits or 'unearned increment' made out of specifically environmental processes, it is therefore suggested, should be expropriated, and used to repair damage done to the environment elsewhere, by those same environmental processes. This would include not only those places defined by the private sector as not worth investing in or living in, and best left to their fate, but also all those other places and populations affected by any other kind of pollution, environmental degradation or externality effect which the 'environmental protection service' has not succeeded in dealing with by other means. Featuring very largely on this list of 'other' problems, one might suggest, would be the isolating of motorways and other heavily trafficked roads from the residential areas through which they pass.[10]

What kind of money are we talking of, and how far might it go towards providing the different classes in society with somewhat more equal standards of environment? In 1948, it was estimated that the 'development charge' or recoupment of betterment to be levied under the 1947 Act, at 100 per cent, would yield £9 million per annum. By the time that the 1967 Act was on its way through Parliament, the yield was estimated at £80 million per annum, even though this time the rate was to be only 40–50 per cent.[11] At 100 per cent, then, this 1967 figure would be about £178 million per annum. The estimated rise in yield, over this twenty-year period, is therefore about twentyfold. The level of prices *generally* in 1968 however, as measured by the Retail Price Index, was only about 2¼ times what it had been in 1948. In other words, the price of land with development potential had risen about 9 times faster than had prices in general.[12] If we assume that the price of land with development potential rose again in the *next* twenty-year period, 1968 to 1988, at a rate nine times greater than the rate of inflation generally, we arrive at an estimated 'yield', from a hypothetical 100 per cent betterment tax imposed in 1988, of some £9612m. If, then, on the grounds that it is perhaps desirable to keep the market in existence, in order to provide some indication of consumer preferences and opportunity costs, we were to recoup betterment at (say) 45 per cent, the annual income thus provided would, on these admittedly rough figures, be £4325 m.[13]

Even funding at this kind of level may seem inadequate however, when we consider the magnitude of the resources available to those whose activities the interventions would be required to counteract. Already by 1982, for example, the pension funds alone held £64 billion.[14]

Nevertheless, one may feel, funding at the level made possible by the recoupment of betterment would at least be rather more adequate than the resources *currently* devoted to the task of reviving 'outworn' areas. The low levels of funding of all the various types of aid given both to the inner cities and to the economically depressed areas have already been referred to. The general view, it has been noted, is that all such efforts can best be understood as having largely symbolic rather than real functions. As an outstanding example of this kind of misrepresentation of the scale of the forces which produce the existing spatial pattern as compared with the scale of the resources which would be required in order to modify it, one can mention for example a speech of Mr King, Minister of State for Local Government, at a private conference of directors of leading British and American firms held at Sunningdale in April 1980. King urged his guests to hand over a part of their profits to the 'inner cities', partly in their own interests, but partly also in recognition of the fact that government had helped industry by establishing 'enterprise zones', and continued: 'If British Petroleum, which made £1,600m this year, were to hand over £100,000 to the inner cities it would make a big difference. Yet that sum of money is within the margin of error accountants accept in drawing up the balance sheets and would pass unnoticed.'[15] Quite apart from King's apparent assumption that such falsification of company accounts is perfectly moral, one can only note the magnitude of the insult. This is 'conscience money', given by those who, like primitive farmers, miners or those who fell tropical rain forest, have extracted what they could, and have moved on, leaving the areas and their populations to their fate.

How might betterment be recouped? One obvious way, of course, is by requiring all land to pass through the hands of public authorities before it is developed, as under the 1967 and 1975 Acts. This is a perfectly reasonable solution, provided that this time, it could be ensured that political support could be secured for it from all parties, rather than as on the two previous occasions, simply attempting to 'impose' it. In Sweden, the effective recoupment of all development value by this means forced developers to get their profits out of the construction process, rather than out of increases in land values, with the result that they were obliged to increase their economic efficiency. By 1980, the construction costs of small houses were only 98 per cent of 1965 levels in real terms, while building labour productivity rose by almost 250 per cent from 1950 to 1980.[16]

What I would suggest, however, is that taxation should apply to *all* land, and not only to that which is developed. As Ashworth[17] points out, the real weakness of the 1947 Act was not that it kept land off the market or discouraged development, but that it created unfairness as between those who developed their land (or sold it for development) and those who did not. For *existing* use values can rise, and as a result of exactly the same processes as those which create development value. For all the 'usual' reasons, including such things as an enhanced level of economic activity either nationally or in the area in question, urban growth, provision of infrastructure, removal of negative externalities or provision of positive ones, changes in relative transport costs, and so on, the existing use values of all kinds of property can rise at a rate which exceeds the general rate of increase of prices. And owners, whether individuals or firms, can of course *realize* this rise in existing use value, either by selling, or, for example, by raising larger mortgages. Had these rises in existing use value been taxed under the 1947 Act, just as realized development value was taxed in the form of the development charge, the comparative advantage of (as it were) 'denying the existence' of development value, by keeping one's land off the market, would have been lost. The market, then, would presumably *not* have 'dried up', as it is so widely accepted it did. Putting the matter a little differently, we can say that the 1947 Act allowed the owner himself to decide whether any development value attaching to his land should or should not be realized; *this*, we might say, was its central weakness.

If, then, recoupment were to be imposed *both* on rises in existing use value *and* on development value, whether realized or not, and if it were government, rather than the owner, which had the power to decide whether development value should be realized (by 'zoning', or determining the use of all land), then there would seem to be little likelihood of such recoupment of betterment leading to any drying up of the market. On the contrary, such a tax would stimulate the market; owners of land with development value would now be unable to afford *not* to develop it, since only by this means could they pay the tax.

It is sometimes seen as surprising that the Labour Party has advocated such a system of site value taxation, for, it is pointed out, it would simply lead to all land being put to its most profitable use, irrespective of social considerations. This is of course true, but it is only true in the absence of planning. If there is a planning system, then it is the planning system which, by zoning land for various purposes, determines whether it shall have development value. If planning 'intervention' takes the form of decreeing that land which in a free-market situation would have development value shall not be developed, then that development value is destroyed (or forced elsewhere). In this case, some tax is forgone (though it may be collected elsewhere), and this is part of the cost of the intervention.

What 'Uthwatt' recommended, at least for all those parts of the country already developed,[18] was a form of this site value taxation. The Report recommended that all increases in annual site value should be subject to a 75 per cent annual tax, 'site value' here including both value in existing use and development value. If annual site value rose for example from £200 to £300, the annual tax payable would be £75. If such a tax were imposed nationally, if it were applied to developed and undeveloped land alike, and especially, perhaps, if it were applied in the same way to land, especially in central areas, with potential for *re*development, then in the light of the figures set out above it would seem likely to produce a significant revenue. For it is important to remember that the figures set out above related only to the recoupment of *realized development value*. Here, by contrast, we are talking of a tax which would *also be imposed on rises in existing use value and on unrealized development value*.

As well as producing a significant revenue, such a tax would of course reduce land and property prices, and thus reduce itself. At the same time, however, this would have the advantage of reducing the cost, if compulsory acquisition of land for public purposes were to continue, as it now is, to be at 'market' value. Above all, however, such a tax would radically shift the division of the profits to be made out of the development of land, and thus the distribution of economic and political power in society more generally.

As an example of such a tax (though in this case taking the form of a *single* levy on unrealized development gains, rather than an annual tax), we can look at the way in which urban development is promoted in Denmark. Here, development is permitted only in a relatively restricted number of defined zones, each, generally speaking, immediately adjoining an existing built-up area. For each such zone, a plan is prepared, providing sufficient land for all the private—and public—sector development judged economically feasible and desirable. No development is allowed elsewhere, and no local authority is allowed to provide new infrastructure elsewhere. At the time the plan is made public, a betterment levy is imposed on all the land covered by it, representing between 40 and 60 per cent of the difference between the values of the various holdings in their existing, agricultural use, and their values in their new, planned, uses. These taxes are usually sufficient to 'drive out' existing owners. The only way they can raise the money to pay them, is by selling to developers, and the latter, since they have nowhere else to go, have no other way to continue in business than to buy the land in question, and to develop it in the way which the plan requires.

It is the *combination* of an efficient form of tax with strict and unalterable zoning decisions, then, which enables the planning authorities to achieve their objectives. The result is, we might say, virtually a kind of 'positive planning' even though achieved by purely regulatory means; the public sector requires neither to carry out the development itself, nor even to acquire the land for subsequent disposal to developers.[19]

Another example, though this time one based on annual site value taxation, and which shows that the approach does however have its problems, can be taken from Sweden. In parts of the archipelego of wooded islands off the coast east of Stockholm, site value taxation is driving out the remaining small farmers. The taxation authorities see the land as capable of being converted to the much more profitable use of plots for summer cottages, and therefore tax it as if it were *already* thus converted. The problem here, apparently, is that it is difficult to maintain that an area should be kept as farmland, forest, or wilderness, in order to meet public recreational needs, when much of it is *already* used for summer cottages.

In principle, however, the example does not invalidate the arguments set out above. Zoning for less profitable uses, if judged socially desirable, *can* be combined with this form of taxation. If, for example, the authorities had stepped in soon enough, and before too many summer cottages had been built, they would then have been able to zone these parts of the archipelego for farming, forestry and so on, in order to produce a landscape more suited to the recreational needs of those who do not own summer cottages. Those able to afford to build such cottages would then have had to go elsewhere. The tax revenues would have been lower, here in the protected area, than they otherwise might have been, but tax revenues would have been higher (if not necessarily by the same amount) in the areas to which the summer cottage development had been diverted. Land use would thus have been 'rearranged', and social costs and benefits thus redistributed, in favour of the less privileged. If the total tax revenue *were* lower, this would be a cost of 'intervention', one of the factors on the basis of which the social benefit produced could be compared with the cost of producing it.

And even now, of course, when fewer farmers are left, it is still open to the authorities to keep the land as farms, if they both consider that this would enable the area to be enjoyed by visitors without summer cottages, and if they are prepared to forgo the tax revenues in question. But in this case, I would suggest, the valuations for tax purposes of those summer cottages which already are in the area should be greatly increased, for they would then have the benefit both of being in areas protected at public expense against further development, and of the proximity of the very attractive small farms. Again, the example shows the importance of devising land-use controls and taxation policies jointly, as two parts of a single operation.

The *second* feature of the alternative approach which I am outlining was that it should be piecemeal. The whole idea of 'planning', I suggested, should be abandoned, and we should instead think in terms of specific interventions. Hallet[20] comes to similar conclusions, if for different reasons. It is because he sees the free market as inherently superior to state control in terms of efficiency that Hallet proposes a piecemeal approach; his concern is that the interventions should be subordinate to the market, and operate within the general framework which it provides. My own reasons for advocating a piecemeal approach, by contrast, centre on the quite different problem of the intellectual muddle which pervades planning in Britain. It is because the present system is *portrayed* as regulating all land use, I have argued, that we are confused, for the planners seem quite uninterested in explaining *when* and *where* and *to what extent* their regulation has resulted in the criteria of the market being replaced by other, 'planning', criteria. 'Planning' in Britain thus constitutes an impenetrable facade, concealing the operations of the property development industry. To overcome this, I have suggested, it is necessary to break down this nebulous notion of 'planning', and to compel the planners to tell us exactly *which* shortcomings of the market they are concerned to combat, one by one, and to explain how intervention works in the case of each one of them.

To continue for a moment with Hallett, however, we can note that he takes as his preferred model the so-called 'social market' economy of West Germany. In the land and property sector, just as in any other, the market is assumed to provide the basic framework, and governmental interventions must be conceived and effectuated within it. This means, of course, that where there is thought to be a case for intervention the case must be made, and to this extent, perhaps, one can go along with Hallett.

But it also means that where it is desired to provide any particular kind of public facility or non-market land use, the land must be bought at market price, just as in Britain, and here it is less easy to agree. Hallett's argument is, however, at least in so far as it applies to West Germany, that the public sector can well afford to pay this market price, since the high level of national prosperity produced by the economy at large has produced an affluent society, well able to afford to tax itself at high levels to provide those social facilities which the market fails to provide. And certainly, the 'interventions' need not be small. Large areas of agricultural land around the major cities in West Germany, for example, are bought by the public authorities and converted into forest, a solution far more effective in providing for the recreational needs of the urban population than is the British practice of merely preserving 'green belts'. Much land is also taken out of the market for co-operative and other non-profit-making forms of 'social housing'.

It is when we come to the question of betterment, then, that the problems arise. In principle, and in contrast to Hallett, I would suggest that all development value should be the property of the community rather than of the landowner or developer. The problem, however, is that if it is recouped at 100 per cent, this destroys the land market altogether, producing a situation in which it is difficult to obtain any idea of consumer preferences and opportunity costs, and in which all land must therefore be allocated administratively. If, on the other hand, it is recouped at *less* than 100 per cent, in order to keep the market in being, we then have the problems both of knowing at what level *compensation* should be paid, where planning clearly destroys development value, and of knowing what *price* should be paid, in the case of compulsory purchase. If we see development value as socially created, however, both acquisition at market value and compensation for planning restrictions seem unjust. The approach in which we 'split the difference', collecting betterment at less than 100 per cent, is in any case a retreat from pure principle; logic requires, as explained in Chapter 1, that we make up our minds one way or the other, legally defining development value either as the property of the state, or as the property of the landowner.

Yet such an abandonment of pure principle may still offer the best answer. It

would provide a solution both more workable and more equitable than has yet
existed in Britain, and if to pay planning compensation and to buy land for public
purposes at market prices offends our sense of justice, we at least have the comfort
of knowing that these market prices would be themselves very much depressed, by
the system of taxation. The only workable alternative, land nationalization
combined with allocation through competitive 'market' bidding, also has its
problems; it would mean that unless the overall distribution of wealth in society
were *also* changed, then only to the extent that government were prepared to
forgo the bids offered, could the pattern of land use be other than it is.

The case for a piecemeal approach, then, rests on the belief that solutions are
only found when problems are carefully defined. It is because so many different
perceived problems and policy responses are confusingly lumped together under
the name of 'planning', it has been argued, that this 'planning' is so difficult to
disentangle, so poorly understood, and therefore so lacking in public and political
support. The problem with 'planning' as it is at present constituted, it has been
argued, is that so many different and sometimes quite opposed things can be done
in its name, and that any interest which is sufficiently powerful can bend it to its
own purposes. If it were instead broken down into a number of discrete forms of
intervention, each of them being justified, formulated, operated, researched and
evaluated by its own networks of experts, publicists, and political commentators
and analysts, this would both facilitate clearer thought about the nature of the
problems, and reduce to manageable proportions the tasks of those who attempt
to deal with them.

One way of visualizing how this breakdown might work lies in reducing the
'package' of planning ideas of the 1940s to a series of policy hypotheses. There is,
for example, the hypothesis that the new towns would help to improve working
class housing conditions in London, the hypothesis that the green belt would
provide opportunities for outdoor recreation for Londoners, and the hypothesis
that over the region as a whole it would become decreasingly necessary for people
to travel long distances to work. If the achievement of each such objective had
been monitored by its own band of political analysts and policy researchers,
planning in the London region would have been far less likely to have been
rendered, as it in fact was, into an impenetrable mystery, in which everything was
supposedly being balanced against everything else. It is also less likely that the
planning system would have been misused, for example as a means of preserving
the exclusiveness of privileged residential areas.

Another illustration of the value of the single-issue, 'piecemeal' approach can
be seen in the case of an issue *not* uppermost in the minds of the framers of the
1947 Act, but which has certainly become a major problem since. Suppose that
planners had concentrated their efforts on the one single objective of reducing
traffic noise and nuisance. It might, for example, have been forbidden to carry out
any new development within one mile of a proposed motorway or other main
road, and elsewhere, the provision of embankments, acoustic screens and so on
could have been made obligatory. It seems likely that the pursuit of this one single
objective, precisely because it can be understood, and would therefore have

attracted public support, would have provided far greater benefits for society than
has all the mysterious 'balancing of conflicting demands' with which planners have
instead concerned themselves. The test of a good policy, it might be suggested, is
that the average person knows of it, knows its purpose, and the way it works, so
that he could, for example, explain it to a visitor from abroad.

The result of the opposite assumption, that we should instead leave experts to
decide the extent to which any given objective is compatible with the achievement
of any other, is that we have no means of knowing the trade-offs which have been
made. And these trade-offs, we should remember, are *political* trade-offs. Planners
claim to balance all desirable objectives one against another, and to co-ordinate
their achievement, but this claim is unsubstantiated. Indeed, it is unsubstantiable.
True co-ordination, I would suggest, is achieved by contrast 'from the bottom up'.
*If* and *when* the achievement of any given policy objective is found to be in practice
impeded by the pursuit of some other policy objective, *then* would seem soon
enough to research the 'collision' between the two.

In reality, such researching of policy 'collisions' is rare, in planning. It is rare, of
course, because the monitoring of the achievement of *individual* objectives is rare.
Assertion of the need to formulate policies 'comprehensively', however, is
extremely useful to those in power, for it distracts attention away from the fact
that many individual objectives are not receiving the attention they might be
thought to deserve. The assertion of this comprehensive approach can also serve to
conceal the fact that behind the screen thus provided, certain powerful interests
are pursuing their own particular objectives not at all 'comprehensively', but very
single-mindedly indeed.[21]

The *third* feature of the approach urged here is that it is based on research into
past policies. This was discussed in Chapters 3 and 4, and it seems unnecessary
here to provide any more than a brief summary. The gist of the argument, it will be
remembered, is that in fact the *only* way in which we can assess the likely effects of
our future actions is by studying the effects which they have had in the past. Laws
explaining causal relationships are not specific to time or place. The operation of
such laws, especially in such a complex area as public policy, is admittedly much
modified by other factors, and these, of course, *do* vary from time to time and from
place to place. It seems often to be overlooked by planners, however, that the only
real reason for studying these contextual factors is to try to assess the ways in
which they might *modify* the operations of laws of causation which *are* themselves
already broadly understood. To study the likely future contextual factors *before*
the general laws which explain the effects of various types of intervention are
understood, seems to put the cart before the horse, and it is for this reason that I
have tried in Chapter 5 to identify those fundamental laws on which any
intervention in the property development process should in fact be based. The
mistaken stress placed in planning on such data as opposed to these
fundamental laws is accompanied by an equally mistaken stress on 'forecasting'
future economic and social conditions as opposed to discovering the effects of past
policies.

Yet in reality, the future simply *cannot* be known.[22] While worrying much about the distant future, planners often fail to keep up with the future as it actually arrives; up-to-date statistics are probably worth more than futurology.

The *fourth* feature of this alternative approach is that it implies a clear separation between *the formulation and researching of policy,* on the one hand, and its *effectuation,* on the other. In arguing that planners should insist on responsibility for the objectives of policy being shouldered to a much greater extent by the politicians, I have also argued for a correspondingly increased division of functions within the ranks of the planners themselves. Some, of course, whether as policy analysts or as researchers, must be involved with the politicians in clarifying and formulating policies. Others, however, will be required to put into effect, in the field, the rules and regulations into which, in practice, policy finally resolves itself. One of the unfortunate effects of the ideology of professionalism, I have argued, is that it leads to misleading 'job specification'. Occupational groups which aspire to professional status tend both to constantly enlarge the apparent content of their training, and to exaggerate the time required for this training, in order to make their work look impressively difficult, to restrict numbers, and thus to keep up their salaries.[23] But beyond this, the 'collegial' assumptions underlying the ideology of professionalism lead them to claim that *the same* long training is required by all their members, irrespective of the work they do.

To some extent, of course, these status-seeking ploys have succeeded. It is widely accepted by the politicians, by the public, and by the universities and polytechnics which authorize the forms of training demanded, both that the planner's job is very 'technical', and that it involves a considerable measure of sound judgment. Planners therefore assess development proposals 'on their merits'. In practice, however, this assessment of 'merit' may mean little more than shrewdly discovering the extent to which the various interests involved are too powerful to be resisted. But this, of course, explains *why* it is that planners are accorded this privilege of assessing 'merit'; from the politicians' point of view, it has the useful function of concealing the varying extent to which control over sectional interests is in fact exercised. And though it is the source of such power as they have, this privilege of supposedly assessing merit and exercising professional judgement also has disadvantages, even for the planners themselves.

In reality, the rank and file discover, they are only able to exercise such judgment to a limited degree, or concerning relatively trivial matters. There *are* of course rules, even (or especially) concerning the matter of how one proceeds when there are no rules; the point is simply that in this case the rules are perhaps not sufficiently respectable to be enunciated. The result, then, is professional frustration; the intellectual pretensions which underlie the professional training are shown to be a sham.

And in fact, of course, one can see that even in terms of simple logic this notion of assessing merit is a sham. Those who claim to be able to discern merit should be able to *describe* this 'merit', to explain *why* it is meritable, and how they *weigh* one kind of merit against another. If they *cannot* provide such explanations, we must doubt their claim. And if they *can* provide such explanations, there is clearly no need for the privileges of judgment which they enjoy; once made explicit, the processes of 'judgment' described can be performed by anyone.

On the one hand, then, reliance upon the ideology of professionalism means that we have nobody who has been trained and who is prepared to operate as an ordinary official, faithfully and impartially giving effect to the regulations which the politicians have approved; all, on the contrary, have been socialized into the expectation of being able to operate as 'fixers', 'wheeler-dealers' and negotiators, getting their kicks out of the astuteness of the bargains they drive (even if in reality the extent to which they can extract concessions from developers is strictly limited).

On the other hand, equally, reliance upon the ideology of professionalism means that we have nobody who has been trained to look critically and impartially at the operations of the planning system 'from above', in terms of its purposes and its effectiveness in achieving these purposes.

All, rather, have been socialized into 'middle-level', 'managerial' expectations, into the assumption that their task is to operate within a framework of social values, practices, and above all relationships of power, which they take as 'given'. Control by such a middle-level managerialist stratum, I would suggest, gives us the worst of both worlds. Such people have neither the capacity to shape policy, nor the humility to faithfully carry it out. What they *have* got, is the power to shape policy in use, which means to complicate, to mystify and to muddy it, and then to use the resulting confusion as a pretext for claiming for themselves even greater powers of 'discretion.' If we look at such matters as immigration laws, public health regulations, or the control of traffic offences, we readily see the dangers of 'discretion'. Exactly the same dangers, I would suggest, exist in the administration of land-use controls.

In fact, of course, the trend of events is in precisely the opposite direction from that advocated here. Observers note an increasing tendency for development-control decisions to be unrelated to statutory plans,[24] while there is at the same time an increasing reliance on bargaining with developers rather than on clearly stated policies or standards. And these trends, I would suggest, are not unrelated to the continued growth of the planning profession. If large numbers of graduates are produced by the planning schools, it seems only to be expected that their colleagues within the planning bureaucracy will attempt to provide for them an equally large number of places within their own ranks, and will seek to enhance the status of the profession by according to this 'rank and file' as high a degree of perceived discretion in its work as can be achieved for it.

Separation of policy-making from routine administration, then, seems unlikely to be an objective viewed favourably by planners. But it may well be resisted by politicians, too. Those officials who define their role 'modestly', as that of faithfully putting policies into effect, throw onto politicians themselves the task of clarifying the purpose of those policies, a task which is indeed properly the task of the politicians, but one which they may not relish.

Those who claim the right to subject policy to critical analysis, on the other hand, may be equally resented by politicians, even if again mistakenly, for apparently usurping the politicians' own prerogatives. The way in which the planning profession *in fact* defines its role, however, as I have outlined it above, is probably one which many politicians find rather useful. The professional planners are probably highly valued by the politicians, both for their characteristic loyalty to 'the authority',[25] and for their useful capacity to weld political and technical considerations together into an impenetrable 'professional judgment'.

The *fifth* characteristic of the approach urged here is that 'rule of law' should replace 'discretion'. This, of course, is merely a corollary of the previous point, that policy-making be separated from implementation. It is difficult to go quite as far in this respect as Coleman does, however,[26] for her approach rests on a rather questionable assumption of environmental determinism. Nevertheless, the principle implicit in her proposals is accepted; legislation should, so far as possible, explain its own purposes.

But if planning law urgently needs rethinking, it also needs simplifying. Town and country planning is not one of the major institutions in society, and it therefore seems rather unreasonable that such a relatively large proportion of all extant statute should be devoted to it. Indeed, it has become so complex that it seems likely to add more to the incomes of lawyers than it contributes to the solution of environmental problems. Proposals for simplification, such as those of 'Dobry',[27] or the present government's proposal that conforming development be authorized automatically by the plan itself rather than requiring specific permission, tend also to be strongly resisted by the planning profession, for it, too, has a vested interest in the job opportunities made available by unnecessary complexity. It is true, of course, that the planning profession has been subjected in recent years to criticism, but very much more criticism will clearly be necessary, and at a more fundamental level, if a more rational approach to the control of land use is to emerge. So far, the criticism has tended to focus mainly on the authorization of specific types of development, and on particular local issues. There is a clear need, however, for it to focus instead on the fundamental purposes served by land-use planning, and the progressive reconsideration and clarification of planning law would obviously be an integral part of this process of questioning. Eventually, one would hope, this would lead to the emergence of clear policies and regulations, whose purposes were widely understood. The public is at present rightly suspicious, on the one hand of local planning committees on which developers, estate agents and property owners tend to be so strongly represented, and on the other hand of a planning profession which renders such relatively simple matters of property development into supposedly highly technical questions, thus enhancing its own status.

Many, indeed, suspect that these two things may be linked. And such 'local fiefdom', as Healey calls it,[28] is in any case a very strange basis on which to found any governmental initiative which claims to be concerned with the redistributive aims of a modern welfare state.[29]

The *sixth* feature of the 'alternative approach' urged here is that planning policies should be national rather than local; the power of local authorities to operate their own planning policies, I would suggest, should be withdrawn. There are a number of arguments pointing to this conclusion. I have already discussed what I see as the dangers of 'local corporatism', but more fundamentally, perhaps, there is the point that to the extent that policies become based on 'rule of law' rather than 'discretion', this in itself implies central control. Local authorities cannot legislate, and if the purpose of planning policy were to become more explicit in the legislation, public knowledge and understanding of its objectives would become more widespread. To the public, it would seem unreasonable that the law should vary as between one local authority area and another. Public support would probably also increase; while there is in general support for the law, there is far less for 'local fiefdom'.

Another argument for planning controls to be formulated at central level hinges on the knowledge base on which policy rests. In discussing monitoring, it was argued that if statistically valid inferences are to be drawn, this implies that policies must be both uniformly imposed over relatively wide areas, and kept in operation in unaltered form long enough for the effects to be discerned.[30] To the extent that local authorities can deal with planning applications 'on their merits' according to particularistic criteria, the possibility of learning anything about their effects is enormously reduced. 'Policy', in such a situation, will in effect vary from case to case, for criteria of 'merit' are ranked differently from one case to another. Monitoring in any statistically valid sense, therefore, will clearly be impossible. This, of course, was the problem faced by Hall, in his attempt to discover the effects of planning;[31] the *land-use patterns* produced by planning could be observed, but the *reasons why* planning powers had been used in such ways as to create those patterns was quite unclear. On further analysis, it was concluded that these reasons included such things as the desire to keep working-class people out of exclusive areas, the desire to keep up residential property values, the desire to keep Labour voters within the cities, and the availability of generous central government subsidies for high-rise council flats. In a very real sense, Hall was not studying the effects of *policy* at all, but the effects of the very various more (and less) respectable uses made by various interests of various *powers*. These various powers had been lumped together by the professionals in the field, in order to enhance their own perceived importance, under the apparently impressive yet in fact highly misleading title of 'planning'.

If there is to be *policy*, then, in the sense of legislation whose aims are both reasonably clear and reasonably 'respectable', it seems difficult to believe that this could emerge out of anything other than open and critical debate at the national level. I will return to this point below, where I consider the politicization of planning.

A further argument against allowing land-use controls to be formulated at local level centres on questions of equity. To the extent that local authorities are allowed to formulate and operate their own land-use policies, this is a clear encouragement to the creation of even greater environmental inequalities than already exist. It seems both inequitable and in conflict with the fundamental assumptions of parliamentary sovereignty that the same legislation can be used in various areas in pursuit of different class interests.[32] Yet again, Hall's research (*inter alia*) suggests that this is exactly how planning legislation is in fact used. Up to three-quarters of the population of England and Wales lives within local authority areas whose party-political control is normally rather unlikely to change,[33] and it seems inequitable that in the case of anything so fundamentally political as the control of land use, the very large political minorities in these extensive areas should be more or less permanently subjected to policies to which they may be opposed. This seems especially so, if one accepts as argued above that such controls over land use require to be operated as an integral part of a system for the recoupment of betterment; this, clearly, could hardly be a local tax.

Next, there is the fact that the institutions with which the planning system deals are themselves organized at national level. Developers themselves, their professional advisers and the financial institutions on which they depend all tend to be organized nationally, and even in the case of firms with more geographically restricted areas of operation, these exist within a national network of interest associations. To formulate land-use policies is to formulate policies towards these major economic interests as well as towards major nationally organized environmentalist and conservationist movements. To suppose that local authorities, and even the largest in the land, could deal with such interests other than on the basis of predetermined inferiority, seems unrealistic. The subculture of the planning profession itself is also national rather than local, and it is clearly difficult for local politicians to counter or even to question systems of professional ideas of the kind described in this book.[34]

Most fundamentally of all, however, in this statement of the case against allowing local authorities to formulate their own land-use policies, there is the fact that if planning is anything at all, it is the attempt to determine *where* development shall go. Land-use planning rests on the assumption that on the basis of some politically negotiated conception of what is socially equitable or likely to be economically efficient, development is steered to certain places rather than others; of necessity, this often means certain *local authority* areas rather than others. Since land-use planning is thus an attempt to influence the settlement pattern, it seems quite unreasonable, and likely to prove ineffective, to attempt to impose this control from *within* the settlements or localities themselves. Ever since it was decided at the time of the drafting of the 1947 Act *not* to entrust the planning system to a national planning authority, but instead to entrust it to the local authorities, the assumption has been that this steering of development to one place rather than another is achieved both through the power of central government to require amendments in statutory local plans submitted to it for approval, and through 'regional policy'; in reality, however, the extent to which either of these two forms of control has led to the imposition upon the local authorities of any kind of 'national plan' seems strictly limited.

Having made a case against local government autonomy in land use planning, however, it is perhaps important to emphasize that this case is not intended to apply to any local government activity other than planning; such wider questions are quite beyond the scope of this book.

The *seventh*, and final, characteristic of the approach urged here is a much enhanced level of politicization. Perhaps the main point to emphasize here is that if any effective land-use policies are to be formulated, there must first be found a politically acceptable and lasting solution to the problem of recoupment of betterment; the present see-saw situation renders planning in any real sense impossible. The public support necessary for the achievement of effective legislation, however, is unlikely to be obtained without considerable efforts of public education. And in fact virtually the same can be said about most of the other questions involved in land-use planning. All such questions hinge basically on economic theory, for the whole idea of governmental regulation of land use is predicated upon the desirability of social redistribution. Thus, it would be necessary to achieve a wider public understanding of the concept of externalities, of the workings of the property development industry, of the importance of the pension funds and insurance funds, and so on, and to seek to promote public and political debate of all such matters in terms of the kind of ethical and economic 'justifications for intervention' set out in Chapter 5.

In principle, however, one would not think that the public clarification of such questions would pose any great problem. Journalists working for the more serious newspapers, as well as television, have already done much to publicize these issues, and they are in any case ones which readily attract interest. The problem of the 'unearned increment' becomes actual whenever, as a result of the peculiarly unstable nature of the British property market, profits rise to 'unacceptable' levels, while the implications of the rapid growth of the financial institutions as a factor in the economy literally 'invite' serious investigative journalism.

The conclusion to which this book seems to point is that the reform of the planning system depends primarily upon pressure exerted at the parliamentary level and at the level of the national political parties. Though such politicization can lead to a simplification of the issues, it does at least succeed in bringing those issues to light. The very fact that an oversimplification can be recognized as such is in any case evidence that a less superficial understanding of the matter is claimed, or at least, sought. Eighty years of statutory town and country planning, in which the 'definition of the problem' has, by contrast, been permitted to be conducted in professional and bureaucratic circles, has led to no improved understanding, but rather to an ever-increasing confusion and obfuscation of the issues. Nor can it be said that the problems have been dealt with. In many ways the problems caused by the pattern of development and the institutions of the property industry seem even more intractable today than they did at the time of Ebenezer Howard.

A decreased level of spending on the planning bureaucracy and on planning education, therefore, and a correspondingly increased level of expenditure within those quarters which would clarify the issues by politicizing them, would seem to offer the best hope for the reform of the planning system, and within this broad framework I would mention two possibilities.

The first of these lies in public subsidization of the research departments of the political parties. The issues involved in any matter of public policy can by definition only be understood in political terms, and it seems misguided to pretend otherwise. Only political arguments, therefore, can make the issues involved in land-use .planning clear to the public, and money spent on such political clarification is therefore more cost-effective in promoting understanding than is money spent on the kind of supposedly neutral research advocated by planners themselves. If there is to be public control of the property development process, this should be because there is an informed political demand for it, and not merely because those who operate such controls have succeeded in establishing themselves within the governmental and educational bureaucracies.

The second possibility lies in parliamentary select committee procedure. The Conservative government of 1979 showed considerable enthusiasm for this procedure, creating a relatively large number of new committees; while it is clear that it was motivated primarily by a desire to strengthen the position of the government relative to Whitehall, and in particular, of course, to strengthen its financial control, the existence of these committees could in time come to have quite other consequences. The hope, of course, is that service on these committees could eventually open up an alternative career path for MPs, independent of the system of prime ministerial preferment and appointment to ministerial posts. Especially if something more nearly approaching a three-party system were to emerge, and if the members who serve on these committees were to be paid, they could eventually come to constitute a strengthening of the power of the House itself, and not only of the individual back-bencher, relative to that of the party machines and the prime minister. Specialization of interest among Members, a development which would seem highly desirable, would also be greatly encouraged. So far, of course, these hopes do not seem to have been realized to any significant extent, and prime ministerial patronage remains the only real career path, but there seems no reason to suppose that those who believe in the need to strengthen the status of Parliament will relax their efforts. One power which it has been conceded these committees do have is the power to publish evidence presented to them, and this could be very valuable in promoting informed debate in an area which, like planning, has become far too much the province of bureaucrats and professionals.

Also especially relevant in the present context is that the new committees established since 1979 are used not as previously for the purpose of reporting on specific Bills, but rather with a more general remit to oversee the work of specific departments. Though there is thus now an Environmental Committee, with a watching brief over the Department of the Environment, it must be said that if supervision is to be adequate, the existence of a single committee to cover the work of a governmental department with such diverse responsibilities seems hardly likely to be sufficient. If further environmental committees were established, therefore, and if it became increasingly the practice for researchers, pressure groups and those offering specialist advice to operate through these committees rather than through the channels provided by Whitehall, this would seem to offer the possibility of a much-needed enhanced capacity for linking political purpose with technical understanding. Eventually, perhaps, this would lead to demands for the statutory division of planning legislation into a series of more specific and more clearly analysed types of control over land use, each having its own rationale.[35]

Other means of politicization would of course also be needed. It seems clearly
desirable, for example that greater political control be established over the central
government bureaucracy, by the appointment to ministers' own staffs of advisers
capable of countering the arguments of the civil servants.[36] And if it be accepted
that the research departments of the political parties be publicly subsidized, why
not those of voluntary organizations too? Protest movements and voluntary
bodies, and especially those whose members work with their own hands, as for
example in restoring derelict canals, have arguably done more to improve the
physical environment in recent decades than has the system of statutory planning
control.

I should like to summarize the argument of this book as urging greater
intellectual clarity, an enhanced level of democratic control, and more economic
realism. The forces militating against such changes, however, which might be
summed up as a mistaken conception of professionalism together with an
unconscious corporatism, are probably very difficult to deflect from their course,
for they are so firmly institutionalized. The implicit and unspoken 'corporatist
bargain', I have argued, as it operates in this particular field of public policy,
provides benefits for three interests. For government, it provides legitimation, or
the public belief that the potentially environmentally—and socially-damaging
effects of sectional greed 'are' regulated and controlled in the public interest. For
the planners, it provides professional reward, not only in the material sense but
also in the form of an almost evangelical belief in their own mission, fostered by
the government's collusion in portraying them as important people. For the
developers, or at least for the more powerful among them, it provides more
tangible benefit, the benefit of retaining at least as much economic power as they
would have anyway, in the absence of all this 'planning'. Only in the case of the
'public' are the benefits of planning unclear. And the public, in any case, consists of
a multiplicity of quite different interests. I have argued that the professional
planners should so far as possible endeavour to extricate themselves from this
'corporatist bargain', and instead insist on their right as policy analysts to clarify all
these multifarious impacts. To advance such an argument, however, as the reader
will know, is not easy. The strength of any such social institution as the
'corporatist bargain' lies in the fact that even to suggest its existence is to lay
oneself open to the charges of being socially cynical, professionally irresponsible
and academically simplistic.

# Notes

## Notes to Chapter 1

1. For a discussion of the relationships between planning policy and some other policies with environmental effects, see, for example, Hall *et al.*, 1973, vol. 2, Chapter 13.
2. 'Uthwatt', 1942, p. 13, as cited in Cullingworth, 1982, p. 170. For an even more outspoken contemporary statement of this view, see Abercrombie, 1933, as cited in Ravetz, 1980, p. 64. For comments, see, for example, Hallett, 1977, pp. 119, 125.
3. White Paper *The Land Commission*, Cmnd. 2771 (London, HMSO, 1965), as cited in Cullingworth, 1980, p. 553.
4. White Paper *Land*, Cmnd. 5730 (London, HMSO, 1974), as cited in Cullingworth, 1982, p. 187.
5. This argument will be developed in Chapter 3, Section 3. It should be noted here that there is also a third meaning implicit in the word 'planning' as used by town and country planners, though this will not greatly obtrude until we reach Chapter 2. This third meaning describes a tendency towards a 'command' as opposed to a 'market' economy. For other discussions of the meanings of 'planning', see Cross and Bristow, 1983, Chapter 11 and Midgley and Piachaud, 1984.
6. Further justifications for 'intervention' will be discussed below, Chapter 5, Section 3.
7. Cf., for example, Hall *et al.*, 1973, vol. 2, pp. 422–6.
8. The obvious example is in the attempt by the 'Roskill' Commission to establish the 'objectively' best location for the third London airport. See Self, 1970 and 1975, *passim*; P. Hall, 1980, pp. 15–55.
9. Notable contributions include M.L. Harrison 1972, 1975, 1978 and 1979; McAuslan, 1975 and 1980; Roberts, 1976; Loughlin, 1980; Stephen and Young, 1985.
10. Some of these analyses, and the empirical evidence on which they are based, will be discussed in Chapter 3.
11. See, for example, Musil, 1968; Taubman, 1973, pp. 41–6; Stretton, 1978, Chapters 10 and 12; Hallett, 1979, Chapter 7; Bater, 1980, pp. 32–55; Pallot and Shaw, 1981, pp. 125, 134–5 and 151–3.
12. The standard descriptive text is Cullingworth, 1985.
13. Town and Country Planning Act 1971, s. 22 (1). For interesting comments on this, see Pearce, 1980, p. 126.
14. See Hallett, 1979, Chapter 8; Healey, 1983a, p. 38.
15. For comments on this, see, for example, Ambrose and Colenutt, 1975, pp. 61–64, 148 and 178–80; Broadbent, 1977, pp. 156–7; Ravetz, 1980, pp. 82–3.
16. For example, 'Dobry', 1975; Shoard, 1980, pp. 204–17 (see also Shoard, 1986). For detailed descriptions of rural development control in practice, see, for example, Blacksell and Gilg, 1981, Chapter 5; Cloke, 1983, Chapter 8.

17. Wildlife and Countryside Act 1981.

18. For discussions of structure planning in practice, see, for example, Bruton and Fisher, 1980; Cross and Bristow, 1983; Healey, 1983a; Bruton and Nicholson, 1985.

19. Though increasingly, apparently, local plans too are prepared in a rather informal and 'flexible' style. On the preparation and use of local plans in practice, see, for example, Hall, 1982; Bruton, 1983; Bruton, Crispin and Fidler, 1983; Farnell, 1983; Field, 1983; Healey, 1983a.

20. Cherry, 1982, pp. 125–31 and 135–8; Healey, 1983a, Chapter 1.

21. 'Joint Circular on Structure Plans, DOE Circular 98/74. For comments, see, for example, Donnison and Soto, 1980, pp. 20–1; Jowell and Noble, 1980; Healey, 1983a, pp. 37–38, 62 and 240; Stephen and Young, 1985, pp. 137 and 148–9. For the background, see, for example, McLoughlin, 1973.

22. For a good brief summary, see McKay and Cox, 1979, Chapter 6. For planners' views, see, for example, Alden and Morgan, 1974; Cooke, 1983. For more analytical accounts, see, for example, Budd, 1978; Law, 1981; and for more critical views, Hallett, Randall and West, 1973; Pickvance, 1981.

23. Nominally, of course, decisions are made by the full Council of the local authority, but it is unusual for a council to go against the recommendations of its planning committee. For discussions of development control in practice, see, for example, McLoughlin, 1973; H.W.E. Davies, 1980; Underwood, 1981; Pearce, 1984 and 1984; Beer, 1983; Boot, 1983; Healey, 1983a; Pountney and Kingsbury, 1983; Fleming and Short, 1984; Davies et al., 1986; Healey, 1986c.

24. On this particular use of 'Section 52 agreements', see, for example, Willis, 1980, pp. 86–8; Shucksmith, 1981 and 1983; Rogers, 1985. 'Planning agreements' more generally will be discussed in Chapter 3, Section 4.

25. For an interesting insight on the capacity of the Minister and of the Department of the Environment to make policy, see Switzer, 1984. The number of planning applications has in recent years tended to vary between 400,000 and 600,000, of which some 80–90 per cent are granted permission. The number of appeals against refusal of permission (or against conditions imposed) runs at between 10,000 and 20,000 per annum. Of these, around 80 per cent are dealt with on 'written representations' only (without holding a public local enquiry). The percentage of refusals of planning permission allowed on appeal rose fairly steadily from about 22 per cent in 1973 to about 32 per cent in 1984. By the last two quarters of 1985 it had reached 41 per cent (Davies, et al., 1986, p. 14). For discussions of the way in which the appeals system is administratively organized, see Barker and Couper, 1984 and 1985. Where applicants regard the Minister's decision on appeal as questionable in terms of law (as opposed to policy) they can then go to the High Court; it is in the analysis of the decisions of the latter that observers are able to study the extent to which the planning system is in practice interpreted by government as having social, economic, or purely 'amenity' objectives. See notes 9 and 21, above.

26. It is also subjected to an 'inquiry in public' at the local level. See, for example, Bridges, 1979; Darke, 1979; Friend, Laffin and Norris, 1981; Healey, 1983a, passim.

27. For criticisms of this 'loose connection' between plan and development control, see, for example, McAuslan, 1980, pp. 145ff; Davies et al., 1986.

28. This is an important point, if we are trying to clarify the nature of the planning system; see my typology of varieties of governmental intervention, above.

29. The standard account here is Cox, 1984. For shorter summaries, see Parker, 1965 and 1985; McKay and Cox, 1979, Chapter 3; Lichfield and Darin-Drabkin, 1980, pp. 129–168. The legislative background is documented in the 'official histories', Cullingworth, 1975 and 1980. Wenban-Smith (1986, p. 24) states that the planning system employs some 14,000 people at a net cost in 1982/83 of £110m., while the construction industry had an output valued at about £9 billion and employed about 1m. people. Thus, he suggests, the planning system is about 1½ percent of the size of 'the main industry whose operations it affects'. I would question this, however. Planning affects (and is affected by) not only the property development industry, but also the major financial institutions of society, on which this industry is dependent. For an excellent recent analysis of 'planning', explaining these relationships very clearly, see Ambrose, 1986.

30. The concepts of 'floating' and 'shifting' value are those used in the Uthwatt (1941 and 1942) Report. For comments, see, for example, Cullingworth, 1980, pp. 4–7; Hallet, 1977, p. 112–41; Leung, 1979; Hallett, 1979, Chapter 9. For a recent application of the concept of floating value to an analysis of British planning policy, see Ball, 1983.

31. Cullingworth, 1982, p. 5.

32. For arguments *against* the very wide interpretation adopted here, see Hallett, 1977 and 1979.

33. This is 'site value rating', or 'site value tax'. See Clarke, 1965; Hallett, 1977, pp. 112–23; Lichfield and Darin Drabkin, 1980, pp. 92–3 and 196–7.

34. A fallacy in this assumption that planning merely rearranges what is a 'given' volume of development spatially, of course, is that some potential development may be discouraged altogether, or may go abroad. But the proportion of development thus lost may be relatively small, and the assumption may, therefore, be valid subject to some qualification.

35. This argument does *not* of course imply that no compensation be paid to owners whose *existing* use value is depreciated by public action (as, for example, due to motorway or airport noise). This is usually called 'injurious affection'.

36. Unless it was shown on the plan as needed for public purposes. But in this case, of course, it would be compulsorily purchased; the price paid would be its existing use value.

37. Cullingworth, 1980, p. 5; Lichfield and Darin-Drabkin, 1980, p. 140.

38. Cullingworth, 1975, pp. 234–41; 1980, p. 7.

39. Except for two comparatively short periods when further relatively unsuccessful attempts have been made to recoup betterment. These will be discussed below.

40. On this, see, for example, Lichfield and Darin-Drabkin, 1980, pp. 142–4.

41. For a contrary view, see, for example, Hallett, 1979, pp. 177–9.

42. Perhaps not only for ideological reasons, but because it was in fact yielding very little, giving abolition merely symbolic value; it was reported that developers had found ways of avoiding development land tax even before it was introduced. See The *Economist*, 1978a.

43. For fuller typologies, which do not merely distinguish, as here, between 'regulative' and 'positive' planning, see Stretton, 1978, Chapter 4; Pearce, 1980; Lichfield and Darin-Drabkin, 1980, pp. 86–99, and (especially useful, since it is applied to an empirical analysis of British planning policy over time) McKay and Cox, 1979, Chapter 2. For statements *urging* 'positive planning', see, for example, Morley, 1981 and (perhaps the most thoroughgoing) Broadbent, 1977. One very interesting attempt by an economist to interpret 'positive planning' suggests that planning authorities could in principle write out planning permissions for all the development they *would* like to see, and auction these ready-made permissions to the highest bidder: see Pennance, 1967, pp. 53–60.

44. Though it abolished the development charge in 1953, the Conservative government kept in force until 1959 the arrangement whereby land needed for public purposes was acquired at existing use value. See below, Chapter 2, Section 5.

45. The 'third type' of government intervention (Section 1, above) also has very significant effects, both on the overall spatial pattern, and on the structure and operations of financial institutions. But it is not *intended* to. Thus, few would describe the subsidization of commuter railways or the system of financing local government as parts of a programme of 'positive planning'.

46. This public–private sector 'partnership' was advocated officially in the Sheaf (1972), and Pilcher (1975) reports, and was increasingly urged by the DoE in the late 1970s (especially in Circulars 71/77, 44/78, 9/80 and 22/80). It is also urged from the Right (for example, Denman, 1980), and by professional planners (Morley, 1981; Cherry, 1982, pp. 134–5; H.W.E. Davies, 1981). See also Ambrose and Colenutt, 1975, Chapter 7; Healey, 1983a, pp. 39–40 and 266–7; Hague, 1984, p. 78.

47. 'Uthwatt' (1941 and 1942), for example, in its analysis of the nature of planning, assumed this. Things might have been clearer if we had been told subsequently whether or not this is indeed what the planning system seeks to do.

48. I.e. the compulsory purchase price would be the existing use value plus 60 per cent of the difference between this existing use value and the price which a profit-seeking private developer, able to convert the land to a more profitable use, might be expected to have paid for it.

49. Eventually, it was intended, acquisition would be not merely net of tax, but at existing use value. But in the 1975–6 scheme, it will be remembered, the tax was at a far higher rate than the 40 per cent of the 1967 scheme.
50. On Sweden, see Passow, 1970; Anton, 1975; Darin-Drabkin, 1977, Chapter 13; Strong, 1979; Lichfield and Darin-Drabkin, 1980, pp. 192–226; Goldfield, 1982; Duncan, 1985 and especially useful, Dickens *et al.*, 1985.
51. Under the 1975 Community Land Act, responsibility to acquire land and subsequently to make it available to developers was not, as in England, placed with the local authority, but with a specially constituted Land Authority for Wales. In 1980, when the Act was repealed, the Land Authority for Wales was inconsistently kept in existence.

## Notes to Chapter 2

1. Examples include the writings of Cherry (1970, 1972, 1974, 1981 and 1982), and to a somewhat lesser extent those of Hall (1975), and Cullingworth (for example, 1985). For comments on this approach, see, for example, J.G. Davies, 1972, esp. pp. 93–104 and 119–22; Ravetz, 1980, p. 14 and Hebbert, 1983b. For an 'anti-professional' (or 'radical-professional') history, see Hague, 1984, and for other, rather more sceptical interpretations of the role of the profession Rees and Lambert, 1985 and Ravetz, 1986.
2. As both McKay and Cox (1979) and Ravetz (1980) make clear, the professions involved in planning include architects, surveyors, valuers and arguably other local government professions, too; that the present book restricts its attention to the members of the Royal Town Planning Institute is dictated purely by the need to keep it within manageable proportions.
3. The ongoing 'official history' (Cherry, 1975; Cullingworth, 1975, 1979, 1980) provides a detailed account of the various currents at work within the Whitehall bureaucracy, but does not relate these to political forces in the wider society.
4. For example, Mellor, 1977, pp. 127–66; Donnison and Soto, 1980, pp. 3–37; Ravetz, 1980 and 1986; Cherry, 1982.
5. This concept of a 'truce situation' is taken from Rex, 1961.
6. My interpretation rests on the concept of corporatism in that it sees the various interests involved as having tended always fairly readily to agree on an interpretation of the scope of planning which seemed to be to their mutual advantage. A fuller discussion of the concept of corporatism is to be found in Chapter 4, Section 4.
7. Here, the planning profession is heir to a strongly developed strand in nineteenth-century thought. See, for example, Mellor, 1982.
8. Cf. Hayek, 1962, p. 40.
9. Glass, 1959. Foley (1960) said much the same thing.
10. The term 'town planning' appears to date from about 1906. See, for example, Cherry, 1974, p. 49.
11. The 'architectural history' approach is characteristic of the work of the Planning History Group. See, for examaple, Sutcliffe 1980, 1981a, 1981b. The 'standard' history of the period up to the 1947 Act (Ashworth, 1954) is written by an economic historian and while detailed and thorough, contains little political or economic analysis. One of the few works which *does* attempt political analysis is Benevolo (1967), but this examines the planning movements in the major European countries, and not only in Britain. Its thesis of 'depoliticization through professionalization', however, is broadly similar to the argument presented here.
12. For the development of this school of thought, see Offer, 1981, esp. pp. 184ff. Other useful sources include Douglas, 1971 and 1976; Hamer, 1972 and Emy, 1973, pp. 189–234.
13. George became very influential in Britain after his visits here in 1881–4. His book, *Progress and Poverty*, had appeared in 1879, and was very quickly translated into the major European languages. The gist of George's argument is expressed thus: 'It is not necessary to confiscate land; it is only necessary to confiscate rent . . . In this way the State may become the universal

landlord without calling herself so, and without assuming a single new function' (George, 1884, pp. 313–14).

14. Perkin, 1973, p. 180; McDougall, 1979, p. 370; Murray, 1980, pp. 39–40; Offer, 1981, p. 184.
15. In the Lords, and on most of the county councils, landed interests were still dominant until at least the First World War, and in many cases until after the Second, and indeed, until quite recently: Thompson, 1966; Newby, 1979; p. 32.
16. Gray, 1946, pp. 389–93; Douglas, 1971, p. 163. C. Llewellyn Davies, Secretary to the English League for the Taxation of Land Values, is said to have reported to Lloyd George that Ramsay MacDonald, Keir Hardie and Snowden could not afford to identify Labour with the land issue 'for fear of losing their independent position and bringing grist to the Liberal mill' (quoted in Emy, 1973, p. 219).
17. Analyses concurring with this Labour view include Hobsbawm, (1968, p. 170) and Emy (1973, p. 233). Perkin (1973) suggests that its continued concentration on the land issue even contributed to the eclipse of the Liberal Party itself. But Labour continued its formal commitment to land nationalization up to and including its 1945 election manifesto.
18. Hamer, 1971.
19. Offer, 1981, pp. 317–19.
20. Emy, 1973, p. 209.
21. Fishman, 1977, p. 77.
22. Briggs, 1964, as quoted in McDougall, 1979, p. 370.
23. Possibly the most important of the other 'intellectual' thinkers was Patrick Geddes: See, for example, Boardman, 1978; Tyrwhitt 1947a and 1947b; Kitchen, 1975; Meller 1979. Among the 'professional men' (who arguably had far more direct influence) can be named Thomas Adams and Raymond Unwin. For discussions of the various intellectual influences on the development of British planning thought, see Eversley, 1973; Mellor, 1977, Chapter 4; Ravetz, 1980.
24. Howard, 1965, esp. Chapters 2–5 and 13.
25. Ibid., title of Chapter 10.
26. Ibid., p. 131.
27. For an account which gives particular attention to the competition for town planning between the various local government professions, see Cherry, 1974, esp. pp. 43–8, 56, 134–5, 166 72, and 201–17.
28. That professional planners tend to see Howard's scheme as more utopian than do other observers seems to be explained by their concentration on its architectural aspects (which were simplistic), and neglect of its economic basis. See, for example, Hall et al., 1973, vol. 2, pp. 42–6.
29. Fishman, 1977, pp. 52–67.
30. Ibid., p. 65; cf. Hall et al., 1973, vol. 2, p. 370.
31. Miller, 1981, pp. 79–80; Backwell and Dickens, 1978, p. 1.
32. Howard, 1965, pp. 147–9 and 154–9.
33. Though they are, of course, 'positive planning', as this term was used in Chapter 1, Section 5.
34. There seems to be some doubt concerning the impacts of these more general land taxes. Douglas(1971, p. 150), Emy (1973) and Perkin (1973, p. 206) suggest that they contributed only marginally to revenue requirements, and that Lloyd George himself seems to have agreed fairly readily to their repeal in 1922. Newby (1979), however, suggests that they produced a 'deluge' of land sales: 'In four years between 1918 and 1922, England, in the words of a famous Times leader of the day "changed hands". One quarter of the area of England was bought and sold in this hectic period of transaction, a disposal of land which was unprecedented since the Dissolution of the Monasteries in the sixteenth century'. Newby (idem., pp. 35–6) suggests that these taxes produced 'a decisive shift in the class structure of rural society', the sales being mainly to owner-occupier farmers. He states, however, that the landowners were in the main glad to sell out, being 'physically and emotionally exhausted' by the war, and 'robbed of their heirs by the carnage in Flanders'. Bruce (1973, p. 15), however, suggests that these taxes discouraged the building of council housing, by keeping land off the market. See also Murray, 1980, Chapter 11; Offer, 1981, p. 391 and Ambrose, 1986, pp. 11–12.
35. McDougall, 1979, p. 364. Powers to enable this had, however, existed since Acts of 1890 and

1900 and had already been fairly extensively used by the London County Council (Bruce, 1973, p. 101).

36. McDougall, 1979, p. 364.

37. Murray, 1980, passim.

38. Emy, 1973, pp. 189–234; Douglas, 1974; Read, 1979, pp. 467–8, 237–40 and 473; Offer, 1981, pp. 317–27 and 363–80.

39. Douglas, 1974, pp. 152–3; Offer, 1981, p. 388; Cherry, 1982, p. 12; Gauldie, 1974, p. 304. Cole and Postgate (1961, p. 462) describe the 1909 Act as having been 'utterly wrecked in action by John Burns' unsatisfactory administration at the Local Government Board'.

40. McDougall, 1979, pp. 376–7.

41. *Ibid.*, pp. 378–9. See also Minett, 1974.

42. Halliday, 1968; Mumford, 1948.

43. Miller, 1981.

44. Simpson, 1981.

45. Hebbert, 1981, p. 187.

46. Though, as stated, the inter-war years saw no very significant *actual* changes, the 1932 Town and Country Planning Act can be seen as a vestige, all that finally remained after an interesting but brief period of *attempted* change. The Labour government of 1929–31 in effect provided what was almost a 'pre-run' of the very radical initiatives which were eventually to bear fruit in the mid-1940s. It set up committees to advise on a government programme of garden cities and satellite towns, on regional development, and on the creation of national parks. In the 1931 budget, it imposed land taxes similar to those of 1910. These were subsequently repealed by the National government in 1934. But perceptions, at least, became clearer; as Ravetz (1980, p. 46) says: 'From the 1932 Act onwards it was axiomatic that British planning was always 'town and country planning.' See also, for example, Perkin, 1973; S. Ward, 1974, Aldridge, 1979, p. 16; Ravetz, 1980, p. 28.

47. 'Uthwatt', 1942, p. 123, paras 291–2.

48. The Garden City Association was founded in 1899, in the offices of the Secretary to the Land Nationalization Society (Fishman, 1977, p. 56). In 1907 it changed its name to the Garden Cities and Town Planning Association, and in 1942 it became the Town and Country Planning Association (TCPA). For a statement 'from the inside' of the Association's success, see, for example, Osborn and Whittick, 1977. For independent assessments of the Association's very influential role in shaping both professional attitudes and official policy, see, for example, Creese, 1966; Peterson, 1968; Rodwin, 1956; Foley, 1962 and Aldridge, 1979. Altshuler (1965, pp. 444–5) goes so far as to say that '[n]early all British planning ideas emerge from the Town and Country Planning Association'. But there *were* (and are) other propagandist bodies, such as the National Housing and Town Planning Council, in this field.

49. The Town Planning Institute was founded in 1914, but despite its attempts to secure monopoly in this field it continued to share responsibility for planning with other local government professions (municipal engineers, surveyors, housing architects) throughout the inter-war period. It only became a significant force in its own right after the passing of the Town and Country Planning Act of 1947 created a vastly increased demand for local government planners. It obtained a royal charter, becoming the Royal Town Planning Institute (RTPI), in 1959.

50. '[I]t was not until the 1920s and 1930s that a mass "amenity movement" was born. This movement had its roots in two areas: first, the newly affluent and mobile middle classes of home counties suburbia, and second, the dedicated Sunday ramblers of the northern industrial towns.' Blacksell and Gilg (1981, p. 1).

51. Bank rate was held at 2 per cent from 1932 to 1951 (Mellor, 1977, p. 112).

52. See, for example, Marwick, 1968, pp. 119–26.

53. Hall *et al.*, 1973, vol. 1, p. 83.

54. Aldridge, 1979, pp. 13–16. These two estates were the subjectss of classic 'community studies', by Ruth Durant (later Ruth Glass) and Terence Young respectively.

55. See, for example, Jackson, 1973.

56. Newby, 1979, p. 230.

57. See below.
58. Abercrombie, 1933, as cited in Newby, 1979, p. 230.
59. Osborn, the Secretary of the TCPA, was for a time editor of the *Journal* of the Town Planning
Institute, but was asked to resign this position in 1936. See Cherry, 1974, p. 117.
60. Aldridge, 1979, pp. 198–9. For a devastating contemporary critique of conditions in London, see
Sinclair, 1937.
61. Evidence of widespread support among intellectuals for the objective of curbing 'urban sprawl' is
reflected in Williams-Ellis (1938), a book which included contributions from J.M. Keynes, E.M.
Forster, C.E.M. Joad and G.M. Trevelyan, with prefatory remarks by Lloyd George, George
Lansbury, Stafford Cripps, Julian Huxley and J.B. Priestley. See also Allison, 1975, Chapter 4.
62. Ashworth, 1954, pp. 222–3; Cherry, 1974, pp. 81 and 109. The Ministry of Health, at this time
the central government department responsible for town and country planning, was itself
concerned, apparently, to ensure that town and country planning powers were not linked with
any wider economic policies for the depressed regions; see S. Ward, 1986.
63. Huxley, 1943; Lepawski, 1976; Akin, 1977; Schaffer, 1986.
64. Here, we come up against the 'third' meaning of 'planning' as this word is used by town and
country planners, to describe a movement away from a 'market' economy and towards a
'command' economy (see Chapter 1, note 5). Often, such planners defend their activity by
suggesting that the case for it was demonstrated long ago, when it was shown to be necessitated
by the whole trend of historical development of modern society. In saying this, they are referring
to the 'planning movement' described here, and to the so-called 'great planning debate' which
emerged out of it. Even assuming that this debate *was* in fact 'decided' in the way that planners
suggest, however, what is still left unclear is the connection between the case for the planning of
the economy in general and the case for the planning of the property development industry (or of
land use). The arguments for the former are not the same as those for the latter. Indeed, it is the
last-named, ironically, which are arguably the stronger. Political and Economic Planning, one of
the main groups within this planning movement, was founded in 1931 (see Pinder, 1981). For
brief accounts of the movement, see, for example, Marwick, 1964; Harris, 1972. For an excellent
longer analysis, relating this movement to the growth of corporatist trends in British politics, see
Smith, 1979, pp. 3–92. Harold Macmillan, as a result of his involvement in these circles,
formulated his doctrine of the 'middle way': see Macmillan, 1938 and 1966, pp. 368–75 and
481–512. For brief accounts of the 'planning debate', see Flybjerg and Petersen, 1982; Deakin,
1985. For the view that planning (in this 'third' sense) is *not* historically necessary, see Hayek,
1962, p. 32; Popper, 1956, p. 75; Jewkes, 1968.
65. 'Barlow' (1940), as quoted in Cullingworth, 1982, pp. 9–10.
66. See Chapter 1, Section 4.
67. Reith, 1949; Titmuss, 1958, Chapter 4; Calder, 1968; Addison, 1977, pp. 173ff; McLaine, 1979;
Backwell and Dickens, 1978; Hague, 1984, pp. 101–2, n. 21.
68. Marwick, 1968, pp. 300–14; Westergaard and Resler, 1975, pp. 39–40.
69. Marwick, 1968.
70. Aldridge, 1979, p. 189.
71. Backwell and Dickens, 1978, p. 14.
72. Marriott, 1967; *The Economist* (no. 5084, 1941, p. 144; and no. 5125, 1941, p. 591), as cited in
Backwell and Dickens, 1978.
73. Backwell and Dickens, 1978, p. 12.
74. Newby, 1979, pp. 230–1.
75. Hall *et al.*, vol. 2, p. 52. See also *ibid*, vol. 2, p. 371. That the majority 'Scott' Report of 1943
was unrealistic, and that the minority report of Professor Dennison was far more economically
sound, seems nowadays to be quite generally accepted. See, for example, Aldridge, 1979, p. 24;
Hallett, 1979, p. 156; Gilg, 1978; Cloke, 1983, pp. 77–8; Wibberley, 1985.
76. The notion of a 'package' is used in Hall *et al.*, 1973, vol. 2, pp. 67ff.
77. In fact, however, quite a lot of high-density (especially five-storey) housing was built in the cities
immediately after the war.
78. See for example Sharp, 1940, pp. 92–102.

79. The post-war planning legislation which gave effect to this programme is traditionally seen as consisting of five main acts, the Distribution of Industry Act 1945, the New Towns Act 1946, the Town and Country Planning Act 1947, the National Parks and Access to the Countryside Act 1949, and the Town Expansion Act 1952. The intellectual and political roots, however, are obviously of far wider provenance; all this was an integral part of the wider attempt at post-war social reconstruction. On the specifically town and country planning aspects of these intellectual currents there is a considerable contemporary literature. See, for example (other than items already mentioned), Boumphrey, 1940; Adshead, 1941; Robson, 1941; Osborn, 1942; Tubbs, 1942; Cole, 1943; Gutkind, 1943; Huxley, 1943; McCallum, 1945; McAllister and McAllister, 1945; Simon, 1945; Wolfe, 1945; Fogarty, 1948; Silkin, 1948; Tyrwhitt, 1950; Hughes, 1971. Planning in the wider, socio-economic sense, was advocated especially in Mannheim, 1940 and 1951 and Wootton, 1945. Commentaries on the post-war British town and country planning system were at first almost entirely American: see Haar, 1951; Orlans, 1952; Rodwin, 1956; Mandelker, 1962; Foley, 1960, 1962, 1963, and 1972. Later, British, analyses are discussed in Chapter 3.

80. Indeed, as the example of the Scott (1943) report suggests, expert opinion seems sometimes to have been rejected: see note 75 above. For an interesting account of the involvement of social scientists in planning in the 1940s, however, see Hebbert, 1983a; see also Glass, 1948, 1950 and 1955.

81. Especially Kuper, 1951; Rodwin, 1956; Glass, 1959.

82. Notably, the Modern Architecture Research Group. See, for example, Ravetz, 1980, p. 21.

83. See, for example, Allison, 1975, esp. pp. 41–54.

84. For example, Wolfe, 1945; Purdom, 1946.

85. Cullingworth, 1975, pp. 251–8. See also McKay and Cox, 1979, p. 34.

86. Foot, 1962, pp. 470–4.

87. Cullingworth, 1975, pp. 241–9; Cherry, 1974, p. 161.

88. See, for example, Ravetz, 1980, pp. 68–9.

89. In 1939, the Town Planning Institute had 927 members, of whom 145 were students. By 1950, it had 3,098 members, of whom 964 were students: Backwell and Dickens, 1978, p. 16.

90. 'Schuster', 1950. For discussion of this, see, for example, Healey and Samuels, 1981, pp. 5–8; Hague, 1984, pp. 104–6.

91. Hague, 1984, p. 105.

92. By a reversal of 'mood', here, is meant a general move in the 'consensus', away from 'controls' and collectivist solutions. But this had already been reflected in the policy of the Labour government from about 1948 onwards. And in 1951, ironically, Labour obtained more votes in the country as a whole than every before, or since.

93. From 1943 to 1951 the central department responsible for the planning system was the Ministry of Town and Country Planning. In 1951, it became part of a new Ministry of Local Government and Planning, and later in the same year this was renamed the Ministry of Housing and Local Government. In 1970 this became part of a wider Department of the Environment (DoE), which included transport, though at the insistence of the road transport and road construction lobby a separate Ministry of Transport was re-established in 1976.

94. Altshuler, 1965, p. 451.

95. Ibid., p. 449; Westergaard, 1964, p. 235.

96. Healey (1983a, p. 33) makes the very valid point that it is in a sense surprising that the 1947 planning system was left in existence at all, once its essential financial basis had thus been removed. This point will be taken up in Chapter 6. One, possibly typical, professional response to the 'eclipse' of planning in the 1950s is Keeble (1961).

97. Merrett, 1979, pp. 68–9. Ravetz (1980, p. 67) comments on the Conservatives that 'towards landowners they were more ruthless than the Labour government had perhaps dared to be'.

98. Self, 1961, Chapter 6. On the Conservative government's desire to reduce the level of state intervention more generally, see for example, Harris, 1972, pp. 249–73 and 77–154.

99. Town and Country Planning Association, 1962.

100. Cf. Hall et al., 1973, vol. 2, p. 425.

101. M.L. Harrison, 1972, p. 257.

102. Editorial, *Town Planning Review*, 1959, vol. 30, p. 185.

103. In 1945, the Town Planning Institute had 1,600 members, in 1962 it had 2,350, and in 1973 this had risen to 9,500 (all figures including student members): Mellor, 1977, p. 277. In the summer of 1986 the RTPI reached a corporate membership (that is, excluding student members) of 10,000.

104. Mellor, 1977, p. 150; Cf Hague, 1984, p. 115.

105. McKay and Cox, 1979, pp. 40-1.

106. Rodwin, 1956, p. 48.

107. Osborn and Whittick, 1969, p. 417.

108. See Chapter 1, Sections 4 and 5. *Until* the Commission was in a position to ensure that land could only be developed if it had passsed through its own hands, it had the secondary task of imposing a tax, at the rather modest rate of 40 per cent, on all betterment. One important difference from the 1947 Act, however, was that this recoupment of betterment was not to occur only on the granting of planning permission. It could also be collected in the case of certain other statutorily defined 'events', notably on the *sale* of land.

109. As this term was defined in Chapter 1, Section 5.

110. As quoted in Hall *et al.*, 1973, vol. 2, p. 242.

111. *Ibid.* Cf. Cullingworth, 1980, Chapter 13, pp. 412-14.

112. Crossman, 1975, vol. 1, p. 158.

113. Though the Conservatives did say, in the campaign leading up to the 1970 general election, that the Land Commission 'had no place in a free society': Cullingworth, 1982, p. 185.

114. In 1950, there had been ten centres offering courses leading to qualifications 'recognized' for membership by the Town Planning Institute. By 1970, there were 30 such courses. But in addition, there were 19 other new courses intended as providing this training, and awaiting 'recognition'. There were also 91 further new 'non-professional' undergraduate and postgraduate planning courses of various kinds, classified as 'spatial planning' (30), 'transport planning' (16) and 'social and economic planning and management' (45), all of which must be seen as having been brought into existence by the new vogue for 'planning' in society: Healey and Samuels, 1981, pp. 8 and 14.

115. It was the Federation of British Industries (as it then was) which had urged economic planning, at its national conference in 1960. And it was the Conservative government which had set up the National Economic Development Council, in effect a kind of tripartite corporatist 'economic parliament', in 1962. For analyses of this revived all-party consensus on the need for 'planning' in the widest sense, see, for example, Shonfield, 1965, pp. 160-3 and 230-3; Harris, 1972, pp. 228 246; Winkler, 1976, pp. 114-16; Turner and Collis, 1977, Chapter 5. The Labour governments of 1964 and 1966, therefore, merely continued and reinforced these tendencies. The regional planning approaches emanating from the division of the country into ten economic planning regions, in 1965, would presumably have eventually come to completely replace the machinery established under the Distribution of Industry Act 1945 and its successors, but in the event the Department of Economic Affairs met strong resistance from other established ministries (especially, of course, the Treasury), and was wound up in 1969.

116. This refers in particular to the reports of the Community Development Project Information and Intelligence Unit (for example, Benington, 1976; Community Development Project, 1976 and 1977). The whole notion of reducing economic and social inequality by directing extra resources to specific *places* seems fundamentally illogical. As a number of observers have pointed out, the fact is that even on the most 'generous' definition of such 'areas of deprivation', most of the poorest people in society will still be living outside these areas, while most of those within them will not be 'deprived'. Nevertheless, the approach has continued to be used under various names from the mid-1960s to the present day. The generally accepted explanation is that this is because such programmes combine the highest possible appearance of action with the lowest possible level of expenditure. For discussions of this phenomenon, see, for example, Marris and Rein, 1974; McKay and Cox, 1979, Chapter 7; Higgins *et al.*, 1983; Loney, 1983; Rees and Lambert, 1985. For planners' attitudes, see, for example, Cherry, 1970; Lawless, 1979 and 1981.

117. Especially in two books by J.D. Stewart (1971 and 1974). (See also Stewart and Eddison, 1971; Eddison, 1973) The high-point of this vogue for corporate planning is marked by the 'Bains' Report (1972). For critiques of corporate planning in practice, see, for example, Benington, 1976; Cockburn, 1977; Dearlove, 1979. For later assessments by previous advocates, accepting in effect the failure of the approach to secure the supremacy of the officers over the politicians, see, for example, Haynes, 1978; Skelcher, 1980; Norton and Wedgwood-Oppenheim, 1981; Stewart, 1983, Chapter 13.

118. See, for example, The Economist, 1972; Counter Information Services, 1973; Ambrose and Colenutt, 1975.

119. McKay and Cox, 1979, p. 56. For a thought-provoking analysis of the programme of the 1974 Labour government, see T. Smith, 1979, pp. 161–93. This programme was to a significant extent based on ideas set out in Holland, 1975 (see also Holland, 1976). The general background is described in Ionescu, 1975.

120. Though with many 'exceptions' and 'exemptions'; the legislation was notable for its complexity.

121. For evaluations of this legislation, see, for example, Hallett, 1977, pp. 137–41; Massey and Catalano, 1978, Chapter 8; Grant, 1979; McKay and Cox, 1979, Chapter 3; McAuslan, 1980, Chapter 5; Barrett, 1981; Cox, 1984, Chapter 8.

122. The evidence on these points will be set out in Chapter 3, Section 2.

123. This will be taken up in Chapter 6, Section 2. This argument that the Thatcher government's 'attack on planning' is more apparent than real is suggested in Robinson and Lloyd (1986).

124. See Chapter 1, note 42.

125. For a brief historical account of the development of state aid to British agriculture, see Cox, Lowe and Winter, 1986 and 1987.

126. The events surrounding the 'reversal' of the new towns policy are discussed in Higgins et al., 1983, Chapter 5.


# Notes to Chapter 3

1. Cf A.J. Harrison, 1977, p. 89.
2. Popper, 1945 and 1957.
3. Magee, 1973, pp. 75–7. See also James, 1980.
4. Young and Mason (1983, p. 217), discussing the tendency for economic policy to be purely symbolic rather than realistically designed to achieve social benefits, suggest that one aspect of this symbolic action is reflected in a 'deep-seated reluctance to monitor and assess the impact of economic policies'. 'Monitoring', they continue, 'is often dismissed as a costly and academic irrelevance. The stridency of the dismissal suggests a tacit recognition that many economic initiatives could not survive a rigorous monitoring exercise'.
5. Chapter 1, Section 1 and Chapter 2, Section 1.
6. Ferris, 1972. For comments, see, for example, Counter Information Services, 1973; Kirk, 1980, pp. 62–4 and 169–170.
7. Lee et al., 1974. See also Lee, 1967.
8. Muchnik, 1970. Other studies focusing on the bureaucracy itself include Dennis, 1970 and 1972; Davies, 1972; Harloe, 1975 and Levin, 1976. Orlans (1952) and Mullan (1980) both analyse the decision-making processes in the development of Stevenage New Town.
9. Elkin, 1974.
10. See the various examples in Marriott, 1967; Gregory, 1971; Ambrose and Colenutt, 1975; P.J. Smith, 1975; Ambrose, 1976; Blowers, 1980 and 1984; Counter Information Services, 1973; Gladstone, 1976; Monahan 1976; Wates, 1976; Saunders, 1979 (on this, see also Young and Kramer, 1978); Cox and Johnston, 1982; J.M. Hall, 1982.
11. Newby, 1979, p. 242, emphasis in original.
12. Cullingworth, 1982, p. 343.
13. Gregory, 1970; Thomas, 1970; Elson, 1986. Cf. Munton, 1983, who does go on to investigate

economic and social effects. For some reason, there seem to have been more attempts to assess the effects of planning in the countryside than in urban areas. See, for example, Mandelker, 1962; Martin and Voorhees Associates, 1981; Council for the Preservation of Rural England, 1981; Blacksell and Gilg, 1981, pp. 137–217.

14. Chapter 2, Section 1, above.
15. Coleman, 1976. There is support for Coleman's conclusions in a report of the Standing Conference on London and South East Regional Planning (1976), and in Munton, 1983.
16. Coleman, 1976, p. 428.
17. Newman, 1972.
18. Coleman, 1976, p. 430. See also Coleman, 1985, in which this approach is applied to council housing. For a more sceptical view, see, for example, Reade, 1982b, 1984b and 1985a.
19. Simmie, 1981. See also Simmie, 1985.
20. Hague, 1984.
21. Hall et al., 1973. For comments, see, for example, Broadbent, 1977, pp. 162–5.
22. Hall et al., 1973, vol. 2, p. 22.
23. Ibid., vol. 1, Chapter 3 and vol. 2, Chapter 1. Broadly, this list of factors corresponds to the 'package' of ideas and policies discussed above in Chapter 2, Section 4.
24. Ibid., vol. 2, p. 69. All subsequent references are to vol. 2.
25. Ibid., pp. 69–70.
26. Ibid., p. 367.
27. Ibid., pp. 370–1.
28. Ibid., p. 371.
29. For example, Glass, 1959; Foley, 1960 and 1963, Chapter 8; Altshuler, 1965, pp. 439ff.
30. Hall et al., 1973, p. 408.
31. Ibid., p. 408.
32. See above, Chapter 1, Section 4.
33. Hall et al., 1973, pp. 386–90.
34. Ibid., p. 387.
35. See above, Chapter 2, Section 2.
36. Hall et al., 1973, p. 393. One thing which is known about the effects of planning is that the amount of agricultural land taken for development in England and Wales has been halved, from over 60,000 acres per annum in the inter-war years to something like 30,000 acres per annum in the period from 1945 to the present day. As Allison (1975, p. 63) points out, this is a significant effect; over a twenty-five-year period, for example, it means that over 1,000 square miles, or the equivalent of an average-sized English county, has been 'saved' from development.
37. Ibid., p. 395.
38. Ibid.
39. Ibid.
40. This helps to explain the high-rise system building of the 1960s.
41. Ibid., p. 398.
42. Ibid., p. 399. The negative externality effects produced by the construction of motorways through the older inner suburbs, of course, fell mainly on lower-income groups.
43. Ibid., p. 404.
44. Ibid., p. 399. Note that this does not take account of the even higher prices which were to occur during the 1971–3 property boom.
45. Ibid., p. 385.
46. For example, Hallett, 1979, pp. 83–92; Boddy, 1980; Ball, 1983. See, however, Massey and Catalano, 1978, pp. 145–8.
47. Counter Information Services, 1973, p. 7; Ambrose and Colenutt, 1975, pp. 165–9; Broadbent, 1977, p. 27; Massey and Catalano, 1978, pp. 1, 171–2 and 162–6.
48. Hall et al., 1973, p. 405.
49. Ibid., p. 374.
50. Ibid., p. 375.
51. Ibid.

52. Ibid., p. 406.
53. Ibid., p. 397.
54. Ibid., p. 408.
55. Collison, 1953; Dennis, 1968; Sarkissian, 1976.
56. Healey (1986a) provides one of the few examples in which a planner *does* urge the need for research into the effects of planning . But see note 65, below.
57. A notable exception is Hague, 1984.
58. Kingston (1981) interviewed five senior local government planning officers, two of whom had explicit responsibility for monitoring. None of them, apparently, considered it important that efforts should be made to discover the effects of planning. They interpreted 'monitoring' quite differently. See below.
59. Popper, 1945, p. 158.
60. Popper, 1957, p. 67.
61. Kingston, 1981. This finding is corroborated by Masser's research on structure plan monitoring: see Masser, 1983, pp. xx and 217–22.
62. Reade, 1983b and 1983d.
63. Sillince (1986) not only uses the word 'evaluation' in the way which I have identified as characteristic of planners, but also argues that planning policies can *only* be evaluated before being put into effect, since monitoring in the sense in which I urge it here is quite impossible. Monitoring in this sense, Sillince argues, can be advocated only by those who subscribe to the philosophy of utilitarianism, which he shows in detail to be incapable of practical application in policy making. The paradox here is that I would *also* reject utilitarianism; rather than spelling out the case against it, however, I have taken it as 'given' that utilitarianism is simply a non-starter. The explanation of this apparent paradox lies in the fact that while arguing the necessity of researching the effects of policy, I assume that any such effect can only be judged desirable or undesirable *from a particular standpoint*. Where the term 'evaluation' *has* crept into the present text, it should be interpreted as synonymous with what I term 'monitoring'.
64. The approach adopted in this book assumes that there is no significant distinction between 'pure' and 'applied' research, and similarly that there is no meaningful distinction to be made between 'theory' and 'practice'. Briefly, these assumptions rest on the fact that the word 'theory' is used to mean no more than the explanation of what is in fact done, or 'practiced' (or what it is known *could* be done). For a fuller discussion, however, see, for example, Bulmer, 1982, Chapter 2. Planners, by contrast, tend to make a sharp distinction between theory and practice, between theoretical knowledge and practical knowledge. For a discussion of this, see Reade, 1981.
65. Eversley and Moody, 1976, p. 73. That planners in general share the view expressed by Eversley and Moody seems hardly to require substantiation. It is reflected in the fact that one searches in vain in the planning literature for any discussion of the empirical research reviewed in this present chapter. Eversley and Moody's view, however, seems unfortunately to be also shared by the funding bodies, and especially the Socal Science Research Council (currently called the Economic and Social Research Council). Healey (1986a), who goes some way towards questioning this conventional view, does not however make clear *why* it is that research is needed into the effects of planning. She urges such research in order to clarify 'the interrelation of State activity with economic and social process, to identify and generalize about whose interests are furthered and hindered by State programmes and the way they operate', and also because it is 'of normantive significance since planners, politicians and interest groups from time to time seek to discover what the effects of policies have been' (Healey, 1986a, p. 113). In fact it is *planners* who most need this research, to do 'planning'. It is a *technical* necessity.
66. Platt, 1972. The approach adopted here is I would suggest broadly compatible with the 'mainstream' of explanations of the relationship between research and public policy. See, for example, Gouldner and Miller, 1966; Pinker, 1971; Argyris and Schon, 1974; Lazarsfeld *et al.*, 1975; Bailey, 1975 and 1980; Bulmer, 1978; Jenkins, 1978; McAllister, 1980; Bulmer, 1982. What is argued here, however, is *not* so compatible with the rather technocratic 'policy sciences' approach of, for example, Cherns *et al.*, 1979 or of Cherns, 1972, or that of the journal *Policy Sciences*, since this seems to me to rest on very much the same epistemological fallacies as does the

ideology of 'planning'; on this, see, for example, Fay, 1975.

67. See Note 58, above.

68. Healey, personal communication. Elsewhere (1983b, p. 38) Healey suggests that 'the retention of the model of plan-based action has been a serious impediment to the development of effective and accountable land-use policy in Britain' but goes on to suggest that 'if statutory development plans are abolished, we must be very wary of losing rational method, open public debate and semijudicial review as well'. I would suggest that if our concern is for accountability, there *must* be clear statements (plans), explaining what is and what is not allowed to be built, and planning officials must be bound by these plans.

69. See the discussion on 'discretion', in Chapter 1, Section 3, and the discussion on 'corporatism', in Chapter 4, Section 4. Healey (1983a) uses the term 'negotiative planning' to describe the approach which I discuss here, and which I would argue is incipiently corporatist: see Healey, 1983a, esp. pp. 14–17 and 242–3. On 'planning gain' and 'planning by agreement', see, for example, Kirk, 1980; Pearce, 1980; Reade, 1982a; Keogh, 1985; Loughlin, 1985, and, for an interesting American comparison, Lefcoe, 1980. For discussions of British land-use planning which interpret it specifically in corporatist terms, see Cawson, 1977, 1982 and 1985a; Jowell, 1977; Azmon, 1980; Simmie, 1981 and 1985; Flynn, 1983 and Reade, 1984a.

70. As discussed above, Chapter 1, Section 5.

71. Few writers suggest that there is a significant level of corruption in British planning. But see Pinto-Duschinsky, 1977; Ravetz, 1980, pp. 72 and 177; Goldsmith, 1980, p. 131; Dawson, 1984, pp. 44–7 and 63–4; Goldsmith, 1984, pp. 71 and 74; Gyford, 1985, pp. 7–9; Wachs. (ed.), 1985; Nuffield Foundation, 1986, pp. 13–14. With the emergence of the approach which Healey calls 'negotiative planning' and which I have termed 'incipient corporatism', however, the line between integrity and corruption becomes very difficult to discern. On the planners' desire to be involved in the decision-making processes of developers, see, for example, Cuddy and Hollingsworth, 1986, p. 168.

72. R. Smith (1981) provides a good brief summary of the policy research field and its problems. For discussions specifically related to land use planning, see Lichfield, 1979; McAllister, 1980. For a discussion of the problems of assessing the financial cost of planning administration (which should of course be weighed against its 'effects'), see Hayton, 1981.

73. Aaron Wildavsky, *The Art and Craft of Policy Analysis* (London, Macmillan, 1980), p. 234, quoted in Smith, 1981, p. 233.

74. Rossi, source unclear, cited in Smith, 1981, p. 232.

75. In Chapter 6, part 3.

# Notes to Chapter 4

1. It is commonly said that much has been written on 'planners' ideology' and 'planners' values', and even that too much importance has been attached to this matter. In reality, however, there have been few, if any, systematic or even sustained attempts to identify what is distinctive in the way planners tend to think, let alone to explain *why* they tend to think as they do; the purportedly exaggerated attention given to this matter thus turns out on inspection to consist mainly of impressionistic commentaries. Most of the sources are referred to in other chapters of this book, therefore, in the context of attempts to clarify various specific questions. Among the main sources of evidence on the historical development of planning thought, however, might be mentioned Eversley, 1973; Cherry, 1974; Hebbert, 1977; Mellor, 1977, and Hague, 1984, while evidence on planners' ideology as revealed in their everyday work is provided in Albrow, 1970; Dennis, 1970 and 1972; Davies, 1972; Pahl, 1977a, Underwood, 1980 and Kiernan, 1983. Much can also be learned, of course, from the pages of the monthly journal of the Royal Town Planning Institute, *The Planner*, and especially, since it is independent and tends to be fairly critical, from the weekly *Planning Newspaper*. A rare example of an empirical study of planners' values is Knox and Cullen, 1981. W.H. Cox, 1976; pp. 135–68; Regan, 1978 and D.M. Hill, 1980.

2. Healey, (1985, p. 502) also comes to this conclusion.

3. Among the more influential texts may be mentioned McLoughlin, 1969; Chadwick, 1970 and 1978; Faludi, 1973a and 1973b; Friend and Jessop, 1969; Friend, Power and Yewlett, 1974; Solesbury, 1974; Hambleton, 1978; Lichfield, Kettle and Whitbread, 1974; Roberts, 1974; Hall, 1975; Bracken, 1981 and Bruton, 1984. The general approach of the 'new planning' is also apparent in many reports and discussion documents (for example, Centre for Environmental Studies, 1973, and Royal Town Planning Institute, 1976; on this last, see also Raab, 1977).

4. This is made clear especially in Jameson, 1971. Few, if any, of the other British commentators on 'sociology in planning' have pointed it out.

5. For example, Williams, 1971; Lofland, 1973; Bassett and Short, 1980.

6. Cf., for example, Broady, 1968; Heraud, 1979, pp. 79–116; Pahl, 1975. For a particularly useful discussion, see Tucker, 1966.

7. On the inapplicability of systems theory, see, for example, Hoos, 1971; Dimitriou et al., 1973; Bailey, 1975, Chapter 4; Scott and Roweis, 1977; Thomas, 1979. On the epistemological fallacies inherent in cost-benefit analysis, see, for example, Self, 1970 and 1975. On the fallacious assumptions inherent in 'transportation studies', see, for example, Plowden, 1972; Tyme, 1978. For an explanaton of the misleading nature of Faludi's 'procedural planning theory', see Thomas, 1979, and for reviews of the whole field of 'planning theory', Healey, McDougall and Thomas, 1982, and Reade, 1982c. Elsewhere (Reade, 1983b), I have attempted a critical analysis of the idea of planning as a specific method of decision-making. Other writers who have discussed the pseudo-scientific basis of the 'new planning' techniques include Mellor, 1977, pp. 127–66; Stretton, 1978, Chapter 6; Ravetz, 1980, pp. 201–11, and Hague, 1984, pp. 109–16. That academic debate on planning as rational decision-making still continues, however, is evidenced in such works as Camhis, 1979; McConnell, 1981; Cooke, 1983; Faludi, 1986 and Sillince, 1986. That 'practitioners' still continue to believe that policies can be based on these 'new planning' techniques, rather than on political debate and empirical research, is evidenced in, for example, Hall, 1980, pp. 187–276; the contributions to Masser, 1983; to the October 1984 issue of the *Town Planning Review* (Vol. 55, no. 4), to a recent issue of *Built Environment* (Vol. 10, no. 2, 1984); to Breheny and Hooper (1985); and in Isserman (1985). One should, however, note two recent books which, while written from the planners' own viewpoint, adopt an approach to the use of techniques in planning which is markedly different from that usually characteristic of planners, and very much more sceptical and moderate in tone. These are D.M. McAllister (1980), and Sillince (1986). Sillince even argues that much so-called rational technique in British planning is indeed intellectually unsupportable, and in fact is pure sham, but is a political necessity.

8. It is interesting that this apparently rather odd analysis, placing the blame on the form of the plans rather than on what the plans proposed, was arrived at by a group of professional planners without the benefit of outside observers (Planning Advisory Group, 1965). For comments, see, for example, Donnison and Soto, 1980, Chapter 1; Hague, 1984, pp. 74–7.

9. 'Skeffington', 1969, p. 4.

10. Crossman, 1975, Vol. 1, p. 99.

11. 'Roskill', 1971. Buchanan urged that instead of being built on the site to the north of London, shown by the calculations to be 'objectively' best, the airport should instead be built far down the Thames estuary, at Foulness.

12. The debate over this concept, broadly speaking, is between those who see the 'public interest' as capable of being objectively defined, and those who do not. The latter group, to which the present writer belongs, consider it to be at best a normative idea and at worst a mere slogan, though very useful in mobilizing political consent. Planners tend rather strongly to belong to the first group (see, for example, Friedman, 1973; Klosterman, 1980; Weaver, Jessop and Das, 1985). Political scientists, by contrast, tend equally strongly to adhere to the second group (see, for example, Banfield, 1955; Schubert, 1961; Barry, 1964; Mitnick, 1976). McAuslan (1980), discussing British town and country planning, identifies the way in which planners and developers tend to arrive at a shared perception as to what is in the public interest; concerning this, he shares the political scientists' view.

13. McLoughlin, 1986.

14. This argument is developed in Chapter 6. On the particular point made here, see Healey, 1986d. On planners' use of the concept of rationality, see Altshuler, 1965, p. 305; for a fuller discussion, Reade, 1983a and 1985b. That planners still continue their own usage, however, is shown in, for example, Faludi, 1973a; Roberts, 1974; Chadwick, 1978; Bracken, 1981, and the contributions of Darke, Forester, Harris, Hill, Johnson, Goldberg, Weaver *et al.* and Yewlett to the volume edited by Breheny and Hooper, 1985.

15. Faludi, 1970; Albrow, 1970; Pahl, 1977a.

16. Faludi, 1970; Reade, 1981; Hague, 1984, p. 102.

17. Glazer, 1974.

18. Musgrove, 1973, p. 8. For more favourable views on curriculum integration in professional education, see, for example, Heraud, 1979, pp. 115–16; Rustin, 1981. For views on the way in which vocational training *can* be combined with a liberal education, see, for example, Goodlad, 1975 and 1976.

19. Faludi, 1976. For comments, see Cooke and Rees, 1977; Frost, 1977; Reade, 1981.

20. Hague, 1984.

21. They can, of course, have such functions as mobilizing support for innovatory policies, changing the climate of opinion, and so on (Sillince, 1984). They also have a 'professional' function, in that planners tend to evaluate each other professionally in terms of their plans rather than in terms of the practical consequences of these plans.

22. Lichfield, 1956; cf. Stretton, 1978, pp. 65–74 and 83–6.

23. Chapter 3, Section 3, above.

24. Healey, 1983a, pp. 29–33.

25. For example, H.W.E. Davies, 1981; Batty, 1983; Sillince, 1986.

26. Figures are not easily obtained, but Mellor (1977, p. 227, note 7), quoting a Town Planning Institute membership survey, states that though in 1963–4 the largest single group of students on postgraduate planning courses were architects, by 1972, recruits with a first degree in geography predominated. McLoughlin (1973, pp. 154–5), in a sample survey of local planning authorities carried out in 1970, found that geographer-planers were the largest single group in 'plan' sections, and that only 2 per cent of all the planners in his sample (one person, an economist) were qualified in the social sciences.

27. These conclusions are based on experience of teaching sociology to twelve years' intake of students to a postgraduate planning course, the great majority of whom were geography graduates.

28. See, for example, the responses to the survey of sociologists in planning reported in Faludi, 1970.

29. Ravetz, 1980, pp. 201–5.

30. Ibid., p. 204.

31. Ibid., p. 205, citing Eversley, 1973, p. 243.

32. Joe Bailey, Maurice Broady, Ray Pahl, John Rex and John Westergaard, for example, all made considerable attempts over the 1960s and 1970s to establish a dialogue between sociology and town planning: see, for example, Bailey, 1975 and 1980; Broady, 1968; Pahl, 1970; Rex, 1968 and 1971. See also Buttimer, 1971, and Reade, 1983c.

33. Davies, 1972, esp. pp. 89–122 and 210–32.

34. A.H. Halsey, referring to the two books by Dennis (1970 and 1972), suggests that 'when a person like Norman Dennis protests against the emerging tyranny of government with the authentic voice of deeply-rooted English socialism, he is heard with approval by Sir Keith Joseph and dismissed as a nuisance by the Labour establishment' (as cited in Ward, 1984). For a good explanation of the dangers of applying a 'sociology of knowledge' perspective in this crude way, see Popper, 1945, Chapter 23.

35. Power, 1971; Davies, 1972; Wildavsky, 1973.

36. Kirk, 1980, pp. 55ff.

37. Ibid., pp. 57–66.

38. Ibid., pp. 66–73. This 'managerialist' school is a variety of elite theory, with roots going back to Burnham (1941) and ultimately to such early sociologists as Pareto, Mosca and Michels. The examples cited by Kirk include Rex and Moore, 1967, Eversley, 1973, and Pahl, 1975. English *et*

al. (1976) might also be seen as a contribution to this 'school'. For other attempts both to use the approach and to assess its usefulness, see, for example, Pahl, 1977a, 1977b, 1977c; Elliott, 1980; Elliott and McCrone, 1981; Saunders, 1981b; Batley, 1982; Elliott and McCrone, 1982.

39. Kirk, 1980, pp. 73–78. Writers mentioned by Kirk as reflecting this approach include Donnison (1973) and Ambrose and Colenutt (1975). She also, however, sees such governmental initiatives as the Urban Programme, the creation of General Improvement Areas, and the Home Office's Community Development Projects as embodying the approach.

40. Kirk, 1980, pp. 78–93. Marxist contributions include Harvey, 1973, 1985a and 1985b; Pickvance, 1976; Castells, 1977 and 1978; Cockburn, 1977; Harloe, 1977 and 1981; Scott and Rowels, 1977; Cox, 1978; Scott, 1980; Smith, 1980 and 1984; Dear and Scott, 1981; Harloe and Lebas, 1981; Saunders, 1981a; Lebas, 1982 and 1983; Tabb and Sawers (eds) 1984. For commentaries on this Marxist work, see, for example, Glass, 1977; Dunleavy, 1980; Elliott, 1980; Batley, 1982; Elliott and McCrone, 1982, Chapter 1; Forrest, Henderson and Williams, 1982; Gans, 1984; Ceccarelli, 1984. It should however be emphasized that the extent to which writers of this school look in detail at the institution and practices of land use planning is very limited.

41. The sheer implausibility of pluralism, as Kirk interprets this concept, seems hardly to require comment. That society is a system of structured inequality of power, and that it tends to socialize its members into an acceptance of this structured inequality, both as inevitable and even as beneficial, is an assumption shared by virtually all sociologists, whatever their theoretical and philosophical predilections. Martin (1983, p. 92) notes that 'for many years there has been no school of self-professed "pluralists" expressly committed to staking out pluralism's claim as a theory of politics', and goes on to point out that the term 'pluralist' is normally only used 'as a weapon of attack'. If the reader remains unconvinced, however, and wishes for further evidence of the implausibility of pluralism as explanatory theory, there are, for example, the classic works on 'non-decision-making' (Bachrach and Baratz, 1962, 1963 and 1970; Crenson, 1971), and on the political passivity of those who know they would anyway achieve little by being active. Useful studies in this last category, in areas close to the concerns of the present book, include Dearlove, 1973; Saunders, 1979; Dunleavy, 1981a and Blowers, 1984.

42. Davies, 1972.

43. Dennis, 1970 and 1972.

44. Kirk, 1980, p. 70.

45. Ibid., p. 72.

46. Dennis, 1972, pp. 157, 278–9 and 281. For another commentary on Dennis, see Room, 1979, pp. 119–22.

47. Davies, 1972, p. 229.

48. Ibid., p. 230.

49. For a very convincing statement of the case for theoretical eclecticism in this subject-area, see Bailey, 1980.

50. Chapter 3, Section 3, Notes 69 and 71.

51. Schmitter, 1974, as cited in R.J. Harrison, 1980, pp. 184–5.

52. Ibid., p. 185. The definition of corporatism is however much contested. For an interpretation which stresses the *values* inherent in corporatism, and which is therefore especially relevant to the present discussion, see Winkler, 1976 (in short form in Pahl and Winkler, 1974). For other discussions of the meaning of this concept, see, for example, Wilson, 1983; Coates, 1984; Williamson, 1985; Cawson, 1986.

53. Many theorists of corporatism would insist that the term is appropriate only where *two or more* such *institutionalized* or *incorporated* pressure groups engage in processes of mutual accommodation together with representatives of the governmental bureaucracy. And clearly, not all pressure-group activity is corporatist; some of it is addressed to Members of Parliament, or to electors. Since the analytical utility of corporatism may be seen as depending upon showing it to differ from ordinary old-fashioned pressure group politics, some distinguishing features may usefully be summarized here. *First*, then, and in order to achieve this 'privileged access' or 'incorporation' in the first place, an interest group must demonstrate a 'capacity to do the state's work for it'. Thus, government may value the group in question for its ability to get certain things done in a 'low-profile',

'non-political' way, or for its ability to construct a useful legitimating ideology, or simply for its members' technical expertise. (See, for example, King, 1985). *Second*, therefore, corporatist arrangements are based on mutual interdependence; a mere pressure group, by contrast, will have difficulty in presenting itself to the Whitehall bureaucracy in any other role than that of the supplicant. *Third*, we can note that in thus granting to any specific interest group this privilege of sharing with it the responsibility for a particular area of public policy, the governmental bureaucracy thereby of necessity excludes other groups, even though they may have an equal, and equally legitimate, interest in the matter. *Fourthly*, both this incorporation and this exclusion tend to be semi-permanent. In competitive pressure group politics, by contrast, no interest group is 'finally' excluded, and none has any officially-defined status; all are merely as strong as they can make themselves from time to time, and the relationships which obtain are therefore fluid and shifting. *Fifth*, we can note that in thus sharing responsibility for a specific area of public policy with any particular group, government in effect accords this group public status (Offe, 1981). The group acquires in the public eye an authority and a legitimacy which otherwise, or in the past, was accorded only to government itself. But if the *status* of such a group is public, its operations are far from being so. *Sixth*, therefore, we may say that whereas pressure group activity is public knowledge, a pressure group once incorporated tends to conduct its business with government in great secrecy. *Seventh*, we can note that under corporatist arrangements it becomes difficult to see where policymaking ends and implementation begins. A pressure group campaigns to get a specific change in the law or in administrative practice, and assumes that once adopted, the innovation will be duly implemented by the civil servants. Incorporated interst groups, by contrast, being themselves responsible for the implementation of public policy, tend not to demand particular policies, but rather to evolve policies in the very process of putting them into effect. *Eighth*, therefore, we can note that in the case of 'old-fashioned' pressure group politics it is usually clear to the public and to politicians *what* specific policies are wanted by which specific groups. An 'incorporated' group, by contrast, may quite literally want *no* particular policies, but merely the power to continue to control and to shape policy within its particular areas as seems to it desirable from time to time. *Ninth*, we may suggest that no interest group will generally be granted the privilege of incorporation into the state apparatus unless it can demonstrate a capacity to control the behaviour of its own members. This applies not only to employers' federations or trades unions, but is equally true of groups which have no 'economic' function, and which have a purely 'ideological' or 'legitimatory' role. We may readily imagine, for example, the way in which the relationship of the state to such bodies as the National Union of Teachers or the Royal Town Planning Institute would change, if it became obvious to the public that they had fallen into the control of their respective 'radical' wings. *Tenth*, it is clear under competitive pressure group politics where the state begins and ends. To the extent that corporatist strategems are adopted, however, this becomes far more difficult to discern. Incorporated groups, in fact, tend to be both 'inside' and 'outside' the state apparatus at one and the same time, a point made below in my analysis of the three types of relationship which obtain between government and the planning profession. *Eleventh*, then, and finally, we may note that corporatism as an analytical concept was developed partly to account for the fact that the state is apparently often more active or more 'initiatory' than the older models of 'pluralism' tended to assume. But as is clear from the previous point, such state activity may often reflect no initiative on the part of government itself. On the contrary, the 'active state' is a reflection of the interests of the incorporated groups, which have the capacity, as a result of their thus being both 'inside' and 'outside' the state apparatus, to respond to *their own* demands for state activity.

54. Coates (1984, p. 127) shows that it was a Labour government which 'bullied private industrial capital into one federation' (the CBI), in 1965, and that conversely it was a Conservative government which 'maintained the TUC's monopoly of Labour representation by refusing to recognize a white-collar alternative (the Conference of Professional and Public Service Organizations, COPPSO), in 1962. On the CBI case, see also Newman, 1981, pp 89–94.

55. Thus, the approach adopted here rests on a rejection of the so-called 'dual state' or 'dual politics' thesis. This last suggests that while corporatist arrangements tend often to be adopted at the national level and in relation to production issues, competitive or 'pluralist' pressure group

politics tend to be more characteristic of the local level and of issues relating to consumption or distribution. This thesis is rejected here, firstly, on the grounds that virtually all political issues are by definition issues of production and of consumption/distribution simultaneously. Secondly, it is rejected on the grounds that the possibility of successfully bringing corporatist strategems to bear at the local level depends upon the existence of corporatist networks at the national level. The empirical evidence suggests that any attempt to distinguish between the local and national levels, in British land-use planning, is a non-starter; the *physical development*, obviously, must be located within some local jurisdiction or other, but most of those involved in promoting or preventing it tend to draw whatever strength they may have from far wider power-bases. But certainly, I would agree that in any political issue, those interests which control the means of production are far more likely to be able to call on pre-existing corporatist institutions or understandings than are, for example, the consumers, residents, or environmentalist pressure groups which oppose them. The latter are those which tend to be excluded from 'privileged access', at *any* level of government. On the 'dual politics thesis', see Cawson, 1977, 1982, 1985a and 1986, Chapter 7; Saunders 1981a, 1981b, 1984, 1985 and 1986; Cawson and Saunders, 1983, and for criticisms of the thesis, Harrington, 1982 and Dunleavy, 1984. On the importance of nationally-organized professional networks in enabling such occupational groups as planners to bring corporatist strategems to bear in pursuing their aims, see for example Dunleavy, 1981a and 1981b; Laffin, 1980 and 1986 and Rhodes, 1986. For studies for corporatism in the local context, see Hernes and Selvik, 1981; Cawson, 1985a; Saunders, 1985; King, 1985; Simmie, 1985 and Villadsen, 1986. Dearlove (1973) and Saunders (1979) provide studies of local government in which distinctively corporatist strategems of admitting certain interests and excluding others are shown to play an important role.

56. For attempts to apply such a 'wider' conceptualization of corporatism, see for example Newman 1981; Cawson, 1982; Harrison, 1984. For general accounts of the development of corporatist approaches in the British economy, see for example Beer, 1965; Shonfield, 1965; Harris, 1972; Ionescu, 1975; Carpenter, 1976; Crouch, 1979; Middlemas, 1979; T. Smith, 1979; and especially, Harrison, 1980; Booth, 1982 and Cawson, 1985b. For selections of papers by writers using corporatism as an explanatory concept, see, for example, Schmitter and Lehmbruch, 1979; Berger, 1981; Lembruch and Schmitter, 1982; and especially, W. Grant, 1985. For discussions of corporatism from a broadly Marxist perspective, see, for example, Panitch, 1977, 1980, 1981, and 1984; Jessop, 1978, 1979, 1980 and 1982. For sceptical discussions, questioning the analytical utility of the concept, see, for example, Westergaard, 1977; Cox, 1981; Jordan, 1981; Martin, 1983.

57. These arguments are also advanced in Jessop, 1980, p. 52; Newman, 1981 (especially Chapter 11); Jessop, 1982, pp. 239–40; Rosenberg, 1983, p. 118; and M.L. Harrison, 1984, Chapters 1 and 2.

58. He also advocated the preparation of national economic and social plans: See Ionescu, 1976, 'Introduction'.

59. Durkheim, 1952, pp. 378–92; 1957, pp. 28–41 and 98–109; and 1964, 'Author's Introduction'. Also P. Elliott, 1972, Chapter 1.

60. Durkheim, journal article published in 1908, as quoted in Newman, 1981, p. 8.

61. Winkler, 1977, p. 50.

62. Winkler, 1977 and 1978; Jessop, 1980, p. 54.

63. Winkler, 1977, p. 50.

64. Ibid., pp. 53–4. The way in which the university 'cuts' of the early 1980s were administered—by academics themselves—provides a good example.

65. As Winkler (1977, p. 49) himself makes clear, corporatist mechanisms can be used in pursuit of both egalitarian and inegalitarian objectives, and are in themselves politically neutral. It seems likely that egalitarian outcomes are only possible, however, where the state is both politically strong relative to the other parties, and has a clear political purpose. See also M.J. Hill, 1981, pp. 220–2.

66. See, for example, Rydin 1984; Herington, 1984.

67. Flynn, 1981 and 1983. See also Boaden *et al.*, 1979; Goldsmith, 1980, p. 142.

68. Darke, 1979 and 1982. See also Friend, Laffin and Norris, 1981, esp. p. 457.

69. Cited in Darke, 1982, p. 202. This meant declining coal-mining and industrial areas, especially along the River Dearne, to which the politicians wanted to apply policies of 'positive discrimination'.

70. Cited in Darke, 1982, p. 203.

71. Darke, 1979, p. 351.

72. Corporatist institutions which are open to public scrutiny in a real sense, such as the Dutch 'Economic and Social Parliament', (or (possibly) NEDC; see, for example, Middlemas, 1983), I would see as meriting a completely different kind of consideration from the kind of 'private' administrative corporatism discussed in this book.

73. In Cross and Bristow, 1983, p. 315. For other discussions of the 'Examination in Public', see, for example, Bridges, 1979; Friend, Laffin and Norris, 1981.

74. Eckstein, 1960; Foot, 1962; Mercer, 1984. The arguably even more powerful position of the legal profession is attested by the fact that we still do not have free and equal access to legal services, even today.

75. Bailey, 1980, pp. 88–9. There are of course independent consultants, also members of the RTPI, working in the planning field, and the Institute, predictably, attempts to model the professional self-image upon them, but they seem unimportant in fact both in number and as regards providing us with an understanding of the way in which 'planning' works in reality.

76. Comparisons between the 'older' and the 'newer' professions are to be found in Larson, 1977. For good brief accounts of the way in which the older 'trait' and 'functional' approaches were overturned by these newer explanatory frameworks, see, for example, Bailey, 1980, Chapter 2; Saks, 1983, and especially relevant in the present context, Rosenberg, 1983. Among the main proponents of the newer approach are Johnson, 1972 and 1977; Elliott, 1972 and McKinley, 1973. Writers who have made particular use of the concept of 'social closure' include Parkin, 1974 and 1979 and Parry and Parry, 1977. For comments on it, see for example, Murphy, 1986.

77. And of the two books by Bailey (1975 and 1980). These provide an excellent account of the relationship between planning and its requisite knowledge-base.

78. Jamous and Peloille, 1972; Boreham, 1983. For comments in the context of 'planning', see Broadbent, 1977, pp. 172–4, 212–13 and 246; Bailey, 1980, pp. 30–1; Healey, 1983a, p. 3.

79. It was of course mainly for the 'crime' of having noted that the institution of communism in Eastern Europe had led to the emergence of a 'new class', deriving its power from its effective 'ownership' of the means of administration, that Djilas spent many years in prison. Crossman (1962, pp. 84–5) expresses fears that socialism in Britain could 'create a new leviathan, in which a socialist managerial oligarchy replaces a capitalist managerial oligarchy, or, even worse, shares power with it' unless, he suggests, there can be achieved constitutional reform, in which the government will 'return to the first principles of socialism and decide boldly to make all irresponsible power accountable to the community'.

80. Carchedi (1975) is generally regarded as an influential contribution here. See also, however, Harries-Jenkins, 1970; Freidson, 1973; Oppenheimer, 1973; Laffin, 1980.

81. Gould, 1982 and 1982. Writers who have put forward similar arguments include Parkin, 1974 and 1979; Wilding, 1982 and, at a more general level, Gouldner, 1979.

82. Gould, 1981, p. 412.

83. Ibid., p. 412.

84. Ibid., p. 415. Panitch (in Schmitter and Lehmbruch, 1979, pp. 124–5) makes this same point.

85. Gould, 1981, p. 402.

86. Ibid., p. 415.

87. Dunleavy, 1981a. See also Dunleavy 1981b.

88. Rosenberg, 1983, p. 125.

89. M.L. Harrison (1985) has suggested that such studies are needed in planning. See, however, Healey and Underwood, 1979 and Underwood, 1980.

90. Basch, 1937, pp. 117–34; Herbert, 1963; Pahl and Winkler, 1974.

91. This argument, contrasting the attitudes of 'professionals' who prefer to speak with a single voice, and 'experts', who accept and work within a plurality of viewpoints, is developed in Reade, 1984a.

92. Pahl and Winkler, 1974, p. 72. This is more fully developed in Winkler, 1976 and 1977.
93. Wilding, 1982, p. 61.

## Notes to Chapter 5

1. Cf. N. Taylor, 1980.
2. Archbishop of Canterbury, 1985.
3. Discussed more fully as a 'planning problem' in Reade, 1982, 1984b and 1985a. On the 'high rise' phenomenon, see for example Jephcott and Robinson, 1971; Sutcliffe, 1974; McCutcheon, 1975, and especially, Dunleavy, 1981a. Hallet (1979, p. 25) suggests that the high-rise flats could only have been produced under a command economy, which of course is how they *were* produced.
4. Over public sector development, the local planning authority has no power of veto but only the right to be consulted. But it might be argued that this should be sufficient, if on the one hand the professional planners' judgments had authority, and if on the other hand a sufficient number of powerful elected members were prepared to back 'planning' against the claims of other departments of the local authority.
5. Jessop, 1980, p. 44; Ball, 1983, Chapters 7 and 8; Dawson, 1984, pp. 63–4; Herington, 1984; Rydin, 1984; Chiddick and Dobson, 1986; Hooper, 1986; Cuddy and Hollingsworth, 1986. Cf. Hall *et al.*, 1973, vol. 2, p. 425, and Dunleavy, 1981a, p. 190.
6. Heseltine, 1979, p. 25.
7. Lefcoe, 1980, p. 215.
8. For a discussion of this, see Schaffer, 1970, Chapter 7.
9. Dawson, 1984, p. 66.
10. Shoard, 1980, p. 31. This figure was obtained by dividing the total subsidies paid by the estimated number of whole- and part-time farmers in the United Kingdom, at that time about 293,000.
11. Dawson (1984, pp. 11–12) points out that while the developed countries, which have considerable problems with food surpluses, tend to subsidize their farmers, the Third World countries, which have considerable food shortages, tend to tax their farmers quite heavily, thus depressing output still further; it is obviously difficult for almost any society to grant tax concessions to a *numerically large proportion* of its population. But agriculture is a sphere in which public and political pressure in Britain now increasingly challenges established bureaucratic, economic and corporate power, and in which some significant change in policy therefore now seems possible.
12. In the case of transport policy, as opposed to that of agriculture, there seems little sign of any change in the way things are seen, despite much excellent research. On the power of the roads lobby, and on the social and environmental problems caused by motor vehicles, see, for example, W. Plowden, 1971; S. Plowden, 1972; M. Hamer, 1974; J. Grant, 1977; S. Plowden, 1985. For analysis of these problems as they affect less privileged groups, and on the need to conceptualize the matter in terms of 'accessibility' rather than 'mobility', see the various research reports of Anne Whalley and Mayer Hillman, published by Political and Economic Planning, or the report of the Independent Commission on Transport (1974).
13. Edwards, 1985.
14. Boddy, 1981; *The Economist*, 1978b.
15. Calvocoressi, 1978, p. 145.
16. See Chapter 3, note 71.
17. For example, Bjork, 1980.
18. Williams, 1971; Aronson, 1974 for discussions of the social significance of physical environment more generally, see, for example, Beshers, 1962; Taylor, 1973; Gould and White, 1974; Kirby, 1982; Badcock, 1984; Gregory and Urry, 1985.
19. As identified in Chapter 1, Section 5.
20. See, for example, McKay and Cox, 1979, p. 72.
21. Foster, 1973, pp. 153 and 159. See also Dowall, 1981; Healey, 1983a, pp. 253–4; Broadbent,

1977, p. 164. But the strongest evidence in support of the thesis that land prices are raised by planning is probably Hall *et al.*, 1973.

22. For example, Ball, 1983; Hallet, 1979, p. 51,
23. For example, Stretton, 1978, p. 37; Broadbent, 1977, p. 21 and *passim*. Hallet (1979, p. 151) points out that land-value policies in Britain are formulated and discussed not only without reference to economic theory and research, but also without any attempt to learn from other countries. Darin-Drabkin (1977, Chapters 3, 4 and 5) provides much detailed comparative data on land prices, but does not address the 'theoretical' question posed here.
24. On this debate, see Lean and Goodall, 1966; Lean, 1969, 1970; Evans, 1969, 1970 and 1983; McMillan, 1975; Wiltshaw, 1985.
25. Hallett, 1977, p. 117. But see also Dunleavy, 1981a, p. 72; Westergaard and Resler, 1975, p. 135.
26. See, for example, Darin-Drabkin and Darin, 1980, pp. 220 and 225; Evans, 1983.
27. See above, Chapter 3, Section 3. Also (for example) Lefcoe, 1980, especially the 'summary'.
28. See, for example, Ravetz, 1980, p. 91; Evans, 1974, p. 96.
29. Burnham, 1985. That there is a shortage of land in Britain *in general*, one of the arguments for planning put forward most frequently by planners themselves, is dismissed by Best. See Best, 1981, especially p. 169.
30. For example Broadbent, 1977, especially Chapter 3.
31. For an interesting discussion, see McMahon, 1985.
32. Hall *et al* 1973: see Chapter 3, Section 3, above.
33. For example, Eversley, 1974.
34. See for example Pearce, 1980, p. 137; Hallett, 1979, pp. 15–21.
35. Evans, 1974, p. 91. For a useful discussion, see Willis, 1980, pp. 39–59.
36. Pahl (1965) suggests an interesting reversal of this general tendency. One of the positive externalities enjoyed by those commuters who live in the country, he suggested, is the presence of colourful and quaint 'characters' among the rural working class.
37. See for example Moore, 1978, p. 394.
38. For example, Pearce, 1980, p. 123, and further references quoted therein.
39. It is also very much stressed, of course, by those who urge that planning should be restricted to the 'indicative' level. See for example Foster, 1973; Klosterman, 1985, p. 9; Moore, 1978.
40. Evans, 1974, pp. 94–5. On the IOR, see, for example, Cullingworth, 1982, p. 41.
41. Pearce, 1980, p. 150; see also Klosterman, 1985, p. 11.
42. Some also use the name 'prisoners' dilemma' (for example, Foster, 1973, pp. 149–52), but others suggest that this reflects a misunderstanding.
43. Hardin, 1968.
44. Foster, 1973, pp. 162–3.
45. Purdom, 1946.
46. A recent exploration and restatement of this view, with statistical evidence and arguments, is provided by Donnison and Soto, 1980.
47. Sarkissian, 1976, provides a good summary. See also, for example, Dennis, 1968.
48. Stretton, 1978, p. 40. The school of thought he reflects here derives largely from Jacobs (1961); until the appearance of the latter, the 1933 'Charter of Athens' call for segregation of land uses was the dominant ideology in town planning circles.
49. Familiarity with the pages of *Planning Newspaper*, for example, would support this conclusion.
50. See, for example, Hallett, 1979, pp. 128 and 136; Harvey, 1973, p. 190. As Hague (1984, p. 74) notes, one single company (Ravenseft) built 400 shopping developments in 150 different towns in Britain between 1949 and 1966, at a cost of £60 million.
51. For example, Heywood, 1974.
52. Obvious examples of such alternative conceptions of what constitutes welfare include Galbraith's view that wellbeing would be increased by more public and less private consumption, Schumacher's suggestion that the working environment is qualitatively better in small-scale than in large-scale production, Illich's view that the services we provide for ourselves give us greater satisfaction than those provided for us by professionals, or Mishan's suggestion that a pleasant environment in fact contributes more to material welfare than does an over-abundance of manufactured goods. For a

recent rejection of the view I advance here, however, arguing that 'economic' and 'environmental' considerations *are* in fact mutually incompatible, see Sillince, 1986.

53. For example J.G. Davies, 1972; Dennis, 1970 and 1972.

54. On the problems of intervention, see for example Lichfield, 1980, pp. 196–7; Hallett, 1979, Chapter 2.

55. Nuffield Foundation, 1986.

56. Ratcliffe, 1984, p. 251. See also Hallett, 1979, p. 24.

57. Ravetz, 1980, pp. 72–3.

58. Drewett, in Hall *et al.*, 1973, vol. 2, p. 197.

59. Pointed out in Oxley, 1975. Another example illustrating this mistaken belief that greater economic realism can simply be equated with increased reliance upon the market is Sorensen and Day, 1981.

60. As put forward in Lichfield, 1956. For the contrary view, arguing the utility of CBA in some detail, see Willis, 1980, pp. 91–165 or McAllister, 1980, pp. 85–147.

61. See, for example, Hallett, 1977, pp. 124–6.

62. McKay and Cox, 1979, pp. 89–95; Marriott, 1967, pp. 11–12, pp. 211–13; Hallett, 1977, pp. 138–41; 1979, Chapter 9. It seems quite possible that the public would favour a much greater measure of firm intervention, too, at least if the issues were presented clearly and widely understood. A survey carried out in 1945 found that over half the population favoured complete nationalization of land, and that less than one-third were actually opposed to this measure (Hewitt, 1974). It seems unlikely that after the experience of the 'unacceptable face of capitalism' as manifested in the great property scandals of the 1960s and 1970s, a similar level of support could not be obtained for effective taxation of development value. The widely-accepted view that the 1947 Act went as far as was politically possible in this direction seems to be without foundation.

63. Hallett, 1979, p. 9.

64. McKay and Cox, 1979, p. 21; Evans, 1983, p. 119.

65. Examples include such 'texts' as Button, 1976; Harrison, 1977; Willis, 1980; Balchin and Kieve, 1985 and Evans, 1985. The second and third of these discuss the economics of land-use planning without even mentioning the problem of betterment at all. But this same tendency to discuss far too wide a subject area, and in far too general terms, is often found even in short journal articles, and short 'introductions', too. Examples include Foster, 1973; Evans, 1974; Moore, 1978; Lichfield, 1980; Klosterman, 1985. The planners' over-ambitious conceptions of the scope of planning, on which these economists' discussions are presumably based, continue apace. See, for example, McLoughlin, 1982; *The Planner*, 1985; Royal Town Planning Institute 1986. One lone voice (Coon, 1984), urging planners to restrict themselves to analysis of the control of land use, seems not to have been heeded.

# Notes to Chapter 6

1. Denman, 1980, as quoted in Cherry, 1982, p. 106.

2. Allison, 1975, pp. 20–22.

3. Notably in the 1968 Town and Country Planning Act and the 1969 'Skeffington' report.

4. For comments on this, see for example Cullingworth, 1982, pp. 338–9; Hague, 1984, pp. 112–13.

5. Participation which is *not* promoted by authority as a legitimating device, but which originates with the 'participants' themselves, is generally not called participation by authority, but rather is portrayed as the expression of selfish sectional interests. For discussions of public participation in planning from the period in which this was most avidly sought by planners, see, for example, Dennis, 1970, Chapter 20; 1972, Chapter 19; Damer and Hague, 1971; Davies, 1972; Thornley, 1977; and for a bibliography over the whole phenomenon, Barker, 1979. The main problem, when participation in this sense does occur, is that it is 'unconstitutional', for it bypasses the elected representatives. In political science, by contrast, participation in politics is seen as

*including* activity which goes through the elected representatives. For discussions of participation in this wider, political science, sense, see, for example, Pateman, 1970; D.M. Hill, 1970 and 1974; Parry, 1972; Leonard, 1975.

6. Ironically, the growth of public and especially national pressure-group participation in 'local' inquiries has led to a governmental perception of the latter as offering *too much* scope for debate, and as holding up the decision-making process: see, for example, White, 1986. For other discussions, see Le Las, 1983; Blowers, 1986. That this redefinition of important national political issues as local administrative matters is indeed a *misrepresentation* of them is a point very well made in Lowe and Goyder (1983); see especially pp. 68 and 180.

7. Cherry, 1982, p. 125.

8. See Chapter 4, note 12.

9. As Hall (1983a, pp. 44–5) points out, this Marxist work is 'quietist', in the sense that from its assertion that the planning system will 'inevitably' have the function of promoting capital accumulation and providing legitimation no conclusions for action can be drawn; one cannot change that which is inevitable. Nevertheless, one feels, *some* response is called for. The 'inevitability' itself might be challenged, and it is in any case necessary to clarify the circumstances in which 'planning' will be *more* and *less* merely the unwitting agent of inexorable forces. And admittedly there do exist a few attempts to apply this new urban sociology specifically to the institutions of planning: see, for example, Scott and Roweis, 1977; Fainstein and Fainstein, 1979; Roweis, 1981; McDougall, 1982; Paris, 1982; Cooke, 1983; Beauregard, 1984; Klosterman, 1985; Harvey, 1985a and 1985b; Healey, 1986b, and especially, Ball, 1983.

10. On this point, see Rhodes, 1980 and 1984; Barlow, 1981; McAuslan, 1981; Newton, 1981; Rinder, 1982; Martlew, 1983; Elliott and McCrone, 1984; Goldsmith and Newton, 1984; Harloe and Paris, 1984. On the 'attack' on local government more generally, see Bramely, 1984; Goldsmith, 1985b; Jones and Stewart, 1985; Loughlin *et al.*, 1985; Ranson, Jones and Walsh, 1985; Rhodes, 1986 and especially, Cochrane, 1985. For a brief historical review of the central–local relationship, see Thrasher, 1981.

11. On 'local economic planning', see Underwood and Stewart, 1978; Townroe, 1979; Muller and Bruce, 1981, Young and Mason, 1983, Young and Mills, 1983, Benington, 1985; Chandler and Lawless, 1985; Duncan and Goodwin, 1985; Moore, Richardson and Moon, 1985; Nickson, 1985. On attempts to link such local economic planning with physical planning, see T. Davies, 1981; Greater London Council, 1985a and 1985b.

12. On these trends, see, for example, Whiteley and Gordon, 1980; Alexander, 1981, Alt and Turner, 1982; Gyford and James, 1982; Gyford, 1984; 1985a and 1985b.

13. Bulpitt, 1967; Lee, 1967; Heclo, 1969; Jones, 1969 and 1973; Dearlove, 1973; Elkin, 1974; Lee *et al.*, 1974, Newton, 1976, Jennings, 1982.

14. A 'corporate planning' approach can be used by a political 'cabinet', and does not necessarily lead to officer domination of policy-making. Cf. Norton and Wedgwood-Oppenheim, 1981; Rydin, 1981; Clapham, 1984.

15. On 'local socialism', see, for example, Jennings, 1982; Boddy and Fudge, 1984; Gyford, 1985a. On the 'socialist planners', see, for example, McLeish, 1981; Thompson, 1981; Howl, 1982 and 1985; Hague, 1984 and 1985.

16. See Chapter 5, note 5. These dilemmas, and the ambivalence of Conservative 'planning' policies more generally, are discussed in for example Cox, 1980; McAuslan, 1981; McKay, 1982; Hall, 1983b; Healey, 1983a, pp. 268–70; Howes, 1983; Goldsmith, 1985a and Allison, 1986. McKay and Cox (1979, p. 55) point to the fact that much the same dilemmas were experienced by the previous Conservative government, of 1970–4. That the 'attack on planning' is at the symbolic level is also suggested by Robinson and Lloyd (1986).

17. DoE Circulars 22 of 1980 (on 'Development Control Policy and Practice') and 14 of 1985 (on 'Development and Employment' which accompanied the White Paper *Lifting the Burden*—i.e. of planning) are perhaps the most noteworthy. See, for example, Davies et al., 1986.

18. Especially, perhaps, that of Heseltine (1979). For comments, see for example Cherry, 1982, pp. 67–8.

19. Lloyd and Botham, 1985, p. 52.

20. Ibid.
21. Roger Tym and Partners, *Monitoring Enterprise Zones Year Two Report*, London, DoE, 1983, as quoted in ibid. Balchin and Kieve (1985, p. 181), quoting further research by these same consultants, report that by the end of 1983 'in net terms only about 5375 jobs had been created at a total cost of £252.4m., or as much as £46,958 per job'. For discussions of the origins of Enterprise Zones, see, for example, S. Taylor, 1981; Hall *et al.*, 1983.
22. Urban Development Corporations are discussed in for example Newman and Mayo, 1981 and Adcock, 1984. Further UDCs are in fact proposed.
23. This is the third meaning of 'planning', as identified in this book. See Chapter 1, note 5.
24. Allison, 1975, p. 17.
25. For example, Van Gunsteren, 1976.
26. The 'classic' text here is Braybrooke and Lindblom, 1963. See also Lindblom, 1959; Dror, 1964; Etzioni, 1967.
27. R. Gregory, 1969.
28. Discussed in Cherry, 1974, pp. 201–10 and Hague, 1984, pp. 108–10. I must admit that I myself opposed this, but have for many years thought that I was mistaken in this.
29. Cherry, 1974, pp. 210–17; Hague, 1984, pp. 110–12.
30. Cooke, 1983, *passim.*, esp. pp. 13, 73 and 87. Cooke, however, may not intend that his analysis be restricted to the planning profession as the latter is identified and discussed in the present book, for he uses the term 'planning' very broadly, sometimes, apparently, to mean policy-making in general, and even to include the programmes formulated by workers' co-operatives.
31. Above, for example, I have described the emergence of a neo-Marxist approach in urban studies. But other approaches, and indeed, ones quite critical of this neo-Marxist school, still continued. Conversely, there are many who would question the idea that this Marxist work told us anything about planning which was not already well-known.
32. There are few discussions of this, but see, for example, Jenkins, 1973.
33. Healey, 1983a, pp. 271–86.

## Notes to Chapter 7

1. In its present-day form, in 'planning', this becomes the fallacy of supposing that rationality can govern our choice of objectives. See below.
2. Whether planning graduates are in fact in great demand outside planning, is not altogether clear. Of 583 people who applied for membership in the Royal Town Planning Institute in 1984, just ten, or 1.7 per cent, seem to have been in non-planning jobs. Of 570 members of the Institute who responded to a membership survey in the same year, 25, or 4.4 per cent, appear to have been in non-planning private sector jobs: RTPI, unpublished report on membership, 1985. For statements urging the high quality of planning education and the potential demand for planning graduates in wider areas of employment, see, for example, Batey, 1985; Blowers *et al.*, 1985; Chandler, 1985; Fidler, 1985; Isserman, 1985.
3. Ravetz, 1980, p. 227.
4. Duncan and Goodwin, 1985; Young and Mason, 1983, pp. 216–21. Deakin, 1985. The 2p rate which local authorities are permitted to devote to such purposes as these local economic initiatives produced £40 million in the case of the former Greater London Council area, but only 'hundreds of thousands' in Mid-Glamorgan (Rees and Lambert, 1985, p. 177). In districts, clearly, it would yield much less. Far more urgent than these attempts at 'local economic planning', one might suggest, is the need to politicize the struggle for control over such powerful agents of social change as the Manpower Services Commission, which really *does* have the power to shape the 'quality of life' in the depressed regions.
5. As well as competing with each other, such local authority economic initiatives also reduce the effectiveness of central government's 'regional policies'.
6. See, for example, as a suggestive indication of the ways in which this 'research establishment'

promotes the values of a powerful technocratic and managerialist local government service, Dearlove, 1979, *passim,* esp. pp. 257–9; Deakin, 1982; Gyford, 1985a, pp. 22–23, 43, and 102–3 and Rees and Lambert, 1985, pp. 170–82.

7. Rydin, 1984.

8. Healey, 1983a, pp. 271–86.

9. I am thinking here primarily of Healey (1983a), and of most of the contributions to the book edited by Barrett and Healey (1985). But these assumptions are also reflected in much of the current debate, as for example in the pages of *The Planner.*

10. In principle, this should of course be achieved by means of tolls imposed on vehicles, but clearly this is in most cases probably not possible.

11. Lichfield and Darin-Drabkin, 1980, p. 145.

12. Author's estimates, based on Retail Price Index.

13. *ibid.,* assuming a six-fold increase in the general price level over the period 1968–1988.

14. Duncan and Goodwin, 1985, p. 240.

15. As quoted in Hague, 1984, p. 86.

16. Duncan, 1985, p. 331.

17. Ashworth, 1954, pp. 233–34. See also McKay and Cox, 1979, p. 78.

18. In the case of undeveloped land, the 'Uthwatt' committee recommended that development be permitted only after compulsory purchase by the state at existing use value and resale to the developer at development value, as in the 1967 and 1975 Acts.

19. Lichfield and Darin-Drabkin, 1980, *passim.*

20. Hallett, 1977 and 1979.

21. For a relevant account of the results of co-ordination pursued 'for its own sake', see Painter, 1980.

22. Goldthorpe, 1971.

23. See, for example, Parkin, 1979, Chapter 4; Wilding, 1982, pp. 53–8.

24. McAuslan, 1980; Underwood, 1981; Bruton and Nicholson, 1985; Davies *et al.,* 1986.

25. Cf. Lee *et al.,* 1974.

26. Coleman, 1976 and 1985. See Chapter 3, Section 2, above.

27. 'Dobry', 1975. On this, see for example Broadbent, 1977, p. 250; Hallett, 1979, p. 161 and n. 21; Pearce, 1984.

28. Healey, 1983a, pp. 29–33.

29. What I am advocating might be called a 'standards' approach, in the sense that the same criteria would be used over the whole country. Economists (for example Pearce, 1980, pp. 126–131; Evans, 1985, Chapter 1) often ask why it is that planners prefer physical standards to such economic mechanisms as subsidies and taxes, for the latter, they suggest, are more flexible. I would, however, see such economic tools of control as *more* in line with what I am calling a standards approach than is the 'discretion' in assessing physical criteria calimed by planners; subsidies and taxes are applied uniformly, all like cases being treated alike.

30. Chapter 4, Section 2.

31. Chapter 3, Section 2.

32. Jackman (1985) provides a recent statement of the fact that if local rates are increased to pay for 'welfare' in any sense, the rich will tend to move away, leaving the poor with even *higher* levels of taxation; the same is of course true at the international level.

33. Dunleavy, 1980, Chapter 5; Kirby, 1982, Chapters 4 and 7.

34. Grant and Healey (1985) make clear that both the interests and idea-systems which 'planning' tackles and those on which planning is itself based are all *nationally* organized.

35. For some of the relevant background here, see for example Drewry, 1985; Nixon, 1986.

36. Kellner and Crowther-Hunt, 1980; Blackstone, 1981; Judge, 1981; Delafons, 1982. The Widdicombe (1986) Committee on the Conduct of Local Authority Business recommends that 'small numbers of officers . . . be attached to party groups or their leaders' (i.e. at the local authority level). An editorial in the July 1986 issue of *The Planner* (vol. 72, no. 7, p. 3) opposes this, however, suggesting that 'Planners should guard their independence of judgment and advice or their claim to offer a worthwhile public service will be devalued'. It also opposes this closer contact with the

politicians on the grounds that 'Few genuinely community-oriented planners would be so naive . . . as to imagine that getting closer to the people merely involves getting closer to their elected representatives.'

# Bibliography

Abercrombie, P. (1933), *Town and Country Planning*, Oxford, Oxford University Press.

Adcock, B. (1984), 'Regenerating Merseyside docklands: the Merseyside Development Corporation, 1981–1984', *Town Planning Review*, vol. 55, pp. 265–89.

Addison, P. (1977), *The Road to 1945: British Politics and the Second World War*, London, Cape.

Adshead, S.D. (1941), *A New England*, London, Frederick Muller.

Akin, W.E. (1977), *Technocracy and the American Dream: The Technocrat Movement, 1900–1941*, Berkeley, University of California Press.

Albrow, M. (1970), 'The role of the sociologist as a professional: the case of planning' in *Sociological Review Monograph No. 16, The Sociology of Sociology*, Keele (Staffs.), University of Keele.

Alden, J. and Morgan, R. (1974), *Regional Planning: A Comprehensive View*, Leighton Buzzard (Beds.), Leonard Hill.

Aldridge, M. (1979), *The British New Towns: A Programme Without a Policy*, London, Routledge.

Alexander, A. (1981), 'Officers and members in the new local government system—parallel structures and interactive processes', *Local Government Studies*, vol. 7, pp. 33–44.

Allison, L. (1975), *Environmental Planning: A Political and Philosophical Analysis*, London, Allen & Unwin.

Allison, L. (1986), 'What is planning for?' *Town Planning Review*, vol. 57, pp. 5–16.

Alt, J.E. and Turner, J. (1982), 'The case of the silk-stocking socialists and the calculating children of the middle class', *British Journal of Political Science*, vol. 12, pp. 239–48.

Altshuler, A.A. (1965), *The City Planning Process: A Political Analysis*, Ithaca (N.Y.), Cornell University Press.

Ambrose, P. (1976), *Who Plans Brighton's Housing Crisis?* London, Shelter.

Ambrose, P. (1986), *Whatever Happened to Planning?*, London, Methuen.

Ambrose, P. and Colenutt, B. (1975), *The Property Machine*, Harmondsworth, Penguin.

Anton, T.J. (1975), *Governing Greater Stockholm: A Study of Policy Development and System Change*, Berkeley, University of California Press.

Archbishop of Canterbury (1985), *Faith in the City*, London, Church House Publishing Company.

Argyris, C. and Schon, D. (1974), *Theory in Practice: Increasing Professional Effectiveness*, San Francisco, Jossey-Bass.

Aronson, J.R. (1974), 'Voting with your feet', *New Society*, 29 August, pp. 545–7.

Ashworth, W. (1954), *The Genesis of Modern British Town Planning: A Study in Economic and Social History of the Nineteenth and Twentieth Centuries*, London, Routledge.

Azmon, Y. (1980) 'Bargaining in physical planning in Israel: a comparison with the British experience' *Policy and Politics*, Vol. 8, pp. 443–56.

Bachrach, P. and Baratz, M.S. (1962), 'The two faces of power', *American Political Science Review*, vol. 56, pp. 947–52.

Bachrach, P. and Baratz, M.S. (1963), 'Decisions and nondecisions: an analytical framework', *American Political Science Review*, vol. 57, pp. 641–51.

Bachrach, P. and Baratz, M.S. (1970), *Power and Poverty*, London, Oxford University Press.

Backwell, J. and Dickens, P. (1978), *Town Planning, Mass Loyalty and the Restructuring of Capital: The*

*Origins of the 1947 Planning Legislation Revisited'*, University of Sussex, Urban and Regional Studies Working Paper no. 11.

Badcock, B. (1984), *Unfairly Structured Cities*, Oxford, Blackwell.

Bailey, J. (1975), *Social Theory for Planning*, London, Routledge.

Bailey, J. (1980), *Ideas and Intervention: Social Theory for Practice*, London, Routledge.

'Bains' (1972), *The New Local Authorities: Management and Structure*, London, HMSO.

Balchin, P.N. and Kieve, J.L. (1985), *Urban Land Economics* (3rd. edn), London, Macmillan.

Ball, M. (1983), *Housing Policy and Economic Power: The Political Economy of Owner Occupation*, London, Methuen.

Banfield, E.C. (1955), 'Note on conceptual scheme' in Meyerson, M. and Banfield, E.C., *Politics, Planning and the Public Interest: The Case of Public Housing in Chicago*, New York, The Free Press of Glencoe.

Barker, A. (1979), *Public Participation in Britain: A Classified Bibliography*, London, Bedford Square Press in association with the Royal Town Planning Institute.

Barker, A. and Couper, M. (1984), 'The art of quasi-judicial administration: the planning appeal and inquiry systems in England', *Urban Law and Policy*, vol. 7, pp. 363–476.

Barker, A. and Couper, M. (1985), 'Planning appeals and inquiries: a unique quasi-judicial system, *The Planner*, vol. 71, pp. 18–23.

'Barlow' (1940), *Report of the Royal Commission on the Distribution of the Industrial Population*, London, HMSO.

Barlow, J. (1981), 'The rationale for the control of local government expenditure for the purposes of macro-economic management', *Local Government Studies*, vol. 7, pp. 3–14.

Barrett, S.M. (1981), 'Local authorities and the community land scheme' in Barrett, S.M. and Fudge, C. (eds), *Policy and Action: Essays on the Implementation of Public Policy*, London, Methuen.

Barrett, S.M. and Healey, P. (eds) (1985), *Land Policy: Problems and Alternatives*, Aldershot, Gower.

Barry, B. (1964), 'The public interest', *Proceedings of the Aristotelian Society*, Supp. vol. 38, pp. 1–18, reprinted in Quinton, A. (ed.), *Political Philosophy*, Oxford, Oxford University Press, 1967.

Basch, F. (1937), *The Fascist: His State and his Mind*, New York, Morrow.

Bassett, K. and Short, J. (1980), *Housing and Residential Structure: Alternative Approaches*, London, Routledge.

Bater, J.H. (1980), *The Soviet City: Ideal and Reality*, London, Arnold.

Batey, P.W.J. (1985), 'Postgraduate planning education in Britain: its purpose, context and organization', *Town Planning Review*, vol. 56, pp. 407–20.

Batley, R.A. (1982), 'The politics of administrative allocation' in Forrest, R., Henderson, J. and Williams, P. (eds.), *Urban Political Economy and Social Theory: Critical Essays in Urban Studies*, Aldershot, Gower.

Batty, M. (1983), 'A plan for planning education', *Environment and Planning B*, vol. 10, pp. 245–8.

Beauregard, R.A. (1984), 'Structure, agency and urban redevelopment', in Smith, M.P. (ed.), *Cities in Transformation: Class, Capital and the State*, Beverly Hills, Sage

Beer, A.R. (1983), 'Development control and design quality, Part 2. Attitudes to design', *Town Planning Review*, vol. 54, pp. 383–404.

Beer, S.H. (1965), *Modern British Politics*, London, Faber.

Benevolo, L. (1967), *The Origins of Modern Town Planning* (tr. Judith Landry), London, Routledge.

Benington, J. (1976), *Local Government Becomes Big Business* (2nd edn), London, Home Office Community Development Project, Information and Intelligence Unit.

Benington, J. (1985), 'Local economic initiatives', *Local Government Studies*, vol. 11, pp. 1–8.

Berger, S. (ed.) (1981), *Organizing Interests in Western Europe*, London, Cambridge University Press.

Beshers, J. (1962), *Urban Social Structure*, New York, The Free Press of Glencoe.

Best, R.H. (1981), *Land Use and Living Space*, London, Methuen.

Binder, B.J.A. (1982), 'Relations between central and local government since 1975: are the associations failing?', *Local Government Studies*, vol. 8, pp. 35–44.

Bjork, B.G. (1980), *Life, Liberty and Property: The Economics and Politics of Land Use Planning and Environmental Controls*, Lexington (Mass.), Lexington Books.

Blacksell, M. and Gilg, A. (1981), *The Countryside: Planning and Change*, London, George Allen & Unwin.

Blackstone, T. (1981), 'The entrenched generalists', *New Universities Quarterly*, vol. 35, pp. 280–92.

Blowers, A. (1980), *The Limits of Power: The Politics of Local Planning Policy*, Oxford, Pergamon.

Blowers, A. (1984), *Something in the Air: Corporate Power and the Environment*, London, Harper and Row.

Blowers, A. (1986), 'Environmental politics and policy in the 1980s: a changing challenge', *Policy and Politics*, vol. 14, pp. 1–8.

Blowers, A., Goldsmith, M., Kitchen, T. and Morphet, J. (1985), 'Planning and planning education: the future', *Newsletter of the Education for Planning Association*, vol. 14, pp. 10–15.

Boaden, N., Goldsmith, M., Hampton, W. and Stringer, P. (1979), 'Public participation in planning within a representative local democracy', *Policy and Politics*, vol. 7, pp. 55–67.

Boardman, P.L. (1978), *The Worlds of Patrick Geddes: Biologist, Town Planner, Re-educator, Peace Warrior*, London, Routledge. (Originally published 1944).

Boddy, M. (1980), *The Building Societies*, London, Macmillan.

Boddy, M. (1981), 'The property sector in late capitalism: the case of Britain' in Dear, M. and Scott, A.J. (eds). *Urbanization and Urban Planning in Capitalist Society*, London, Methuen.

Boddy, M. and Fudge, C. (eds)(1984), *Local Socialism? Labour Councils and New Left Alternatives*, London, Macmillan.

Booth, A. (1982), 'Corporatism, capitalism and depression in twentieth century Britain', *British Journal of Sociology*, vol. 32, pp. 200–23.

Booth, P. (1983), 'Development control and design quality, Part I: Conditions: a useful way of controlling design?' *Town Planning Review*, vol. 54, pp. 265–84.

Boreham, P. (1983), 'Indetermination, professional knowledge, organization and control', *Sociological Review*, vol. 31, pp. 693–718.

Boumphrey, G. (1940), *Town and Country Tomorrow*, London, Nelson.

Bracken, I. (1981), *Urban Planning Methods: Research and Policy Analysis* London, Methuen.

Bramley, G. (1984), 'Local government in crisis: a review article', *Policy and Politics*, vol. 12, pp. 311–24.

Braybrooke, D. and Lindblom, C.E. (1963), *A Strategy of Decision*, Glencoe (Ill.), Free Press.

Breheny, M. and Hooper, A. (eds.) (1985), *Rationality in Planning: Critical Essays on the Role of Rationality in Urban and Regional Planning*, London, Pion.

Bridges, L.T. (1979), 'The structure plan examination in public as an instrument of intergovernmental decision making', *Urban Law and Policy*, vol. 2, pp. 241–64.

Briggs, A. (1964), 'The political scene' in Newell-Smith, A. (ed.), *Edwardian England, 1901–1914*, Oxford, Oxford University Press

Broadbent, T.A. (1977), *Planning and Profit in the Urban Economy*, London, Methuen.

Broadbent, T.A. and Key, J.A. (1981), *Review of Research in Planning*, London, Centre for Environmental Studies, CES Paper no. 15.

Broady, M. (1968), *Planning for People: Essays on the Social Context of Planning*, London, National Council of Social Service.

Bruce, M. (ed.) (1973), *The Rise of the Welfare State: English Social Policy, 1601–1971*, London, Weidenfeld and Nicholson.

Bruton, M.J. (1983), 'Local plans, local planning and development schemes in England, 1974–1982, *Town Planning Review*, vol. 54, pp. 4–23.

Bruton, M.J. (ed.) (1984), *The Spirit and Purpose of Planning (2nd edn)* London, Hutchinson.

Bruton M.J., Crispin, G. and Fidler, P.M. (1983), 'The context of local plan inquiries', *Journal of Planning and Environment Law*, May, pp. 276–86.

Bruton, M.J. and Fisher, E.A. (1980), Policy symposium: the future of development plans—PAG revisited, *Town Planning Review*, vol. 51 pp. 131–51.

Bruton, M.J. and Nicholson, D. (1985), 'Strategic land use planning and the British development plan system', *Town Planning Review*, vol. 56, pp. 21–41.

Budd, A. (1978), *The Politics of Economic Planning*, Manchester, Manchester University Press and London, Fontana.

Bulmer, M. (ed.) 1978), *Social Policy Research*, London, Macmillan.

Bulmer, M. (1982), *The Uses of Social Research: Social Investigation in Public Policy-Making*, London, Allen & Unwin.

Bulpitt, J.G. (1967), *Party Politics in English Local Government*, London, Longman.

Burnham, J. (1941), *The Managerial Revolution: What is Happening in the World*, New York, John Day Co. Inc.

Burnham, P. (1985), 'A turning point in British land use policies', *Town and Country Planning*, vol. 54, pp. 188–90

Buttimer, A. (1971), 'Sociology and planning', *Town Planning Review*, vol. 42, pp. 145–80.

Button, K.J. (1976), *Urban Economics: Theory and Policy*, London, Macmillan.

Calder, A. (1968), *The People's War*, London, Cape.

Calvocoressi, P. (1978), *The British Experience, 1945–1975*, London, Bodley Head.

Camhis, M. (1979), *Planning Theory and Philosophy*, London, Tavistock.

Carchedi, G. (1975), 'On the economic identification of the new middle class', *Economy and Society*, vol. 4, pp. 1–86.

Carpenter, L.P. (1976), 'Corporatism in Britain, 1930–1945', *Journal of Contemporary History*, vol. 11, pp. 3–25

Castells, M. (1977), *The Urban Question*, London, Arnold.

Castells, M. (1978), *City, Class and Power* (tr. E. Lebas) London, Macmillan.

Cawson, A. (1977), *Environmental Planning and the Politics of Corporatism*, University of Sussex, Urban and Regional Studies Working Paper no. 7.

Cawson, A. (1982), *Corporatism and Welfare: Social Policy and State Intervention in Britain*, London, Heinemann.

Cawson, A. (1985a), 'Corporatism and local politics' in Grant, W. (ed.), *The Political Economy of Corporatism*, London, Macmillan.

Cawson, A. (1985b) (ed.), *Organized Interests and the State: Studies in Meso-Corporatism*, London, Sage.

Cawson, A. (1986), *Corporatism and Political Theory*, Oxford, Blackwell.

Cawson, A. and Saunders, P. (1983), 'Corporatism, competitive politics and class struggle' in King, R. (ed.), *Capital and Politics*, London, Routledge.

Ceccarelli, P. (1984), 'Ex uno plures: a walk through Marxist urban studies' in Rodwin, L. and Hollister, R.M. *Cities of the Mind: Images and Theories of the City in the Social Sciences*, New York, Plenum Press

Centre for Environmental Studies (1973), *Education for Planning: The Development of Knowledge and Capability for Urban Governance*, Oxford, Pergamon.

Chadwick, G.F. (1970), *A Systems View of Planning: Towards a Theory of the Urban and Regional Planning Process*, Oxford, Pergamon. (2nd. edn., 1978).

Chandler, E.W. (1985), 'The components of design teaching in a planning context', *Town Planning Review*, vol. 56, pp. 468–82.

Chandler, J.A. and Lawless, P. (1985), *Local Authorities and the Creation of Employment*, Aldershot, Gower.

Cherns, A. (1979), *Using the Social Sciences*, London, Routledge.

Cherns, A., Sinclair, R. and Jenkins, W.I. (eds) (1972), *Social Science and Government: Policies and Problems*, London, Tavistock.

Cherry, G. (1970), *Town Planning in its Social Context*, London, Leonard Hill.

Cherry, G. (1972), *Urban Change and Planning: A History of Urban Development in Britain since 1750*, Henley-on-Thames, Foulis.

Cherry, G. (1974), *The Evolution of British Town Planning: A History of Town Planning in the United Kingdom during the Twentieth Century, and of the Royal Town Planning Institute 1914–1974*, Leighton Buzzard, Leonard Hill.

Cherry, G. (1975), *Environmental Planning, 1939–1969. Volume II: National Parks and Recreation in the Countryside*, London, HMSO.

Cherry, G. (1981), 'Biographies and planning history' in Cherry, G. (ed.), *Pioneers in British Planning*, London, Architectural Press.

Cherry, G. (1982), *The Politics of Town Planning*, London, Longman.

Chiddick, D. and Dobson, M. (1986), 'Land for housing: circular arguments', *The Planner*, Vol. 72, pp. 10–13

Clapham, D. (1984), 'Rational planning and politics: the example of local authority corporate planning', *Policy and Politics*, vol. 12, pp. 31–52

Clarke, P.H. (1965), 'Site value rating and the recovery of betterment' in Hall, P. (ed.), *Land Values*, London, Sweet and Maxwell.

Cloke, P.J. (1983), *An Introduction to Rural Settlement Planning*, London, Methuen.

Coates, D. (1984), 'Corporatism and the state in theory and practice' in Harrison, M.L. (ed.), *Corporatism and the Welfare State*, Aldershot, Gower.

Cockburn, C. (1977), *The Local State: Management of Cities and Peoples*, London, Pluto Press.

Cochrane, A. (1985), 'The attack on local government: what it is and what it isn't', *Critical Social Policy*, vol. 12, pp. 44–62.

Cole, G.D.H. (1943), *Britain's Town and Country Pattern*, London, Faber.

Cole, G.D.H. and Postgate, R. (1961), *The Common People, 1746–1946*, London, Methuen.

Coleman, A. (1976) 'Is planning really necessary?', *Geographical Journal*, vol. 142, pp. 411–37.

Coleman, A. (1985), *Utopia on Trial: Vision and Reality in Planned Housing*, London, Hilary Shipman.

Collins, J. (1985), 'Education for practice: a local authority view', *Town Planning Review*, vol. 56, pp. 458–67.

Collison, P. (1953), 'Planning officers and the neighbourhood unit concept', unpublished PhD Thesis, University of Birmingham, Faculty of Commerce.

Community Development Project (1976), *Profits Against Houses: An Alternative Guide to Housing Finance*, London, Home Office Community Development Project, Information and Intelligence Unit.

Community Development Project (1977), *Gilding the Ghetto*, London, Home Office Community Development Project, Information and Intelligence Unit (also in Paris, C. (ed.), *Critical Readings in Planning Theory*, Oxford, Pergamon, 1982).

Cooke, P. (1983), *Theories of Planning and Spatial Development*, London, Hutchinson.

Cooke, P. and Rees, G. (1977), 'Faludi's "Sociology in planning education": a critical comment', *Urban Studies*, vol. 14, 215–18.

Coon, A.G. (1984), 'The research and educational needs of planning', *The Planner*, vol. 70, pp. 22–5.

Council for the Protection of Rural England (1981), *Planning: Friend or Foe?*, London, CPRE.

Counter Information Services (1973), *The Recurrent Crisis of London: Anti-Report on the Property Developers*, London, CIS.

Cox, A. (1980), 'Continuity and discontinuity in Conservative urban policy', *Urban Law and Policy*, vol. 3, pp. 269–92.

Cox, A. (1981), 'Corporatism as reductionism: the analytic limits of the corporatist thesis', *Government and Opposition*, vol. 16, pp. 78–95.

Cox, A. (1984), *Adversary Politics and Land: The Conflict over Land and Property Policy in Post-War Britain*, Cambridge, Cambridge University Press.

Cox, G., Lowe, P. and Winter, M. (1986), 'From state direction to self regulation: the historical development of corporatism in British agriculture', *Policy and Politics*, vol. 14, pp. 475–90.

Cox, G., Lowe, P. and Winter, M. (1987), 'Farmers and the state: a crisis for corporatism', *Political Quarterly*, Vol. 58, pp. 73–81.

Cox, K. (ed.) (1978), *Urbanization and Conflict in Market Societies*, London, Methuen.

Cox, K. and Johnston, R.J. (eds.) (1982), *Conflict Politics and the Urban Scene*, London, Longman.

Cox, W.H. (1976), *Cities: The Public Dimension*, Harmondsworth, Penguin.

Creese, W.L. (1966), *The Search for Environment: The Garden City, Before and After*, New Haven, Yale University Press.

Crenson, M.A. (1971), *The Unpolitics of Air Pollution: A Study of Non-Decision Making in the Cities*, Baltimore and London, Johns Hopkins University Press.

Cross, D.T. and Bristow, M.R. (1983), *English Structure Planning: A Commentary on Procedure and Practice in the Seventies*, London, Pion.

Crossman, R.H.S. (1962), *Planning and Freedom*, London, Hamish Hamilton.

Crossman, R.H.S. (1975), *The Diaries of a Cabinet Minister. Volume I. Minister of Housing, 1964–66*, London, Hamish Hamilton and Jonathan Cape.

Crouch, C. (ed.) (1979), *State and Economy in Contemporary Capitalism*, London, Croom Helm.

Cuddy, M. and Hollingsworth, M. (1986), 'The review process in land availability studies: bargaining positions for builders and planners', in Barrett, S.M. and Healey, P. (eds.), *Land Policy: Problems and Alternatives*, Aldershot, Gower.

Cullingworth, J.B. (1975), *Environmental Planning, 1939–1969. Volume I: Reconstruction and Land Use Planning*, London, HMSO.

Cullingworth, J.B. (1979), *Environmental Planning, 1939–1969. Volume III: New Towns Policy*, London, HMSO.

Cullingworth, J.B. (1980), *Environmental Planning, 1939–1969. Volume IV: Land Values, Compensation and Betterment*, London, HMSO.

Cullingworth, J.B. (1982), *Town and Country Planning in Britain* (8th edn), London, G. Allen & Unwin. (9th edn., 1985).

Damer, S. and Hague, C. (1971), 'Public participation in planning: a review', *Town Planning Review*, vol. 42, pp. 217–32.

Darin-Drabkin, H. and Darin, D. (1980), 'Let the state control!', *Urban Law and Policy*, vol. 3, pp. 217–27.

Darke, R. (1979), 'Public participation and state power: the case of South Yorkshire', *Policy and Politics*, vol. 7, pp. 337–55.

Darke, R. (1982), 'The dialectics of policy-making: form and content' in Healey, P., McDougall, G. and Thomas, M.J. (eds) *Planning Theory: Prospects for the 1980s*, Oxford, Pergamon.

Davies, H.W.E. (1980), 'The relevance of development control', *Town Planning Review*, vol. 51, pp. 7–17.

Davies, H.W.E. (1981), 'Planning Practice: Report to the Social Science Research Council', University of Reading, School of Planning Studies (also in Davies and Healey 1983)

Davies, H.W.E., Edwards, D. and Rowley, A.R. (1986), 'The relationship between development plans, development control and appeals', *The Planner* vol. 72, pp. 11–15 (a shortened version of a research report with the same title, and published as Working Paper no. 10 of the Department of Land Management and Development, University of Reading).

Davies, H.W.E. and Healey, P. (eds.) (1983), *British Planning Practice and Planning Education in the 1970s and 1980s*, Oxford Polytechnic, Department of Town Planning, Working Paper no. 70.

Davies, J.G. (1972), *The Evangelistic Bureaucrat: A Study of a Planning Exercise in Newcastle upon Tyne*, London, Tavistock.

Davies, T. (1981), 'Implementing employment policies in a district authority' in Barrett, S. and Fudge, C. (eds.), *Policy and Action: Essays on the Implementation of Public Policy*, London, Methuen.

Dawson, A.H. (1984), *The Land Problem in the Developed Economy*, London, Croom Helm.

Deakin, N. (1982), 'Research and the policy-making process in local government', *Policy and Politics*, vol. 10, pp. 303–15.

Deakin, N. (1985), 'Vanishing utopias: planning and participation in twentieth century Britain', *Regional Studies*, vol. 19, pp. 291–300.

Dear, M. and Scott, A.J. (eds.) (1981), *Urbanization and Urban Planning in Capitalist Society*, London, Methuen.

Dearlove, J. (1973) *The Politics of Policy in English Local Government: The Making and Maintenance of Public Policy in the Royal Borough of Kensington*, London, Cambridge University Press.

Dearlove, J. (1979), *The Reorganization of British Local Government: Old Orthodoxies and a Political Perspective*, London, Cambridge University Press.

Delafons, J. (1982), 'Working in Whitehall: changes in public administration, 1952–1982', *Public Administration*, vol. 60, pp. 253–72.

Denman, D. (1980), *Land in a Free Society*, London, Centre for Policy Studies.

Dennis, N. (1968), 'The popularity of the neighbourhood community idea' in Pahl, R.E. (ed.), *Readings in Urban Sociology*, Oxford, Pergamon.

Dennis, N. (1970), *People and Planning: The Sociology of Housing in Sunderland*, London, Faber.

Dennis, N. (1972), *Public Participation and Planners' Blight*, London, Faber.

Dickens, P., Duncan, S., Goodwin, M. and Gray, F. (1985), *Housing, States and Localities*, London, Methuen.

Dimitriou, B., Faludi, A., McDougall, G. and Silvester, M.S. (1973), 'Symposium on the systems approach to planning', *Socio-Economic Planning Sciences*, vol. 7, pp. 55–103.

'Dobry' (1975), *Review of Development Control: Final Report by George Dobry*, (Department of the

Environment), London, HMSO.

Donnison, D.V. (1973), 'Micro-politics of the city' in Donnison, D.V. and Eversley, D.E.C. (eds.), *London: Urban Patterns, Problems and Policies*, London, Heinemann.

Donnison, D.V. and Soto, P. (1980) *The Good City: A Study of Urban Development and Policy in Britain*, London, Heinemann.

Douglas, R. (1971), *The History of the Liberal Party, 1985–1970*, London, Sidgwick and Jackson.

Douglas, R. (1974), 'God gave the land to the people', in Morris, A.J.A. (ed.), *Edwardian Radicalism, 1900–1914*, London, Routledge.

Douglas, R. (1976), *Land, People and Politics: A History of the Land Question in the United Kingdom, 1878–1952)*, London, Allison and Busby.

Dowall, D.E. (1981), 'Reducing the cost effects of local land use controls', *Journal of the American Planning Association*, vol. 47, pp. 145–53.

'Dower' (1946), *Report of the National Parks Committee (England and Wales)*, (Ministry of Town and Country Planning), London, HMSO.

Drewry, G. (ed.) (1985), *The New Select Committees*, Oxford, Oxford University Press

Dror, Y. (1964), 'Muddling through: "science" or inertia?', *Public Administration Review*, vol. 24, pp. 153–7.

Duncan, S.S. (1985) 'Land policy in Sweden: separating ownership from development' in Barrett, S.M. and Healey, P. (eds.), *Land Policy: Problems and Alternatives*, Aldershot, Gower.

Duncan, S.S. and Goodwin, M. (1985), 'The local state and local economic policy: why the fuss?', *Policy and Politics*, vol. 13, pp. 227–53.

Dunleavy, P. (1980), *Urban Political Analysis: The Politics of Collective Consumption*, London, Macmillan.

Dunleavy, P. (1981a), *The Politics of Mass Housing in Britain, 1945–1975: A Study of Corporate Power and Professional Influence in the Welfare State*, Oxford, Clarendon.

Dunleavy, P. (1981b), 'Professions and policy change: notes towards a model of ideological corporatism', *Public Administration Bulletin*, vol. 36, pp. 3–16.

Dunleavy, P. (1984), 'The limits to local government', in Boddy, M. and Fudge, C. (eds.), *Local Socialism: Labour Councils and New Left Alternatives*, London, Macmillan.

Durkheim, E. (1952), *Suicide. A Study in Sociology*, London, Routledge (originally published 1897)

Durkheim, E. (1957), *Professional Ethics and Civic Morals*, (tr. Cornelia Brookfield) London, Routledge (originally published 1950).

Durkheim, E. (1964), *On the Division of Labour in Society*, Glencoe, (Ill.), The Free Press (originally published 1893).

Eckstein, H. (1960), *Pressure Group Politics: The Case of the BMA*, London, Allen & Unwin.

The Economist (1972), 'Land at any price', *The Economist*, vol. 243, no. 6711, 8 April, p. 24.

The Economist (1978a), 'Development untaxed', *The Economist*, vol. 266, no. 7010, 7 January, p. 90.

The Economist (1978b), 'The new Leviathans: property and the financial institutions: a survey', *The Economist*, vol. 267, no. 7032, 10 June, special supplement.

Eddison, T. (1973), *Local Government: Management and Corporate Planning*, London, Leonard Hill.

Edwards, M. (1985), 'Planning and the land market: problems, prospects and strategy' in Ball, M., Bentivegna, V., Edwards, M. and Folin, M. (eds.), *Land Rent, Housing and Urban Planning: A European Perspective*, London, Croom Helm.

Elkin, S. (1974), *Politics and Land Use Planning: The London Experience*, Cambridge, Cambridge University Press.

Elliott, B. (1980), 'Manuel Castells and the new urban sociology', *British Journal of Sociology*, vol. 31, pp. 151–8.

Elliott, B. and McCrone, D. (1981), 'Power and protest in the city' in Harloe, M. (ed.), *New Perspectives in Urban Change and Conflict*, London, Heinemann.

Elliott, B. and McCrone, D. (1982), *The City: Patterns of Domination and Conflict*, London, Macmillan.

Elliott, B. and McCrone, D. (1984), 'Austerity and the politics of resistance' in Szelenyi, I., *Cities in Recession: Critical Responses to the Urban Policies of the New Right*, Beverley Hills, Sage.

Elliott, P. (1972), *The Sociology of the Professions*, London, Macmillan.

Elson, M.J. (1986), *Green Belts: Conflict Mediation in the Urban Fringe*, London, Heinemann.

Emy, H.V. (1973), *Liberals, Radicals and Social Politics, 1982–1914*, Cambridge, Cambridge University Press.

English, J., Madigan, R. and Norman, P. (1976), *Slum Clearance*, London, Croom Helm.

Etzioni, A. (1967), 'Mixed scanning: a "third" approach to decision-making', *Public Administration Review* vol. 17, pp. 385–92 (also in Faludi, A. (ed.), *A Reader in Planning Theory*, Oxford, Pergamon, 1973).

Evans, A.W. (1969), 'Two economic rules for town planning: a critical note', *Urban Studies*, vol. 6, pp. 227–34.

Evans, A.W. (1970), 'Two economic rules for town planning: a reply', *Urban Studies*, vol. 7, pp. 90–1.

Evans, A.W. (1974), 'Economics and planning' in Forbes, J. (ed.), *Studies in Social Science and Planning*, Edinburgh, Scottish Academic Press.

Evans, A.W. (1983), 'The determination of the price of land', *Urban Studies*, vol. 20, pp. 119–29.

Evans, A.W. (1985), *Urban Economics: An Introduction*, Oxford, Blackwell.

Eversley, D.E.C. (1973), *The Planner in Society: The Changing Role of a Profession*, London, Faber.

Eversley, D.E.C. (1974), 'Conservation for the minority?', *Built Environment Quarterly*, vol. 3, pp. 14–15.

Eversley, D.E.C. and Moody, M. (1976), *The Growth of Planning Research Since the Early 1960s*, Report to the Social Science Research Council Planning Committee, London, SSRC.

Fainstein, N. and Fainstein, S. (1979), 'New debates in urban planning: the impact of Marxist theory within the United States, *International Journal of Urban and Regional Research*, vol. 3, pp. 381–403. (also in Paris, 1982).

Faludi, A. (1970), *Sociology in Planning Education*, Oxford Polytechnic, Department of Town Planning, Working Paper no. 4.

Faludi, A. (1973a), *Planning Theory*, Oxford, Pergamon.

Faludi, A. (ed.) (1973b), *A Reader in Planning Theory*, Oxford, Pergamon.

Faludi, A. (1976), 'Sociology in planning education', *Urban Studies*, vol. 13, pp. 121–32.

Faludi, A. (1986), *Critical Rationalism and Planning Methodology*, London, Pion.

Farnell, R. (1983), *Local Planning in Four English Cities*, Aldershot, Gower.

Fay, B. (1975), *Social Theory and Political Practice*, London, Allen & Unwin.

Ferris, J. (1972), *Participation in Urban Planning: The Barnsbury Case*, London, Bell.

Fidler, P. (1985), *The Future for Undergraduate Planning Education*, paper presented at the joint Royal Town Planning Institute and Economic and Social Research Council conference 'Planning education in the 1990s'.

Field, B.G. (1983), 'Local plans and local planning in Greater London', *Town Planning Review*, vol. 54, pp. 24–40.

Fishman, R. (1977), *Urban Utopias in the Twentieth Century: Ebenezer Howard, Frank Lloyd Wright and le Corbusier*, New York, Basic Books.

Fleming, S.C. and Short, J.R. (1984), 'Committee rules OK? An examination of planning committee action on officer recommendations', *Environment and Planning A*, vol. 16, pp. 965–73.

Flynn, R. (1981), 'Managing consensus: strategies and rationales in policymaking' in Harloe, M. (ed.), New Perspectives in Urban Change and Conflict', London, Heinemann.

Flynn, R. (1983), 'Cooptation and strategic planning in the local state' in King, R. (ed.), *Capital and Politics*, London, Routledge.

Flyvbjerg, B. and Petersen, V.C. (1982), 'Planning in the 33 years after "1984"' in Healey, P., McDougall, G. and Thomas, M.J. (eds.), *Planning Theory: Prospects for the 1980s*, Oxford, Pergamon.

Fogarty, M.P. (1948), *Town and Country Planning*, London, Hutchinson.

Foley, D.L. (1960), 'British town planning: one ideology or three?', *British Journal of Sociology*, vol. 11, pp. 211–31 (also in Faludi, A. (ed.), *A Reader in Planning Theory*, Oxford, Pergamon, 1973).

Foley, D.L. (1962), 'Idea and influence: the Town and Country Planning Association', *Journal of the American Institute of Planners*, vol. 27, pp. 10–17.

Foley, D.L. (1963), *Controlling London's Growth: Planning the Great Wen, 1940–1960*, Berkeley, University of California Press.

Foley, D.L. (1972), *Governing the London Region: Reorganization and Planning in the 1960s*, Berkeley, University of California Press.

Foot, M. (1962), *Aneurin Bevan, a Biography*, London, McGibbon and Kee.

Forrest, R., Henderson, J. and Williams, P. (eds.) (1982), *Urban Political Economy and Social Theory: Critical Essays in Urban Studies*, Aldershot, Gower.

Foster, C.D. (1973), 'Planning and the market' in Cowan, P. (ed.), *The Future of Planning*, London, Heinemann.

Freidson, E. (1973), 'Professionalization and the organization of middle class labour' in *Sociological Review Monograph No. 20, Professionalization and Social Change*, Keele (Staffs.), University of Keele.

Friedmann, J. (1973), *Retracking America: A Theory of Transactive Planning*, Garden City (NY), Anchor Books.

Friend, J.K. and Jessop, W.N. (1969), *Local Government and Strategic Choice*, London, Tavistock.

Friend, J.K., Laffin, M.J. and Norris, M.E. (1981), 'Competition in public policy: the structure plan as arena', *Public Administration*, vol. 59, pp. 441–63.

Friend, J.K., Power, J.M. and Yewlett, C.J.L. (1974), *Public Planning: The Inter-Corporate Dimension*, London, Tavistock.

Frost, D. (1977), 'Sociology in planning education: a comment', *Urban Studies*, vol. 14, pp. 219–22.

Gans, H.J. (1984), 'American urban theories and urban areas: some observations on contemporary ecological and Marxist paradigms' in Szelenyi, I. (ed.), *Cities in Recession: Critical Responses to the Urban Policies of the New Right*, Beverly Hills, Sage.

Gauldie, E. (1974), *Cruel Habitations: A History of Working Class Housing, 1870–1918*, London, Allen & Unwin.

George, H. (1884), *Progress and Poverty: An Inquiry into the Cause of Industrial Depressions and of Increasing Want with Increase of Wealth: The Remedy*, London, William Reeves (originally published San Francisco, 1879).

Gilg, A.W. (1978), 'Needed: a new "Scott" inquiry', *Town Planning Review*, vol. 49, pp. 353–6.

Gladstone, F. (1976), *The Politics of Planning*, London, Temple Smith.

Glass, R. (ed.) (1948), *The Social Background of a Plan: A Study of Middlesbrough*, London, Routledge.

Glass, R. (1950), 'Social aspects of town planning' in Tyrwhitt, J. (ed.), *Town and Country Planning Textbook*, London, Association for Planning and Regional Reconstruction.

Glass, R. (1955), 'Urban sociology in Great Britain: a trend report', *Current Sociology*, vol. 4, pp. 5–76.

Glass, R. (1959), 'The evaluation of planning: some sociological considerations', *International Social Science Journal*, vol. 11, pp. 393–409 (also in Faludi, A. (ed.), *A Reader in Planning Theory*, Oxford, Pergamon, 1973).

Glass, R. (1977), review of Castells, M. 'The Urban Question' and Harloe, M. (ed.) 'Captive Cities: Studies in the Political Economy of Cities and Regions', *New Society*, 29 September, pp. 667–9.

Glazer, N. (1974), 'The schools of the minor professions', *Minerva*, vol. 12, pp. 346–64.

Goldfield, D.R. (1982), 'National urban policy in Sweden', *Journal of the American Planning Association*, vol. 48, pp. 24–38

Goldsmith, M. (1980), *Politics, Planning and the City*, London, Hutchinson.

Goldsmith, M. (1984), 'The politics of planning' in Bruton, M.J. (ed.), *The Spirit and Purpose of Planning* (2nd edn), London, Hutchinson.

Goldsmith, M. (1985a), 'The Conservatives and local government: 1979 and after' in Bell, D.S. (ed.), *The Conservative Government 1979–1984: An Interim Report*, London, Croom Helm.

Goldsmith, M. (1985b), *New Research in Central–Local Relations*, Aldershot, Gower.

Goldsmith, M. and Newton, K. (1984), 'Central–local government relations: the irresistible rise of 'central power' in Berrington, H. (ed.), *Change in British Politics*, London, Frank Cass.

Goldthorpe, J.H. (1971), 'Theories of industrial society: reflections on the recrudescence of historicism and the future of futorology', *European Journal of Sociology*, vol. 12, pp. 263–88.

Goodlad, S. (ed.) (1975), *Education and Social Action: Community Service and the Curriculum in Higher Education*, London, Allen & Unwin.

Goodlad, S. (1976), *Conflict and Authority in Higher Education*, London, Hodder and Stoughton.

Gould, A. (1981), 'The salaried middle class in the corporatist welfare state', *Policy and Politics*, vol. 9, pp. 401–18.

Gould, A. (1982), 'The salaried middle class and the welfare state in Sweden and Japan', *Policy and Politics*, vol. 10, pp. 417–37.

Gould, P. and White, R. (1974), *Mental Maps*, Harmondsworth, Penguin.

Gouldner, A.W. (1979), *The Future of the Intellectuals and the Rise of the New Class*, London, Macmillan.

Gouldner, A.W. and Miller, S.M. (eds) (1966), *Applied Sociology: Opportunities and Problems*, New York, The Free Press of Glencoe.

Grant, J. (1977), *The Politics of Urban Transport Planning*, London, Earth Resources Research.

Grant, M. (1979), Britain's Community Land Act: a post-mortem, *Urban Law and Policy*, vol. 2, pp. 359–73.

Grant, M. and Healey, P. (1985) 'The rise and fall of planning', in Loughlin, M., Gelfand, M.D. and Young, K. (eds.) *Half a Century of Municipal Decline, 1935–1985*, London, Allen and Unwin.

Grant, W. (1977), 'Corporatism and pressure groups' in Kavanagh, D. and Rose, R. (eds), *New Trends in British Politics: Issues for Research*, London, Sage.

Grant, W. (ed.) (1985), *The Political Economy of Corporatism*, London, Macmillan.

Gray, A. (1946), *The Socialist Tradition: Moses to Lenin*, London, Longman.

Greater London Council (1985a), *Erosion of the Planning System*, London, GLC.

Greater London Council (1985b), *The Future of Planning: London's Proposals*, London, GLC.

Gregory, D. (1970), *Green Belts and Development Control: A Case Study in the West Midlands*, University of Birmingham, Centre for Urban and Regional Studies, Occasional Paper no. 12.

Gregory, D. and Urry, J. (eds.) (1985), *Social Relations and Spatial Structures*, London, Macmillan.

Gregory, R. (1969), 'Local elections and the rule of anticipated reactions', *Political Studies*, vol. 17, pp. 31–47.

Gregory, R. (1971), *The Price of Amenity: Five Studies in Conservation and Government*, London, Macmillan.

Gutkind, E.A. (1943), *Creative Demobilization* (2 vols), London, Routledge.

Gyford, J. (1984) *Local Politics in Britain* (2nd edn), London, Croom Helm.

Gyford, J. (1985a), *The Politics of Local Socialism*, London, Allen & Unwin.

Gyford, J. (1985b). The politicization of local government, in Loughlin, M., Gelfand, M.D. and Young, K. (eds.), *Half a Century of Municipal Decline, 1935–1985*, London, Allen and Unwin.

Gyford, J. and James. M. (1982), 'The development of party politics in the local authority associations', *Local Government Studies*, vol. 8, pp. 23–46.

Haar, C.M. (1951), *Land Planning Law in a Free Society: A Study of the British Town and Country Planning Act*, Cambridge (Mass.), Harvard University Press and Oxford University Press.

Hague, C. (1984), *The Development of Planning Thought: A Critical Perspective*, London, Hutchinson.

Hague, C. (1985), 'The Radical Institute Group: the first ten years', *The Planner*, vol. 71, pp. 22–4.

Hall, J.M. (1982), *The Geography of Planning Decisions: Theory and Practice in Geography*, Oxford, Oxford University Press

Hall, P. (1975), *Urban and Regional Planning*, London, David and Charles.

Hall, P. (1980), *Great Planning Disasters*, London, Weidenfeld and Nicolson.

Hall, P. (1983a), 'The Anglo-American Connection: rival rationalities in planning theory and practice, 1955–1980', *Environment and Planning B*, vol. 10, pp. 41–6.

Hall, P. (1983b), 'Housing, planning, land and local finance: the British experience', *Urban Law and Policy*, vol. 6, pp. 75–86.

Hall, P., Harrison, B., Massey, D. and Goldsmith, W.W. (1982), 'Debate on Urban Enterprise Zones', *International Journal of Urban and Regional Research*, vol. 6, pp. 416–446.

Hall, P., Thomas, R., Gracey, G. and Drewett, R. (1973), *The Containment of Urban England* (2 vols.), London, Allen & Unwin

Hallett, G. (1977), *Housing and Land Policies in West Germany and Britain: A Record of Success and Failure*, London, Macmillan.

Hallett, G. (1979), *Urban Land Economics: Principles and Policy*, London, Macmillan.

Hallett, G., Randall, P. and West, E.G. (1973), *Regional Policy for Ever? Essays on the History, Theory and Political Economy of Forty Years of 'Regionalism'*, London, Institute of Economic Affairs.

Halliday, R.J. (1968), 'The sociological movement, the Sociological Society and the genesis of academic sociology in Britain', *Sociological Review*, vol. 16, pp. 377–98.

Hambleton, R. (1978), *Policy Planning and Local Government*, London, Hutchinson.

Hamer, D.A. (ed.) (1971), *The Radical Programme of 1885*, Brighton, Harvester Press.

Hamer, D.A. (1972), *Liberal Politics in the Age of Gladstone and Rosebery: A Study in Leadership and Policy*, Oxford, Oxford University Press.

Hamer, M. (1974), *Wheels within Wheels: A Study of the Road Lobby*, London, Friends of the Earth.

Hardin, G. (1968), 'The tragedy of the commons', *Science*, vol. 162, pp. 1243–8.

Hardy, D. and Ward, C. (1985), *Arcadia for All: The Legacy of a Makeshift Landscape*, London, Mansell.

Harloe, M. (1975), *Swindon, a Town in Transition: A Study in Urban Development and Overspill Policy*, London, Heinemann.

Harloe, M. (ed.) (1977), *Captive Cities: Studies in the Political Economy of Cities and Regions*, London, Wiley.

Harloe, M. (ed.) (1981), *New Perspectives in Urban Change and Conflict*, London, Heinemann.

Harloe, M. and Lebas, E. (eds.) (1981), *City, Class and Capital*, London, Arnold.

Harloe, M. and Paris, C. (1984), 'The decollectivization of consumption: housing and local government finance in England and Wales, 1979–1981' in Szelenyi, I. (ed.), *Cities in Recession: Critical Responses to the Urban Priorities of the New Right*, Beverly Hills, Sage

Harries-Jenkins, G. (1970), 'Professionals in organizations' in Jackson, J.A. (ed.), *Professionals and Professionalization*, London, Cambridge University Press.

Harrington, T. (1982), 'Explaining state policymaking: a critique of some recent "dualist" models', *International Journal of Urban and Regional Research*, vol. 7, pp. 202–17.

Harris, N. (1972), *Competition and the Corporate Society: British Conservatives, the State and Industry, 1945–1964*, London, Methuen.

Harrison, A.J. (1977), *Economics and Land Use Planning*, London, Croom Helm.

Harrison, M.L. (1972), 'Development control: the influence of political, legal and ideological factors', *Town Planning Review*, vol. 43, pp. 254–74.

Harrison, M.L. (1975), 'British town planning ideology and the welfare state', *Journal of Social Policy*, vol. 4, pp. 259–74.

Harrison, M.L. (1978), 'Social policy and normative theories of town planning', *Urban Law and Policy*, vol. 1, pp. 77–98.

Harrison, M.L. (1979), *Land Planning and Development Control: Aspects of Development Control Policy, Politics and Practice in England and Wales, 1947–1972*, University of Leeds, Department of Social Policy and Administration.

Harrison, M.L. (ed.) (1984), *Corporatism and the Welfare State*, Aldershot, Gower.

Harrison, M.L. (1985), review of Hague C. 'The Development of Planning Thought' (1984), *International Journal of Urban and Regional Research*, vol. 9, pp. 590–1.

Harrison, R.J. (1980), *Pluralism and Corporatism: The Political Evolution of Modern Democracies*, London, Allen & Unwin.

Harvey, D. (1973), *Social Justice and the City*, London, Arnold.

Harvey, D. (1985a), *Consciousness and the Urban Experience*, Oxford, Blackwell.

Harvey, D. (1985b), *The Urbanization of Capital*, Oxford, Blackwell.

Hayek, F.A. (1962), *The Road to Serfdom*, London, Routledge (first published 1944).

Haynes, R. (1978), 'The rejection of corporate management in Birmingham in theoretical perspective', *Local Government Studies*, vol. 4, pp. 25–38

Hayton, K. (1981), 'Performance review in local authority land use planning', *Local Government Studies*, vol. 7, pp. 51–60

Healey, P. (1983a), *Local Plans in British Land Use Planning*, Oxford, Pergamon.

Healey, P. (1983b), 'Rational method as a mode of policy formation and implementation in land-use policy', *Environment and Planning B*, vol. 10, pp. 19–39.

Healey, P. (1985), 'The professionalization of planning in Britain: its form and consequences', *Town Planning Review*, vol. 56, pp. 492–507

Healey, P. (1986a), 'Emerging directions for research on local land-use planning', *Environment and Planning B*, vol. 13, pp. 103–20

Healey, P. (1986b), review of Harvey, D. 'Consciousness and the Urban Experience (1985)' and 'The Urbanization of Capital (1985)', *The Planner*, vol. 72, pp. 24–7

Healey, P. (1986c), 'Planning policies, policy implementation and development plans', *The Planner*, vol. 72, pp. 9–12

Healey, P. (1986d), review of Breheny, M. and Hooper, A. (eds.) 'Rationality in Planning' (London, Pion, 1985), *Urban Studies*, vol. 23, pp. 248–9

Healey, P., McDougall, G. and Thomas, M.J. (1982), 'Theoretical debates in planning: towards a coherent dialogue' in Healey, P., McDougall, G. and Thomas, M.J., *Planning Theory: Prospects for the 1980s*, Oxford, Pergamon.

Healey, P. and Samuels, O. (1981), *British Planning Education in the 1970s and 1980s* (paper commissioned by Social Science Research Council), Oxford Polytechnic, Department of Town Planning (also in Davies, A.W.E. and Healey, P. (eds.), *British Planning Practice and Planning Education in the 1970s and 1980s*, Oxford Polytechnic, Department of Town Planning, Working Paper no. 70, 1983).

Healey, P. and Underwood, J. (1979), 'Professional ideals and planning practice', *Progress in Planning*, vol. 9, no. 2.

Hebbert, M.J. (1977), *The Evolution of British Town and Country Planning*, unpublished PhD thesis, University of Reading.

Hebbert, M.J. (1981) 'Frederic Osborn 1885-1978' in Cherry, G. (ed.), *Pioneers in British Planning*, London, Architectural Press.

Hebbert, M.J. (1983a), 'The daring experiment: social scientists and land-use planning in 1940s Britain', *Environment and Planning B*, vol. 10, pp. 3-17

Hebbert, M.J. (1983b), review of Cherry, G. 'The Politics of Town Planning' (1982), *Environment and Planning A*, vol. 15, pp. 1273-4.

Heclo, H.H. (1969), 'The councillor's job', *Public Administration*, vol. 47, pp. 185-202

Heraud, B. (1979), *Sociology in the Professions*, London, Open Books.

Herbert, G. (1963), 'The organic analogy in town planning', *Journal of the American Institute of Planners*, vol. 29, pp. 198-209

Herington, J. (1984), *The Outer City*, London, Harper and Row.

Hernes, G. and Selvik, A. (1981), 'Local corporatism' in Berger, S. (ed.), *Organizing Interests in Western Europe*, Cambridge, Cambridge University Press.

Heseltine, M. (1979) Secretary of State's Address, *Report of Proceedings, Town and Country Planning Summer School*, London, Royal Town Planning Institute.

Hewitt, C. (1974), 'Policymaking in post-war Britain: a national level test of elitist and pluralist hypotheses', *British Journal of Political Science*, vol. 4, pp. 187-216

Heywood, P. (1974), *Planning for Human Need*, Newton Abbot, David and Charles.

Higgins, J., Deakin, N., Edwards, J. and Wicks, M. (1983), *Government and Urban Poverty: Inside the Policymaking Process*, Oxford, Blackwell.

Hill, D.M. (1970), *Participating in Local Affairs*, Harmondsworth, Penguin.

Hill, D.M. (1974), *Democratic Theory and Local Government*, London, Allen & Unwin.

Hill, D.M. (1980), 'Values and judgments: the case of planning in England since 1947', *International Policy Science Review*, vol. 1, pp. 149-67

Hill, M.J. (1981), 'The policy-implementation distinction: a quest for rational control?' in Barrett, S.M. and Fudge, C. (eds), *Policy and Action: Essays on the Implementation of Public Policy*, London, Methuen.

Hobsbawm, E.J. (1968), *Industry and Empire: An Economic History of Britain Since 1750*, London, Weidenfeld and Nicolson.

Holland, S. (1975), *The Socialist Challenge*, London, Quartet.

Holland, S. (1976), *Capital versus the Regions*, London, Macmillan.

Hooper, A. (1968), 'Land availability studies and private housebuilding', in Barrett, S.M. and Healey, P. (eds.), *Land Policy: Problems and Alternatives*, Aldershot, Gower.

Hoos, I. (1972), *Systems Analysis in Public Policy: A Critique*, Berkeley, University of California Press.

Howard, E. (1965), *Garden Cities of Tomorrow*, London, Faber (first published 1902).

Howes, C.K. (1983), 'Central government redevelopment initiatives in the United Kingdom', *Urban Law and Policy*, vol. 6, pp. 151-68.

Howl, D. (1982), *Alternatives for Planning: Planning and the Alternative Economic Strategy*, University of Liverpool, Department of Civic Design, Working Paper no. 21.

Howl, D. (1985), 'A people-based approach to local economic planning', *The Planner*, vol. 71, pp. 23-5.

Hughes, M.R. (ed.) (1971), *The Letters of Lewis Mumford and Frederic J. Osborn: A Transatlantic Dialogue, 1938-1970*, Bristol, Adams and Dart.

Huxley, J. (1943), *TVA: Adventure in Planning*, London, Architectural Press.

Independent Commission on Transport (1974), *Changing Directions*, London, Hodder and Stoughton.

Ionescu, G. (1975), *Centripetal Politics: Government and the New Centres of Power*, London, Hart-Davis McGibbon.

Ionescu, G. (ed.) (1976), *The Political Thought of Saint-Simon*, Oxford, Oxford University Press.

Isserman, A. (1985), 'Dare to plan: an essay on the role of the future in planning practice and education', *Town Planning Review*, vol. 56, pp. 483–91.

Jackman, R. (1985), 'Local government finance', in Loughlin, M., Gelfand, M.D. and Young, K. (eds.) *Half a Century of Municipal Decline*, London, Alllen and Unwin.

Jackson, A.A. (1973), *Semi-detached London: Suburban Development, Life and Transport, 1900–1939*, London, Allen & Unwin.

Jacobs, J. (1961), *The Death and Life of Great American Cities: The Failure of Town Planning*, New York, Random House (Harmondsworth, Penguin, 1964).

James, R. (1980), *Return to Reason: Popper's Thought in Public Life*, London, Open Books.

Jameson, C. (1971), 'The human specification in architecture', *Architects' Journal*, 27 October, pp. 918–41.

Jamous, H. and Peloille, B. (1972), 'Professions or self-perpetuating systems: changes in the French university-hospital system' in Jackson, J.A. (ed.), *Professions and Professionalization*, Cambridge, Cambridge University Press.

Jenkins, S. (1973), 'The press as politicians in local planning', *Political Quarterly*, vol. 44, pp. 47–57.

Jenkins, W.I. (1978), *Policy Analysis: A Political and Organizational Perspective*, London, Martin Robertson.

Jennings, R.E. (1982), 'The changing representational roles of local councillors in England', *Local Government Studies*, vol. 8, pp. 67–86.

Jephcott, P. and Robinson, H. (1971), *Homes in High Flats: Some of the Human Problems Involved in Multi-Storey Housing*, Edinburgh, Oliver and Boyd.

Jessop, B. (1978), 'Capitalism and democracy: the best possible political shell' in Littlejohn, G. (ed.), *Power and the State*, London, Croom Helm.

Jessop, B. (1979), 'Corporatism, parliamentarianism and social democracy' in Schmitter, P.C. and Lehmbruch, G. (eds.), *Trends Towards Corporatist Intermediation*, London, Sage.

Jessop, B. (1980), 'The transformation of the state in post-war Britain', in Scase, R. (ed.), *The State in Western Europe*, London, Croom Helm.

Jessop, B. (1982), *The Capitalist State: Marxist Theories and Methods*, Oxford, Martin Robertson.

Jewkes, J. (1968), *The New Ordeal by Planning: The Experience of the Forties and Sixties*, London, Macmillan.

Johnson, T. (1972), *Professions and Power*, London, Macmillan.

Johnson, T. (1977), 'The professions in the class structure' in Scase, R. (ed.), *Industrial Society: Class, Cleavage and Control*, London, Allen & Unwin.

Jones, G. (1969), *Borough Politics*, London, Macmillan.

Jones, G. (1973), 'The functions and organization of councillors', *Public Administration*, vol. 51, pp. 135–46.

Jones, G. and Stewart, J. (1985), *The Case for Local Government*, London, Allen & Unwin.

Jordan, A.G. (1981), 'Iron triangles, woolly corporatism and elastic nets: images of the policy process', *Journal of Public Policy*, vol. 1, pp. 95–123.

Jowell, J. (1977) 'Bargaining in development control', *Journal of Planning and Environment Law*, July, pp. 414–33.

Jowell, J. and Noble, D. (1980), 'Planning as social engineering: notes on the first English structure plans', *Urban Law and Policy*, vol. 3, pp. 293–317.

Judge, D. (1981), 'Specialists and generalists in British central government: a political debate', *Public Administration*, vol. 59, pp. 1–14.

Keeble, L. (1961), *Town Planning at the Crossroads*, London, Estates Gazette.

Kellner, P. and Crowther-Hunt, Lord (1980), *The Civil Servants: An Inquiry into Britain's Ruling Class*, London, Macdonald.

Keogh, G. (1985), 'The economics of planning gain' in Barrett, S.M. and Healey, P. (eds.), *Land Policy: Problems and Alternatives*, Aldershot, Gower.

Kiernan, M.J. (1983), 'Ideology, politics and planning: reflections on the theory and practice of urban planning', *Environment and Planning B*, vol. 10, pp. 71–87.

King, R. (1985) 'Corporatism and the local economy, in Grant, W. (ed.) *The Political Economy of Corporatism*, London, Macmillan.

Kingston, M. (1981), *Monitoring in Town and Country Planning*, unpublished MTP thesis, University of Manchester, Department of Town and Country Planning.

Kirby, A. (1982), *The Politics of Location: An Introduction*, London, Methuen.

Kirk, G. (1980), *Urban Planning in a Capitalist Society*, London, Croom Helm.

Kitchen, P. (1975), *A Most Unsettling Person: An Introduction to the Ideas and Life of Patrick Geddes*, London, Gollancz.

Klosterman, R.E. (1980), 'A public interest criterion', *Journal of the American Planning Association* vol. 46, pp. 323–33.

Klosterman, R.E. (1985), 'Arguments for and against planning', *Town Planning Review*, vol. 56, pp. 5–20.

Knox, P. and Cullen, J. (1981), 'Planners as urban managers: an exploration of the attitudes and self-image of senior British planners', *Environment and Planning A*, vol. 13, pp. 885–98.

Kuper, L. (1951), 'Social science research and the planning of urban neighbourhoods', *Social Forces*, vol. 29, pp. 237–43.

Laffin, M. (1980), 'Professionalism in central–local relations' in Jones, G. (ed.), *New Approaches to the Study of Central–Local Government Relationships*, Aldershot, Gower.

Laffin, M. (1986) 'Professional communities and policy communities in central-local relations', in Goldsmith, M. (ed.) *New Research in Central-Local Relations*, Aldershot, Gower.

Larson, M.S. (1978), *The Rise of Professionalism: A Sociological Analysis*, Berkeley, University of California Press.

Law, C. (1981), *British Regional Development Since World War I*, London, Macmillan.

Lawless, P. (1979), *Urban Deprivation and Government Initiative*, London, Faber.

Lawless, P. (1981), *Britain's Inner Cities: Problems and Policies*, London, Harper and Row.

Lazarsfeld, P.F., Reitz, J. and Pasanella, A.K. (1975), *An Introduction to Applied Sociology*, New York, Elsevier.

Lean, W. (1969), *Economics of Land Use Planning: Urban and Regional*, London, Estates Gazette.

Lean, W. (1970), 'Two economic rules for town planning: a comment', *Urban Studies*, vol. 7, pp. 88–9.

Lean, W. and Goodall, B. (1966), *Aspects of Land Economics*, London, Estates Gazette.

Lebas, E. (1982), 'Urban and regional sociology in advanced industrial societies: a decade of Marxist and critical perspectives (annotated bibliography), *Current Sociology*, vol. 30, pp. 1–272.

Lebas, E. (1983), 'The state in British and French urban research, or the crisis of the urban question' in Pons, V. and Francis, R. (eds.), *Urban Social Research: Problems and Prospects*, London, Routledge.

Lee, J.M. (1967), *Social Leaders and Public Persons*, Oxford, Clarendon.

Lee, J.M., Wood, B., Solomon, B.W. and Walters, P. (1974), *The Scope of Local Initiative: A Study of Cheshire County Council, 1961–1974*, London, Martin Robertson.

Lefcoe, G. (1980), 'The market's place in land policy', *Urban Law and Policy*, vol. 3, pp. 205–16.

Lehmbruch, G. and Schmitter, P.C. (eds.) (1982), *Patterns of Corporatist Policy-Making*, London, Sage.

Le Las, W.G. (1983), 'The major public inquiry: politics and the rational verdict', *Urban Law and Policy*, vol. 6, pp. 39–51.

Leonard, P. (ed.) (1975), *The Sociology of Community Action*, University of Keele, Sociological Review Monograph no. 21.

Lepawski, A. (1976), 'The planning apparatus: a vignette of the New Deal', *Journal of the American Institute of Planners*, vol. 42, pp. 16–32.

Leung, H.L. (1979), *Redistribution of Land Values: A Re-examination of the 1947 Scheme*, University of Cambridge, Department of Land Economy, Occasional Paper no. 11.

Levin, P.H. (1976), *Government and the Planning Process: An Analysis and Appraisal of Government Decision-making Processes with Special Reference to the Launching of New Towns and Town Development Schemes*, London, Allen & Unwin.

Lichfield, N. (1956), *Economics of Planned Development*, London, Estates Gazette.

Lichfield, N. (1979), 'Towards an acceptable planning system', *Town Planning Review*, vol. 50, pp. 5–17.

Lichfield, N. (1980), 'Land policy: seeking the right balance in government intervention: an overview', *Urban Law and Policy*, vol. 3, pp. 193–203.

Lichfield, N. and Darin-Drabkin, H. (1980), *Land Policy in Planning*, London, Allen & Unwin.

Lichfield, N., Kettle, P. and Whitbread, M. (1974), *Evaluation in the Planning Process*, Oxford, Pergamon.

Lindblom, C.E. (1959), 'The science of "muddling through"', *Public Administration Review*, vol. 19, pp. 79–88 (also in Faludi, A. (ed.), *A Reader in Planning Theory*, Oxford, Pergamon, 1973).

Lloyd, M.G. and Botham, R.W. (1985), 'The ideology and implementation of Enterprise Zones in Britain', *Urban Law and Policy*, vol. 7, pp. 33–55.

Lofland, L.H. (1973), *A World of Strangers: Order and Action in Urban Public Space*, New York, Basic Books.

Loney, M. (1983), *Community Against Govermment: The British Community Development Project, 1968–1978: A Study of Government Incompetence*, London, Heinemann.

Loughlin, M. (1980), 'Planning control and the property market', *Urban Law and Policy*, vol. 3, pp. 1 22.

Loughlin, M. (1985), 'Apportioning the infrastructure costs of urban land development' in Barrett, S.M. and Healey, P. (eds.), *Land Policy: Problems and Alternatives*, Aldershot, Gower.

Loughlin, M., Gelfand, M.D. and Young, K. (eds.) (1985), *Half a Century of Municipal Decline*, London, Allen & Unwin.

Lowe, P.L and Goyder, J. (1983), *Environmental Groups in Politics*, London, Allen & Unwin.

Macmillan, H. (1938), *The Middle Way: A Study of the Problem of Economic and Social Progress in a Free and Democratic Society*, London, Macmillan.

Macmillan, H. (1966), *Winds of Change, 1914–1939*, London, Macmillan.

Macpherson, C.B. (1978), *Property: Mainstream and Critical Positions*, Oxford, Blackwell.

Magee, B. (1973), *Popper*, London, Collins.

Mandelker, D.R. (1962), *Green Belts and Urban Growth: English Town and Country Planning in Action*, Madison, University of Wisconsin Press.

Mannheim, K. (1940), *Man and Society in an Age of Reconstruction*, London, Routledge.

Mannheim, K. (1951), *Freedom, Power and Democratic Planning*, London, Routledge.

Marriott, O. (1967), *The Property Boom*, London, Hamish Hamilton.

Marris, P. and Rein, M. (1974), *Dilemmas of Social Reform* (2nd edn), Harmondsworth, Penguin.

Martin, R.M. (1983), 'Pluralism and the new corporatism', *Political Studies*, vol. 31, pp. 86–102.

Martin and Woorhees Associates (1981), *Review of Rural Settlement Policies, 1945–1980*, London, Martin and Voorhees.

Martlew, C. (1983), 'The state and local government finance', *Public Administration*, vol. 61, pp. 127 47.

Marwick, A. (1964), 'Middle opinion in the Thirties: planning, progress and political agreement', *English Historical Review*, vol. 79, pp. 285–98.

Marwick, A. (1968), *Britain in the Century of Total War*, London, Bodley Head.

Masser, I. (ed.) (1983), *Evaluating Urban Planning Efforts: Approaches to Policy Analysis*, Aldershot, Gower.

Massey, D. and Catalano, A. (1978), *Capital and Land: Landownership by Capital in Great Britain*, London, Arnold.

'Maud' (1967), *Report on the Management of Local Government* (Ministry of Housing and Local Government) London, HMSO.

McAllister, D.M. (1980), *Evaluation in Urban Planning: Assessing Environmental, Social, Economic and Political Trade-Offs*, Cambridge (Mass.), MIT Press.

McAllister, G. and McAllister, E.G. (1945), *Homes, Towns and Countryside: A Practical Plan for Britain*, London, Batsford.

McAuslan, P. (1975), *Land, Law and Planning: Materials and Text*, London, Weidenfeld and Nicholson.

McAuslan, P. (1980), *The Ideologies of Planning Law*, Oxford, Pergamon.

McAuslan, P. (1981), 'Local government and resource allocation in England: changing ideology, unchanging law', *Urban Law and Policy*, vol. 4, pp. 215–68.

McCallum, I.R.M. (1945), *Physical Planning*, London, Architectural Press.

McConnell, S. (1981), *Theories for Planning*, London, Heinemann.

McCutcheon, R. (1975), 'High flats in Britain, 1945 to 1971', in Conference of Socialist Economists, *Political Economy and the Housing Question*, University of Sussex, School of Cultural and Community Studies.

McDougall, G. (1979), 'The state, capital and land: the history of town planning revisited', *International Journal of Urban and Regional Research*, vol. 3, pp. 361–80.

McDougall, G. (1982), 'Theory and practice: a critique of the political economy approach to planning' in Healey, P., McDougall, G., and Thomas, M.J. (eds.), *Planning Theory: Prospects for the 1980s*, Oxford, Pergamon.

McEwen, J. (1977), *Who Owns Scotland? A Study in Land Ownership*, Edinburgh, EUSPB.

McKay, D.H. (1982), 'Regulative planning in the centralized British state', in McKay, D.H. (ed.), *Planning and Politics in Western Europe*, London, Macmillan.

McKay, D.H. and Cox, A.W. (1979), *The Politics of Urban Change*, London, Croom Helm.

McKinley, J.B. (1973), 'On the professional regulation of change' in Halmos, P. (ed.), *Professionalization and Social Change*, University of Keele, Sociological Review Monograph no. 20.

McLaine, I. (1979), *Ministry of Morale: Home Front Morale and the Ministry of Information in World War Two*, London, Allen & Unwin.

McLeish, H. (1981), 'The alternative strategy at national and local level', *The Planner*, vol. 67, pp. 160–1.

McLoughlin, J.B. (1969), *Urban and Regional Planning: A Systems Approach*, London, Faber.

McLoughlin, J.B. (1973), *Control and Urban Planning*, London, Faber.

McLoughlin, J.B. (1982), *Review of Research and Education in Planning: Final Report to the Social Science Research Council*, London, SSRC.

McLoughlin, J.B. (1986), Review of Breheny, M. and Hooper, A. (eds.) (1985) 'Rationality in Planning,' *Town Planning Review*, vol. 57, 204–5.

McMahon, M. (1985), 'The law of the land: property rights and town planning in modern Britain' in Ball, M. et al., *Land Rent, Housing and Urban Planning: A European Perspective*, London, Croom Helm.

McMillan, M. (1975), 'Economic rules for planners: a reconsideration', *Urban Studies*, vol. 12, pp. 329–33.

Meller, H.E. (ed.) (1979), *The Ideal City*, (Reprint of Barnett, 'The Ideal City', and Geddes, 'Civics as Applied Sociology', with Editor's introductions), Leicester, Leicester University Press.

Mellor, J.R. (1977), *Urban Sociology in an Urbanized Society*, London, Routledge.

Mellor, J.R. (1982), *The Urban Perspective*, Units 1–2 of Open University course on 'Urban Change and Conflict', Milton Keynes, Open University Press.

Mercer, G. (1984), 'Corporatist ways in the NHS?' in Harrison, M.L. (ed.), *Corporatism and the Welfare State*, Aldershot, Gower.

Merrett, S. (1979), *State Housing in Britain*, London, Routledge.

Middlemas, K. (1979), *Politics in Industrial Society: The Experience of the British System since 1911*, London, Macmillan. Andre Deutsch.

Middlemas, K. (1983), *Industry, Unions and Government: Twenty One Years of NEDC*, London.

Midgley, J. and Piachaud, D. (eds.) (1984), *The Fields and Methods of Social Planning*, London, Heinemann.

Miller, M. (1981), 'Raymond Unwin, 1863–1940' in Cherry, G. (ed.), *Pioneers of British Planning*, London, Architectural Press.

Minett, J. (1974) 'The Housing, Town Planning, etc. Act, 1909, *Journal of the Royal Town Planning Institute*, vol. 60, pp. 676–80.

Mitnick, B.M. (1976), 'A typology of conceptions of the public interest', *Administration and Society*, vol. 8, pp. 5–28.

Monahan, J. (1976), 'Up against the planners in Covent Garden' in Hain, P. (ed.), *Community Politics*, London, John Calder.

Moore, C., Richardson, J.J. and Moon, J. (1985), 'New partnerships in local economic development', *Local Government Studies*, vol. 11, pp. 19–33.

Moore, T. (1978), 'Why allow planners to do what they do? A justification from economic theory', *Journal of the American Institute of Planners*, vol. 44, pp. 387–98.

Morley, S. (1981), 'Positive planning and direct development by local authorities', *Town Planning Review*, vol. 52, pp. 298–315.

Muchnik, D.M. (1970), *Urban Renewal in Liverpool*, London, Bell.

Mullan, B. (1980), *Stevenage Ltd: Aspects of the Planning and Politics of Stevenage New Town, 1945–1978*, London, Routledge.

Muller, R. and Bruce, A. (1981), 'Local government in pursuit of an industrial strategy', *Local Government Studies*, vol. 7, pp. 3–18.

Mumford, L. (1948), 'Patrick Geddes, Victor Branford and applied sociology in England: the social survey, regionalism and urban planning' in Barnes, H.E. (ed.), *An Introduction to the History of Sociology*, Chicago, Chicago University Press.

Munton, R. (1983), *London's Green Belt: Containment in Practice*, London, Routledge.

Murray, B.K. (1980), *The People's Budget, 1909–1910: Lloyd George and Liberal Politics*, Oxford, Oxford University Press.

Murphy, R. (1986), 'Weberian closure theory: a contribution to the ongoing assessment', *British Journal of Sociology*, vol. 37, pp. 21–41.

Musgrove, F. (1973), 'Power and the educational curriculum', *Journal of Curriculum Studies*, vol. 5, pp. 3–12.

Musil, J. (1968), 'The development of Prague's ecological structure' in Pahl, R.E. (ed.), *Readings in Urban Sociology*, Oxford, Pergamon.

Newby, H, (1979), *Green and Pleasant Land? Social Change in Rural England*, Harmondsworth, Penguin.

Newman, I. and Mayo, M. (1981), 'Docklands', *International Journal of Urban and Regional Research*, vol. 5, pp. 529–45.

Newman, Otto (1981), *The Challenge of Corporatism*, London, Macmillan.

Newman, Oscar (1972), *Defensible Space: People and Design in the Violent City*, London, Architectural Press.

Newton, K. (1976), *Second City Politics: Democratic Processes and Decision Making in Birmingham*, Oxford, Oxford University Press.

Newton, K. (1981), 'The local financial crisis in Britain: a non-crisis which is neither local nor financial' in Sharpe, L.J. (ed.), *The Local Fiscal Crisis in Western European States: Myths and Realities*, London, Sage.

Nickson, R.A. (1985), 'The role of local authorities in economic development: a rejoinder', *Local Government Studies*, vol. 11, pp. 8–17.

Nixon, J. (1986), 'Evaluating select committees and proposals for an alternative perspective, *Policy and Politics*, vol. 14, pp. 415–38.

Norton, A. and Wedgwood-Oppenheim, F. (1981), 'The concept of corporate planning in English local government: learning from its history', *Local Government Studies*, vol. 7, pp. 55–72.

Nuffield Foundation (1986), *Town and Country Planning: The Report of a Committee of Inquiry*, London, Nuffield Foundation.

Offe, C. (1981), 'The attribution of public status to interest groups' in Berger S. (ed.), *Organizing Interests in Western Europe*, Cambridge, Cambridge University Press.

Offer, A. (1981), *Property and Politics, 1870–1914: Landownership, Law, Ideology and Urban Development in England*, Cambridge, Cambridge University Press.

Oppenheimer, M. (1973), 'The proletarianization of the professional' in. Halmos, P. (ed.), *Professionalization and Social Change*, University of Keele, Sociological Review Monograph no. 20.

Orlans, H. (1952), *Stevenage: A Sociological Study of a New Town*, London, Routledge.

Osborn, F.J. (1942), *New Towns After The War*, London, Dent.

Osborn, F.J. and Whittick, A. (1969), *The New Towns: The Answer to Megalopolis*, London, Leonard Hill.

Osborn, F.J. and Whittick, A. (1977), *New Towns: Their Origins, Achievements and Progress*, London, Routledge.

Oxley, M.J. (1975), 'Economic theory and urban planning', *Environment and Planning A*, vol. 7, pp. 497–508.

Pahl, R.E. (1965), *Urbs in Rure*, London, London School of Economics, Geographical Paper no. 2.

Pahl, R.E. (1970), *Whose City? And Other Essays on Urban Society*, London, Longman (2nd edn. Harmondsworth, Penguin, 1975).

Pahl, R.E. (1977a), 'Playing the rationality game: the sociologist as a hired expert' in Bell, C. and Newby, H. (eds.), *Doing Sociological Research*, London, Allen & Unwin.

Pahl, R.E. (1977b), 'Managers, technical experts and the state: forms of mediation, manipulation and dominance in urban and regional development' in Harloe, M. (ed.), *Captive Cities: Studies in the Political Economy of Cities and Regions*, London, Wiley.

Pahl, R.E. (1977c) "Collective consumption" and the state in capitalist and state socialist societies' in Scase, R. (ed.), *Industrial Society: Class, Cleavage and Control*, London, Allen & Unwin.

Pahl, R.E. and Winkler, J.T. (1974), 'The coming corporatism', *New Society*, 10 October, pp. 72–6.

Painter, M.J. (1980), 'Policy coordination in the Department of the Environment, 1970–1976, *Public Administration*, vol. 58, pp. 135–54.

Pallott, J. and Shaw, D.J.B. (1981), *Planning in the Soviet Union*, London, Croom Helm.

Panitch, L. (1977), 'The development of corporatism in liberal democracies', *Comparative Political Studies*, vol. 10, pp. 61–89 (also in Schmitter, P.C. and Lehmbruch, G. (eds.), *Trends Toward Corporatist Intermediation*, London, Sage, 1979).

Panitch, L. (1980), 'Recent theorizations of corporatism: reflections on a growth industry', *British Journal of Sociology*, vol. 31, pp. 159–87.

Panitch, L. (1981), 'The limits of corporatism: trade unions and the corporate state', *New Left Review*, no. 125, pp. 21–43.

Panitch, L. (1984), *Corporatism and Modern Capitalism*, Glasgow, Fontana.

Paris, C. (ed.) (1982), *Critical Readings in Planning Theory*, Oxford, Pergamon.

Parker, H.R. (1965), 'The history of compensation and betterment since 1900' in Hall, P. (ed.), *Land Values*, London, Sweet and Maxwell.

Parker, H.R. (1985), 'From Uthwatt to Development Land Tax: the end of the road?' *The Planner*, vol. 71, pp. 21–8.

Parkin, F. (1974), 'Strategies of social closure in class formation' in Parkin, F. (ed.), *The Social Analysis of Class Structure*, London, Tavistock/British Sociological Association.

Parkin, F. (1979), *Marxism and Class Theory: A Bourgeois Critique*, London, Tavistock.

Parry, G. (ed.) (1972), *Participation in Politics*, Manchester, Manchester University Press.

Parry, N. and Parry, J. (1977), Social closure and collective social mobility, in Scase, R. (ed.), *Industrial Society: Class, Cleavage and Control*, London, Allen & Unwin.

Passow, S.S. (1970), 'Land reserves and teamwork in planning Stockholm', *Journal of the American Institute of Planners* vol. 36, pp. 179–88.

Pateman, C. (1970), *Participation and Democratic Theory*, Cambridge, Cambridge University Press.

Pearce, B.J. (1980), 'Instruments for land policy: a classification', *Urban Law and Policy*, vol. 3, pp. 115–55.

Pearce, B.J. (1981), 'Property rights versus development control: a preliminary evaluation of alternative planning policy instruments', *Town Planning Review*, vol. 52, pp. 47–60.

Pearce, B.J. (1984), 'Development control: a "neighbour protection service"?' *The Planner*, vol. 70, p. 8.

Pennance, F.G. (1967), *Housing, Town Planning and the Land Commission*, London, Institute for Economic Affairs.

Perkin, H.J. (1973), 'Land reform and class conflict in Victorian Britain' in Butt, J. and Clarke, I.F. (eds.), *The Victorians and Social Protest: A Symposium*, Newton Abbot, David and Charles.

Peterson, W. (1968), 'The ideological origins of Britain's New Towns', *Journal of the American Institute of Planners*, vol. 34, pp. 160–70.

Pickvance, C.G. (ed.) (1976), *Urban Sociology: Critical Essays*, London, Tavistock.

Pickvance, C.G. (1981), 'Policies as chameleons: an interpretation of regional policy and office policy in Britain' in Dear, M. and Scott, A.J. (eds.), *Urbanization and Urban Planning in Capitalist Society*, London, Methuen.

'Pilcher' (1975), *Report on Commercial Property Development* (Department of the Environment), London, HMSO.

Pinder, P. (ed.) (1981), *Fifty Years of Political and Economic Planning: Looking Forward, 1931–1981*, London, Heinemann.

Pinker, R. (1971), *Social Theory and Social Policy*, London, Heinemann.

Pinto-Duschinsky, M. (1977), 'Corruption in Britain', *Political Studies*, vol. 25, pp. 174–84.

*The Planner* (1985) 'Planning education: a special 'Planner' supplement, *The Planner*, vol. 71, pp. 17–32.

Planning Advisory Group (1965), *The Future of Development Plans: A Report of the Planning Advisory Group* (Ministry of Housing and Local Government), London, HMSO.

Platt, J. (1972), 'Survey data and social policy', *British Journal of Sociology*, vol. 23, pp. 77–91.

Plowden, S. (1972), *Towns Against Traffic*, London, Andre Deutsch.

Plowden, S. (1985), *Transport Reform: Changing the Rules*, London, Policy Studies Institute.

Plowden, W. (1971), *The Motor Car and Politics, 1896–1970*, London, Bodley Head.

Popper, K.R. (1945), *The Open Society and its Enemies*, London, Routledge.

Popper, K.R. (1957), *The Poverty of Historicism*, London, Routledge.

Pountney, M.T. and Kingsbury, P.W. (1983), 'Aspects of development control', *Town Planning Review*, vol. 54, pp. 139–54 and 285–303.

Power, J.M. (1971), 'Planning: magic and technique' in Institute for Operational Research/Tavistock Institute, *Beyond Local Government Reform: Some Prospects for Evolution in Public Policy Networks* (conference papers).

Purdom, C.B. (1946), *How Should We Rebuild London?*, London, Dent.

Raab, C.D. (1977), 'From town planning to statecraft', *Political Quarterly*, vol. 48, pp. 361–6.

Ranson, S., Jones, G. and Walsh, K. (eds.) (1985), *Between Centre and Locality*, London, Allen & Unwin.

Ratcliffe, J. (1984), review of Moor, N. 'The Planner and the Market,' (London, Godwin, 1983), *Town Planning Review*, vol. 55, p. 251.

Ravetz, A. (1980), *Remaking Cities: Contradictions of the Recent Urban Environment*, London, Croom Helm.

Ravetz, A. (1986), *The Government of Space: Town Planning in Modern Society*, London, Faber.

Read, D. (1979), *England 1868–1914: The Age of Urban Democracy*, London, Longman.

Reade, E.J. (1981), *Practical Work in Planning Education*, Oxford Polytechnic, Department of Town Planning, Working Paper no. 54.

Reade, E.J. (1982a), 'Section 52 and corporatism in planning', *Journal of Planning and Environment Law*, January, pp. 8–16.

Reade, E.J. (1982b), 'Residential decay, household movement and class structure', *Policy and Politics*, vol. 10, pp. 27–45.

Reade, E.J. (1982c), 'The theory of town and country planning' in Healey, P., McDougall, G. and Thomas, M.J. (eds.), *Planning Theory: Prospects for the 1980s*, Oxford, Pergamon.

Reade, E.J. (1983a), *An Analysis of the Use of the Concept of Rationality in the Literature of Planning*, University of Reading, Department of Land Management and Development, Working Paper no. 1.

Reade, E.J. (1983b), 'If planning is anything, maybe it can be identified', *Urban Studies*, vol. 20, pp. 159–71.

Reade, E.J. (1983c), 'Town planning and sociology' in Pons, V. and Francis, R. (eds.), *Urban Social Research: Problems and Prospects*, London, Routledge.

Reade, E.J. (1983d), 'Monitoring in planning' in Masser, I. (ed.), *Evaluating Urban Planning Efforts: Approaches to Policy Analysis*, Aldershot, Gower.

Reade, E.J. (1984a), 'Town and country planning' in Harrison, M.L. (ed.), *Corporatism and the Welfare State*, Aldershot, Gower.

Reade, E.J. (1984b), 'Vandalism: is household movement a substitute for social control?' in Levy-Leboyer, C. (ed.), *Vandalism: Behaviour and Motivations*, Amsterdam, North Holland Publishers.

Reade, E.J. (1985a), 'Britain and Sweden: premature obsolescence of housing', *Scandinavian Housing and Planning Research*, vol. 2, pp. 27–43.

Reade, E.J. (1985b) 'An analysis of the use of the concept of rationality in the literature of planning' in Breheny, M. and Hooper, A. (eds.), *Rationality in Planning: Critical Essays on the Role of Rationality in Urban and Regional Planning*, London, Pion.

'Redcliffe-Maud' (1969), *Report of the Royal Commission on Local Government in England, 1966–1969* (Ministry of Housing and Local Government), London, HMSO.

Rees, G. and Lambert, J. (1985), *Cities in Crisis: The Political Economy of Urban Development in Post-war Britain*, London, Arnold.

Regan, D.E. (1978), 'The pathology of British land use planning', *Local Government Studies*, vol. 4, pp.

3–23.

'Reith' (1946), *Reports of the New Towns Committee* (Ministry of Town and Country Planning), London, HMSO.

Reith, J.C.W. (1949), *Into the Wind*, London, Hodder and Stoughton.

Rex, J. (1961), *Key Problems of Sociological Theory*, London, Routledge.

Rex, J. (1968), *Economic growth and decline: their consequences for the sociology of planning*, Town and Country Planning Summer School (Town Planning Institute), Report of Proceedings.

Rex, J. (1971), 'Some theses on sociology and planning' in Rex, J. *Race, Colonialism and the City*, London, Routledge.

Rex, J. and Moore, R. (1967), *Race, Community and Conflict: A Study of Sparkbrook*, London, Oxford University Press.

Rhodes, R.A.W. (1980), 'Some myths in central–local relations', *Town Planning Review*, vol. 51, pp. 270–85.

Rhodes, R.A.W. (1984), 'Continuity and change in British central–local relations: "The Conservative Threat", 1979–1983', *British Journal of Political Science*, vol. 14, pp. 261–83.

Rhodes, R.A.W. (1986), ' "Power dependence" theories of central-local relations: a critical assessment', in Goldsmith, M. (ed.), *New Research in Central-Local Relations*, Aldershot, Gower.

Roberts, M. (1974), *An Introduction to Town Planning Techniques*, London, Hutchinson.

Roberts, N.A. (1976), *The Reform of Planning Law*, London, Macmillan.

Robinson, J.R. and Lloyd, M.G. (1986), 'Lifting the burden of planning: a means or an end?' *Local Government Studies*, vol. 12, pp. 51–64.

Robson, W.A. (1941), *The War and the Planning Outlook*, London, Faber.

Rodger, J.J. (1985), 'Natural justice and the big public inquiry: a sociological perspective', *Sociological Review*, vol. 33, pp. 410–29.

Rodwin, L. (1956), *The British New Towns Policy: Problems and Implications*, Cambridge (Mass.), Harvard University Press

Rogers, A. (1985), 'Local claims on rural housing: a review', *Town Planning Review*, vol. 56, pp. 367–80.

Room, G. (1979). *The Sociology of Welfare: Social Policy, Stratification and Political Order*, Oxford, Basil Blackwell and Martin Robertson.

Rosenberg, D. (1983), review of Dunleavy, P. 'The Politics of Mass Housing in Britain' (Oxford, Clarendon, 1981), *Sociological Review*, vol. 31, pp. 116–29.

'Roskill' (1971), *Report of the Commission of Inquiry on the Third London Airport*, London, HMSO.

Roweis, S.T. (1981), 'Urban planning in early and late capitalist societies: an outline of a theoretical perspective', in Dear, M. and Scott, A.J. (eds), *Urbanization and Urban Planning in Capitalist Society*, London, Methuen.

Royal Town Planning Institute (1976), *Planning and the Future*, Report of a joint working party of the Royal Town Planning Institute, the Institution of Civil Engineers and the Royal Institute of Chartered Surveyors (the 'Law Report'), London, RTPI.

Royal Town Planning Institute (1986) *Planning Education Review: Final Report*, London, R.T.P.I.

Rustin, M. (1981), *Integrated Codes and Professional Education*, Organization of Sociologists in Polytechnics, SIP Paper no. 10, Plymouth, Plymouth Polytechnic.

Rydin, F. (1981), 'The corporate approach and the advancement of officer interests: the evaluation of a critique', *Local Government Studies*, vol. 7, pp. 71–9.

Rydin, Y. (1984), 'The struggle for housing land: a case of confused interests', *Policy and Politics*, vol. 12, pp. 345–67.

Saks, M. (1983), 'Removing the blinkers? A critique of recent contributions to the sociology of the professions', *Sociological Review*, vol. 31, pp. 1–21.

Sarkissian, W. (1976), 'The idea of social mix in town planning: an historical review', *Urban Studies*, vol. 13, pp. 231–47.

Saunders, P. (1979), *Urban Politics: A Sociological Interpretation*, London, Hutchinson.

Saunders, P. (1981a), *Social Theory and the Urban Question*, London, Hutchinson.

Saunders, P. (1981b), 'Community power, urban managerialism and the "local state" ' in Harloe, M. (ed.), *New Perspectives in Urban Change and Conflict*, London, Heinemann.

Saunders, P. (1984), 'Rethinking local politics' in Boddy, M. and Fudge, C. (eds), *Local Socialism?*

*Labour Councils and New Left Alternatives*, London, Macmillan.

Saunders, P. (1985), 'Corporatism and urban service provision' in Grant, W. (ed.), *The Political Economy of Pluralism*, London, Macmillan.

Saunders, P. (1986), 'Reflections on the dual politics thesis: the argument, its origins and its critics' in Goldsmith, M. and Valladsen, S. (eds), *Urban Political Theory and the Management of Fiscal Stress*, Aldershot, Gower.

Schaffer, D. (1986), 'Ideal and reality in 1930s regional planning: the case of the Tennessee Valley Authority', *Planning Perspectives*, vol. 1, pp. 27–44.

Schaffer, F. (1970), *The New Town Story*, London, MacGibbon and Key.

Schmitter, P.C. (1974), 'Still the century of corporatism?', *Review of Politics*, vol. 36, pp. 85–131, (also in Schmitter, P.C. and Lehmbruch, G. (eds), *Trends toward Corporatist Intermediation*, London, Sage, 1979).

Schmitter, P.C. and Lehmbruch, G. (eds) (1979), *Trends toward Corporatist Intermediation*, London, Sage.

Schubert, G.A. (1961), *The Public Interest: A Critique of the Theory of a Political Concept*, Glencoe (Ill.), The Free Press.

'Schuster' (1950), *Report of the Committee on the Qualifications of Planners* (Ministry of Town and Country Planning), London, HMSO.

'Scott' (1943), *Report of the Committee on Land Utilization in Rural Areas*, London, HMSO.

Scott, A.J. (1980), *The Urban Land Nexus and the State*, London, Pion.

Scott, A.J. and Roweis, S.T. (1977), 'Urban planning in theory and practice: a reappraisal', *Environment and Planning A*, vol. 9, pp. 1097–1119.

Self, P. (1961), *Cities in Flood: The Problems of Urban Growth* (2nd edn), London, Faber.

Self, P. (1970), 'Nonsense on stilts: cost–benefit analysis and the Roskill Commission', *Political Quarterly*, vol. 41, pp. 249–60.

Self, P. (1975), *Econocrats and the Policy Process: The Politics and Philosophy of Cost–Benefit Analysis*, London, Macmillan.

Sennett, R. (1971), *The Uses of Disorder: Personal Identity and City Life*, London, Allen Lane The Penguin Press.

Sharp, T. (1940), *Town Planning*, London, Penguin.

Sharpe, L.J. (ed.) (1981), *The Local Fiscal Crisis in Western European States: Myths and Realities*, London, Sage.

'Sheaf' (1972), *Report of the Working Party on Local Authority/Private Enterprise Partnership Schemes* (Department of the Environment), London, HMSO.

Shoard, M. (1980), *The Theft of the Countryside*, London, Temple Smith.

Shoard, M. (1986), 'Who owns the countryside?', *New Society*, 28 February, pp. 356–7.

Shonfield, A. (1965), *Modern Capitalism*, London, Oxford University Press.

Shucksmith, M. (1981), *No Homes for Locals*, Aldershot, Gower.

Shucksmith, M. (1983), 'Second homes: a framework for policy', *Town Planning Review*, vol. 54, pp. 174–93.

Silkin, L. (1948), 'The New Towns Act', and 'Address to the 34th. Annual General Meeting', *Journal of the Town Planning Institute*, vol. 34, July/August.

Sillince, J. (1984), 'The evaluation of planning: some political considerations', *The Planner*, vol. 70, pp. 19–22.

Sillince, J. (1986), *A Theory of Planning*, Aldershot, Gower.

Simmie, J. (1981), *Power, Property and Corporatism: The Political Sociology of Planning*, London, Macmillan.

Simmie, J. (1985), 'Corporatism and planning' in Grant, W. (ed.), *The Political Economy of Corporatism*, London, Macmillan.

Simon, E.D. (1945), *Rebuilding Britain: A Twenty Year Plan*, London, Gollancz.

Simpson, M. (1981), 'Thomas Adams 1871–1940' in Cherry, G. (ed.), *Pioneers in British Planning*, London, Architectural Press.

Sinclair, R. (1937), *Metropolitan Man: The Future of the English*, London, Allen & Unwin.

'Skeffington' (1969), *Report of the Committee on Public Participation in Planning* (Ministry of Housing and Local Government), London, HMSO.

Skelcher, C. (1980), 'From programme budgeting to policy analysis: corporate approaches in local government, *Public Administration*, vol. 58, pp. 155–72.

Smith, M.P. (1980), *The City and Social Theory*, Oxford, Blackwell.

Smith, M.P. (ed.) (1984), *Cities in Transformation: Class, Capital and the State*, Beverly Hills, Sage.

Smith, P.J. (ed.) (1975), *The Politics of Physical Resources*, Harmondsworth, Penguin.

Smith, R. (1981), 'Implementing the results of evaluation studies' in Barrett, S.M. and Fudge, C. (eds), *Policy and Action: Essays on the Implementation of Public Policy*, London, Methuen.

Smith, T. (1979), *The Politics of the Corporate Economy*, London, Martin Robertson.

Solesbury, W. (1974), *Policy in Urban Planning: Structure Plans, Programmes and Local Plans*, Oxford, Pergamon.

Sorensen, A.D. and Day, R.A. (1981), 'Libertarian planning', *Town Planning Review*, vol. 52, pp. 390–402.

Standing Conference on London and South East Regional Planning (1976), *The Improvement of London's Green Belt*, London, SCLSERP.

Stephen, F.H. and Young, E. (1985), 'An economic insight on the judicial control of planning authorities' discretion', *Urban Law and Policy*, vol. 7, pp. 133–64.

Stewart, J.D. (1971), *Management in Local Government*, London, Charles Knight.

Stewart, J.D. (1974), *The Responsive Local Authority*, London, Charles Knight.

Stewart, J.D. (1983), *Local Government: The Conditions of Local Choice*, London, Allen & Unwin.

Stewart, J.D. and Eddison, T. (1971), 'Structure planning and corporate planning', *Journal of the Royal Town Planning Institute, vol. 57, pp. 367–9.*

Stretton, H. (1978), *Urban Planning in Rich and Poor Countries*, Oxford, Oxford University Press.

Strong, L.A. (1979), *Land Banking: European Reality, American Prospect*, Baltimore, Johns Hopkins University Press.

Sutcliffe, A. (ed.) (1974), *Multi-storey Living: The British Working Class Experience*, London, Croom Helm.

Sutcliffe, A. (ed.) (1980), *The Rise of Modern Urban Planning, 1800–1914*, London, Mansell.

Sutcliffe, A. (1981a), *British Town Planning: The Formative Years*, Leicester, Leicester University Press.

Sutcliffe, A. (ed.) (1981b), *Towards the Planned City: Germany, Britain, the United States and France, 1780–1914*, Oxford, Blackwell.

Switzer, J.F.Q. (1984), The duty of the Secretary of State for the Environment, *The Planner*, vol. 70, pp. 14–15.

Tabb, W.K. and Sawers, C. (eds) (1984), *Marxism and the Metropolis: New Perspectives in Urban Political Economy* (2nd edn), New York, Oxford University Press.

Tauber W. (1973), *Governing Soviet Cities: Bureaucratic Politics and Urban Development in the USSR*, New York, Praeger.

Taylor, N. (1973), *The Village in the City*, London, Temple Smith.

Taylor, N. (1980), 'Planning theory and the philosophy of planning', *Urban Studies*, vol. 17, pp. 159–72.

Taylor, S. (1981), 'The politics of enterprise zones', *Public Administration*, vol. 59, pp. 421–40.

Thomas, D. (1970), *London's Green Belt*, London, Faber.

Thomas, M.J. (1979), 'The procedural planning theory of A. Faludi', *Planning Outlook*, vol. 22, pp. 72–7.

Thompson, F.L.M. (1966), *English Landed Society in the Nineteenth Century*, London, Routledge.

Thompson, R. (1981), 'An alternative direction', *The Planner*, vol. 67, pp. 16–18.

Thornley, A. (1977), 'Theoretical perspectives on planning participation', *Progress in Planning*, vol. 7, no. 1.

Thrasher, M. (1981), 'The concept of a central–local government partnership: issues obscured by ideas', *Policy and Politics*, vol. 9, pp. 455–70.

Titmuss, R. (1958), *Essays on the Welfare State*, London, Allen & Unwin.

Town and Country Planning Association (1962), *The Paper Metropolist: a Study of London's Office Growth*, London, TCPA.

Townroe, P. (1979), 'The design of local economic development policies', *Town Planning Review*, vol. 50, pp. 148–63.

Tubbs, R. (1942), *Living in Cities*, Harmondsworth, Penguin.

Tucker, J. (1966), *Honourable Estates*, London, Gollancz.

Turner, R.K. and Collis, C. (1977), *The Economics of Planning*, London, Macmillan.

Tyme, J. (1978), *Motorways versus Democracy: Public Inquiries into Road Proposals and their Political Significance*, London, Macmillan.

Tyrwhitt, J. (ed.) (1947a), *Patrick Geddes' 'Cities in Evolution'*, edited by Jacqueline Tyrwhitt, London, Williams and Norgate (Gedde's book originally published 1915).

Tyrwhitt, J. (ed.) (1947b), *Patrick Geddes in India*, London, Lund Humphries.

Tyrwhitt, J. (ed.) (1950), *Town and Country Planning Textbook*, London, Association for Planning and Regional Reconstruction.

Underwood, J. (1980), *Town Planners in Search of a Role: A Participant Observation Study of Local Planners in a London Borough*, University of Bristol, School for Advanced Urban Studies, Occasional Paper no. 6.

Underwood, J. (1981), 'Development control: a case study of discretion in action' in Barrett, S.M. and Fudge, C. (eds), *Policy and Action: Essays on the Implementation of Public Policy*, London Methuen.

Underwood, J. and Stewart, M. (1978), 'Local economic initiatives by local authorities', *The Planner*, vol. 64, pp. 110–12.

'Uthwatt' (1941), *Interim Report of the Expert Committee on Compensation and Betterment*, London, HMSO.

'Uthwatt' (1942), *Final Report of the Expert Committee on Compensation and Betterment*, London, HMSO.

Van Gunsteren, H.R. (1976) 'Constructing a city in speech: planning as political theory', in Barry, B. (ed.) *Power and Political Theory: Some European Perspectives*, London, Wiley.

Villadsen, S, (1986) 'Local corporatism?: the role of organizations and local movements in the local welfare state', *Policy and Politics*, vol. 14, pp. 247–66.

Wachs, M. (ed.) (1985), *Ethics in Planning*, New Brunswick (N.J.), Rutgers University Press.

Ward, C. (1984), 'George Orwell and the politics of planning', *The Planner*, vol. 70, pp. 4–6.

Ward, S. (1974), 'The Town and Country Planning Act 1932', *Journal of the Royal Town Planning Institute*, vol. 60, pp. 685–9.

Ward, S. (1986), 'Implementation versus planmaking: the example of List Q and the depressed areas, 1922–1939', *Planning Perspectives*, vol. 1, pp. 3–26.

Wates, N. (1976), *The Battle for Tolmers Square*, London, Routledge.

Weaver, C., Jessop, J. and Das, V. (1985), 'Rationality in the public interest: notes toward a new synthesis' in Breheny, M. and Hooper, A. (eds), *Rationality in Planning: Critical Essays on the Role of Rationality in Urban and Regional Planning*, London, Pion.

Westergaard, J. (1964), 'Land use planning since 1951: the legislative and administrative framework in England and Wales', *Town Planning Review*, vol. 35, pp. 219–37.

Westergaard, J. (1977), 'Class, inequality and "corporatism" ' in Hunt, A. (ed.), *Class and Class Structure*, London, Lawrence and Wishart.

Westergaard, J. and Resler, H. (1975), *Class in a Capitalist Society: A Study of Contemporary Britain*, London, Heinemann.

White, D. (1986), 'Public inquiries under threat', *New Society*, 9 May, pp. 13–14.

Whiteley, P. and Gordon, I. (1980), 'Middle class, militant and male', *New Statesman*, 6 January.

Wibberley, G. (1985), 'The famous Scott Report: a text for all time?', *The Planner*, vol. 71, pp. 13–20.

'Widdicombe' (1986), *Report of the Committee on the Conduct of Local Authority Business* (Department of the Environment), London, HMSO.

Wildavsky, A. (1973), 'If planning is everything, maybe it's nothing', *Policy Sciences*, vol. 4, pp. 127–53.

Wilding, P. (1982), *Professional Power and Social Welfare*, London, Routledge.

Williams, O.P. (1971), *Metropolitan Political Analysis: a Social Access Approach*, New York, The Free Press of Glencoe and London, Collier Macmillan.

Williams-Ellis, C. (ed.) (1938), *Britain and the Beast*, London, Dent.

Williamson, P.J. (1985), *Varieties of Corporatism: A Conceptual Discussion*, Cambridge, Cambridge University Press.

Willis, K.G. (1980), *The Economics of Town and Country Planning*, London, Granada.

Wilson, F.L. (1983), 'Interest groups and politics in Western Europe: the neo-corporatist approach', *Comparative Politics*, vol. 16, pp. 105–23.

Wiltshaw, D.G. (1985), 'The supply of land', *Urban Studies*, vol. 22, pp. 49–56.

Winkler, J.T. (1976), 'Corporatism', *European Journal of Sociology*, vol. 17, pp. 100–36.

Winkler, J.T. (1977), 'The corporate economy: theory and administration' in Scase, R. (ed.), *Industrial Society: Class, Cleavage and Control*, London, Allen & Unwin.

Wolfe, C. (1945), *The Reilly Plan: A New Way of Life*, London, Nicholson and Watson.

Wootton, B. (1945), *Freedom Under Planning*, London, Allen & Unwin.

Young, K. and Kramer, J. (1978), *Strategy and Conflict in Metropolitan Housing: Suburbia versus the Greater London Council, 1965–1975*, London, Heinemann.

Young, K. and Mason, C. (eds) (1983), *Urban Economic Development: New Roles and Relationships*, London, Macmillan.

Young, K. and Mills, L. (1983), *Managing the Post-Industrial City*, London, Heinemann.

# Index